THE
ENCYCLOPEDIA
of
HERBS,
SPICES
& FLAVOURINGS

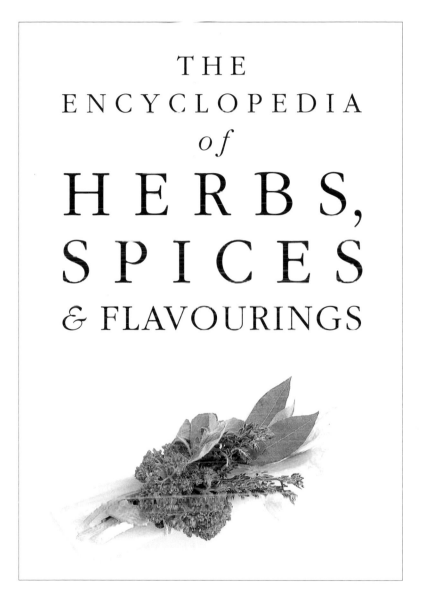

THE
ENCYCLOPEDIA
of
HERBS,
SPICES
& FLAVOURINGS

CONTRIBUTING EDITOR
ELISABETH LAMBERT ORTIZ

DORLING KINDERSLEY
London · New York · Stuttgart

DK

A DORLING KINDERSLEY BOOK

Created and Produced by
CARROLL & BROWN LTD
5 Lonsdale Road
London NW6 6RA

Editor **Laura Washburn**
Art Editor **Lisa Tai**
Photographer **David Murray**
Computer Operator **Debra Lelliott**
Production Controller **Lorraine Baird**

First published in Great Britain in 1992
by Dorling Kindersley Limited
9 Henrietta Street, London WC2E 8PS

A CIP catalogue record for this book is available
from the British Library
ISBN 0-86318-982-2

Reproduced by Colourscan, Singapore
Printed and bound in Italy

FOREWORD

Since the art of cookery was developed, herbs have been used to enliven and enhance meals. The number of herbs are legion, and they may be used medicinally as well as in the kitchen. Herbs are always bracketed with spices, but the difference between the two is easily defined. Herbs are the leaves of fresh or dried plants, while spices are the aromatic parts: buds, fruit, berries, roots or bark, usually dried, from plants that thrive in tropical regions. Their role in the kitchen is the same: to enhance the flavour of foods. Herbs, which are not confined to the tropics, are outdoor plants though some can be grown indoors in sunny places. The categories can overlap as a plant can supply both a spice and a herb, coriander for example with its fresh leaves and aromatic seeds, or celery and celery seed. It is herbs and spices in combination that give the flavour and aromas which are a mingled sensation of smell and taste.

Herb cultivation and use has always been a peaceful enterprise. Spices, on the other hand, have upset and altered history, caused fortune or mishap, and have been prime movers in great events. The nations of Europe, especially Portugal, Spain, the Low Countries (Holland and Belgium), England and France became embroiled in colonial wars as a result of Columbus's search for a quick route to the Spice Islands. It was this search for spices that ended with Columbus discovering the Americas – an event with far-reaching consequences; he found not only a new world but new foods, including the capsicums that greatly influenced world cooking and spread with astonishing rapidity over the globe.

Nowadays, an ever-widening range of reliable seeds are available for sowing in home gardens, patio tubs, window boxes or pots on ledges. In addition, more fresh herbs are on sale in supermarkets and greengrocers as well as a wide variety of dried herbs, freeze dried herbs and packaged spice mixtures. The world of herbs, spices and flavourings from faraway places, as well as the familiar ones of home, can add immeasurably to our gustatory pleasure, whether we are dining on family favourites or entertaining friends with new and exciting dishes. Our culinary horizons are expanded and our imaginations stirred. And, travel away from home is more fulfilling when we have some knowledge of unfamiliar dishes and can choose with confidence from a menu in a foreign land. The flavours of the world are yours to discover, they are just waiting for you to try them, so accept their invitation and go and experiment, go and enjoy.

ELISABETH LAMBERT ORTIZ

CONTENTS

INTRODUCTION:
A WORLD OF FLAVOURINGS

KITCHEN HERBS

Herbs, the fragrant plants that are used for seasoning dishes, were probably first cultivated thousands of years ago, before the dawn of civilization: perhaps their cultivation signalled the beginning of civilization itself. Records exist which testify to a very early knowledge of their cultivation and use in Egypt, China, India, Arabia, Persia and Greece, and the culinary use of herbs remains a firmly-rooted tradition. Today they are more important than ever and more accessible; they are cultivated on a small scale in private gardens, on a large scale for sale to supermarkets and greengrocers, and by chefs for use in their restaurant kitchens. They are increasingly sold fresh, which is best, and dried stocks mean they are available year round; many dried herbs happily retain their aromas. Their extra advantage as garden plants is that they are easy to grow, undemanding for the most part of special soils and conditions. Attractive in the garden and on the plate, they improve the flavour of our food and are also good for us.

Borage

KITCHEN SPICES

Today, all supermarkets and most corner shops have well-stocked spice shelves, offering a selection of seasonings from around the world. These spices are now all modestly priced, yet there was once a time when they were worth their weight in gold.

The Queen of Sheba brought spices, precious stones and gold to King Solomon, proof that spices with a temporary life were rated as highly as enduring metals and gems. Aside from flavouring and preserving foods, spices also played a considerable role in religion, an even greater role in medicine, and their role in politics was greater still. The spice trade virtually made the Dutch empire and turned the small city-state of Venice into a great power.

Spice jars

8

Many spices originated in the Asian tropics: cinnamon, cloves, nutmeg, pepper and ginger. The Americas contributed allspice, vanilla and chillies; the Mediterranean countries provided coriander, mustard, fennel, poppy seeds and fenugreek; Europe's cooler regions brought forth caraway, dill and juniper.

There was a time when spices were so precious that they were kept locked away in special boxes and an exuberant use of spices was an indication of the provider's wealth. Nowadays we look to spices to capture the exotic flavours of faraway places without ever leaving our own kitchens.

FLAVOURS OF THE WORLD

The great dishes of the world's cuisines are characterized by specific combinations of herbs, spices and flavourings. These mixtures have developed over the centuries, influenced largely by the foodstuffs native to each region, the foodstuffs being determined by climate, soil and local culture.

The scent of curry will instantly transport you to India, where the preferred spices are highly aromatic, with as many as 10 used to flavour a single dish. Thai curries, though very hot, are more delicate with a far greater use of fresh herbs and it is more likely to be the aroma of lemon grass, kaffir lime and fresh coriander leaves that evoke Thailand and its deliciously subtle cuisine. Chinese cooking is immensely diverse yet it still has a uniform characteristic flavour, a mingling of smell and taste that can bring a whole country into being in our imagination. It may be the perfume of five-spice powder blended in soy sauce, or a stir-fry with black bean sauce, ginger and garlic that is the trigger. The flavours of Indonesia are an intricate mixture of sweet and sour, with lemon grass, tamarind, kaffir lime, chillies and pungent dried shrimp combined. Soy sauce is also important in Japanese cooking – the most elegantly simple in the world – relying on the pure flavour of fresh seasonal ingredients. Though all these countries are in the Far East, their cuisines could not be more richly diverse.

North Africa uses many of the spices of Asia in ways that produce wholly different flavours. Europe uses spices more sparingly – mainly for pickling and baking – while in the Mediterranean, the use of herbs is predominant, with healthy doses of thyme, sage, bay, oregano and rosemary. With a culinary history closely linked to Europe, North America uses herbs and spices in much the same way, though western regions are influenced by Mexico and the Pacific. The flavours of Mexico are hard to mistake; the aroma of baking corn tortillas and chillies being toasted are characteristic of the region.

Highly spiced foods also are a feature of Central and South America, and the Caribbean. Here, as in the rest of the world, the individual combinations of herbs, spices and flavourings transform ordinary ingredients into culinary classics, which can be enjoyed throughout the year, in the comfort of our own dining rooms.

Chat masala

VEGETABLE AND FRUIT FLAVOURINGS

Vegetables and fruit are as important as their close relatives herbs and spices in turning our daily meals into sources of pleasure as well as sources of nutrition, and so nourish both spirit and body. Mushrooms of many kinds, all with different flavours, are essential in an array of dishes from East to West. Life without the onion family would be a sorry thing as there is scarcely a savoury dish that does not welcome one or other of the *allium*, whether it be the everyday onion, the delicate chive or the robust garlic clove. Pungent roots like horseradish and wasabi add piquancy to foods as diverse as roast beef or raw fish. Olives bring with them the salty, sunny flavours of the Mediterranean, and it is hard to imagine how barren the culinary landscape would be without the tomato. From Mexico comes chocolate, the royal drink of the Aztecs and the modern-day ingredient in sweets and desserts the world over. The citrus family – limes, lemons, oranges and others – are infinitely useful in the kitchen; a few drops of their juices accent flavours of both savoury and sweet dishes. They could well be called indispensable. Nuts are good just by themselves, and their texture and their varied flavours make them a welcome and often essential ingredient in sauces, snacks, main course dishes and desserts.

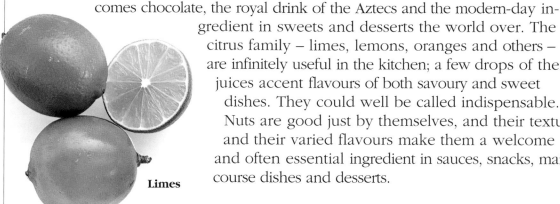

Limes

EXTRACTS, ESSENCES AND SWEETENERS

Natural extracts and essences bring a wonderful flavour into our cooking, conveniently bottled so that they will keep almost indefinitely. From Asia comes the soy bean, and from around the world comes the variety of flavoursome table condiments. For sweetness, the bees work hard, but we get the honey, and the sugar maple gives us the subtle flavour of its syrup. The fruits of summer are captured in purées, essences and syrups, to bring the warmth and brightness of that season into our winter kitchens.

EDIBLE FLOWERS AND LEAVES

Flower gardens, as much as herb gardens, can be a valuable source of ingredients for the kitchen. Likewise, many plants have leaves that are not edible but do make valuable wrappings. Clambakes in New England and *curantos* in Chile would lose a great deal without the seaweed used in their preparation, and Japanese cooking would not be half as delectable if the seaweeds were taken away. Most flowers are used more for beauty than for flavour, though courgette blossoms make a splendid soup and a fine first course when stuffed. Crystallized violets and rose petals are both beautiful to look at and delicious to eat; bringing the best of both worlds to the kitchen.

Salad with flowers

Oils, Vinegars and Dairy Products

The fats – oil, butter and cream – give food a rich and satisfying quality. Soured cream, buttermilk and yogurt add a richness and tang to any dish, from soup to dessert. The acidic quality of vinegar is vital both for flavour and preserving. It is essential in vinaigrette, the mustardy salad dressing of French cuisine, and it adds the tartness that characterizes sweet-and-sour dishes.

Pickles and relishes

Sauces, Preserves and Condiments

All the good things of summer can be harvested and transformed into pickles, relishes, preserves and chutneys, though nowadays modern agriculture and transport mean that many fruits and vegetables are available all year round. Many sauces can be made fresh whenever needed, making the winter table a very lavish one indeed. In addition, there is a myriad of commercial cooking and table sauces that can be used directly on cooked food, or added during cooking. Sweet or savoury, these sauces, preserves and condiments deserve a place on our kitchen shelves.

Coffee, Tea and Spiced Drinks

Tea and coffee are both ancient drinks in their countries of origin: China and Ethiopia. Today, they are both firmly established beverages in most countries of the world. Tisanes, or herb teas, have long been appreciated for their soothing and mildly medicinal properties, and they are gaining popularity as a flavoursome and healthy alternative to coffee and tea. Fruit and vegetable juices, wines, spirits, and even yogurt, are the perfect base for drinks, both hot and cold, to be flavoured with herbs and spices.

Iced tea

Flavourings at Home

Nothing quite equals the pleasure of going into the garden, or to the window box, and picking fresh herbs for the next meal. The flavour is incomparable and, beyond that, it allows for last-minute decisions, improvization and even the possibility to improve an old favourite. As the summer moves inevitably to autumn, the crisp, cooler days are perfect for canning, preserving and bottling the last of the season's fruit for the store-cupboard or holiday gift-giving. Any time of year, a gift from one kitchen to another is always welcome.

GROWING HERBS

Most culinary herbs are ideally suited to container growing, both indoors in pots on the window-sill and outside in tubs, window boxes and hanging baskets. Not only does this result in extremely attractive additions to the garden environment, but it puts herbs immediately at hand for cooking.

Tubs and large pots can be conveniently placed near the back door, on the terrace or balcony, or if space is really at a premium, small pots of herbs on a kitchen windowsill also work very well. With access to a bright window ledge, no cook has to be denied the authentic taste of fresh herbs for culinary creations.

A large tub will allow for a number of herbs in a relatively small area, but some attention to compatibility is necessary. Herbs such as rosemary, thyme, marjoram and sage love a very sunny spot, whereas the mint family, chervil and chives prefer filtered sunlight and a more moist atmosphere. Fussy herbs, such as basil, thrive indoors where their needs can be monitored more easily. Invasive herbs, such as tarragon and mint, should be planted in separate pots so they do not encroach on other herbs.

A well thought out herb garden can enhance the landscape as much as it enhances the stockpot and salad bowl. With many green, purple, gold and silver-leaved herbs, as well as the many variegated types, there is an overwhelming choice for the home cook and gardener. The striking sage tricolour, with pink-tinged new growth, the gold-green lemon thyme and the blue-green narrow-leaved rosemary column, amongst others, offer limitless opportunities to design with not only form and colour, but also flavour.

Some herbs have beautiful flowers as well as flavoursome leaves: borage, hyssop, rosemary, thyme, chives, mint and sage, for example. In the kitchen, they can be used as last-minute garnishes for salads or cheese platters. In the garden, however, flowers detract from the plant's ability to devote all of its flavour to the leaves, so prune frequently.

Potted herbs

HOW TO PLANT

If only one plant is required, it is probably best to purchase a small herb from a specialist nursery or garden centre and progressively pot it on to larger containers. For multiple plants, some herbs grow well from seed: tarragon, parsley, chives or basil can all be sown directly into individual pots of quality compost. Place them in a warm spot and cover with polythene bin liners until germination, and then position on the windowsill to grow to maturity.

In all instances, remember that the larger and deeper the pot, the more leaves the plant will be able to produce.

HERBS INDOORS

There is a vast array of terracotta and plastic pots available for indoor planting. As many herbs are native to the Mediterranean region, terracotta pots complement them visually while also allowing moisture to evaporate, which helps the roots to breathe. Whatever the material you choose, always use containers with proper drainage holes and crock well with a few pieces of broken pot or a layer of gravel to prevent water-logging. When potting up, incorporate a half-inch of horticultural sand two-thirds down from the rim of the pot which will assist drainage and keep the soil from impacting and suffocating the roots.

Watering can

Herbs appreciate a moist atmosphere, particularly indoors. To increase humidity, stand the pots on a gravel bed in a saucer, if possible, with water not quite covering the gravel. The exception is basil, which will tolerate a moderate level of dryness.

Treat your herbs as you would wish to be treated; they will thrive in a comfortable environment – a stable temperature between 16-21°C (60°-70°F), free from draughts. Water regularly but err on the dry side. If in doubt, touch the soil; if it feels dry, the herb requires watering. Always use tepid water, not cold. Windows can reduce the available light quite substantially, so turn the pots regularly to expose all parts of the plant to some sun. Herbs such as marjoram, oregano, thyme and basil require full sun to thrive. Chives, parsley, chervil and mint prefer less direct sun and a cooler position.

Remember to pinch out the growing tips of the herbs to encourage a bushier plant. If the herb is used regularly for cooking, this natural pruning will be adequate for a long supply.

HERBS OUTDOORS

Wooden half barrels, old basins, chimney pots and the myriad of terracotta pots are all suitable

Hanging basket

for herb growing. The final choice depends entirely on personal taste and available space. However, wood or clay do seem to set off herbs to their best advantage.

Several herbs grown together in one large tub often seem to fare better than plants grown in individual pots. For balconies or patios, this creates an instant herb garden that is both decorative and very useful. Try a combination of annuals, such as sweet basil, dill and summer savory, surrounding a central, taller herb such as rosemary or bay. Fill in any gaps with lemon thyme, marjoram and purple sage.

Some herbs are not compatible. Fennel should not be mixed with caraway, dill or coriander, and parsley does not do well with mint.

Another idea if space is limited, is to fill a large strawberry pot with a different herb for each opening, thus creating an unusual focal point for the terrace. This type of container does need careful monitoring, as it tends to require more watering than conventional tubs.

If grown in single pots, remember that the bigger the pot, the better the leaf-production. Raise large tubs and pots off the ground by balancing on two battens of wood; this frees the drainage hole and prevents water-logging. Invasive herbs, such as tarragon and the mints, are more suited to individual planting. These smaller pots look very attractive in groups, which also encourages the more humid environment that they appreciate and thrive in.

Hanging baskets are an attractive way to display low-growing and compact herbs. Exposure to the wind can be a problem as they will have little shelter from other plants and structures.

Sturdy herbs, such as various thymes, curled parsley, prostrate rosemary and nasturtiums, are most suitable.

CARE AND MAINTENANCE

All container plants need careful monitoring. Check topsoil daily and water as required. Bear in mind that smaller tubs and pots dry out quicker. When watering, try to maintain an even moistness throughout, not wet in parts and parched elsewhere.

Pinch out the growing tips to encourage full, bushy plants, particularly sage, which tends to become untidy.

Watch out for the usual garden pests, such as greenfly, slugs and caterpillars, as these can decimate plants in a very short time. An environmentally-friendly method of controlling the onslaught is to spray with a diluted detergent at the first indications. Be sure to wash any treated herbs thoroughly before using in foods.

In the autumn, re-site tubs and pots that are in exposed parts of the garden to more sheltered areas, and mulch the roots well with organic matter. In extremely cold snaps, wrap a handful of straw around the top growth of perennial herbs, such as bay and rosemary, with a layer of polythene (bin liners) as insulation until the worst is over. Individual pots can be wintered in an unheated greenhouse or conservatory.

Strawberry pot with herbs

HARVESTING HERBS

Having successfully grown the various herbs on the windowsill or in the garden, there are a few principles that should be observed when it comes to harvest time.

Different parts of the herb are gathered at different times and in a variety of ways. It is advisable to use a trug or flat-bottomed container, so that the herbs can be placed in a single layer, which prevents damage by bruising.

Obviously, with roots and bulbs, such as garlic, the entire plant is forfeited at the end of the season, but annual leafy herbs, such as basil, can be successfully maintained in the garden until late autumn by judicious picking and pruning of leaves. It is very important to take into account the type, size and age of the plant. Perennial herbs, such as sage, thyme and rosemary, should not be weakened by severe pruning or over-stripping of the leaves before winter sets in, particularly if the plant is small, or quite young, or only just recently established.

When harvesting any plant, in the garden or indoors in pots, do not take more than a maximum of 10 per cent of the growth, otherwise the shock effect can be detrimental. Careful harvesting of all leafy perennial herbs results in more vigorous leaf production and healthier plants.

LEAVES

These can be picked throughout the year, particularly from herbs such as rosemary, thyme, parsley, chives and chervil. The flavour is best just before the herb flowers. Try to pick the young leaves from the parent plant in the morning, when the dew has evaporated. Discard any imperfect leaves or those damaged by insects. Handle as little as possible, as bruising or crushing the leaves releases the volatile oils, thereby reducing the flavour.

FLOWERS AND BULBS

Herb flowers – chives, marigolds, borage and chamomile – should be picked carefully when they are fully open. Lavender is best when the flowers have only just begun to open. In all cases, avoid old, damaged or wilted specimens. Place in an open container, uncovered, until needed, and do not harvest too far in advance. Harvest bulbs, such as garlic, in late summer, when the leaves start to die off.

SEEDS

When the seed heads and pods have formed, keep a close eye on their progress, since timing is all-important to their harvest. There should be no green colouring on the seeds, and the pods, if any, should be very dry. If there is a risk of scattering, as with fennel, carefully cut off the entire stalk holding the seeds and invert into a paper bag or over a container.

Place the seeds or seed heads in a warm, well ventilated room for a few days to dry thoroughly. As they dry, the seeds will drop into the bag or container, so there will be no waste. It is a good idea to label the seed container when harvesting begins, to avoid identification problems later. Store the dried seeds in a dark, air-sealed glass jar. If they are required for next year's planting, store them in a cool, dry place until required.

Trug for harvesting herbs

DRYING HERBS

For centuries cooks have endeavoured to maintain good supplies of herbs year round. Originally, this was achieved by drying, or by infusing in oils and vinegars. Nowadays, with greatly improved methods of transportation, there is an extended season for fresh herbs, and these traditional techniques are often overlooked. This is a disadvantage to the modern cook as these preserving methods extend the flavouring potential of both herbs and spices.

To retain most of the flavour and colour of the herb, speed is vital as is the freshness of the herbs at harvest.

DRYING

This is one of the most popular methods of preservation, and in some cases, it actually improves the flavour of the herb, especially with bay leaves.

Brush off any loose soil from the leaves and dust with a soft pastry brush or similar implement; washing is only necessary if they are very gritty. The easiest procedure is to hang the herbs in small, loose bunches from a rack in a warm room. The temperature should not exceed 30°C (86°F) or the essential oils will evaporate.

Drying rack

Do not let leaves become so dry that they disintegrate into a powder when touched. Also, despite the attractive appearance of herbs hanging in bunches, try to avoid drying them in the kitchen, which is often full of condensation from cooking. To avoid dust settling on the bunches, place a paper bag over the herbs, leaving the bottom of the bag open to the air.

When the leaves are crisp and dry, after about one week (but this depends on the thickness of the leaf and the warmth of the room), they are ready for storage. Strip the leaves whole from the stems and place in a jar, without crushing them. After one day, check for condensation inside the jar; this is a sign leaves are not yet dry enough. If condensation is present, remove the leaves for further drying, otherwise the batch will spoil. For small quantities, make a herb-drying rack by covering an oven shelf, or a simple wooden frame, with fine wire mesh, and place the herbs on top in a single layer. Leave in a warm place, as before, checking periodically on the progress of the drying herbs.

It is not advisable to dry herbs in the oven, however low the temperature, as this treatment does seem to diminish the flavour.

Microwave ovens, however, are useful for drying herbs. Place a single layer of herbs on a paper towel and cook on full power. Time will depend on quantity and oven wattage; see manufacturer's instructions for best results. After about one minute, turn the herbs and continue cooking until dry

Bundles of herbs for drying

15

PRESERVING AND STORING

Storage jars

Dried herbs should be stored in airtight dark glass or pottery jars. Clear glass containers should be stored inside kitchen cupboards. Light and exposure to air and moisture makes the herbs deteriorate more quickly, which is why it is important to use well-sealed containers and keep in a dark place.

Freezing is another effective means of extending the availability of herbs, especially dill, fennel, basil and parsley. Clean the herbs as appropriate and seal in small quantities – two or three tablespoons worth – in freezer bags. Freeze alone or in favourite combinations, such as the traditional bouquet garni (see page 55) or a tomato sauce seasoning with oregano, thyme and parsley. Label clearly and choose a large, rigid container for an assortment of frozen herb bags. This avoids having to empty the entire freezer searching for the individual items. It also lessens damage to the frozen herbs.

Another method, which also makes it easier to flavour individual dishes, involves ice-cube trays. Finely chop the herbs, half-fill each cube compartment with the chopped herbs and top up with water. Freeze, then remove the cubes and place meal-size quantities in to freezer bags, or store in a large, rigid container for easy access.

To regain the taste of summer herbs in the winter, look to oils, vinegars and butters as a means of preserving.

Herb-infused vinegars are made by bruising the herbs slightly, placing in a clean glass jar and pouring over warmed vinegar. Good-quality wine and sherry vinegars work best for flavour; light coloured vinegars are the most attractive as the herbs can be seen. Do not use a metal container, such as one of untreated aluminium, which reacts to the acid in the vinegar, imparting a metallic taste. Leave to infuse for about three weeks, stirring daily. Taste at the end of the period. If it is not strong enough, discard the infused herbs and add fresh ones, and leave for a further week or so.

Herbs for freezing

Strain the vinegar to remove the old herbs. If desired, transfer to a decorative bottle and add a fresh sprig of the herb for decoration and identification. Use only caps and seals that have plastic linings with vinegar; an old vinegar bottle is the perfect choice, cleaned of course. Some flavoursome vinegar and herb combinations include cider vinegar with apple mint, red wine vinegar with garlic and rosemary, or white wine vinegar with tarragon, summer savory and thyme.

The method is the same for herb-infused oils. The less strongly flavoured oils, such as sunflower or safflower, are generally suitable, since the herb taste is more prominent. However, olive oil, with a flavour reminiscent of the Mediterranean area, makes a wonderful partner for the earthy flavour of many herbs and spices. If using garlic as well, remove the cloves after a couple of days as they do tend to overpower the other herbs. Prolific summer herbs, such as basil, can be enjoyed throughout the winter by preserving them in the form of paste. Place the whole leaves in a blender or food processor with a few tablespoons of lemon juice, some cloves of garlic and olive oil just to cover. Process until thoroughly mixed. Transfer to a clean jar with an airtight lid and refrigerate, or freeze in ice-cube trays.

Peaches in alcohol

Basil oil

EDIBLE GIFTS

The bounty of an herb garden can be kept for home use, or it can be used as a source of innumerable edible gifts. Likewise, shop-bought herbs, spices and other ingredients can be pressed into service for an array of flavoursome offerings that are as satisfying to make as to give.

The first step in preparing edible gifts is to find suitable containers. A collection of glass jars will prove most useful, just be sure to remove all traces of the labels. Usually, a long soak in hot, soapy water will suffice, and any remaining bits of glue and paper can be removed with steel wool, or even nail polish remover. It is best to compile an assortment of jars, being sure there is a good supply of plastic-lined lids, as foods containing vinegar should not come in contact with metal lids. Also, take into consideration the size of the jar. Wide-neck jars are best for preserving fruit in alcohol (see page 253), while small jars are best for herb and spice sugar mixtures (see page 195) or flavoured mustards (see page 66). Baby food jars are a handy, uniform size for an assortment of gifts, such as chutneys and relishes (see page 254). Wine, vinegar, fruit juice and mineral water bottles can be used for presenting fruit syrups (see page 204), plum sauce (see page 250) or home-made ginger beer (see page 277). If the caps cannot be re-used, second-hand bottles can be corked (see page 233).

Ceramic jars or hand-made pottery flasks are ideal when offering seasoned salt mixtures (see page 104) or herb and spice mixtures (see Index) that do not need a large container, but do require an airtight, dark one.

Airtight biscuit tins can house a large number of gingerbread men (see page 109), butterscotch sweets wrapped in cellophane (see page 197) or fruit jellies in paper cases (see page 205).

Alternatively, any gift that goes in a box can also be presented in an attractive basket on top of colourful shredded cellophane and secured with a sheet of cling film that is taped on the bottom.

Labels also play an important role, not only as decoration and identification but to indicate a use-by date wherever necessary.

A calligraphy pen filled with black or coloured ink is best for pretty lettering, or sheets of rub-off type can be purchased in stationers, though this can prove time-consuming. A simple solution for the amateur artist is to type out the labels on a typewriter and then trace over the letters with a black pen. This gives an unusually attractive handwritten effect.

Once the goods have been bottled and labelled, all that is required is a bit of embellishment. Ribbons and fabric swatches are easy to obtain and they can be used separately or together. Use similar colours and textures, or mix and match for a more dramatic effect. Dried flowers and herbs can be tied up in bunches or tucked into the ribbons, or the jars can be wrapped in coloured tissue paper and tied with metallic string that has been beaded. The country associated with the food is also a good guideline for presentation. For example, a green- or ochre-coloured earthenware jar is most appropriate when filled with *herbes de Provence* (see page 51), while warm reds and golds would be best for wrapping an Indian chutney.

Herb and spice decorations

Decorative jars

KITCHEN
HERBS

CHIVES

OTHER NAMES
Onion chives

FORMS
Stems: Fresh, chopped,
freeze-dried and frozen
Flowers: Fresh, in season

AFFINITY WITH OTHER HERBS/SPICES
Parsley, tarragon, chervil

HOW TO STORE
Stems: Refrigerate in an
airtight container, or freeze
in ice-cube trays.

HOW TO DRY
Suspend from heads on
wire mesh for use in
arrangements or as garnish.

Rich in vitamins A and C, chives are a member of the
onion family. Indeed, the flavour is reminiscent of
onion, but more delicate because they contain less sulphur. When finely snipped, their bright green colour
makes them an attractive as well as flavoursome addition
to dishes. They are one of the classic *fines herbes* (see
page 24) along with parsley, tarragon and chervil, and
they marry well with egg dishes, like omelettes, and
with egg-based sauces. Long cooking will diminish their
flavour, so it is best to add them to dishes at the last
minute. Chive flowers can be sprinkled into salads for
added eye-appeal and flavour. A handful of chopped
chives is the perfect finish for just about any salad, soup
or sauce, adding to the taste as well as the presentation.

*Flowers are light purple with a
delicate chive flavour*

*Fresh stems are
long, hollow and
grass-like, with a
bright green
colour*

Chinese chives
*(Allium tuberosum)
have grey stems
which are wider
and flatter*

TASTES GOOD WITH/IN
Stems: Eggs, salads, soft
cheese, sauces, soups.
Flowers: Salads.

COOK'S CHOICE
CHIVE AND GARLIC DIP

Serves 2–3

*125 g (4 oz) low-fat soft cheese
2 tbsp mayonnaise
1 garlic clove, crushed
2 tbsp snipped chives
Salt
Freshly ground black pepper*

In a bowl, whisk together the
cheese, mayonnaise, garlic and
chives. Add salt and pepper to
taste. Turn into a serving bowl
and smooth the surface with
the back of a spoon.
Refrigerate for at least 30
minutes before serving.

COOKING TIPS
Add at the last minute as
long cooking destroys their
flavour. For chopping
stems, a pair of scissors is
the best tool. Use *flowers*
for salads and garnishes.

DILL

For the ancient Romans, dill was a symbol of vitality; for the Greeks, it was a remedy for the hiccups. In the Middle Ages it was believed to be a protection against witchcraft, though in fact, dill was an ingredient in many magic potions. In the kitchen, dill is prized both for its seeds and its leaves, and each have their own distinctive taste. Both forms are widely used in the cuisines of Scandinavia, Germany, and Central and Eastern Europe. In addition to culinary use, dill seeds are also known for their soothing, digestive properties.

OTHER NAMES
Dry leaves also known as dillweed

FORMS
Leaves: Fresh and dried
Seeds: Whole and ground

HOW TO STORE
Fresh leaves: Can be kept in a plastic bag in the refrigerator. To freeze, chop finely, mix with water, and freeze in ice-cube trays.
Dried leaves and seeds: Keep in airtight jars in a cool, dark place.

HOW TO DRY
Hang bunches in a warm, dry, well-ventilated place.

Seeds *are tiny, flat and oval*

Dried leaves *are a dark green colour*

Chopped fresh dill

COOKING TIPS
For best flavour, use *fresh leaves*. Cooking diminishes the flavour of fresh dill, so add just before serving. *Dried leaves* do not retain much flavour, so use generously.

Fresh leaves are aromatic, feathery, and green in colour

TASTES GOOD WITH/IN

Leaves: Soft cheeses such as cream cheese or cottage cheese, omelettes, seafood, mustard-based sauces, cold soups, stuffed vine leaves, herring, salmon, potato salads, cucumber, veal, green beans.
Seeds: Breads, braised cabbage, meat stews, rice, cooked root vegetables.

COOK'S CHOICE
DILL PICKLES

Makes 10 pickles

About 10 pickling cucumbers, scrubbed clean

1 bunch fresh dill

75 g (2 ½ oz) coarse sea salt

1 tsp dill seeds

125 ml (4 fl oz) white wine vinegar

1 tsp black peppercorns

1 tbsp pickling spice (see page 75)

Put the cucumbers and fresh dill in a 2 litre (3½ pt) sterilized, clamp-top jar. In a saucepan, combine 1200 ml (2 pt) of water with the salt, dill seeds, vinegar, peppercorns and pickling spice. Bring to the boil over high heat for 3 minutes. Leave to cool. Pour the cooled mixture over the cucumbers; if there is an excess of liquid, be sure to add all the spices to the cucumbers and discard any remaining liquid. Seal the jar and store in a cool, dark place for 3 weeks before serving. Refrigerate after opening.

ANGELICA

(see page 204)

OTHER NAMES
Garden angelica, wild angelica, American angelica, Japanese angelica

FORMS
Stems: Crystallized *Leaves:* Fresh, crystallized and dried *Seeds:* Fresh and dried

HOW TO STORE
Crystallized stems: Wrap in aluminium foil and store in a cool, dry place; do not refrigerate.
Dried leaves: Strip from the stems and store in airtight glass bottles away from light and moisture.
Seeds: If fresh, dry in a warm place before storing.

HOW TO DRY
Collect the *leaves* before the plant begins to flower, then hang them in a warm, dry, well-ventilated place.

COOKING TIPS
If the *crystallized stems* are somewhat dry and brittle, soak them briefly in warm water to soften, then pat dry with paper towels.

Stems are hollow, thick and ridged and should be cut early in the season for crystallizing

Although best known in the form of crystallized stems used as decoration on cakes and desserts, all parts of this strongly aromatic plant can be eaten. The fresh leaves can be added to tart fruit dishes, such as stewed rhubarb or gooseberries, where they will help to reduce acidity and their sweetness minimize the need for sugar. The young shoots can be blanched and added to salads, and all parts of the plant, fresh or crystallized, can be used to imbue home-made jellies and jams with a delicate flavour. Angelica can be used in fruit syrups (see page 204) to make a pleasant summertime drink or enhance a salad of winter fruits. The dried leaves, when infused as a tisane, are said to calm the nerves and remedy indigestion. The dried seeds can be added, along with the stems, to flavour spirits such as gin, vodka or vermouth. In some countries, the stems and roots are boiled and served as a vegetable.

The leaves are large and bright green with serrated edges and a sweet, pungent smell

Fresh stems

TASTES GOOD WITH/IN
Fresh leaves: Vegetable salads, custards, tart fruit such as rhubarb and plums, court-bouillon for poached seafood.

COOK'S CHOICE
CRYSTALLIZED ANGELICA

Makes 350 g (12 oz)

350 g (12 oz) fresh young angelica leaves and stems
250 g (8 oz) sugar
Caster sugar for coating

Separate the leaves from the stems and cut stems and leaf stems into pieces about 12 cm (5 in) long. Place in a heat-proof bowl. In a saucepan, combine the sugar with 300 ml (1/2 pt) water and bring to the boil. Pour the boiling syrup over the angelica – there should be enough to cover it generously. Let it stand in a cool place for at least 24 hours. Transfer the angelica and syrup to a saucepan and bring to the boil. Simmer until the stems and leaves turn bright green. Drain, cool completely, then coat with sugar.

Crystallizing fresh angelica
After cooking and cooling, the stems and leaves are rolled in caster sugar to coat. Then spread the crystallized pieces out on a cake rack and allow to dry thoroughly. If you don't intend on using right away, store in an airtight container.

CHERVIL

OTHER NAMES
Garden chervil

FORMS
Leaves: Fresh and dried

AFFINITY WITH OTHER HERBS/SPICES
Saffron, tarragon, parsley

HOW TO STORE
Leaves are best when used fresh but they can be kept in a plastic bag in the refrigerator. Though much of the flavour is lost, chervil can be dried and stored in an airtight jar.

HOW TO DRY
Spread the *leaves* on wire trays and dry in a cool, well-ventilated place, away from light. When dry strip the leaves and crumble.

COOKING TIPS
To retain the delicate flavour, add *leaves* at the end of cooking time.

Chopped fresh leaves *can be sprinkled over dishes just before serving*

Dried leaves *have little flavour so add generously*

Chervil grows wild in southern Russia and was introduced to the rest of Europe by the Romans. An annual herb, and among the first to appear in spring, it is easy to grow, and prefers a cool, moist climate. One of the *fines herbes* (see page 24), it is essential in French cooking, often supplanting parsley, which it does resemble though the leaves are more feathery, and the flavour is reminiscent of anise. It is very delicate, so long cooking or high temperatures should be avoided. Use chervil much like parsley, though it is at its best when sprinkled over a salad just before serving.

Sprigs are delicate and fern-like, with a bright green colour

TASTES GOOD WITH/IN
Poached fish and shellfish, cream-based soups, omelettes and scrambled eggs, chicken, delicate butter sauces, soft cheeses, glazed vegetables such as carrots, smoked fish and green salads.

COOK'S CHOICE
CREAM OF CHICKEN SOUP WITH CHERVIL

Serves 6

1 large potato, peeled
2 tbsp unsalted butter
60 g (2 oz) fresh chervil sprigs, chopped
1.5 litres (2 ½ pt) chicken stock
60 ml (2 fl oz) whipping cream
Salt
Freshly ground black pepper
Chervil sprigs for garnish

Place the potato in a saucepan of cold water and bring to the boil. When cooked, drain and set aside. Heat the butter in a saucepan, add the chervil, cover and cook over very low heat for 5 minutes. Stir in the chicken stock and simmer for 10 minutes. Pour into a food processor, add the cooked potato and mix until smooth. Return to the saucepan and stir in the cream. Season to taste and cook until heated through. Garnish with chervil sprigs. Serve either hot or cold.

Whole fresh leaves *are a flavoursome garnish for both hot and cold dishes*

TARRAGON

FORMS
Leaves: Fresh and dried

HOW TO STORE
Fresh leaves: Can be stored
in a plastic bag in the
refrigerator, frozen in ice-
cube trays or preserved in
white wine vinegar or oil
and packed in sealed,
sterilized jars.
Dried leaves: Should be
kept in a cool, preferably
dark place in airtight
containers.

HOW TO DRY
Dry in a warm, well-
ventilated place. Strip *leaves*
from stems before storing.

Tarragon Vinegar
White-wine vinegar
flavoured with tarragon is
a useful and flavourful
condiment. Use in salad
dressings, or to deglaze
frying pans (see page 249).
Place a large sprig in a
sterilized bottle or glass jar,
bring the vinegar to the boil
and pour in enough to
cover. Seal and store away
from light.

Tarragon, with its subtle and sophisticated flavour, is
an essential herb in French cuisine. Native to
Siberia, it became a common culinary herb throughout
Europe by the 15th century. The Latin name, meaning
"little dragon", derives from the medieval belief that it
was an antidote for the bites of venomous animals.
Wine vinegar perfumed with tarragon is a classic, while
the reverse – tarragon leaves preserved in vinegar – is a
delicious and practical use for abundant plants. Fresh or
preserved leaves can be mixed with soft cheese, or
puréed with cream and used for canapés.
There are two closely related forms of this valuable
culinary herb: French, or "true" tarragon, and Russian
tarragon. Because of its delicate anise-like flavour,
French tarragon is the preferable type, though it is
harder to cultivate as it seldom sets viable seed. Russian
tarragon grows easily from seed and has a slightly bitter,
more pungent flavour.

Many classic French sauces
such as *béarnaise* or
tartare, with *oeufs en gelée*
(eggs in aspic), omelettes,
poached fish, mushrooms,
poultry, especially chicken,
mustard sauces and salad
dressings.

COOKING TIPS
Tarragon has a flavour
which, although subtle,
diffuses quickly through
dishes, so it must be used
sparingly. Tarragon butter is
simple to make and can be
stored in the freezer. For
each 30 g (1 oz) softened
butter, add 1 tsp finely
chopped tarragon and 1 tsp
lemon juice.

FINES HERBES

This is a traditional French blend of four subtle herbs:
parsley, chervil, chives and tarragon. Finely chopped and
used fresh, it brings an aromatic bouquet to simple green
salads, and the delicate flavours marry well with egg
dishes – especially omelettes – and poached chicken and
fish. Heat diminishes the taste, so it is best to add this
seasoning at the end of the cooking time or sprinkle on
for a delicious garnish.

Dried fines herbes
*Mix together equal
quantities of parsley,
chives, tarragon and
chervil.*

Fresh fines herbes
*With a sharp knife, chop equal
amounts of each of the four
herbs and combine.*

Tarragon

Parsley

Chervil

Chives

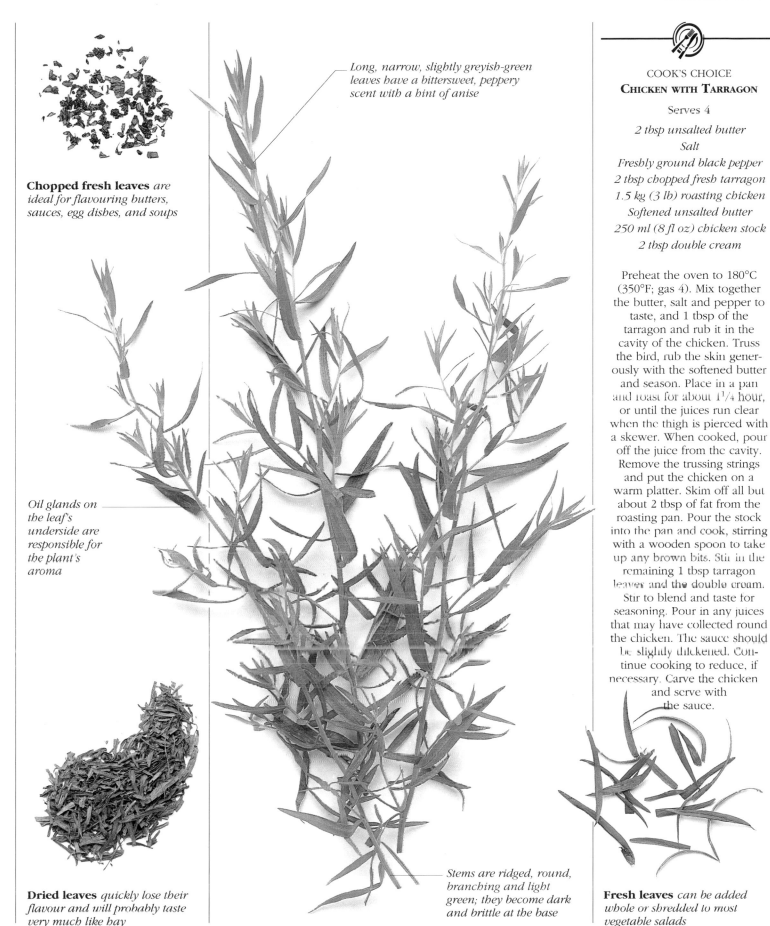

Chopped fresh leaves *are ideal for flavouring butters, sauces, egg dishes, and soups*

Long, narrow, slightly greyish-green leaves have a bittersweet, peppery scent with a hint of anise

Oil glands on the leaf's underside are responsible for the plant's aroma

Dried leaves *quickly lose their flavour and will probably taste very much like hay*

Stems are ridged, round, branching and light green; they become dark and brittle at the base

COOK'S CHOICE
Chicken with Tarragon
Serves 4

2 tbsp unsalted butter
Salt
Freshly ground black pepper
2 tbsp chopped fresh tarragon
1.5 kg (3 lb) roasting chicken
Softened unsalted butter
250 ml (8 fl oz) chicken stock
2 tbsp double cream

Preheat the oven to 180°C (350°F; gas 4). Mix together the butter, salt and pepper to taste, and 1 tbsp of the tarragon and rub it in the cavity of the chicken. Truss the bird, rub the skin generously with the softened butter and season. Place in a pan and roast for about 1¼ hour, or until the juices run clear when the thigh is pierced with a skewer. When cooked, pour off the juice from the cavity. Remove the trussing strings and put the chicken on a warm platter. Skim off all but about 2 tbsp of fat from the roasting pan. Pour the stock into the pan and cook, stirring with a wooden spoon to take up any brown bits. Stir in the remaining 1 tbsp tarragon leaves and the double cream. Stir to blend and taste for seasoning. Pour in any juices that may have collected round the chicken. The sauce should be slightly thickened. Continue cooking to reduce, if necessary. Carve the chicken and serve with the sauce.

Fresh leaves *can be added whole or shredded to most vegetable salads*

BORAGE

FORMS
Leaves: Fresh, dried
Flowers: Crystallized, fresh
Sprigs: Fresh

HOW TO STORE
Fresh leaves: These wilt too rapidly for successful storage.
Dried leaves: In airtight containers.

HOW TO DRY
Remove *leaves* immediately after picking. Dry on wire racks in a well-ventilated place free from humidity.

COOKING TIPS
Always chop the *leaves* finely before using as they have a disagreeable texture. When using *flowers* for a dressed salad, add at the very last moment as the dressing will discolour the flowers and make them wilt. For *crystallized flowers,* brush the petals with a solution of gum arabic and rose water, dip in sugar and dry on wire racks (see page 211).

Borage flowers *are bright purple and star-shaped with distinctive black stamen tips*

Borage came originally from the Middle East and arrived in England via the Romans. It is a very large pretty plant, with velvety grey-green leaves and beautiful, star-shaped, vivid purple flowers; it is said to lift the spirits, banish melancholy and give courage. It is a favourite of bees, as the flowers are filled with nectar and will attract them to the garden. Though its use in the kitchen is limited, the leaves give a refreshing cucumber-like flavour to drinks and salads. In China, the leaves are stuffed and rolled like vine leaves, while the Germans add the large leaves to stews and court-bouillons. It is a traditional part of the Pimm's No. 1, a gin-based drink, which was created about 100 years ago by the proprietor of Pimm's London restaurant. For a more elaborate garnish, crystallized flowers can be used.

Flowers can be scattered over salads

The grey-green leaves are wide and oval, with a fuzzy texture

TASTES GOOD WITH/IN

Fresh leaves: Tossed with boiled, buttered vegetables; finely chopped in salads; as a sandwich or pasta filling; in flavoured butters, yogurt and soft cheese.
Sprigs: Punches, wine cups or drinks such as Pimm's.
Flowers: Green salad, cold fruit and vegetable soups.

COOK'S CHOICE
BORAGE SOUP

Serves 4

2 tbsp unsalted butter
1 medium onion, finely chopped
750 ml (1 ¼ pt) chicken stock
125 g (4 oz) young borage leaves, chopped
500 g (1 lb) potatoes, peeled and sliced
175 ml (6 fl oz) single cream
Salt
Freshly ground black pepper
Chopped borage leaves for garnish (optional)

Heat the butter in a large heavy saucepan and cook the onion over moderate heat until soft but not browned. Stir in the stock, borage and potatoes. Simmer gently, covered, until the potatoes are very soft. Pour the soup through a fine sieve set over a bowl. Return the liquid to the saucepan and transfer the solids to a food processor to purée. Return the mixture to the saucepan, taste for seasoning and pipe or stir in cream. Heat until warmed through; sprinkle with the chopped borage, if desired, and serve. This soup can also be served chilled.

TANSY

Tansy is a hardy perennial herb native to Europe. With its yellow button-like clusters of flowers and fern-like leaves it makes a decorative garden plant. The Greeks and Romans regarded it as a symbol of immortality, while in Tudor England the dried leaves were placed in beds and closets to repel insects and vermin. In the 16th and 17th centuries, tansy tea was regarded as a stimulating tonic. It was once widely used for its internal cleansing and purifying properties, though this is now considered dangerous. Tansy is also one of the bitter herbs of the Jewish Passover. Because of its bitter flavour, culinary uses for tansy are limited though it has been a traditional ingredient in many cakes and puddings. A "tansy" can also refer to a dessert made with tansy leaves, served at Easter, and young leaves and shoots can be used in salads, omelettes and stuffings.

OTHER NAMES
Cow bitters, butter bitters

FORMS
Leaves: Fresh

HOW TO STORE
Tansy is best used fresh but it can be kept briefly in a plastic bag in the refrigerator, or chopped and frozen in ice-cube trays.

HOW TO DRY
Leaves: Hang in a dark, warm, well-ventilated place.

COOKING TIPS
Chop *fresh leaves* finely to use in stews, but use only in small amounts.

Flowers are used for yellow dyes

Fresh leaves are aromatic, toothed, fern-like and dark green, with a bitter taste

Whole leaves *can be rubbed on meat before grilling to impart flavour without bitterness*

TASTES GOOD WITH/IN

Leaves: When finely chopped, add sparingly to salads, omelettes, custards, cakes, or minced meat for savoury pie fillings.

COOK'S CHOICE
TANSY CUSTARD

Serves 6

Butter for custard cups
60 g (2 oz) fresh young tansy leaves, coarsely chopped
750 ml (1 ¼ pt) single cream
4 large eggs, lightly beaten
60 g (2 oz) caster sugar
Pinch of salt
⅛ tsp freshly grated nutmeg
60 g (2 oz) ground almonds

Preheat the oven to 180°C (350°F, gas 4); butter six custard cups. Make the tansy juice: put the tansy leaves into a food processor and reduce to a purée, using a little water if necessary. Scrape the purée into a sieve set over a bowl. Press down hard with a wooden spoon to extract the juice (about 1 tbsp). Set aside. Pour the cream into a small saucepan and scald. Set aside. In a bowl, combine the eggs, sugar, salt, nutmeg and almonds. Mix in the tansy juice a little at a time, to taste. Stir in the cream and pour into the custard cups. Set in a pan of hot water and bake, 30–40 minutes, or until the custard is set and a knife inserted into the centre comes out clean. (Do not let the water boil during baking.) When cool, turn out and serve.

Chopped fresh leaves *can be added to stuffing mixtures*

CORIANDER

OTHER NAMES
Chinese parsley, cilantro, culantro

FORMS
Leaves: Fresh, dried *Roots:* Fresh *Seeds:* Whole, ground

AFFINITY WITH OTHER HERBS/SPICES
Fresh mint, cumin

HOW TO STORE
Fresh leaves: Fresh coriander does not keep well and the flavour of dried is not comparable. Store wrapped in paper towels in a plastic bag or place stem-ends in a glass filled with water in the refrigerator; remove any leaves as they wilt or discolour. Do not remove the roots or rinse the herb until ready to use.
To freeze, finely chop the leaves, place in ice-cube trays and add water to fill.
Seeds: Keep in airtight containers in a cool place away from light.

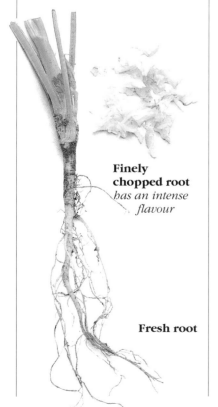

Finely chopped root
has an intense flavour

Fresh root

Native to southern Europe and the Middle East, this ancient annual herb, a member of the carrot family, is one of the most popular herbs in cuisines around the world. Coriander is a pretty plant, with white, pink or pale mauve flowers and delicate light green leaves, a little like flat-leaf parsley. Bunches of the fresh herb are available in many greengrocers, and seeds are always on spice shelves. All parts of the plant are used, and each has its own distinctive flavour. The leaves have a faint overtone of anise, and the seeds are sweet and vaguely reminiscent of orange peel. The root is widely used in Thai curries and other Southeast Asian dishes, and it tastes like an intensified version of the leaves.

One of the bitter herbs eaten at Passover, coriander is mentioned in the Bible, and seeds were found in the tombs of the pharaohs. The leaves are favoured in cuisines throughout the Middle East, Spain, Portugal and Mexico. In Northern Europe, where the seeds have always been more popular than the leaves, they are used for flavouring gin or as an ingredient in pickling spices. But it is on the Indian sub-continent that leaves and seeds are exploited to the full, both being essential ingredients in curries. While leaves and seeds are widely used, the flavour of each is particular, and many consider them to be an acquired taste. In Central and South America the *Conquistadores* introduced the herb to Mexico and Peru, where it became an indispensable companion to the native chillis.

Moroccan seeds

Moroccan powder

Indian seeds

Indian powder

Seeds are sweet and strongly aromatic with a slightly bitter edge, a bit like orange peel

Ground coriander can be bought or ground at home; roast seeds before grinding

TASTES GOOD WITH/IN

Fresh leaves. Soups, stews, curries, stir-fries, vegetables, salads, fish, poultry, yogurt, fresh chutneys, relishes and tomato sauces. *Seeds:* Curries, meat or poultry dishes, vegetables, pickles and chutneys.

COOKING TIPS
Fresh leaves produce the best flavour when added to the dish at the very last minute. Chop the *roots* finely and add to curries or stews for a more intense flavour. Keep the *seeds* whole until needed as they quickly lose their flavour. Roast lightly before crushing or grinding with a mortar and pestle.

COOK'S CHOICE
GUACAMOLE

Serves 2–4

1 large ripe avocado
1 medium tomato, peeled and chopped
1/2 small white onion, finely chopped
1 small fresh hot green chilli, seeded and chopped (optional)
2 tbsp chopped fresh coriander leaves
1 tbsp lemon juice
2–3 tbsp single cream (optional)
Salt
Freshly ground black pepper

Cut the avocado in half and remove the stone. Holding one avocado half in the palm of your hand, mash the flesh with a fork then scoop it out into a bowl. Repeat with the other half. It should retain some texture. Add the tomato, onion, chilli if using, coriander and lemon juice and stir to blend. Add the cream if using. Taste for seasoning. Serve as a dip with crudités or tortilla chips, or as an accompaniment to grilled meats.

White or pale pink
flowers appear in
early summer

Chopped fresh leaves *are
widely used in Mexican and
Tex-Mex cooking where they are
combined with chillies and
added to salsas, guacamole and
seasoned rice dishes*

COOK'S CHOICE
COLD BRAISED CELERY WITH CORIANDER

Serves 4

*4 medium celery sticks, trimmed
and cut into 15 cm (6 in) pieces*
Salt
3 tbsp unsalted butter
*3 spring onions, white and green
parts, chopped*
350 ml (12 fl oz) chicken stock
1 tbsp coriander seeds, crushed
2 tbsp lemon juice
*Fresh coriander sprigs
for garnish*

Blanch the celery pieces in
boiling salted water for 2
minutes. Drain and set aside.
Melt the butter in a frying pan,
preferably non-stick, add the
onions and cook until soft.
Add the celery, pour in the
stock and season to taste.
Cover and cook over low heat
for 15 minutes. Add the
coriander seeds and lemon
juice and continue cooking
until the celery is tender, a
further 15 minutes. If there is
more than about 125 ml
(4 fl oz) liquid, remove the
celery and reduce over high
heat. Combine the celery and
liquid in a shallow dish, cover
with cling film and leave to
cool in the liquid. Drain, and
serve chilled or at room
temperature, garnished with
the sprigs of fresh coriander.

Fresh leaves *make an attractive garnish but they should be
used sparingly with delicate
ingredients as their taste easily
dominates others*

*Lower leaves are
broad and finely
scalloped; their
taste is preferable
to the upper leaves*

*Fresh green leaves look a bit like
flat-leaf parsley, but coriander
can always be identified by its
distinctive aroma*

29

LEMON GRASS

FORMS
Whole stalk: Fresh, dried
and ground

HOW TO STORE
Fresh: In plastic bags in the
refrigerator, or freeze.
Dried: Keep in airtight
containers in a cool place,
or refrigerate but protect
from humidity.
Ground: In an airtight jar
kept in a cool, dark place.

COOKING TIPS
Use *fresh stalk* whole or
chopped. Bruise stem to
release flavour. Use only
lower 10–15 cm (4–6 in),
discarding upper fibrous
part (see below). Soak
dried stalks in hot water
before use. When substituting, one teaspoon *ground*
is roughly equivalent to
one stalk.

Common in the tropics of Southeast Asia, though
also widely grown in many parts of the world
including India, Africa, Australia, South America and
parts of the United States, lemon grass is characterized
by a strong citrus flavour. Typical of much of the
cooking of Thailand and Vietnam, it is not always easy
to find in Western markets. If it is unavailable, substitute
lemon peel with a tiny amount of fresh grated ginger.

*Lemon grass has long spear-shaped
leaves and a bulbous base that is
fibrous and woody*

Ground stalks *can be
added directly to the dish*

Dried shredded stalks
*must be soaked in hot
water before using*

**Fresh chopped
stalks**

TASTES GOOD WITH/IN

Curries, soups, stews and
casseroles, particularly
those made with chicken
and seafood.

COOK'S CHOICE
HOT AND SOUR PRAWN SOUP

Serves 4

1200 ml (2 pt) chicken stock

*4 spring onions, white and green
parts, chopped*

*2 tbsp chopped fresh coriander
leaves*

*1 small fresh hot green chilli,
seeded and chopped*

*3 lemon grass stalks cut into
2.5 cm (1 in) pieces*

*1 tbsp Asian fish sauce
(see page 244)*

Salt

*2.5 cm (1 in) piece lime or
lemon peel*

2 tbsp lime or lemon juice

*500 g (1 lb) frozen prawns,
defrosted*

*Chopped spring onions and
coriander leaves for garnish*

In a saucepan, combine all the
ingredients, except the
prawns. Bring to a simmer,
cover, and cook over low heat
for 20 minutes to blend the
flavours. Strain and discard the
solids. Return the liquid to the
saucepan, add the prawns and
cook until the prawns are just
heated through, 1–2 minutes.
Pour into a soup tureen,
garnish with the chopped
spring onions and coriander
and serve.

FENNEL

Tis hardy perennial, native to Southern Europe, has been used as a herb, spice and vegetable for thousands of years. Popular with the Romans and Greeks, it was also known in ancient China, India and Egypt. All over Europe it was, and still is, widely used with fresh and cured fish. Several varieties exist, but wild or common fennel, grown primarily in Central Europe and Russia, has the most bitter taste. Florence fennel, an annual plant, is grown for its bulbous stalk bases, and also for the young stalks which are cooked and eaten as a vegetable. Florence fennel leaves taste of anise and are not bitter, making them a pleasing addition to dishes both raw and cooked. Florence fennel is smaller than common fennel, though both forms have blue-green feathery leaves and bear attractive bright yellow flowers which last through the summer.

OTHER NAMES
Wild fennel, Roman fennel, Florence fennel, *finocchio*

FORMS
Leaves: Fresh and dried
Stalks: Fresh and dried
Seeds: Dried

AFFINITY WITH OTHER HERBS/SPICES
Parsley, oregano, sage, thyme, chilli

HOW TO STORE
Fresh leaves: Keep in a plastic bag in the refrigerator, or chop finely and freeze in ice-cube trays. They can also be infused in olive oil or wine vinegar. *Dried stalks and seeds:* Keep in airtight containers in a cool, dark place.

Seeds *are small, aromatic, flat ovals with yellow ridges*

Feathery blue-green leaves are similar to dill in appearance, but not in taste

COOKING TIPS
Use *fresh leaves* in a bouquet garni to flavour fish dishes. With a mortar and pestle, lightly crush *seeds* to release their flavour. For Indian dishes, roast before use. The seeds can also be sprouted and added to green salads.

TASTES GOOD WITH/IN
Whole fresh leaves: Baked or grilled seafood, court-bouillons. *Chopped fresh leaves:* Mayonnaise, sauces, stuffings, soups, vinaigrette dressings, vegetable and seafood salads, pork. *Seeds:* Breads, savoury biscuits, sausages, spicy meat mixtures, curries, cabbage dishes and apple pie.

COOK'S CHOICE
SEA BASS WITH FENNEL
Serves 4–6

2 kg (5 lb) sea bass, scaled, gutted and rinsed
Salt
Freshly ground black pepper
10 stalks fresh or dried fennel
Olive oil
4 tbsp anise-flavoured liqueur, such as Pernod (optional)

Preheat oven to 180°C (350°F, gas 4). Season the fish with salt and pepper and stuff the cavity with 2 fennel stalks. Brush the fish with oil, then brush a baking dish with oil. Arrange the remaining fennel stalks in the dish, lay the fish on top and bake until the flesh feels firm to the touch, 30–40 minutes. If using anise-flavoured liqueur, transfer the baking dish to a work surface. Warm the liqueur, pour it over the fish and ignite. When the flames die out, transfer the fish to a warmed platter and serve immediately, or separate the fillets and serve on warmed, individual plates.

Chopped fresh leaves *can be sprinkled over soups or salads as a garnish*

HYSSOP

FORMS
Leaves: Fresh and dried
Flowers: Fresh

HOW TO STORE
Fresh leaves and flowers: In tightly sealed plastic bags kept in the refrigerator. *Dried leaves:* Keep in airtight containers in a cool, dark place.

HOW TO DRY
Hang in warm, dark, well-ventilated place.

COOKING TIPS
Hyssop flowers from June to September and the tiny buds can be sprinkled over a salad of mixed lettuce and sliced, hard-boiled eggs. Use fresh chopped *leaves* in green salads.
Do not use both leaves and flowers in the same dish as the stronger flavour of the leaves will dominate that of the delicate flowers.

This is a herb of great antiquity. Frequently mentioned in the Bible from Moses to John the Baptist, it was also venerated by the Arabs. The ancient Greeks boiled it with rue and honey, and used it as a cough remedy. Much used as a medicinal herb in the past, hyssop is also used to flavour liqueurs, such as the well-known Chartreuse. The flavour is rather bitter with a trace of mint, and some herbalists even find an overtone of rue. In the kitchen it can be added to soups and stews, and a few fresh leaves will enliven a salad. Hyssop is also used in tisanes and, when infused in a sugar syrup (see page 196), it can be added to fruit desserts. A fragrant plant in the garden, it attracts both bees and butterflies, and has been said to discourage the cabbage butterfly from damaging the vegetable patch.

Flowers are generally purple but may be pink or white

Chopped fresh leaves

Fresh leaves *have a slightly bitter, slightly minty flavour*

Leaves are aromatic, pointed and narrow

TASTES GOOD WITH/IN

Dried leaves: Soups, stews, herbal teas. *Fresh leaves:* Soft cheeses such as goat cheese and cottage cheese, flavoured butters, sandwiches, sauces, dips, hot or cold pasta dishes. *Flowers:* Green salads.

COOK'S CHOICE
GLAZED CARROTS WITH HYSSOP

Serves 4

500 g (1 lb) young carrots, scraped and thinly sliced

250 ml (8 fl oz) chicken stock

1 tbsp clear honey

1 tbsp unsalted butter

Salt

Freshly ground white pepper

1 tbsp finely chopped fresh hyssop leaves

In a saucepan, combine the carrots, stock, honey, butter, and salt and pepper to taste. Bring to a simmer over medium heat. Cover and cook over low heat until the carrots are tender and the liquid is a syrupy glaze, about 20 minutes. Toss the carrots with the hyssop and serve immediately.

BAY

HOW TO STORE
Fresh leaves: Should be used immediately though they will keep for a few days in a plastic bag in the refrigerator.
Dried leaves: Keep in an airtight container in a cool, dark place.

HOW TO DRY
Hang in a dry, dark, well-ventilated place. Once dried, remove *leaves* from stems before storing.

COOKING TIPS
The strong, spicy flavour of bay intensifies with drying, however, *old leaves* lose their flavour and should be discarded. *Fresh leaves* have a slightly bitter flavour, which dissipates if left for a few days to wilt. *Whole leaves* release more flavour when shredded or chopped. Remove whole leaves before serving.

The bay tree may have come originally from Asia Minor but it has been in the Mediterranean region for so long that it is thought of as a native. A small tree with glossy dark green leaves, it can reach a considerable height, but is often grown in tubs and pruned into attractive round shapes. It has waxy, creamy blossoms much loved by bees. In ancient Greece and Rome, bay leaves were used to make the crowns of laurel worn by victors in battle or sports contests. Poets were also honoured with a wreath of bay leaves, and were hailed as poet laureate, which is a term still in use today.
In the kitchen, the bay leaf is indispensable. It seems to go in and with almost everything: from savoury meat and fish dishes, to pasta sauces, and even sweet dishes such as baked milk pudding. Cuisines the world over make use of this most versatile and flavoursome herb.
Bay is one of the vital ingredients of a bouquet garni (see page 55) and, at a pinch, a single bay leaf is flavourful enough to act as a substitute for the whole bundle.

(see page 55)

TASTES GOOD WITH/IN

Bouquet garni, soups, meat and poultry dishes, pasta sauces, fish dishes and even some desserts.

COOK'S CHOICE
POTATOES WITH BAY LEAVES

Serves 4–6

Olive oil
1 kg (2 lb) potatoes, peeled and cut into 1.5 cm (1/2 in) slices
2 large garlic cloves, chopped
4 large bay leaves
Salt
Freshly ground black pepper
450 ml (3/4 pt) chicken stock

Brush a shallow, flameproof casserole with olive oil. Make a layer of half the potatoes, garlic and bay leaves. Season with salt and pepper to taste, and drizzle with 2 tbsp olive oil. Repeat with the remaining potatoes, garlic, bay leaves, 2 tbsp olive oil and salt and pepper. Pour in the chicken stock, bring to a simmer and cook, covered, over low heat until the potatoes are tender and the liquid is absorbed, 25–30 minutes. If any liquid remains, pour it off. Discard the bay leaves before serving

Fresh leaves should be glossy and unblemished

Dried bay leaves *can be used either whole or crumbled*

Fresh bay leaves *should be shredded before use*

LOVAGE

Love parsley, garden
lovage, Italian lovage

FORMS

Leaves: Fresh, dried,
crystallized *Seeds*: Dried
Stems: Fresh, crystallized

HOW TO STORE

Dried leaves and seeds:
Keep in airtight containers
in a cool, dark place.
Fresh leaves: Can be frozen
whole in ice-cube trays.

HOW TO DRY

Hang in a dry, well-
ventilated place away from
light. Separate *leaves* from
stems before storing.

Seeds *are small, brown and
aromatic*

*Leaves are large, toothed and
glossy green with a strong
celery-like flavour*

COOKING TIPS

Use lovage sparingly as the
flavour can be overwhelm-
ing if used too lavishly.
Tender *young leaves* can be
added raw to salads, while
old leaves can be used in
soups, stocks, stews, and
with soft cheeses. *Stems* can
be crystallized, or they can
be chopped and added to
soups and stews. The stems
can also be steamed, but
must be peeled or scraped
before cooking. *Crystallized
leaves* can be used for
decoration. *Seeds* can be
added to cakes and breads
or sprinkled on salads.

Lovage is a tall perennial herb with hollow stems
and serrated green leaves which resemble celery.
A fast-growing plant, it is one of the earliest herbs to
appear in the garden at the beginning of spring and the
flowers come out as pale yellow umbels. The seeds,
roots and leaves were widely used by the ancient
Greeks and Romans, but these uses have been lost for
the most part. Lovage tastes very strongly of celery but,
unlike celery, it does stand up well to long cooking, so
only a few leaves or chopped young stalks are needed
to flavour a slow-simmering stew or soup. Its leaves and
stalks can be crystallized and used like angelica for cake
decoration. In parts of Czechoslovakia and Italy, the
roots are peeled to remove the bitter skin, cooked, and
served as a vegetable.

*Top leaves are
smaller and
contain less stalk
than those lower
down*

*Stems are hollow
and ridged*

Soups, salads, stuffings,
stews and meat dishes.

COOK'S CHOICE
**LOVAGE SOUP WITH
TOMATO AND APPLE**

Serves 4–6

4 tbsp unsalted butter

1 medium onion, finely chopped

*500 g (1 lb) tomatoes, peeled,
seeded and chopped*

*4 large cooking apples, peeled,
cored and chopped*

*125 g (4 oz) lovage leaves,
coarsely chopped*

1 litre (1 3/4 pt) chicken stock

Salt

Freshly ground black pepper

*Finely chopped lovage leaves or
yogurt for garnish*

In a large saucepan, heat the
butter and cook the onion
until soft. Add the tomatoes,
apples and lovage leaves and
cook for 2–3 minutes, stirring
occasionally. Pour in the
chicken stock, bring to a boil,
cover, lower the heat and
simmer for 30 minutes. Purée
in batches in a food processor
until smooth. Place a sieve
over a clean saucepan and
pour the soup through. Season
to taste with salt and
pepper, and heat
through. This soup is
delicious hot or cold. If
serving hot, garnish with
fresh lovage and serve immediately. For a cold soup,
refrigerate until sufficiently
chilled, then serve in bowls,
each one topped with a dollop
of yogurt.

Dried leaves *retain their
strong flavour*

LEMON BALM

OTHER NAMES
Balm gentle, balm mint, sweet balm, melissa, bee herb

FORMS
Leaves: Fresh and dried

HOW TO STORE
Fresh leaves: Best to use fresh, but may be stored in plastic bags in the refrigerator for a few days.
Dried leaves: Keep in an airtight container in a cool, dark place, but the flavour lessens with time.

HOW TO DRY
Use the second crop of *leaves* as they are smaller. Hang bunches in a warm, dark, well ventilated place.

COOKING TIPS
Prefer *fresh* over *dried*. Add fresh chopped leaves to a fruit salad. Infuse *fresh* or *dried leaves* for a refreshing and relaxing tea.

Chopped fresh leaves
will add zest to sweet or savoury dishes

Fresh leaves

Lemon balm enhances a wide variety of dishes, and most cooks will agree that any dish using lemon juice will be improved by the addition of a few balm leaves. It is a pretty plant in the garden or in a tub, with fragrant, attractive white flowers, though they should be cut back if the leaves are needed in the kitchen. *Melissa* derives from the Greek for honey-bee, and lemon balm, with heart-shaped, crinkled and serrated leaves, attracts bees with its sweet, lemon-scented perfume. The plant almost certainly originated in the Middle East but spread quickly to the Mediterranean where it has been cultivated for more than 2,000 years. It is the basis of the cordial *eau des Carmes* and is used in various liqueurs. It makes a delicious addition to all kinds of stewed fruits.

Leaves are light green, deeply veined with jagged edges, and have an aroma of lemon with a trace of mint

TASTES GOOD WITH/IN

Egg dishes, especially omelettes; herbal teas; milk infused for drinking or custards; salads; soups; casseroles, especially those made with game birds, white wine cups.

COOK'S CHOICE
MELISSA WINE CUP

Makes 3 litres (5 pt)

500 g (1 lb) peaches, preferably white peaches, peeled, pitted and puréed

Sugar

125 g (4 oz) fresh lemon balm leaves, coarsely chopped

3 litres (5 pt) medium-dry white wine, chilled

A few fresh lemon balm sprigs for garnish

Put the puréed peaches in a small bowl and add sugar to taste. Add the lemon balm leaves and 600 ml (1 pt) of the wine. Stir to blend. Leave to macerate in the refrigerator for at least 2 hours. When ready to serve, strain, discarding the lemon balm. Pour into a punch bowl and stir in the remainder of the chilled wine. Garnish with lemon balm sprigs and serve.

MINT

OTHER NAMES
Spearmint, peppermint, apple mint, lemon mint, water mint, raripila, round-leaved mint

FORMS
Leaves: Fresh and dried

AFFINITY WITH OTHER HERBS/SPICES
Parsley, coriander, chilli, garlic, cardamom, basil

HOW TO STORE
Fresh leaves: All the mints are best used fresh and should be stored only briefly, in plastic bags in the refrigerator. They may be frozen in ice-cube trays.
Dried leaves: Should be kept in an airtight container in a cool dark place.

The many varieties of mint can be used in both sweet and savoury dishes, and there are many recipes which feature mints of all kinds. The great number of species of this perennial herb leads to confusion, though fortunately there are several whose flavour does not differ widely and they can be used interchangeably. Spearmint is the preferred type for mint sauce or mint jelly to accompany lamb, and it is equally good with new potatoes, peas and carrots. Spearmint is also used for the tea that is such a favourite in North Africa and the Middle East, and for the mint julep from the American state of Kentucky, made with Kentucky bourbon and fresh mint, and served in a special silver cup. In the West, peppermint is rarely found in savoury dishes, but is used to flavour cordials, liqueurs, sweets and desserts. Lemon mint is not a culinary herb, though sometimes it is used in drinks.

TASTES GOOD WITH/IN
Fresh and dried: Herb tea, soups, salads, sauces, plain meats, fish, poultry, stews, sweet dishes, chocolate-covered sweets and lemon-based desserts such as mousses and tarts.

COOKING TIPS
Though *fresh* mint is usually preferred, *dried* mint can be used in Middle Eastern dishes, especially those with curd-cheese pastry fillings, yogurt dressings and sauces, and in stuffings for vegetables such as aubergines, peppers and tomatoes. It can also be used to make a mint sauce.

The variegated dappled cream and pale green leaves are known for their fruity flavour

The most widely known and used of the mints has leaves that are closely set, toothed and bright green

Leaves are hairy and bright green

Pineapple mint

Red raripila spearmint *is characterized by pointed, dark green leaves, dark stems and purple flowers; it has a sweet minty flavour*

Apple mint *has rounded woolly leaves full of the flavour of apples and is sweeter and more mellow than other varieties*

Moroccan spearmint

CRYSTALLIZED MINT

Crystallized mint leaves make attractive decorations for puddings and cakes, especially when used with crystallized violets, rose petals (see page 211) or angelica. They can also be served instead of traditional mints with after-dinner coffee.

Gather the best and largest leaves and inspect carefully for blemishes. In a shallow bowl, dissolve 60 g (2 oz) gum arabic (also known as *edible gum*) in 300 ml (½ pt) water. Have ready a bowl of caster sugar and a pastry brush. Using the pastry brush, thoroughly paint each side of the mint leaves with the gum solution to coat completely. Dip the leaves into the sugar to cover both sides, shaking gently to remove the excess. For a strong mint flavour, let the leaves remain submerged in the sugar for several hours or sprinkle a few drops of peppermint oil over the sugar-coated leaves. Spread the leaves out to dry on a wire cake rack. Allow to dry for 24 hours, then turn and dry the other side for a further 24 hours. When both sides are dry, pack them into airtight containers and store in a cool place away from light.

Dried leaves *can be used in certain sauces, though fresh are preferred, and are ideal for creating soothing teas*

Chopped fresh leaves

MINT VARIETIES

With more than 600 known varieties of mint, there are quite a number with distinct flavours and scents. The two most common flavourings used in cookery are spearmint and peppermint. The spearmint bought at any greengrocer is likely to be the Moroccan variety shown. The easily cultivated red raripila variety has a strong flavour and is recognizable by its red stems. For a milder spearmint flavour, any variety of the apple mints can be used. With their distinctive scents, apple mint and its variegated relative, pineapple mint, are attractive and useful herbs to have in the garden. Peppermint is always easily recognized by its strong aroma; it is most often used in the form of peppermint oil for flavouring sweets or chocolates. Basil mint, so named for its similarity in appearance to basil, has a very pleasant lemon scent, and is delicious when stirred into cake or biscuit batters.

Look for bright green, unblemished leaves and a fresh, minty fragrance

Leaves are darker and less crinkly than spearmint with a cool, stimulating scent and a slightly heavier taste

Basil mint

Black peppermint

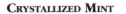

COOK'S CHOICE
CUCUMBER, YOGURT AND MINT DIP

Serves 4

½ *cucumber, peeled, seeded and finely chopped*
10 *fresh mint leaves, preferably spearmint, very finely chopped*
400 g (14 oz) *yogurt, preferably Greek yogurt*
Salt

In a bowl, mix together the cucumber, mint leaves and yogurt. Season to taste with salt and serve with pitta bread as an hors d'oeuvre.

BERGAMOT

FORMS
Flowers: Fresh and
crystallized
Leaves: Fresh and dried

HOW TO STORE
Fresh flowers and leaves:
Can be kept for a short time
in a plastic bag in the
refrigerator.
Dried leaves: Should be
kept in airtight containers in
a cool, dark place.
Crystallized flowers: Should
be wrapped in foil and
kept in a cool place.

HOW TO DRY
Pick *leaves* when young,
preferably in spring or
summer, as flowers form.
Hang to dry in a warm,
well-ventilated place.

COOKING TIPS
Both *fresh leaves* and
flowers, gently torn apart or
coarsely chopped, add
greatly to green salads. Try
fresh leaves in recipes
calling for fresh mint.

A member of the mint family, bergamot is native to
North America. Its botanical name, *Monarda,*
derives from the Spanish physician, Nicholas Monardes,
who first discovered and described it. The North American Oswego Indians made a herb tea from the leaves. At
the time of the Boston Tea Party, settlers called it
Oswego tea and drank it instead of tea imported from
Britain. The young leaves can be used sparingly in
salads or added to stuffings. The flowers make a colourful garnish, either fresh or crystallized. Two other plants
are sometimes called bergamot: eau de cologne mint
and bergamot orange. The latter is a small citrus plant
with a sweet perfume that is grown in southern Italy, but
both of these are quite separate from the herb.

*Flower head clusters
are shaggy, tubular
and scarlet*

*Leaves are
toothed and
oval shaped
with red
veining*

*A pretty plant with
red pin-cushion
flowers which are
sweet-tasting, full of
nectar and a
favourite of bees,
hence its name bee
balm*

*Stem is hairy, hard,
ridged and square in
shape*

Whole leaves
*One of these can be added to
a cup of fresh China tea
to reproduce the flavour
of Earl Grey.*

TASTES GOOD WITH/IN

Salads, herb teas, summer
drinks, vegetable dishes,
stews, poultry and meats,
especially pork.

COOK'S CHOICE
**BERGAMOT SAUCE FOR
PORK**

Makes about 250 ml (8 fl oz)

2 tbsp unsalted butter
*1 medium onion, finely
chopped*
1 tbsp plain flour
250 ml (8 fl oz) chicken stock
1 tbsp lemon juice
Salt
Freshly ground black pepper
*1 tbsp finely chopped fresh
bergamot leaves*

Heat the butter in a small
saucepan, add the onion and
cook until it is soft. Add the
flour and cook, stirring with a
wooden spoon, for about 2
minutes. Gradually stir in the
chicken stock and cook until
the sauce is smooth and
thickened. Stir in the lemon
juice and season to taste with
salt and pepper. Add the
bergamot leaves and cook for
a further 2 minutes. Transfer to
a gravy boat and serve hot,
with roast pork.

Chopped fresh leaves
*These can be added in judicious
amounts to stuffings and salads.*

SWEET CICELY

HOW TO STORE
Fresh leaves: Can be kept in tightly sealed plastic bags in the vegetable bin of the refrigerator. To freeze, chop finely, place in ice-cube trays and add water to fill.

COOKING TIPS
Sweet cicely is a useful sugar substitute. Use it to add sweetness to fruit desserts and drinks, and as a pleasant alternative to sugar for sweetening cream or yogurt. It will enhance the flavour of any herb with which it is used.

Chopped fresh leaves can be sprinkled into drinks or whipped into cream to add sweetness and a delicate anise taste. Make a tea from the leaves to help cure indigestion

Sweet cicely, a perennial herb native to the mountains of the Savoy region of France, owes its charming name to its fern-like, pale green leaves which have a sugary taste. An attractive plant, its kitchen use is fairly limited though its natural sweetness can be put to good use. It will reduce the need for added sugar when cooked with sour fruit such as rhubarb and gooseberries. The seeds are the most flavourful part, tasting strongly of anise or liquorice. Chopped unripe seeds can be used in salads or creamy desserts; whole ripe seeds can be used like cloves. However, it does have a place in the garden not just for its fragrance but because of its persistence: it is one of the first herbs to appear in spring and one of the last to go in the autumn. Boiled sweet cicely roots were once served as a salad, dressed with oil and vinegar.

Unripe seeds are green and are used chopped

Ripe seeds are glossy brown and are used whole

Clusters of white flowers are soon followed by seeds

The stems are hollow; the leaves fern-like

COOK'S CHOICE
FRUIT AND WINE CUP

Makes about 8 servings

500 ml (16 fl oz) orange juice
250 ml (8 fl oz) lemon juice
1 bottle dry red wine
2 tsp finely chopped fresh sweet cicely

Combine all the ingredients in a large glass jug. Stir to mix and refrigerate until ready to serve. Put 2–3 ice cubes into each 250 ml (8 fl oz) goblet and pour in the wine cup.

BASIL

OTHER NAMES
Sweet basil

FORMS
Leaves: Fresh and dried

AFFINITY WITH OTHER HERBS/SPICES
Parsley, rosemary, oregano, thyme, sage, saffron

HOW TO STORE
Fresh leaves: Can be kept briefly in plastic bags in the refrigerator, preserved in olive oil or vinegar, or frozen. To freeze, leaves should be puréed with a little water and put into ice-cube trays. When frozen, the cubes can be stored in the freezer in plastic bags.
Dried leaves: Keep in airtight containers at room temperature away from light and heat.

Basil is one of the most important of the culinary herbs. The Greek name for it means "king," which shows how highly it has been regarded throughout the ages. There are many types of basil, which vary in size, colour and flavour, and all can be used for culinary purposes. Purple ruffle and dark opal are two of the more unusual but useful varieties. Basil goes with almost everything, but it has a special affinity with tomatoes. Fresh torn basil leaves are delicious on a salad of sliced tomatoes, lightly seasoned with salt and freshly ground pepper, and drizzled with a fruity extra-virgin olive oil, accompanied by crusty bread. Perhaps the greatest basil dish is pesto – an Italian basil, garlic, cheese and pine nut sauce – which turns spaghetti into a feast, though it can also be used as a marinade. Bottled pesto can be bought during the months when it is too cold for basil to grow, which is certainly better than having no basil at all. Italian cooks preserve their prolific basil crops by filling a jar with the leaves, lightly salting them, topping up the jar with olive oil, closing it tightly and storing it in the refrigerator.

TASTES GOOD WITH/IN
Tomatoes, spaghetti sauces such as pesto, with fish, especially red mullet, mushroom dishes, soups, stews, salads, chicken, egg and rice dishes, and mixed with other herbs.

Dried basil *does not have the same flavour as fresh; a more minty taste predominates*

Fresh torn leaves

Chiffonade strips
Evenly cut shreds of basil leaves make a delightful soup garnish.

Whole fresh leaves

Pestle, pesto and pistou
Italian pesto, known as **pistou** *in France, is best made with a mortar and pestle.*

Flowers are creamy white or purple-tinged

The young leaves at the top of the plant are sweetest

Look for soft, green, unbruised leaves with a strong scent

Sweet basil

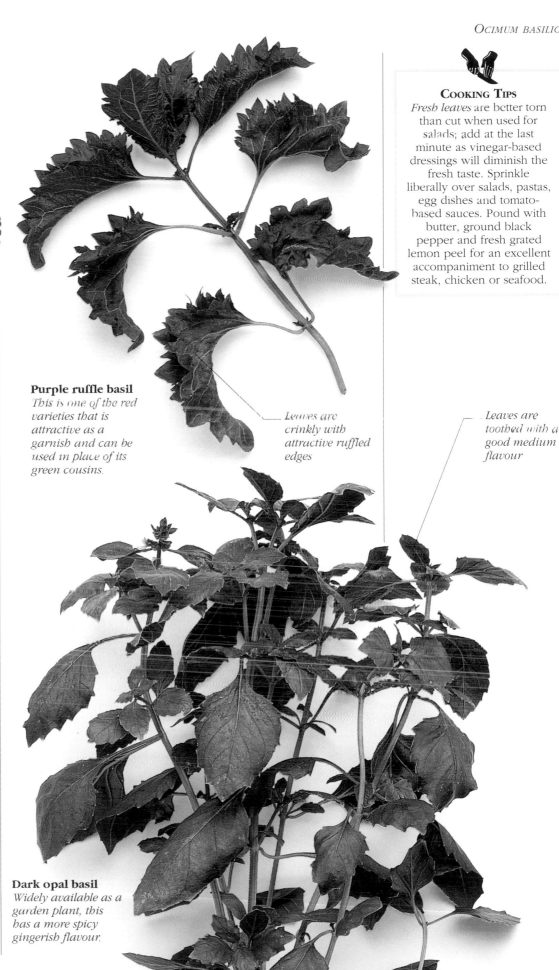

COOK'S CHOICE
FRESH SPAGHETTI WITH PESTO

Serves 2–4

60 g (2 oz) fresh basil leaves
2–4 garlic cloves, or to taste
30 g (1 oz) pine nuts
4 tbsp extra-virgin olive oil
4 tbsp freshly grated Parmesan cheese
Salt
500 g (1 lb) fresh spaghetti

Combine the basil, garlic and pine nuts in a food processor and reduce to a purée. With the machine running, slowly add the oil, pouring in a steady stream. When the mixture is well emulsified, add the cheese and process briefly. Scrape out into a bowl, taste for seasoning, and add a little salt if necessary. Cook the spaghetti in a large pot of boiling, salted water. Drain, transfer to a bowl and toss with the pesto. Serve hot or at room temperature.

Greek basil
This has tiny green leaves with a good flavour and is a compact garden plant.

Purple ruffle basil
This is one of the red varieties that is attractive as a garnish and can be used in place of its green cousins.

Leaves are crinkly with attractive ruffled edges

Dark opal basil
Widely available as a garden plant, this has a more spicy gingerish flavour.

Leaves are toothed with a good medium flavour

COOKING TIPS
Fresh leaves are better torn than cut when used for salads; add at the last minute as vinegar-based dressings will diminish the fresh taste. Sprinkle liberally over salads, pastas, egg dishes and tomato-based sauces. Pound with butter, ground black pepper and fresh grated lemon peel for an excellent accompaniment to grilled steak, chicken or seafood.

MARJORAM AND OREGANO

HOW TO STORE
Fresh leaves: Can be kept in a plastic bag in the refrigerator, or frozen. To freeze, mix finely chopped leaves with a little water in ice-cube trays. Store frozen cubes in the freezer in plastic bags until needed. *Dried leaves:* Should be stored in airtight containers in a cool, dark place.

HOW TO DRY
Tie stems together and hang in a warm, well-ventilated place.

These two perennial herbs are so closely related that they need not be classified separately. The name oregano derives from the Greek for "joy of the mountains", which is where the wild varieties of this herb thrive. They are similar in appearance, with small, soft, sometimes mottled green leaves and small white or pink flowers that form clusters. Marjoram has a more delicate flavour and is a gentler herb than oregano, which is actually a wild variety of marjoram, and has a more potent flavour. These herbs are native to the Mediterranean region, appearing in many French and Italian dishes, especially tomato-based sauces. The more robust flavour of oregano is the quintessential pizza flavouring, and it is also a favourite herb in Greece. In Mexico, it is one of the ingredients of chilli powder. There are many more wild species, most of which grow in Greece where they are all called by one name, *rigani*. These are not commercially available, and are more strongly flavoured and coarser than either ordinary marjoram or oregano.

TASTES GOOD WITH/IN
Oil and vinegar salad dressings, fresh or tinned anchovies, Italian and Greek dishes, poultry, game, seafood, soups, beans, aubergines, pasta, grilled meats, tomato-based sauces.

COOKING TIPS
The powerful flavour of *oregano* comes through quite well when *dried*, but *marjoram*, which is more delicate, is best added *fresh* at the end of cooking.

Can be infused as an aromatic tea

Chopped fresh marjoram *can be added to salads and butter sauces for fish*

Leaves will turn golden when grown in full sun

White or pale pink flowers appear in summer

A compact, bushy plant with small, dark green leaves

Golden curly marjoram

Fresh marjoram

Dried marjoram

Gold splash marjoram

Golden marjoram

Oregano

A hardy perennial, the flavour of oregano varies, depending on climate and soil

COOK'S CHOICE
CORN SOUP WITH FRESH MARJORAM

Serves 4

350 g (12 oz) frozen sweet corn kernels, defrosted

1 litre (1 3/4 pt) chicken stock

30 g (1 oz) fresh marjoram, finely chopped

Salt

Freshly ground black pepper

Marjoram sprigs for garnish

Purée the sweet corn in a food processor with a little of the chicken stock then force the mixture through a sieve. Combine the corn purée with the remaining chicken stock in a saucepan, cover, and simmer for 5 minutes. Stir in the marjoram, season to taste with salt and pepper, and simmer for a further 5 minutes. Garnish with marjoram sprigs and serve in soup bowls.

An attractive garnish, this is created by placing several leaves on top of each other and cutting them into thin lengthwise strips

Oregano chiffonade

Dried oregano *retains its original flavour well and is good used in sauces, stews and soups, particularly those with a tomato base*

43

PARSLEY

This popular herb, originally from Southern Europe, is now grown in all of the world's temperate regions. There are two main types – curly and flat-leaf. Both types are a rich source of vitamins and minerals. Flat-leaf parsley, with its dark green foliage, is best for cooking as it is more flavourful and stands up better to heat. The curly variety is ideal for garnishing a wide variety of dishes. Although less flavoursome, it does keep well when refrigerated. A sprinkling of finely chopped parsley, added just before serving, provides colour and gives a fresh flavour to sauces, salads or buttered new potatoes. The stems and leaves should be used in bouquet garni (see page 55), and the leaves are essential to the classic seasoning mixtures persillade and gremolada. Deep-fried sprigs of whole parsley are delicious partnering seafood or grilled meats. Hamburg parsley is used not as a herb, but for its root which has a flavour that is rather like a mixture of celeriac and parsley. Sold as parsley root, it is very pleasant when boiled and added to mashed potatoes.

OTHER NAMES
Curly parsley, flat-leaf parsley, Italian parsley, continental parsley

FORMS
Leaves: Fresh and dried

HOW TO STORE
Fresh leaves: Keep in a plastic bag in the refrigerator or sprinkle with water and wrap in paper towels. For maximum freshness, put cut-ends in cold water.
Dried leaves: Keep in an airtight container away from light and moisture.

COOKING TIPS
When available, use *flat-leaf parsley* as the flavour is much better than that of *curly parsley.*

Persillade
A mixture of finely chopped parsley leaves and garlic which is sautéed and added at the last minute to numerous dishes such as grilled lamb or beef steaks, fried fish, chicken or vegetables.

Gremolada
A Milanese flavouring mixture consisting of sautéed orange and lemon rind, finely chopped garlic and parsley. Traditionally, gremolada is sprinkled over osso buco just before serving, though it can be used to enhance any braised meat dish. It should always be added at the last minute.

Look for bright green, unblemished leaves

Flat-leaf parsley

TASTES GOOD WITH/IN
Omelettes, salads, stews, vegetables, soups, eggs, sauces, rice and pasta dishes, fish, shellfish, any meat and poultry, mixed with soft cheeses such as ricotta or cottage cheese.

COOK'S CHOICE
COURGETTE AND PARSLEY FRITTATA

Serves 2–3

2 tbsp unsalted butter
1 tbsp olive oil
1 small onion, finely chopped
250 g (8 oz) courgettes, trimmed and chopped
250 g (8 oz) tomatoes, peeled, seeded and chopped
3 tbsp finely chopped flat-leaf parsley
Salt
Freshly ground black pepper
4 large eggs
Curly parsley sprigs for garnish

Heat the butter and oil in a non-stick frying pan and sauté the onion until it is golden and tender. Add the courgettes, tomatoes, parsley and salt and pepper to taste. Cook over low heat until the courgettes are tender, about 8 minutes. Break the eggs into a bowl and beat them lightly; season lightly. Pour over the courgette mixture, stirring with a wooden spoon to mix. Turn the heat to very low and cook until the eggs have set. Run the pan under a grill to brown the top, if liked. Slide out of the pan and serve hot. Garnish with a few curly parsley sprigs.

Chopped fresh leaves *can be used as a garnish*

BURNET

OTHER NAMES
Garden burnet, lesser
burnet, salad burnet

FORMS
Leaves: Fresh and dried

HOW TO STORE
Fresh leaves: These wilt
easily, so they should be
kept in a plastic bag and
refrigerated as quickly as
possible after picking. Can
be frozen, finely chopped,
in ice-cube trays.
Dried leaves: Keep in an
airtight container in a cool,
dark place. This herb does
not dry well, though it can
be grown year round for
use fresh.

COOKING TIPS
Old leaves of burnet tend to
be tough and should be
avoided. *Young leaves* wilt
rather quickly, so use while
still fresh in order to best
savour their pleasant
cucumber taste.

Chopped leaves

*The lacy, fine-toothed leaves are
on long, graceful stems and have
a faint cucumber-like scent*

A delicate-looking, pretty plant with reddish-pink
flowers, salad burnet is nonetheless hardy enough
to produce green leaves throughout most winters. A
perennial herb, it is native to Europe. A very popular
herb in Elizabethan England, it has fallen out of use in
most places, though it can still be found in some French
or Italian dishes. Burnet is useful in salads and sauces,
where its delicate, cucumber-like flavour adds freshness.
This herb should not be confused with great burnet
(*Sanguisorba officinalis*), which is similar in appearance.
Great burnet was once known as bloodwort because it
was believed to be useful in stopping wounds from
bleeding. Yet another plant is called burnet; this is
burnet saxifrage (*Pimpinella saxifraga*), which is not a
burnet at all but a member of the parsley family.

TASTES GOOD WITH/IN
Fresh sprigs: White wine
cups, cold poached
chicken, seafood, green
salads, as a flavouring for
vinegar, cold soups.

COOK'S CHOICE
**BURNET SAUCE FOR
POACHED FISH**

Serves 4

*450 ml (¾ pt) fish stock made
with white wine*

1 tbsp red wine vinegar

*60 g (2 oz) young burnet
leaves, finely chopped*

*60 g (2 oz) unsalted butter,
chilled and cubed*

*1 kg (2 lb) boneless, skinless,
poached fish fillets, such as sole*

Pour the fish stock into a
saucepan and reduce to half
its volume over brisk heat.
Reduce the heat, stir in the
vinegar and burnet leaves and
simmer for a further 2–3
minutes. Lower the heat and
whisk the butter into the
liquid, a piece at a time, to
obtain a creamy sauce. Taste
for seasoning. Do not allow
the sauce to boil or it will
separate. Pour over the fish
and serve with plain rice.

Young leaves
*are more tender
and best suited
to salads*

ROSEMARY

FORMS
Leaves: Fresh, dried *Sprigs·*
Fresh *Flowers:* Fresh

HOW TO STORE
Fresh sprigs: Keep for
several days in a plastic bag
in the refrigerator, or place
stem ends in water.
Dried leaves: Keep in an
airtight container in a cool
place away from light.

HOW TO DRY
Hang *fresh sprigs* to dry in a
warm, dry place. Be sure to
strip off *leaves* before
storing.

COOKING TIPS
To release the flavourful
aroma of *dried leaves,* crush
just before using.
The needle-like form and
tough texture of *fresh leaves*
can be unpleasant when
encountered in a finished
dish. It is best to chop them
very finely or crush in a
mortar and pestle before
use. Alternatively, use *sprigs*
to infuse long cooking
dishes with flavour and
remove before serving.
Sprinkle *flowers* over salads
or use as a garnish.

Herb skewers
*Rosemary stems stripped of
their leaves can be used to
thread vegetables or tender
cuts of meat for grilling.*

The name of this lovely aromatic herb, with its
needle-like leaves and delicate light blue flowers,
is derived from from Latin and means "dew of the sea".
This is most appropriate as the plant is indigenous to the
Mediterranean region, where it thrives in the calcium-
rich soil, the dry climate and the salty sea spray.
It has a strong flavour that is pungent but undeniably
pleasant. In Italy, it is the preferred herb with veal,
poultry or lamb dishes, especially those simmered with
wine, olive oil and garlic. Other Mediterranean countries
do use it, though less lavishly, while in northern Europe,
it often finds its way into sausage mixtures. This versatile
herb tastes good with strongly-flavoured vegetables, jams
and jellies, and even wine cups. It should always be
paired with lamb; a sprig placed on a roasting joint
lends the meat an incomparable flavour.

*The thin, dark green,
needle-like leaves are very
aromatic with a crisp,
woodsy perfume*

TASTES GOOD WITH/IN
Meat dishes, especially lamb
and pork, chicken, tomato-
based sauces, breads,
stuffed vegetables, pizza,
potato gratins, apple jelly.

COOK'S CHOICE
BEETROOT WITH ROSEMARY
Serves 4

12 small beetroots, with tops
Salt
2 rosemary sprigs
3 tbsp unsalted butter
Freshly ground black pepper

Place the beetroots in a
saucepan. Add water to cover,
salt, and simmer, covered,
until the beetroots are tender,
30–45 minutes depending on
the size and age of the
vegetable. When cool, peel
and slice. Strip the leaves from
the rosemary sprigs and chop
finely. In a saucepan, toss the
sliced beetroots with the
rosemary, butter, and salt and
pepper to taste for 2–3
minutes just to blend the
flavours; do not let the butter
brown. Serve immediately.

Fresh leaves *can be tied up in
a square of muslin to make them
easier to remove*

Chopped fresh leaves *can be
used to add flavour to sauces,
stews and marinades*

SORREL

HOW TO STORE
Fresh leaves: Can be kept briefly in plastic bags in the refrigerator. Sorrel does not dry well, but it can be frozen successfully.

COOKING TIPS
Sorrel's high acidity causes it to discolour when it is cooked in iron pots, or when it is chopped with other than stainless steel knives.

Sorrel Chiffonade
A chiffonade is an attractive and flavoursome way to diffuse sorrel through a dish. To proceed, wash the sorrel and pat dry. Trim the stems and then stack the leaves one upon the other. Roll up tightly then slice thinly crosswise (see above). Use the chiffonade as is, or make a purée: combine 250 g (8 oz) sorrel chiffonade with 2 tbsp butter in a small saucepan and cook over low heat, stirring often, until the leaves have melted into a purée, about 10 minutes. Serve with poached fish.

Young shoots are less acidic and ideal for use in salads and sandwiches

G arden sorrel and French sorrel are two of several allied species cultivated for use as green vegetables or herbs. The slightly less acidic French sorrel, *Rumex scutatus,* is preferred by cooks. Another member of the group, *Rumex patienta*, known also as spinach dock, is of lesser culinary importance. All of the sorrels, whose name derives from the Teutonic word for "sour", are very ancient herbs. They were used in Pharaonic Egypt, and they are still employed in modern Egyptian cooking. The ancient Greeks and Romans used the acidity of sorrel to aid digestion and offset the effects of rich food. Sorrel has always been popular throughout Europe, especially in France, where it still enjoys its greatest popularity, most notably in sorrel soup and *saumon à l'oseille,* or salmon with sorrel sauce. The leaves are a very rich source of potassium and vitamins A and C. Sorrel is very easily puréed, making it the ideal base for an excellent sauce to accompany poached fish or eggs. Because of its acidity, it acts as a meat tenderizer, and can be wrapped around cubes of tough meat before stewing or braising.

Garden sorrel has large green, lance-shaped leaves with a broad base

COOK'S CHOICE
VEAL STEW WITH SORREL

Serves 6

2 tbsp vegetable oil

2 tbsp butter

1 kg (2 lb) boneless veal , cut into 4 cm (1¹/₂ in) cubes

2 medium onions, finely chopped

250 g (8 oz) mushrooms, sliced

250 ml (8 fl oz) dry white wine

250 ml (8 fl oz) chicken stock

Bouquet garni

Salt

Freshly ground black pepper

Fresh sorrel chiffonade (see left)

Heat the oil and butter in a frying pan, add the veal and sauté until golden. Transfer to a casserole. Sauté the onions and mushrooms in the same frying pan until they are tender. Add to the casserole with the wine, stock, bouquet garni and salt and pepper to taste. Cover and simmer until the veal is tender, about 1¹/₂ hours. Transfer the veal cubes to a serving dish. Remove the bouquet garni. Reduce the cooking liquid to half, stir in the sorrel chiffonade and heat through. Pour over the veal and serve with plain boiled rice.

Finely chopped leaves

SAGE

FORMS
Leaves: Fresh, dried and ground

AFFINITY WITH OTHER HERBS/SPICES
Rosemary, thyme, oregano, parsley and bay leaf

HOW TO STORE
Fresh leaves: Can be kept for a few days in plastic bags in the refrigerator.
Dried leaves: Must be kept in containers in a cool, dark place to retain the grey-green colour and powerful flavour.
Ground leaves: Must be stored in airtight containers.

HOW TO DRY
Cut in the spring before the flower stalks begin to lengthen; hang to dry in a warm, well-ventilated place.

Sage, a universal flavouring herb, is a native of the North Mediterranean coast. A medium-sized perennial shrub, it is very aromatic with blue or lilac flowers that appear at the end of spring. Sage is one of many herbs not restricted to culinary use; in the past it was believed to have healing qualities and was used medicinally for a long time before it found its way into the kitchen. Greeks, Romans and Arabs all used sage for its curative powers, as a general tonic and for snake bites; in the Middle Ages it was considered a cure-all. Just when its use in the kitchen overtook its use in the sickroom is not clear, but it has certainly kept its place in cookery for several centuries. The Italians use it in meat dishes, particularly with calves' liver and veal, the Germans add sage to eel dishes, and in France, it is cooked with pork, veal and some charcuterie. In many countries, especially Greece, sage tea is popular. In the Middle East, it is added to salads, and British cooks use it for flavouring fresh sausages, in the traditional stuffing for pork or goose and in Derby cheese. It is one of the few herbs whose flavour strengthens when it is dried and, since it has a powerful flavour, the dried and ground versions should be added discreetly.

Dried sage *is more powerful than its fresh form and should be used sparingly*

Leaves are long and narrow with a pungent flavour

Garden sage has thick, downy grey-green leaves

Broad-leaf garden sage

Narrow-leaf garden sage

Chopped fresh leaves *are a flavoursome addition to pasta sauces and stuffings*

Whole leaves *may be threaded on kebabs*

COOKING TIPS

This is a strongly flavoured herb with overtones of camphor and should be used with discretion. It is good with fatty meats as it aids digestion. *Fresh leaves* are milder in flavour than the *dried* version and can be added more freely. The pretty grey-green *leaves* can be used whole in many dishes. Very small young sage *leaves* are mild enough to be used in a green salad, provided that they are shredded into small bits beforehand. Thread sage *leaves* between pieces of meat or vegetables when preparing kebabs.

A half hardy variety, the leaves are green, splashed with pink, and have white margins

Tricolour sage

Sage varieties
Purple leaf, purple variegated and gold variegated sage make an attractive garden trio and can be used like common grey-green sage in the kitchen.

When mature, the leaves are soft and deep purple

Purple sage

Plant contains both green and yellow leaves

Golden sage

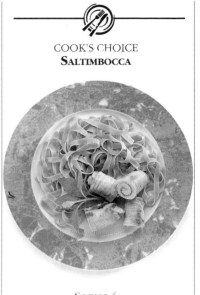

COOK'S CHOICE
SALTIMBOCCA

Serves 4

8 small veal escalopes
8 small slices dry-cured ham, preferably Parma ham
8 large, fresh young sage leaves
Freshly ground black pepper
1 tbsp olive oil
3 tbsp unsalted butter
175 ml (6 fl oz) marsala or port

With a meat mallet or rolling pin, pound the escalopes until thin. Lay a slice of ham and a sage leaf on top of each escalope. Season with pepper and roll up to enclose the filling; secure with a toothpick or kitchen string. Heat the oil and butter in a frying pan and sauté the rolls over moderate heat until they are browned all over. Pour in the marsala or port and bring to a simmer. Cover and cook over low heat for 10-15 minutes. Serve hot, with buttered pasta.

Adding the sage
Centre the ham and sage leaf on the meat and roll up.

SAVORY

FORMS
Leaves: Fresh and dried

AFFINITY WITH OTHER HERBS/SPICES
Rosemary, thyme, sage, fennel, bay leaf

HOW TO STORE
Fresh leaves: Keep in a plastic bag in the refrigerator, or chop finely and freeze in ice-cube trays.
Dried leaves: These retain their flavour for a considerable time if kept in airtight containers, away from light.

HOW TO DRY
For best results, summer and winter savory *leaves* should be harvested just before the plant flowers. Hang in a dark, warm, well-ventilated place.

There are two varieties of this herb, one annual and one perennial. Both come from the Mediterranean and are attractive for gardeners and cooks. They have a strong, slightly peppery taste thought by some to be reminiscent of thyme. In very early times, the Romans made a sauce of vinegar and summer savory, very much like the mint sauce of today. All beans and peas are greatly enhanced by this herb with which they have a particular affinity, and sausages, stuffings and herb mixtures often contain savory. Winter savory, an evergreen, is a shrub-like plant, growing up to 30 cm (12 in) high, with glossy, bright green leaves and pinkish flowers. The flavour is stronger, sharper and spicier than that of summer savory. The latter grows much higher, to about 45 cm (18 in) tall, and has narrow, dark green leaves and lilac flowers. Summer and winter savory are commonly grown alongside each other.

TASTES GOOD WITH/IN
Pulses, especially lentils and white beans, cooked vegetable salads, grilled veal and pork, poultry, rabbit, soups, horseradish sauce, cucumbers, stuffings and charcuterie, goat cheese, tomato-based sauces, marinades, fish, especially trout.

COOKING TIPS
Savory is useful for those on a salt-restricted diet as the *leaves* have a strong, persistent flavour. Use summer savory with fresh beans and winter savory with dried ones. For a more subtle savory flavour, infuse wine vinegar with *fresh sprigs* and use in dressings for salads containing fresh or dried beans, or in marinades.

Winter savory is a hardy perennial with narrow green leaves and a strong, spicy flavour

Pale purple or white flowers bloom from midsummer to autumn

Leaves are sharp-tipped and shiny on upper surface

Chopped fresh leaves *are an excellent addition to horseradish sauce*

Dried leaves *keep their flavour well*

Winter savory *has a less pleasing texture than that of the annual variety*

Whole fresh leaves

COOK'S CHOICE
GREEN BEANS WITH SUMMER SAVORY

Serves 4–6

1 kg (2 lb) fresh young green beans, trimmed

Salt

4 tbsp unsalted butter

2 tbsp finely chopped fresh summer savory leaves

Freshly ground black pepper

Place the beans in a large saucepan of briskly boiling water. Add salt and continue to boil beans over high heat, uncovered, for 8–10 minutes, depending on the age and freshness of the beans. They should be tender but still crisp. Drain, rinse under cold running water, drain again and return to the saucepan. Add the butter and savory. Season with pepper to taste and a little salt if necessary. Cook for 1–2 minutes and serve hot.

Summer savory, an annual, is intensely aromatic and bears small white or lilac flowers in late summer

Leaves are slightly larger and more rounded than those of winter savory; they are dotted with oil glands

HERBES DE PROVENCE

This a mixture of the herbs that flourish in the hills of southern France during the hot summer months. Used in handfuls when fresh, they can also be dried for use until the next season. Herbes de Provence is a useful addition to any dish from the Mediterranean region and is especially good in stews, with baked tomatoes, added to pizza toppings or sprinkled over kebabs before grilling.

Traditional terracotta jars *are ideal for storing this herb mixture until a fresh supply can be gathered*

Oregano

Savory

Thyme

Rosemary

Marjoram

Stems are pale purple and slightly downy

Summer savory *has an aroma reminiscent of both mint and thyme. One or two chopped leaves are effective when added to salads, cheese dishes or herb mixtures*

THYME

There are believed to be about 100 species of thyme, but for most culinary purposes three are sufficient. Used extensively in ancient Greece, this herb may well have been employed in the Mediterranean region even earlier. It is one of the great culinary herbs of European cookery; lacking thyme, a bouquet garni becomes a less valuable flavouring ingredient. Few are the dishes that cannot be improved by thyme. Its amiable and positive flavour blends well with many other herbs, especially rosemary, enhancing them without ever overpowering them when combined in the cookpot. Thyme is a herb that aids the digestion of fatty foods and it is therefore useful in dishes of mutton, pork, duck or goose. Wild French thyme, *serpolet,* grows profusely in Provence, and gives the cooking of that region much of its distinctive flavour. Lemon thyme has an attractive citrus perfume and makes an excellent herb tea. All the thymes are wonderfully aromatic and are to be encouraged in the garden – or, failing a garden, in window-boxes, balcony planters or pots on kitchen counters.

TASTES GOOD WITH/IN

Any slowly cooked dish, especially stews and soups, sautéed or baked vegetables, tomato-based sauces, stuffings, roast poultry, grilled or roasted meat, breads, sauces.
Lemon thyme: Can be used sparingly with fish and chicken, and in some fresh fruit desserts.

Chopped fresh leaves *are much more pungent than dried. If using in place of dried leaves in a recipe, add more sparingly*

Dried leaves *retain their aroma and flavour well*

Variegated varieties can be used wherever ordinary thyme is called for, but they are more difficult to grow

Leaves are aromatic, pointed oval and mid-green; they are covered in fine hairs

Garden thyme bears pale lilac blooms in summer and has a woody stem

Fresh leaves *are useful in just about any savoury dish*

Variegated thyme   **Garden thyme**

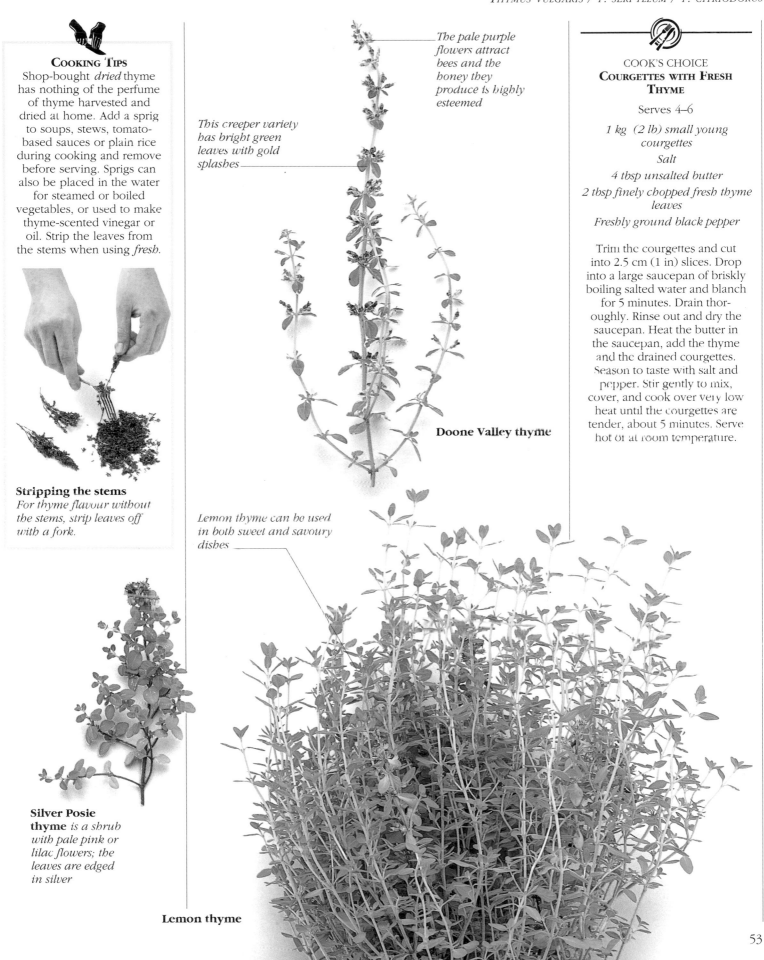

COOKING TIPS

Shop-bought *dried* thyme has nothing of the perfume of thyme harvested and dried at home. Add a sprig to soups, stews, tomato-based sauces or plain rice during cooking and remove before serving. Sprigs can also be placed in the water for steamed or boiled vegetables, or used to make thyme-scented vinegar or oil. Strip the leaves from the stems when using *fresh*.

Stripping the stems
For thyme flavour without the stems, strip leaves off with a fork.

Silver Posie thyme *is a shrub with pale pink or lilac flowers; the leaves are edged in silver*

The pale purple flowers attract bees and the honey they produce is highly esteemed

This creeper variety has bright green leaves with gold splashes

Doone Valley thyme

Lemon thyme can be used in both sweet and savoury dishes

Lemon thyme

COOK'S CHOICE
COURGETTES WITH FRESH THYME

Serves 4–6

1 kg (2 lb) small young courgettes

Salt

4 tbsp unsalted butter

2 tbsp finely chopped fresh thyme leaves

Freshly ground black pepper

Trim the courgettes and cut into 2.5 cm (1 in) slices. Drop into a large saucepan of briskly boiling salted water and blanch for 5 minutes. Drain thoroughly. Rinse out and dry the saucepan. Heat the butter in the saucepan, add the thyme and the drained courgettes. Season to taste with salt and pepper. Stir gently to mix, cover, and cook over very low heat until the courgettes are tender, about 5 minutes. Serve hot or at room temperature.

53

OTHER NAMES
Lemon-scented verbena

FORMS
Leaves: Fresh and dried

HOW TO STORE
Fresh leaves: Keep in tightly
sealed plastic bags in the
refrigerator.
Dried leaves: Keep in
airtight containers in a cool,
dark place.

COOKING TIPS
A few *fresh leaves* can be
added to fruit salads, but
use sparingly as the flavour
can be reminiscent of
lemon-scented cosmetics.

LEMON VERBENA

Lemon verbena is a small deciduous shrub that grows
not higher than 4.5 metres (15 ft) high in warm
climates and far less in cooler ones. The leaves are
strongly perfumed, filling the air with their scent of
lemons. The plant is native to Chile and was brought to
Europe by the Spaniards, where it was first put to use
scenting soaps and cosmetics. The leaves are long,
pointed and light green in colour with mauve flowerets
that appear in clusters at the ends of the branches. Use
as a substitute for lemon grass in oriental recipes as the
lemon flavour is very pronounced. It should not be
confused with vervain, although they are both members
of the same botanical family.

*Leaves are long, pointed
and rough-textured with a
strong lemon scent; they
grow in groups of three on
the branch*

Fresh leaves *taken from
the top of the plant can be
chopped and added to fruit
or vegetable salads*

**Chopped fresh
leaves**

TASTES GOOD WITH/IN

Fresh fruit drinks, especially
those made with peaches
or strawberries; herb teas
made with liquorice or
mint; fruit salads, and
infused in custard-based
dessert sauces.

COOK'S CHOICE
LEMON VERBENA RICE PUDDING

Serves 4–6

250 g (8 oz) short-grain rice
1/2 tsp salt
600 ml (1 pt) milk
2–3 fresh lemon verbena leaves
125 g (4 oz) sugar
1 tbsp unsalted butter
4 large egg yolks, lightly beaten
*Fresh lemon verbena leaves for
garnish*

In a saucepan, combine the
rice, 500 ml (16 fl oz) water
and the salt. Bring to the boil
and cook, uncovered, over
moderate heat until the rice
has absorbed all the water,
about 10 minutes. In another
saucepan, scald the milk and
pour it over the rice, stirring to
mix. Bury the verbena leaves
in the rice and cook, uncovered, over very low heat,
stirring gently from time to
time until the milk is almost
absorbed. Remove and discard
the verbena leaves. Add the
sugar, butter and egg yolks
and continue to cook, stirring
from time to time, until the
sugar, butter and eggs have
been absorbed and the
mixture is creamy. Turn the
pudding into a serving dish,
cool, then refrigerate to chill.
Serve garnished with lemon
verbena leaves.

HERB BUNDLES

Certain herbs and foods have an affinity with each other: rosemary with lamb, sage with pork and veal, fennel with fish and basil with tomatoes. There are also combinations of herbs that marry particularly well. These range from a few fresh sprigs tied together, to a simple bouquet garni, to more elaborate mixtures which are used to flavour soups, stews, sauces and many other dishes. Fresh herbs can be tied in bundles with string; dried herbs should be tied in a muslin bag. Always remove them at the end of cooking time.

For example, for long-cooking poultry dishes, combine a celery stalk with a sprig each of parsley, thyme, marjoram, tarragon and a bay leaf, and tie in a muslin bag; for game birds add six juniper berries. With lamb, tie together sprigs of rosemary, thyme, savory, mint and parsley; for beef stews, add orange peel and remove the mint. Add sprigs of fresh sage, thyme and marjoram to pork, or use the dried forms of these herbs, with oregano added and tied in a muslin bag. Seafood is best with dill, tarragon and lemon peel.

FRESH BOUQUET GARNI

Bouquet garni is the French term for a bundle of herbs. Indispensable in the kitchen, the classic combination calls for 3 stalks of parsley, 1 small sprig of thyme and 1 small bay leaf. It can be enclosed in an aromatic vegetable wrapping, with a celery stalk or the green part of a leek being the most common. When creating these bundles, be sure to use herbs that complement one another; remember that bay leaf is potent and parsley is mild. Size depends only on the volume of the dish; a small bouquet garni will be lost in a big pot of soup and a large one may over-power a small pan of sauce.

Use a piece of string to secure when the herb stalks are sufficiently long

Traditional bouquet garni
The classic combination of three stalks parsley, 1 bay leaf and 1 sprig thyme can be altered to suit the make-up of the dish. This is a larger than average arrangement.

Bouquet garni with a celery stalk, a twist of orange peel and oregano

Mixed dried herbs can be tied in a square of muslin

Thyme

Bay

Parsley

Muslin bags

DRIED BOUQUET GARNI

A bouquet garni made up of dried bay, parsley and thyme can either be shop-bought or made at home. Mix together equal quantities of the dried herbs and place in a square of muslin. Tie the muslin with kitchen string or cotton thread. The bag should be removed at the end of cooking time. Home-made dried bouquet garni make excellent presents, and the choice of herbs can be varied to suit different types of dishes.

Teabag-style bouquet garni

KITCHEN
SPICES

GALANGAL

Both the galangals are closely related members of the ginger family, *Zingiberacae,* and are important in the cooking of Southeast Asia. Greater galangal *(Alpinia galanga),* which is native to Indonesia, has large spicy roots which are knobby like ginger, with a reddish brown or pale creamy coloured skin. With its ginger-like flavour, galangal is much used in the cuisine of Thailand, where it almost replaces ginger as a spice. The lesser galangal *(Alpinia officinarum)* it is used more as a vegetable than a spice in Southeast Asia, and is peeled or shredded before being added to curries or stews. In China, it is used mostly for medicinal purposes. Kempferia galangal is another type, rarely available in the West. Once widely used in European cooking, it is still used in liqueurs and bitters. In the Middle Ages, galangal was called galingale in England, a name also used for the roots of sedge.

COOK'S CHOICE
SOUTHEAST ASIAN-STYLE CHICKEN

Serves 2–4

6 large garlic cloves, crushed
1 tbsp ground black peppercorns
2 tbsp ground galangal, or
1 tbsp grated fresh ginger
$1/2$ tsp salt, or to taste
8 chicken thighs
Oil for deep-frying

In a bowl, mix together the garlic, peppercorns, galangal or ginger and the salt. Rub the mixture into the chicken thighs, put into a bowl, cover, and refrigerate for 3–4 hours to marinate. Pour enough oil into a frying pan to reach a depth of 5 cm (2 in). Heat to 190°C (375°F) on a frying thermometer, or until hot but not smoking. Add the chicken thighs and fry until golden brown and cooked through. Drain on paper towels and serve with rice.

Similar to ginger rhizomes, with a peppery, ginger-like flavour

Greater galangal

Fresh slices

Kempferia galangal

Dried slices

Ground galangal

CELERY SEED

FORMS
Seeds: Whole and ground

HOW TO STORE
Whole and ground: Keep in airtight containers in a cool, dark place to retain their celery-like, slightly bitter flavour.
Celery seasoning: Keep in an airtight container in a cool, dark place.

COOKING TIPS
The *whole* seed retains its flavour well and should be used sparingly as it can be bitter; crush before using. *Celery seasoning* is apt to stale, though it will retain a fresh taste if stored in the refrigerator.

Celery was developed in the 17th century from smallage, or wild celery, found in the salt marshes of Europe. There are three main types: white, green and turnip-rooted celery. The latter is called celeriac, or celery root, and is cooked as a vegetable or eaten raw in salads. Celery seeds are tiny and brown with five lighter ridges; they taste strongly of the plant and are aromatic and slightly bitter. The flavour is pleasant though, and the slight bitterness enhances other flavours. They are sometimes used where celery itself would not be appropriate, such as kneaded into bread doughs or sprinkled on savoury biscuits. They can be used whole, tossed in salads or over cooked vegetables just before serving, or they can be ground and added to cooked dishes. Celery seasoning is salt flavoured with ground celery seeds and other herbs, and is a useful addition to many dishes such as soups, stews and salads – almost anywhere an aromatic salt is needed.

The tiny seeds are brown with lighter ridges and have a slightly bitter taste.

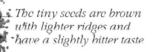

Whole seeds

Celery stalks

Celery seasoning *is especially good when sprinkled on meats before grilling*

TASTES GOOD WITH/IN

Soups, sauces, stews, fish, breads, savoury biscuits, tomato juice, relishes, pickles, chutneys, egg dishes, especially omelettes, salad dressings.

COOK'S CHOICE
POACHED CUCUMBERS WITH CELERY SEED

Serves 6

1 kg (2 lb) cucumbers, peeled and cut widthwise into 2.5 cm (1 in) slices

Chicken stock or water

1–2 tbsp unsalted butter

2 tsp finely ground celery seed

2–3 tbsp double cream (optional)

In a saucepan, combine the cucumber slices with enough chicken stock or water to barely cover. Bring to a simmer and cook, covered, over low heat until the cucumbers are tender, about 5 minutes. Drain thoroughly and return to the saucepan. Melt the butter in a small saucepan and stir in the ground celery seed; add the cream if using. Pour the mixture over the cucumbers and toss gently. Transfer to a warmed serving dish and serve hot as a vegetable. (The celery seed may be left whole.)

ANNATTO

OTHER NAMES
Achiote, bija, bijol, roucou, lipstick tree

FORMS
Seeds: Whole and ground

HOW TO STORE
Seeds: In airtight containers, kept in a cool, dark place. If brick-red in colour, they will keep indefinitely; avoid brownish seeds.

COOKING TIPS
Colour rather than flavour is annatto's main role in the kitchen, however, oil that has been coloured and gently imbued with annatto is a valuable ingredient in the cooking of the Caribbean. To make annatto oil, heat 250 ml (8 fl oz) corn or peanut oil in a small saucepan. Add 60 g (2 oz) annatto seeds and cook, stirring, until the oil turns a deep orange colour, about 2–5 minutes; timing depends on the potency of the seeds. Once the colour is rich and deep, remove the pan from the heat. Cool, strain and store the oil in a glass jar in the refrigerator; it will keep indefinitely.

The annatto tree is an extremely attractive small flowering tree of the *Bixaceae* family which grows throughout the Caribbean, Mexico, and Central and South America. It bears large pink flowers that look like wild roses. However, it is the dye from the pulp that surrounds the 50 or so seeds inside the heart-shaped prickly scarlet fruits that makes the tree commercially important. The warlike Carib Indians used the dye to paint their bodies and it was also used by the ancient Mayas in Guatemala. Annatto is exploited to its fullest in the cooking of the Caribbean and Latin America, being used primarily as a colouring though also as a gentle flavouring. It is an ingredient in the spicy sauce which is served over the Jamaican national dish of ackee and salt cod. In Mexico, annatto seeds are ground with other herbs and spices, among them cumin and oregano, for a seasoning mixture that has a fragrant and flowery taste.

Annatto was introduced to the Philippines by the Spaniards, and it has since become an important ingredient in many dishes. In Europe, annatto is used to colour many cheeses, including Munster, Livarot, Leicester and Red Cheshire. Annatto has a great many names, which vary from island to island and country to country.

The seeds are extracted from the pods

Annatto oil

Seeds

TASTES GOOD WITH/IN

Pulses, grains, rice, poultry, fish, especially salt cod, pork, beef or lamb stews, soups, okra, pumpkins, bell peppers, onions, tomatoes, curries, spice mixtures, shellfish, especially prawns, chilli sauces, egg dishes, sweet potatoes, plantains.

COOK'S CHOICE
PILAU RICE

Serves 4–6

300 g (10 oz) long-grain rice
4 tbsp annatto oil (see left)
600 ml (1 pt) chicken stock
Salt

Rinse and drain the rice. Heat the oil in a pan. Add the rice, stir, and cook until translucent, about 2 minutes. Add the stock and salt to taste. Bring to the boil, then simmer, covered, until the liquid is absorbed, about 20 minutes. Let stand 10 minutes. Fluff with a fork before serving. This goes well with spicy chicken dishes.

SASSAFRAS

FORMS
Leaves: Dried *Bark:* Dried

HOW TO STORE
Leaves: Keep in airtight containers in a cool, dark place.

COOKING TIPS
Filé powder is added after the dish is removed from the heat but while the liquid is still near boiling; it is stirred in and blended thoroughly. The dish must not be allowed to boil after the filé powder is added or it will go stringy.

It was Louisiana's Choctaw Indians who were the first users of sassafras, a handsome tree of the laurel family native to North America. It grows to a considerable height and can reach nearly 27 metres (90 ft). It is aromatic with yellow-green flowers and dark blue fruits with red stalks. It has bright green leaves of three different shapes, all of which appear on the same tree. In the past, sassafras leaves and bark were used to make tea, to flavour medicines and, combined with other ingredients, to make a cordial. Its principal use today is as filé powder, which is obtained from the dried, ground leaves of the tree. The powder is used as a thickening agent in gumbo, a dish that is a cross between soup and stew, most popular in the southern states of America. Gumbos are the result of the meshing of American Indian, French, Spanish and African cuisines. The name "gumbo" probably derives from an African Bantu word for okra, *gombo*, which arrived in the area via the French Caribbean; the two ingredients are easily confused as okra is also used as a thickening agent. If very young, tender leaves are available, they make a pleasant addition to green salads.

Ground bark

Dried bark

**Ground leaves
(filé powder)**

TASTES GOOD WITH/IN

Any Cajun or Creole gumbo, soups, fish, shellfish, poultry, game, highly spiced meat and vegetable stews, any savoury dish that requires thickening.

COOK'S CHOICE
PRAWN AND CRAB GUMBO

Serves 6

4 tbsp vegetable oil
1 medium onion, finely chopped
4 spring onions, chopped
4 celery stalks, chopped
1 medium green pepper, seeded and chopped
3 tbsp plain flour
Salt
500 g (1 lb) cooked prawns
500 g (1 lb) cooked crabmeat, picked over to remove any shell and cartilage
1/2 tsp chilli sauce
4 tsp chopped flat leaf parsley
1 tbsp filé powder

In a saucepan, combine the oil, onion, spring onions, celery and green pepper, and sauté until soft. Sift in the flour and cook for 2–3 minutes without letting the mixture brown. Gradually stir in 2 litres (3 1/2 pt) water; season to taste. Bring to a simmer and cook, covered, for 15 minutes. Add the prawns and crabmeat and cook just long enough to heat them through. Stir in the chilli sauce and the parsley; taste for seasoning. Remove from the heat and stir in the filé powder, blending thoroughly. Serve with plain rice.

MUSTARD

FORMS
Seeds: Dry, whole, oil
Prepared: Strong, mild, flavoured

HOW TO STORE
Seeds: In airtight containers in a cool, dry place.
Prepared: In airtight jars in the refrigerator.

COOKING TIPS
For strongest flavour, mix *dry mustard* with cold water and let it stand about 15 minutes before using. Japanese mustard is always mixed with boiling water, covered and allowed to stand before using. In cooking, add mustard towards the end and heat gently. For stews, dry mustard can be added to the oil in which onions and/or garlic are sautéed. When making mayonnaise, always use a *prepared mustard* such as Dijon, never a dry mustard.

The name mustard derives from the Latin *mustum ardens*, or burning must. The spice was so named for, as the seeds were pounded with unfermented grape juice, or must, their pungent qualities developed, hence "burning." All mustards, and they are legion, derive from three members of the cabbage family, two of them closely related. The close relatives are *nigra*, or black mustard, which can grow as tall as 2 metres (7 ft), and *juncea*, or brown mustard. Both plants bear small round seeds, though brown mustard has largely replaced the black type because its smaller size makes it easier to harvest. These mustards have the strongest flavour; black mustard in particular is prized for the distinctive taste it lends to the cuisine of India. The third mustard, *alba*, or white mustard, is native to the Mediterranean region and bears large yellowish seeds. This is more commonly known as the mustard of mustard cress and it is far less pungent than the black or brown types. White mustard is used extensively in the production of American prepared mustards, occasionally in English mustards but not at all in Dijon-style mustards.

Dry: Soups, stews. *Strong prepared:* Sauces for poultry, roasts, cold meats, charcuterie, mayonnaise, salad dressings.
Mild prepared: Sauces, fish, especially salmon and herring.

SPROUTING SEEDS
White mustard sprouts, *Brassica alba*, are usually grown with garden cress, *Lepidium sativum*, to produce a crisp and slightly peppery salad herb. Growing these seeds together became popular in Victorian England when they used earthenware cones which were grooved to hold the seeds. Mustard can be grown from seed on a thin layer of soil in small trays, on a piece of damp cloth or even on cotton wool. Kept moist, the sprouts should be ready to eat in about two weeks, or when they are about 5 cm (2 in) high. If grown with cress, plant the cress 3–4 days after the mustard as it germinates more quickly. Use the delicate shoots in salads, sandwiches or as a garnish.

The pale, sandy-brown or yellow seeds of the white form are the largest kind

Strong and pungent in flavour but smaller in size than white

White seeds

Black seeds

Bitter, hot and aromatic, brown seeds are more commonly grown than black and used in place of them

The bright yellow colour of a prepared mustard is usually due to the addition of turmeric

Brown seeds

Dry mustard

Prepared mustard *is the most commonly used form of the spice, particularly in its use as a condiment*

MAKING MUSTARD SAUCE

The fiery flavour of mustard is best savoured when used uncooked. While a dollop on a platter of cold meats is often the only required seasoning, some dishes call for a more elaborate treatment. Many cold sauces, such as vinaigrette, mayonnaise or the dill sauce shown here, are flavoured with mustard. All of these sauces go well with vegetable salads, but this dill sauce is particularly suited to Gravad Lax (see page 102).

1 Dissolve 1–2 tbsp sugar in 1½ tbsp white wine vinegar. Gradually whisk in 125 ml (4 fl oz) extra-virgin olive oil until well blended.

2 Add 6 tbsp Dijon mustard, 2–3 sprigs chopped fresh dill and freshly ground white pepper to taste. Whisk to blend.

PREPARED MUSTARD

This condiment is a long-standing tradition in many cuisines around the world. It has been on the tables of the ancient Egyptians, Greeks and Romans, and Pope John XXII was said to have appointed a private mustard maker to the palace in Avignon to ensure the high quality of the papal jars. During the 18th and 19th centuries, when mustard came into fashion, there were at least 93 varieties available for consumption. The manufacturing process has also been handed down through the ages. In modern factories, as in the Middle Ages, the seeds are blended and then left to macerate in a liquid: grape juice, grape must, wine, vinegar, cider or water. Finally, the seeds are ground to a fine paste. The temperature must never exceed 40°C (104°F) during manufacture or the volatile oils in the seeds, which are the source of the flavour, will evaporate. The culinary usage of prepared mustard has also changed little through the ages. It can be used to accompany cold meats, as an ingredient in cold sauces, or it can be added to hot dishes at the end of cooking time. As a condiment, this fiery mixture has universal appeal and there is a mustard flavour to fit every occasion.

STORING MUSTARD

Prepared mustard can be kept up to one year before it loses strength, but as soon as the jar is opened, the flavour begins to deteriorate and it is best used quickly. The shape of the traditional mustard pot, with a small neck, evolved because it was easier to seal, and it prevented a large surface area from coming into contact with the air, keeping it fresh longer.

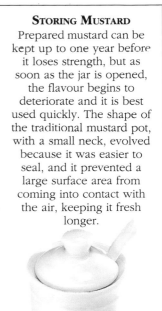

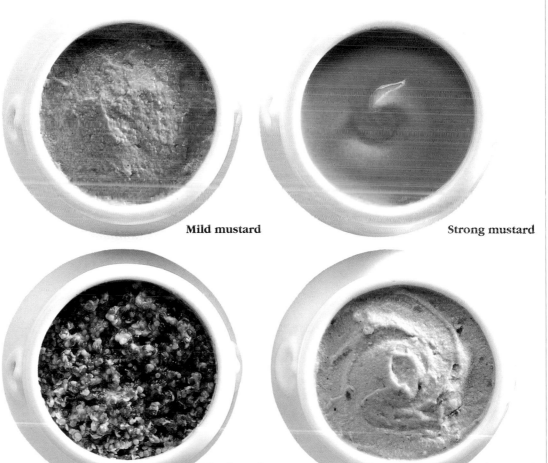

Mild mustard

Strong mustard

Whole-grain mustard

Flavoured mustard

WHOLE-GRAIN MUSTARD

Whole grain mustards are mild Dijon-style mustards made of partly crushed and partly ground brown seeds blended with vinegar and spices. The most well-known type is *moutarde de Meaux,* identified by its attractive stoneware jar with a red wax seal; English mustard was much like this before sifting and straining were introduced. Nowadays both crunchy and smooth mustards are popular. Whole-grain mustard is relatively mild as the seed husk is not completely removed.

MILD AND STRONG MUSTARD

Although there is an astonishing range of mustards, there are two basic types: mild and strong. The seed determines the difference between the two. For mild mustard, the seed coat, or husk, is left on, completely or partially; for strong mustard, it is sifted out. The most popular strong mustard is Dijon. Mild prepared mustards contain a higher percentage of the husk and not less than 20 per cent dry mustard powder. Bordeaux, Beaujolais and whole-grain mustards are the most commonly available mild types. German mustards are generally dark and smooth, made from a blend of black or brown dry mustard and vinegar, and vary in strength. American mustards are made from the milder, ground white mustard seeds, blended with vinegar, sugar, spices and often turmeric, which is the source of the characteristic yellow colour.

COOK'S CHOICE
MUSTARD CREAM SAUCE

Makes about 175 ml (6 fl oz)

60 g (2 oz) unsalted butter
125 ml (4 fl oz) double cream
1 tsp lemon juice, or to taste
Salt
Freshly ground black pepper
1–2 tsp whole-grain mustard
2–3 tbsp snipped fresh chives

Melt the butter in a shallow saucepan over moderate heat. When foaming, pour in the cream. Bring to the boil and allow to cook until slightly thickened, about 5 minutes. Add the lemon juice, salt and pepper; stir in the mustard. Taste for seasoning. Remove from the heat and stir in the chives. Serve immediately with grilled fish, meat or poultry. If it cannot be brought to the table immediately, put the sauce into a bowl and keep it warm on a rack over a pan of warm water. It can be kept warm for approximately 15 minutes but cannot be kept further than this or reheated.

Dijon mustard

Bordeaux mustard

German mustard

American mustard

Beaujolais mustard

Sweet mustard

FLAVOURED MUSTARD

FLAVOURINGS FOR PREPARED MUSTARDS

Commercially prepared flavoured mustards are now widely available. A delicious condiment for cold meats, fish, poultry, pâtés and vegetables, they can also be used in recipes which call for ordinary prepared mustard, as long as the flavours marry.

These mustards can also be made at home for a fraction of the cost. Use about 2 tsp fresh herbs, or other flavouring, for every 125 g (4 oz) mustard and let stand at least 10 minutes before using. For stronger flavours, adjust to taste. Mix with yogurt or soured cream for a quick and delicious sauce for steamed vegetables or poached seafood.

Flavoured mustards are prepared mustards with the addition of a herb, spice or other flavouring. As early as the 16th century, when Tewkesbury was the centre of English mustard production, a pungent mustard infused with horseradish enjoyed great popularity. Today, there are many flavoured mustards on the market. They can be gently imbued with delicate herbs such as basil, tarragon or mint; with spicier ingredients such as green peppercorns, chillies or ginger; or with fruits such as lemon, lime or berries. Some manufacturers are very inventive. *Moutarde aux quatre fruits*, is a French four-fruit mustard, which is flavoured with summer fruits and beetroot. In England, mustard is often flavoured with honey, malt whisky or real ale. Despite its name, the Italian *mostarda di Cremona*, which combines candied fruit in a sweet mustard syrup, is more like a chutney than a mustard.

Chillies

Lemon

Green peppercorns

Mint

Many-flavoured mustards

Mustard is a good base on which to build a custom flavouring. Herbs, spices, vegetables and fruit are among the many additions that can be combined with it.

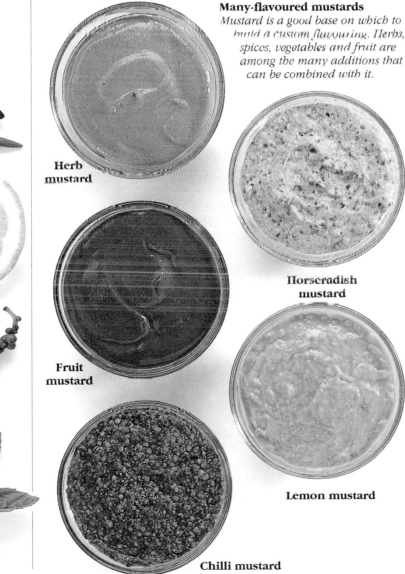

Herb mustard

Fruit mustard

Horseradish mustard

Lemon mustard

Chilli mustard

Serves 4

*4 salmon steaks, weighing about 175 g (6 oz) each
Juice of 1 large lemon
Juice of 1 large orange
60 g (2 oz) unsalted butter
Salt
125 ml (4 fl oz) double cream
Freshly ground black pepper
1 tbsp lemon flavoured Dijon-style mustard
Chopped fresh parsley for garnish (optional)*

Rinse the salmon and pat dry. Place in a shallow dish and pour over the lemon and orange juice. Cover with cling film and refrigerate for about 1 hour to marinate, turn occasionally. Remove the fish from the marinade and pat dry with paper towels; reserve the marinade. Heat the butter in a large non-stick frying pan. When foaming, add the salmon, sprinkle with salt and cook for 2 minutes, turn, salt, and cook the other side for a further 2 minutes. Total cooking time depends upon the thickness of the steaks; cook longer if necessary. Transfer the salmon steaks to a dish and keep warm. Add the marinade to the same non-stick pan and bring to the boil. Cook until reduced by two-thirds. Add the cream and continue reducing, 2–3 minutes. Season with pepper and stir in the mustard. Pour the sauce over the salmon, garnish with the parsley if using, and serve immediately with plain rice.

DRY MUSTARD

Developed in the early 18th century, dry mustard powder was obtained from black and white mustard seeds which were ground together. The blend was then sifted to produce a very smooth powder and this mixture replaced the milder, grainy type used at the time. The technique for producing dry mustard has changed little since then; nowadays wheat flour is added to the seeds as well as turmeric for colour, and some sugar, salt and spices. Dry mustard also acts as a preservative and is often included in pickle and chutney recipes. Even hotter than dry mustard is the spicy Chinese mustard called *gai* made from the brown mustard seed. The hottest of all mustards is the Japanese *karashi* used in soy dipping sauces and, in very small quantities, to accompany Japanese dishes. Use both sparingly, they are very potent.

Once in its powdered form, mustard must be mixed with water to develop its pungent flavour

Dry mustard powder

Chilli mustard powder

Peppercorn mustard powder

Whole-grain mustard powder with mint

Chive mustard powder

CHILLI

DRYING CHILLIES
Fully mature red or yellow chillies are most suitable for drying. Place them on racks which allow air to circulate underneath, but turn them frequently to prevent mould developing. Alternatively, they can be strung. Using a needle and heavy cotton thread, puncture each chilli at the top, just below the stem, and string. Hang in a warm, dry place, where they will dry in about a week.

PREPARING CHILLIES
Fresh and dried chillies should be handled with care. Capsaicin (see right) can be painful if it gets on skin or into the eyes or nose. Wear rubber gloves when handling, and afterwards, wash hands and all surfaces which came into contact with the chillies. Should your hands get a chilli "burn," it can sometimes be remedied by rinsing in a mild bleach solution which renders the capsaicin water-soluble.

Peppers, sweet and hot, are members of *Solanaceae*, a vast assemblage of plants to which potato, tomato and aubergine also belong. They were first cultivated in the Valley of Mexico in North America about 9,000 years ago. Their name in Nahuatl, the language of the region, was *chilli* and this term was applied to all members of the genus. All chillies fall into the genus of *Capsicum* and most of the readily available ones belong to the *Annuum* species. Despite their antiquity, the capsicums remained one of the most well-kept secrets of the New World until Columbus introduced them to Europe at the end of the 15th century. That was the first leg of the capsicums long journey around the cuisines of the world. The Portuguese then took them to the East Indies, Asia and Africa. During the Ottoman invasions of the 16th century, Europeans rediscovered chillies, and the circle was completed when they were re-introduced to the Americas by European immigrants in the 17th century.

There are hundreds of chilli varieties – over 150 in Mexico alone – ranging in pungency from sweet to fiery hot. Chillies are rich in vitamin C, an extra bonus to their mouth-tingling flavour. Used in cuisines around the world, chillies spice up many savoury dishes and are quite frequently made into "hot sauces." Thailand has its hot sauce, *nam prik*, Indonesia has a relish, *sambal*, which uses both sweet peppers and hot chillies (see page 69), Mexico has its *salsas*, and Tunisians make the fiery *harissa*, which is also found in Algeria and Morocco (see page 71). In Mexican cuisine and the cooking of the American south-west, chillies are commonly used as a main ingredient.

Dried chillies

Crushed chillies

Fresh unripe chilli

Fresh ripe chilli

THE HEAT SCALE
Chillies contain capsaicin, which is the source of their fiery flavour. It is an oily substance, not water-soluble, which can be painful when it comes in contact with the eyes or other sensitive areas. The heat of a chilli is measured in Scoville units. The mildest chillies, such as sweet banana chillies, have a rating of 0 as they contain no heat. The hottest chilli, the habanero, ranges from 100,000 to 300,000 Scoville units.

COOKING TIPS
• The longer a chilli is cooked, the hotter the flavour. Simmering results in a dish which is hot overall; stir-frying adds flavour and a bit of spice.
• Small pieces of chopped chilli provide a uniform hotness, but larger pieces can be more easily separated from a dish.
• To reduce their heat, soak fresh or dried chillies in a solution of 3 parts mild wine vinegar to 1 part salt for 1 hour.

Seeds are hot and are usually removed before cooking

Ribs also contain capsaicin, the source of a chilli's heat; remove before use

Skin is usually removed; the distinctive flavour is found inside the meat

COOK'S CHOICE
CHILES RELLENOS

Serves 6

6 large green chilli peppers, such as poblanos, with stems

500 g (1 lb) mozzarella or mild Cheddar cheese, cut in sticks

2 eggs, separated

Salt

Oil for frying

Sifted flour for coating

Tomato sauce (see page 171)

Remove the skins from the chillies (see page 69), taking care not to break off the stems. Make a lengthwise slit and remove the seeds. Place the cheese inside the peppers; secure the slit and any minor tears with toothpicks. Place the egg whites in a bowl and add a pinch of salt. Beat until they hold stiff peaks. Lightly beat the egg yolks then fold into the whites. Heat the oil in a large, heavy frying pan. When hot, lightly coat the peppers in flour, dip into the egg mixture and place in the hot oil. Cook until browned on one side, then turn and brown the other side. Transfer to paper towels to drain. If necessary, cook the chillies in batches. Place the sauce in another large, shallow pan and heat until warm. Add the drained, cooked chillies and cook just long enough to heat through. Serve immediately with boiled rice.

FRESH CHILLIES

In the cooking of Mexico and the south-western United States, it is traditional to use only fresh chillies for certain dishes, and dried for others. Generally, it is the small, hot chillies which are used fresh. Jalapenos, serranos, poblanos, anaheims and banana chillies are the most common. They can be pickled and served on their own; or milder varieties can be added to fresh sauces or *salsas*. Usually they require peeling (see page 69) before being added to a dish. Shapes and sizes vary, as do levels of pungency. Jalapenos and banana chillies, sometimes called Hungarian wax peppers, are medium-hot and juicy. Poblanos are also medium-hot though the flesh is less juicy, while serranos are strong, hot and less juicy. It is the seeds and ribs which contain the capsaicin and the flesh that carries the distinctive flavour of each variety. For this reason, substituting one chilli for another is a delicate task.

Fresh chillies should be firm and smooth to make removal of the skin easier

Serrano chillies

Anaheim chilli

Hot green chillies

Habanero chillies

Bullet chillies

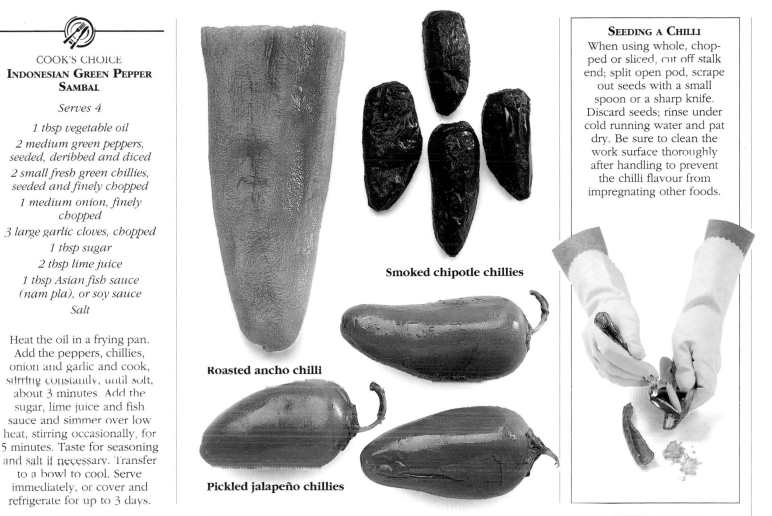

Smoked chipotle chillies

Roasted ancho chilli

Pickled jalapeño chillies

COOK'S CHOICE
INDONESIAN GREEN PEPPER SAMBAL

Serves 4

1 tbsp vegetable oil
2 medium green peppers, seeded, deribbed and diced
2 small fresh green chillies, seeded and finely chopped
1 medium onion, finely chopped
3 large garlic cloves, chopped
1 tbsp sugar
2 tbsp lime juice
1 tbsp Asian fish sauce (nam pla), or soy sauce
Salt

Heat the oil in a frying pan. Add the peppers, chillies, onion and garlic and cook, stirring constantly, until soft, about 3 minutes. Add the sugar, lime juice and fish sauce and simmer over low heat, stirring occasionally, for 5 minutes. Taste for seasoning and salt if necessary. Transfer to a bowl to cool. Serve immediately, or cover and refrigerate for up to 3 days.

SEEDING A CHILLI

When using whole, chopped or sliced, cut off stalk end; split open pod, scrape out seeds with a small spoon or a sharp knife. Discard seeds; rinse under cold running water and pat dry. Be sure to clean the work surface thoroughly after handling to prevent the chilli flavour from impregnating other foods.

PEELING CHILLIES

Most fresh chillies have a thick skin which needs to be removed before cooking. Unless a recipe specifies a method, any of the illustrated ones can be used, or for thick meated chillies, try a vegetable peeler. When cooking fresh and dried chillies, watch cooking stages carefully. Do not let them burn as the fumes from burning chillies can irritate the eyes and nose. After cooking, peel away the skin with gloved fingers under running water or "sweat."

Charring
When only a couple of chillies need to be prepared, this is a quick and easy method, though due caution must be taken. Hold the chilli over a gas burner or electric ring with tongs. Turn frequently until all sides are blistered and blackened.

Roasting
Preheat the oven to 200° C (400°F, gas 6). Rub the chillies with oil (wear rubber gloves), then place on an oven rack. Roast, turning occasionally, until charred on all sides.

Frying
Heat vegetable oil in a heavy-bottomed saucepan. Dip chillies into hot oil and submerge completely for 5 seconds. Remove and cool before handling.

Sweating chillies
Place hot, roasted chillies in a plastic bag or wrap in a damp cloth and allow to sweat for 5–10 minutes, or until skin slips away easily. Remove any clinging skin with gloved fingertips or a small, sharp paring knife.

DRIED CHILLIES

COOKING TIPS

- To bring out the most intense flavour, larger varieties should be dry roasted before use.
- In recipes which require the chillies to be puréed, they are best soaked beforehand to soften. Wearing rubber gloves, tear the chillies into pieces and soak in hot water for 1 hour.
- A pair of scissors is often the best tool for chopping dried chillies. Always be sure to clean the scissors thoroughly after use to rid them of all traces of spicy capsaicin.
- For a more complex flavour, combine several different varieties of dried chillies and grind together to a fine powder. Use wherever ground chilli is required.

Dry Roasting

Heat a dry cast-iron or non-stick frying pan. When hot, add the chillies and press with a wooden spatula to sear. Remove from the heat as soon as they begin to plump and soften, only a few minutes depending on the size of the chilli. Do not allow the chillies to undergo any colour change or become crisp.

As a rule, large dried chillies tend to be milder than small ones, though there are always exceptions. Dried chillies are a useful ingredient to have on hand as they have a fairly long shelf life if stored properly. When choosing dried chillies, suppleness is a sign of freshness; larger chillies tend to stay supple longer than small ones. Always buy in clear plastic packaging which allows a view of the contents. Don't be dismayed if chillies are dusty: this does not reflect age but the state of the packing house. Simply wipe gently before use with a soft, dry cloth. A wide variety of chillies are available dried. Ancho chillies are dried poblanos; the freshest ones smell vaguely of prunes. Guajillos are medium-hot dried chillies which are rarely available fresh, and pasillas are somewhat hotter. Avoid those which have light-coloured spots as this is a sign of moth larvae.

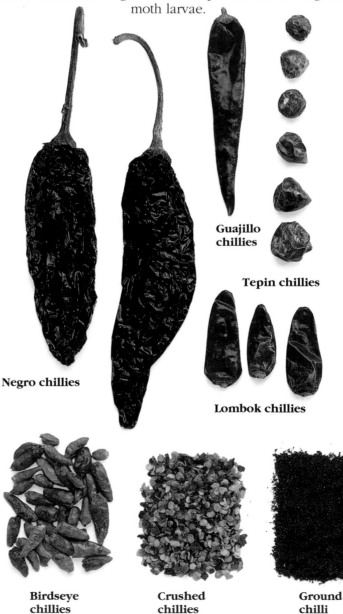

Guajillo chillies

Tepin chillies

Negro chillies

Lombok chillies

Birdseye chillies

Crushed chillies

Ground chilli

HOW TO STORE

Whole: Should be kept in a tightly sealed plastic bag in the refrigerator.
Ground: Keep in airtight containers in a cool, dark place.

COOK'S CHOICE
MEXICAN BEANS WITH CHORIZO AND CHILLIES

Serves 6

500 g (1 lb) dried black or pinto beans, soaked overnight

1 tbsp lard or oil

1 medium onion, chopped

250 g (8 oz) chorizo sausage, thickly sliced

2 poblano chillies, roasted, peeled, seeded and chopped (or 2 ancho chillies, ground)

2 tomatoes, peeled, cored, seeded and chopped

Salt

Chopped fresh coriander for garnish

Place the beans in a saucepan with 2 litres (3½ pt) cold water to cover. Bring to the boil and simmer until tender, 1–2 hours; set aside. In a large frying pan, heat the lard or oil. Add the onion, chorizo and chillies and cook until golden brown, 5–10 minutes. Add the beans with their liquid and the tomatoes. Season to taste and simmer, uncovered, for 30 minutes. Sprinkle with the coriander and serve.

Ancho chilli

Chillies

Harissa

Garlic

Salt

Mint

Cumin

Coriander seeds

COOK'S CHOICE
HARISSA

Makes 60 g (2 oz)

60 g (2 oz) dried red chillies
2 garlic cloves
Salt
2 tsp coriander seeds
1¹/₂ tsp ground cumin
1 tsp caraway seeds
1 tsp crumbled dried mint
Extra-virgin olive oil

Seed the chillies and tear into pieces. Soak in warm water until soft, about 20 minutes. Drain and pound with a mortar and pestle or use a food processor. Crush the garlic with a little salt. Blend all the dry ingredients into a paste. Stir in 2 tbsp oil. Transfer to a jar, cover with a layer of oil and refrigerate. This will keep up to 6 weeks. Use as a marinade for grilled chicken, lamb or fish, as a table condiment, or with North African dishes such as couscous.

GROUND CHILLIES

Many commonly available chilli powders are blends of a number of spices and seasonings, although almost all dried chillies can be ground and used as a pure powder. For a home-made mixture, experiment with herbs and spices.

String fresh chillies to dry, then crush in a spice grinder for home-made ground chilli

Commercial chilli powders
In addition to ground dried chillies, powders can contain garlic, onion, cumin, oregano, allspice, salt and other spices. Not to be used in place of ground chillies, these powders are often used to season chile con carne.

Ground cayenne
Ground from small red chilli peppers of the Capsicum frutescens *variety, cayenne has been used to spice up Western dishes since the 18th century. It is about as spicy as other dried ground chillies and is sometimes used as a table condiment.*

Crushed chillies
A fiery seasoning, crushed chillies can be purchased or made at home from dried chillies. It is more traditional to crush in a mortar, though fumes and chilli dust can irritate eyes and nose. An electric spice grinder is best.

71

PAPRIKA

OTHER NAMES

Tomato pepper, tomato-squash pepper, *pimientó*, tomato pimento, *pimentón*, Hungarian paprika, noble paprika, sweet paprika

FORMS

Fresh: Whole *Dried:* Ground

HOW TO STORE

Dried: Keep in airtight containers in a cool, dark place. Paprika loses its flavour and aroma quickly, becoming brown and stale-tasting if kept too long.

COOKING TIPS

Buy the best quality of sweet paprika available, it is worthwhile for the superior flavour. Be careful to check the label; some are labelled hot and can be very hot indeed. For example, tins that are labelled "Spanish paprika" are not mild like paprika, they are actually spicy, like cayenne.

The sweet peppers which are dried and ground for paprika have a complex history. The plant originated in the southernmost tip of Mexico, was taken to Spain and Morocco by the Spanish and then found its way to Hungary, where it became naturalized and an essential ingredient in local cuisine. The thick-fleshed peppers are as broad as they are long and similar to other members of their large family, and are excellent sources of vitamin C. Whole fresh peppers can be difficult to find, but with their slightly piquant flavour, they make excellent peppers for stuffing. Ground paprika lends an attractive flavour to foods as well as a beautiful deep red colour. Spain has a similar pepper, called *pimientó*. It is a pointed, heart-shaped fruit which is used to make *pimentón*, a spice similar to paprika. It is most familiar, however, as the red stuffing inside green Spanish cocktail olives.

Colour can vary from bright red to light pink; flavour can range from sweet to fiercely hot

Spanish pimentón

Fresh pepper

Hungarian paprika

TASTES GOOD WITH/IN

Egg dishes, meat and poultry stews, game, rabbit, fish and shellfish, soups, boiled or steamed vegetables, rice and cream-based sauces.

COOK'S CHOICE
PAPRIKA CHICKEN

Serves 4

2 tbsp vegetable oil

2 medium onions, finely chopped

1.5 kg (3 lb) chicken, cut into serving pieces

250 g (8 oz) tomatoes, peeled, seeded and chopped

1 ¹/₂ tbsp paprika

Salt

Freshly ground black pepper

2 tbsp soured cream

1 tbsp plain flour, sifted

1 medium green pepper, seeded, deribbed and sliced

2 tbsp double cream

Heat the oil in a heavy, flame-proof casserole. Add the onions and cook over low heat until soft, but not browned. Add the chicken and tomatoes and cook, covered, over low heat for 10 minutes. Stir in the paprika and season to taste. Pour in 175 ml (6 fl oz) water, cover, and continue to cook over low heat for 30 minutes. Remove the lid if there is too much liquid and continue to cook, uncovered, until the liquid has evaporated, a further 15 minutes. Mix the soured cream and flour together to make a smooth paste. Lift out the chicken pieces and keep them warm. Stir the soured cream mixture into the juices remaining in the casserole and cook, stirring constantly, until the sauce is thick and smooth, a further 5–10 minutes. Add the green pepper and double cream and stir. Return the chicken to the casserole and cook for a further 5–7 minutes. Serve with boiled rice.

AJOWAN

FORMS
Seeds: Whole and ground

HOW TO STORE
If kept in an airtight container in a cool, dark place, this spice will keep indefinitely.

COOKING TIPS
Use in rich pastry hors d'oeuvres or crackers, or with beans and pulses to minimize flatulence. As it gives food a very strong flavour of thyme, it should be used sparingly.

Native to southern India, ajowan is closely related to caraway and cumin though it tastes strongly of thyme. The seeds look similar to large celery seeds, and the taste, in addition to the thyme-like flavour, is hot and bitter. The plant, which also flourishes in Egypt, Iran, Pakistan and Afghanistan, is pretty, and resembles wild parsley. It has seeds that range from light brown to red in colour. It is also cultivated for its essential oil, thymol, which is used as a germicide and antiseptic as well as for culinary purposes. Like many spices used in Indian cookery, it serves a dual purpose: alongside flavour, it has medicinal properties which help to control problems of digestion such as flatulence. Thus, for reasons of both flavour and practicality, its natural affinity is with starchy foods and pulses.

The crushed seeds are highly aromatic

Ground ajowan

Seeds *are similar to large celery seeds, with a strong, pungent flavour of thyme*

Naan

Indian breads, *such as naan, pakora and paratha, are made with ajowan; this imparts a thyme-like flavour to the dough*

Pakora

TASTES GOOD WITH/IN
Pickles, Indian breads, Indian savoury snack mixes of nuts and pulses, pastry, starchy foods including root vegetables and pulses.

COOK'S CHOICE
SPICY BROWN LENTILS

Serves 4

250 g (8 oz) brown lentils
2 tbsp vegetable oil
1 medium onion, finely chopped
1 garlic clove, chopped
1/4 tsp ground ajowan seeds, or to taste
1/4 tsp cayenne pepper, or to taste
Salt

Combine the lentils and 450 ml (3/4 pt) water in a saucepan and soak for about 1 hour. Heat the oil in a frying pan and sauté the onion until soft. Add the garlic and sauté for a further 30 seconds. Scrape the contents of the frying pan into the saucepan and add the ajowan, cayenne and salt to taste. Bring to a simmer over moderate heat. Cover and cook until the lentils are tender and the liquid is absorbed, about 1–1 1/2 hours. Serve hot.

CARAWAY

HOW TO STORE

Seeds: Both dried and ground should be stored in airtight containers and kept well away from light. *Leaves and tap roots:* Store briefly in plastic bags in the refrigerator.

COOKING TIPS

Seeds enhance the flavour of many vegetables; they are especially delicious when tossed with boiled, buttered new potatoes or cabbage. *Tap roots* can be boiled or baked and eaten as a vegetable.

Caraway has been used as a spice for about 5,000 years; there is evidence of its culinary use in the Stone Age. Originally from the countries of temperate Asia, including Iran and Turkey, it has since spread widely in Europe and North America. Its name comes from the ancient Arabic, *karawiya*, by which it is still known in the region. A biennial plant, caraway grows up to 60 cm (2 ft) in height with feathery leaves and creamy white flowers. It was once popular in English cookery; seed cake is a very old favourite in Britain and Shakespeare's Falstaff is invited to partake in "a pippin and a dish of caraways." Later, during the reign of Queen Victoria, use of the seeds was revived, in keeping with the fashion for things German. Nowadays, caraway is most popular in Austrian and German cooking, where it is used to flavour breads and pastries; in other countries, its use is limited. Its kitchen contribution is greatest when it is used sparingly. Medicinally, it serves as an aid to digestion; the seeds are chewed after a meal, or can be infused and served as a tisane.

Ground caraway

Fresh leaves *are feathery with a mild flavour*

Dried seeds *are dark brown with light brown ridges and have an aromatic and spicy flavour*

TASTES GOOD WITH/IN

Young leaves: Finely chopped, add to salad, as a garnish, or any dish where parsley would be used. *Seeds:* Cakes, breads, vegetables, especially potatoes, cabbage, carrots and mushrooms, sausages, rich meats such as pork, duck and goose.

COOK'S CHOICE
SEED CAKE

Makes one 23 cm (9 in) cake

Butter and flour for preparing the tin
250 g (8 oz) unsalted butter
250 g (8 oz) sugar
4 eggs
250 g (8 oz) plain flour
¹/₂ tsp salt
1 tsp baking powder
1 tsp vanilla essence
1 tbsp caraway seeds

Preheat the oven to 180°C (350°F, gas 4). Grease and flour a 23 cm (9 in) cake tin. In a bowl, cream together the butter and sugar until light and fluffy. Add the eggs, one by one, beating well after each addition. Sift the flour, salt and baking powder together and add to the butter mixture, blending thoroughly. Stir in the vanilla and caraway seeds and pour the batter into the prepared tin. Bake until the cake is golden brown and pulls away from the sides of the tin, about 50 minutes. Let the cake stand for 10 minutes before turning out. Place on a cake rack to cool. This makes a delicious tea bread served just as it is but to "dress it up" you can cover it with a butter cream frosting (see page 197).

Spice Mixtures

In the past, a store cupboard full of exotic spices was a symbol of wealth, and spice mixtures were a lavish mark of prestige. Nowadays, with spices so readily available, cooks tend to prefer individual spices and mixtures have fallen from favour. However, some traditional European blends survive: quatre-épices, mixed or pudding spice and pickling spice. In India and Asia, spice mixtures such as curry powder retain their importance, and there are some, often based on chillies, which are prevalent in the Americas. Middle-Eastern and North African blends are also well known.

Pickling Spice

This is an English mixture used when making pickled fruits, vegetables and chutneys, and spiced vinegar. The proportions of the spices vary, and so do the spices used – this is a representative recipe. Fennel seed could also be included, and a pinch of freshly grated nutmeg could replace the mace.

Combine 1 tablespoon each whole black peppercorns, white mustard seeds, bird's eye chillies, allspice berries, dill seed and crushed mace. To this, add one 5 cm (2 in) crushed cinnamon stick, 2 crumbled bay leaves, 1 teaspoon whole cloves and 2 tablespoons ground ginger. Use in pickle-making brines, or tie in a small square of muslin and remove after pickling.

Mixed Spice

From the 17th century onwards, cookery books began to list spices separately with each individual recipe, rather than as basic mixtures at the front, but a few popular blends are still in use. This traditional English blend of spices, also called pudding spice, is used in puddings, cakes and biscuits. Like all mixtures, the proportions and the ingredients vary according to personal taste.

Grind together 1 tablespoon coriander seeds, one crushed 5 cm (2 in) cinnamon stick, 1 teaspoon allspice berries and 1 teaspoon whole cloves. Stir in 1 tablespoon freshly grated nutmeg and 2 teaspoons ground ginger. Store in an airtight container and keep in a cool place away from light.

Quatre-Epices

A French spice mixture, the name means "four-spices." It is much used in the preparation of French charcuterie, and to a lesser extent in slowly cooked meat and poultry dishes. The composition varies, but is generally based on black peppercorns, nutmeg, cloves and ginger. Allspice and cinnamon are sometimes substituted for other spices in the blend.

In a spice grinder or coffee mill, grind 1 heaped tablespoon black peppercorns and 2 teaspoons whole cloves. Combine with 2 teaspoons freshly grated nutmeg and 1 teaspoon ground ginger. Store in an airtight container and keep in a cool place away from light.

CASSIA

COOKING TIPS
Ground cassia goes stale quite quickly, so make sure it is stored properly, away from light. Use in any recipe where cinnamon is called for as the flavour is almost, if not quite, identical. When substituting, however, use slightly less cassia than cinnamon as the taste is stronger.

Although closely related to cinnamon and often confused with it, cassia originated in Burma – a long way from cinnamon's birthplace in Sri Lanka. Cultivated extensively in southern China and Indonesia, cassia is one of the oldest of the spices. It was used in China as far back as 2500 B.C. and it reached Europe by the old spice routes from the East. Indeed, most cinnamon and cassia still come from the Orient. Like cinnamon, cassia comes from the bark of an evergreen laurel tree. The bark is peeled from thin branches which are dried in the sun to form "quills", or cassia sticks. Cassia quills are larger and coarser than cinnamon quills and their flavour is sweet and aromatic though it has been described as a coarser species of cinnamon. The leaves also have a cassia flavour and they can be used as a flavouring like bay leaves. The buds, which look a little like cloves, are useful where a slight cinnamon flavour is needed. Cassia is one of the ingredients in the Chinese five-spice mixture, and it is less expensive than cinnamon which makes it a popular substitute.

TASTES GOOD WITH/IN

Curries, pickles, especially pickled beetroot, relishes, tomato ketchup, rhubarb, and baked goods.

COOK'S CHOICE
CASSIA TOAST

Serves 4

Day-old bread, cut into 8 slices
6–8 tbsp unsalted butter, at room temperature
4 tbsp sugar
1 ½ tsp ground cassia, or to taste

Preheat the grill. Generously butter the bread and cut it into triangles or halves. Combine the sugar and cassia and sprinkle over the bread. Grill just until the sugar melts; serve the toast hot.

Cassia has a sweet, strong flavour reminiscent of cinnamon

Cassia toast

Cassia bark

Cassia buds

Ground cassia *is dark and ruddy with a warm aroma*

CINNAMON

FORMS
Dried: Rolled sticks, quills, ground

HOW TO STORE
In airtight containers kept in a cool, dark place.

COOKING TIP
A pinch of *ground* cinnamon will enhance most meat stews, especially those made with lamb. It is also good in stuffings for duck or goose, or in any stuffing made with dried fruit such as apricots or prunes. Cinnamon *sticks* are useful for flavouring hot beverages such as mulled wine, hot chocolate or coffee.

This delicately fragrant, slightly sweet spice is native to Sri Lanka though it is now grown in most hot, wet tropical regions. One of the oldest known spices, cinnamon is mentioned in the Bible and in Sanskrit manuscripts. The first mention of cinnamon comes from ancient China, where it was known as *kwei*. From very early times, there has been a confusion between cassia and cinnamon. Today, the cinnamon sold in Britain comes from Sri Lanka and is considered to be true cinnamon, while most of the cinnamon sold in North America is actually cassia. Cinnamon comes from a small, evergreen laurel-like tree. The spice itself is the bark, peeled from thin branches. The outer bark is then peeled away and the inner bark is rolled up into a quill about 2.5 cm (1 in) in diameter. While the use of cinnamon in most European countries is limited to sweets, in the Middle East it is commonly added to meat stews, especially those made with lamb. It is also combined with dried fruit for poultry or pork stuffings and is delicious on buttered acorn squash or sweet potatoes.

TASTES GOOD WITH/IN

Cakes, puddings, biscuits and breads, meat and game stews, vegetables, stewed fruit and curries.

COOK'S CHOICE
CINNAMON CUSTARD SAUCE

Makes 500 ml (16 fl oz)

350 ml (12 fl oz) milk
125 ml (4 fl oz) single cream
1 cinnamon stick
5 egg yolks
60 g (2 oz) caster sugar

Place the milk, cream and cinnamon in a saucepan and bring to the boil. Off the heat, leave to infuse for at least 15 minutes. In a large bowl, whisk together the yolks and sugar until thick and lemon-coloured. If necessary, reheat the milk and cream. Pour the hot liquid onto the yolk mixture, stirring constantly. Return to the saucepan and place over low heat. Cook gently to thicken, stirring constantly with a wooden spoon. The sauce is done when a finger drawn across the back of the spoon leaves a mark. Strain into a clean bowl. Cover and refrigerate until needed. This custard sauce can be served with puddings, cakes or pies, especially those made with apples.

Cinnamon bark

Cinnamon can be used to flavour many dishes, both sweet and savoury

Cinnamon sticks

Cinnamon quillings

Ground cinnamon

SAFFRON

OTHER NAMES
Hay saffron, saffron crocus

FORMS
Dried: Threads, ground

HOW TO STORE
In airtight containers kept away from light. For best results, buy in small quantities as saffron quickly loses its flavour.

COOKING TIPS
To bring out the strongest saffron colour and flavour grind *threads* in a small ceramic mortar. Transfer the ground saffron to the dish and rinse the mortar and pestle in the cooking liquid so as not to lose any of the saffron. When adding *threads* to dishes with very little liquid, it is best to soak the saffron first in tepid water and add towards the end of cooking. *Ground* saffron can be added directly to dishes.

Over a quarter of a million crocus flowers must be harvested to obtain one pound of saffron, and the three stigmas from each crocus must be collected by hand, which explains why saffron is the single most expensive spice. Fortunately, very little saffron is needed in most dishes, sometimes as little as a pinch. Saffron has been used in cookery since the 10th century B.C., the time of Solomon. It was a great favourite of the Phoenician traders who took it with them wherever they went. It is cultivated in a number of Mediterranean countries, though Spain is the main producer. Some authorities believe it was the Phoenicians who introduced saffron to Spain, and later to Cornwall, where they traded it for tin. Saffron buns are still made in both these areas, a legacy, no doubt, from this trade. Pungent, with a beautiful yellow colour, saffron is indispensable in a number of dishes, such as *bouillabaisse* and *paella*, and saffron bread is a traditional part of the Swedish Christmas feast. It is used also in liqueurs, the best known being Chartreuse. Saffron threads are preferable to the ground form as the latter can easily be adulterated. The spice should not be confused with meadow saffron, *(Colchicum autumnale),* which is poisonous.

TASTES GOOD WITH/IN
Fish dishes, especially those with garlic, such as French *bouillabaisse,* Spanish *zarsuela* and *paella,* poultry and beef stews, tomato-based sauces, sweet breads and biscuits.

COOK'S CHOICE
MONKFISH WITH SAFFRON SAUCE

Serves 6

1 kg (2 lb) monkfish fillets, cut into 5 cm (2 in) pieces
Salt
Freshly ground black pepper
250 ml (8 fl oz) dry white wine
125 ml (4 fl oz) fish stock
125 ml (4 fl oz) double cream
4 tbsp chilled, unsalted butter, cut into pieces
1/2 tsp saffron threads, ground

Place the fish in a deep frying pan and season to taste. Add the wine and stock and bring to a simmer. Cover and cook gently until the fish is cooked through, 7–10 minutes. Remove the fish and keep warm. Add the cream to the liquid in the pan. Whisk in the butter, bit by bit; do not boil. Stir in the saffron. Add the fish with any juices that may have collected and warm before serving.

Ground saffron

Threads are wiry and about 2.5 cm (1 in) long

Saffron threads *are a rich, red-orange; the deeper the colour, the better the quality*

To impart an even saffron-yellow colour, soak threads before using

CUMIN

HOW TO STORE
In airtight containers away from light.

COOKING TIPS
It is best to use *whole seeds* and grind in a mortar just before use as the flavour-some oil escapes rapidly after grinding. Dry roasting the seeds before grinding enhances their warm flavour. Unless a strong cumin flavour is sought, use sparingly as this spice is potent and will dominate most others.

Garam masala *is a traditional spice mixture from Northern India, most often combining cumin with coriander seeds, cardamom, black peppercorns, cloves, mace, bay leaf and cinnamon*

An annual, originally from the East, cumin has been grown in India, Egypt, Arabia and the Mediterranean countries from very early times. It is grown even more widely today, needing only a warm, equable climate to flourish. The spice comes from the seed of this plant, which grows to about 30 cm (1 ft) high and has flowers that range in colour from mauve or rose pink to white. In ancient Rome, cumin was used as a substitute for black peppercorns and it was also ground into a paste for spreading on bread. The essential oil extracted from cumin is used by the perfume industry and it was once believed to have medicinal properties. According to Pliny, his students used it to encourage their pallor in order to make him believe they were overworked. Because of its resemblance to caraway, these spices are often confused, and black cumin is sometimes confused with nigella. However, cumin's distinctive warm flavour is unique and makes a valuable contribution to many savoury dishes. Cumin will evoke Indian and Mexican cuisines as it is a vital flavouring in both; it is also used extensively in North Africa and the Middle East.

Cumin seeds

Ground cumin

Black cumin seeds

Ground black cumin

TASTES GOOD WITH/IN

Pickles, cabbage, Mexican dishes, especially those from the Yucatan, *chili con carne*, North African dishes such as couscous, Indian dishes such as curries, meat stews, some cheeses, sausages, tomato-based sauces.

COOK'S CHOICE
SPICY PORK STEW

Serves 6

1 large onion, chopped
2 garlic cloves, chopped
¹/₂ tsp salt
¹/₂ tsp cumin seeds, ground
¹/₄ tsp black peppercorns, ground
1.5 kg (3 lb) lean boneless pork, cut into 5 cm (2 in) cubes
1 litre (1 ³/₄ pt) lamb stock or water
125 g (4 oz) hulled pumpkin seeds, finely ground
1 tbsp lemon juice

In a heavy flame-proof casserole, combine all the ingredients, except the pumpkin seeds and lemon juice. Simmer, covered, over low heat until the pork is tender, about 2 hours. Add the pumpkin seeds and simmer until the liquid is thickened, about 5 minutes. Taste for seasoning and add salt if necessary; stir in the lemon juice and serve immediately with boiled rice.

HOW TO STORE
In airtight containers kept in
a cool, dark place

COOKING TIPS
Although lacking in the
exquisitely aromatic flavour
of saffron, turmeric can be
used as a substitute. The
taste will be more mild and
musky, but the colour will
be a brilliant golden-yellow.
It can also be used as a
substitute for annatto (see
page 60) which is also
yellow, and for the less
well-known Peruvian spice,
palillo, which imparts a
bright, sunshine yellow
colour to food.

TURMERIC

A handsome perennial with large lily-like leaves and yellow flowers, turmeric is a member of the ginger family and, like ginger, it is the underground rhizome of the plant. Turmeric has been cultivated for over 2,000 years in India, China and the Middle East, and is now grown in all the tropical regions of the world. It is thought to be one of the ancient Persian yellow spices which were associated with sun worship. Although sometimes available fresh, turmeric is most often sold dried and ground. It adds a warm, mild aroma and distinctive yellow colour to foods. It is essential to curry powders, and it is also used to flavour many Indian vegetarian dishes. In both India and China, turmeric is used as a dye for cloth, and in India as a mild digestive and a remedy for liver ailments.

A colourful spice
*The plant is known for
its brilliant golden
yellow colour,
which has
long been
exploited
for dye
making
purposes*

Fresh turmeric *has a
brownish skin with
bright orange flesh*

Dried turmeric

Ground turmeric

TASTES GOOD WITH/IN

Curry powders, pickles,
especially piccalilli, chutneys, devilled eggs, bean
and lentil dishes, kedgeree,
rice and pilaus, poultry,
fish, shellfish, vegetables,
especially cauliflower and
potato.

COOK'S CHOICE
CHICKEN WITH TURMERIC

Serves 4

2 tbsp corn or peanut oil
*1 medium onion, finely
chopped*
1 garlic clove, finely chopped
1 tsp ground turmeric
*1.5 kg (3 lb) chicken, cut into
serving pieces*
Salt
Freshly ground black pepper
500 ml (16 fl oz) chicken stock
2 tbsp lemon juice
Flat-leaf parsley for garnish

In a large casserole, combine
the oil and onion and cook
over low heat until soft, about
5 minutes. Add the garlic and
cook for a further 2 minutes.
Stir in the turmeric. Raise the
heat, add the chicken and
cook until browned. Season to
taste and add the chicken
stock. Bring to a simmer,
cover, and cook over very low
heat until the chicken is
tender, about 45 minutes. Stir
in the lemon juice. Remove
the chicken. Reduce the sauce
over brisk heat to thicken
slightly. Pour over the chicken.
Garnish with parsley and serve
with basmati and wild rice.

CURRY POWDERS

Although curry powders are associated with the cuisines of India, the word "curry" is actually a term coined by British colonials in India. Curries are savoury dishes of meat, fish or vegetables served in a hot and spicy sauce. Each sauce may be based on a different blend of spices, mixed according to personal taste. These blends, known as *masalas*, are intricate mixtures of ground or whole spices, which may be mild or strong. There is no one specific blend, and they are based on the spices native to India: turmeric, ginger, pepper, coriander, cumin and chillies. Some masalas may include all these spices and more, such as cloves, cinnamon and nutmeg; others may use only two or three spices. In general, the spices are dry roasted in a frying pan before grinding. While most curry blends are thought of as dry mixtures, there are, in fact, many which are pastes.

POUDRE DE COLOMBO

This is an example of a spice blend used in the curries of the West Indies. In the 19th century, Indian immigrant workers brought their cooking to the region, and it soon became popular with the inhabitants. Taking their name from Colombo, the capital of Sri Lanka, *colombos* are fiery stews made with pork, chicken, kid or tropical vegetables. White wine, stock, coconut milk and even rum can be added for the sauce.

Peel and crush 3 garlic cloves; seed and finely chop 2 fresh chillies (see page 69), and place in a small bowl. Combine ¹/₂ teaspoon ground turmeric, ¹/₂ teaspoon ground coriander and 1 teaspoon dry mustard and blend. Add to the garlic mixture and blend thoroughly. Stored in an airtight container in the refrigerator, this will keep for 4–6 weeks.

BASIC CURRY POWDER

Spice blending is essential for Indian cooking and the hundreds of mixtures used throughout the sub-continent reflect its different regions, dishes and cooks' temperaments. This recipe is simply a blueprint; for a more aromatic and less spicy mixture, reduce the number of chillies and add a teaspoon of ground cinnamon and a few ground cloves. Use dry, or blend with lukewarm water to obtain a paste.

Combine 6 dried red chillies, 30 g (1 oz) coriander seeds, ¹/₂ teaspoon mustard seeds, 1 teaspoon black peppercorns and 1 teaspoon fenugreek seeds in a heavy, cast-iron frying pan. Roast over medium heat until dark, taking care not to burn. Leave to cool, then grind to a powder with a mortar and pestle. Blend in ¹/₂ teaspoon ground ginger and ¹/₂ teaspoon ground turmeric. Store in an airtight jar, kept in a cool, dark place, for up to 3 months.

Though called a powder, this powerful mixture is, in fact, a paste

THAI RED CURRY PASTE

Thai curries tend to be fiery. They are often served with Oriental-style noodles or salads which serve to balance the heat of chillies. *Trassi* is a firm paste made from fermented shrimp. It is sometimes known as *blachan* and can be bought from oriental grocers. This paste is best used with beef.

Heat a frying pan, combine 1 teaspoon cumin and 1 tablespoon coriander seeds and dry roast, 2–3 minutes. Cool. With a mortar and pestle, grind to a powder together with 1 teaspoon black peppercorns. Add 3 chopped shallots, 2 crushed garlic cloves and 2 chopped lemon grass stalks, and grind to a smooth paste. Seed and chop 10 dried red chillies, and add to mix, along with 1 tablespoon ground galangal, 2 teaspoons grated lime zest, a small piece of trassi and salt to taste. Store in an airtight container in the refrigerator for 2–3 days.

FORMS
Dried: Pods, loose seeds, ground seeds

HOW TO STORE
In airtight containers kept in a cool, dry place.

COOKING TIPS
Loose and *ground seeds* lose flavour quickly so it is best to buy whole *pods*. Discard the papery pods before grinding the seeds. Avoid brown cardamoms which are not true cardamoms and have a flavour reminiscent of camphor.

Loose seeds and ground cardamom lose their flavour quickly, so it is best to buy whole pods and grind at home

CARDAMOM

This is a spice of great antiquity used first by the early Egyptians and then by the ancient Greeks and Romans. It came into Europe by way of the old caravan routes and, after saffron and vanilla, it is the third most expensive spice. Cardamom is used most extensively in India and the Middle East, though it does enter into the cakes and pastries of Germany, Russia and Scandinavia. In France and the United States, the essential oil is used in perfumery. The plant grows profusely on the Malabar coast of India, while another variety grows in Sri Lanka, Mexico and Guatemala. A member of the ginger family, it is a tall perennial shrub with lance-shaped leaves and short flowering stems. After flowering, the stems carry small green seed capsules which must be harvested by hand; these capsules can contain up to 20 aromatic seeds. Green cardamom pods are the most common, and white cardamon pods are simply green ones which have been bleached. Brown cardamom pods are not true cardamom, but a related variety. The flavour and texture are not as delicate as those of the green variety, in fact they are rather unpleasant. For best results, the highly aromatic seeds should only be taken from green or white pods just before use.

TASTES GOOD WITH/IN

Cakes, pastries, liqueurs, coffee, curries, pilaus, pickles, pickled herrings, meat dishes, punches, spiced wine, custard and fruit dishes.

GRAINS OF PARADISE
Grains of paradise, or Melegueta pepper, is a spice related to cardamom. The tiny grains have a hot and peppery taste. The aroma, however, is very similar to cardamom.

Seeds

Green cardamom pods

Ground cardamom

White cardamom pods

Brown cardamom pods

COOKING WITH CARDAMOM

ROASTING CARDAMOM

To bring out the best flavour of cardamom seeds before using in savoury dishes, the seeds should be dry roasted. Split open the pod and remove the sticky brown-black seeds. Heat a frying pan, add the seeds and cook until roasted.

The strong, almost lemony flavour of cardamom will enhance both savoury and sweet dishes. Cardamom is a constant ingredient in Indian cookery, essential in pilaus and curries, especially those from North India and Pakistan, and in creamy dessert dishes such as *kulfi*, a rich pistachio and almond flavoured ice-cream. Used extensively throughout the Middle East, cardamom is a frequent flavouring, especially in the many sweetmeats and sweet pastries of the region. In both the Middle East and North Africa, cardamom is used to mellow the flavour of the traditionally strong, bitter coffee, while other African countries prefer it in tea. Its digestive properties have made it popular as an after-dinner infusion, and it acts as a breath freshener when chewed. In northern European countries, cardamom is associated with warmth, and it is often added to warm, winter punches and mulled wines. In Germany, it is added to some charcuterie preparations, and in Scandinavia cardamom finds its way into spice buns, breads and pastries. Cardamom marries well with fruit: use when poaching pears, baking apples, or add ground cardamom to a fruit salad. Delicious ice-cream can be made by infusing the hot cream or milk with bruised cardomom pods.

CARDAMOM DRINKS

An after-dinner infusion of cardamom pods is not only refreshing and delicious, but an aid to digestion as well. In the Middle East, strong black espresso-type coffee is often flavoured with ground cardamom. To prepare an infusion, add 12 whole crushed pods to 1.5 litres (2 $\frac{1}{2}$ pt) boiling water. Add a strip of orange peel and leave to infuse for 10 minutes. Add 2–3 tablespoons tea leaves. Infuse to desired strength, strain, and serve with hot milk and sugar.

Green cardamom pods

Cardamom tea

Cardamom-flavoured coffee

COOK'S CHOICE
FRUIT SALAD WITH CARDAMOM

Serves 4

2 tbsp sugar
125 ml (4 fl oz) orange juice
$\frac{1}{2}$ tsp ground cardamom
2 oranges, segmented or sliced (see page 172)
1 apple, diced
1 pear, diced
2 bananas, sliced
2 plums, diced
Assorted soft fruit for garnish such as grapes, cherries, blueberries and raspberries
Fresh mint for garnish

In a small saucepan, combine the sugar and 125 ml (4 fl oz) water over medium heat. Simmer until the sugar is dissolved. Leave to cool. Add the orange juice and cardamom. Combine the oranges, apple, pear, bananas and plums in a glass bowl and pour over the cardamom mixture. Chill for at least 30 minutes, garnish with the soft fruit and mint, and serve.

CLOVES

FORMS
Buds: Dried, whole and ground

HOW TO STORE
Keep in airtight containers in a cool, dark place.

COOKING TIPS
Use a clove-studded onion to flavour chicken stock. Add a clove to the bouquet garni used for long-cooking meat dishes such as *daubes* or *pot-au-feu*.

The name for this spice comes from the Latin *clavus*, meaning a nail. Indeed, these dried, unopened flower buds of the evergreen clove tree do resemble nails. Cloves have a long and fascinating history. They originated in the Moluccas, or Spice Islands, in Southeast Asia, and were used by Chinese cooks hundreds of years before the Christian era. When the Western nations sought spices, it was the Dutch who established a monopoly in the islands after driving out the Portuguese in 1605. They restricted cultivation of cloves to one island, but by 1770, the French had succeeded in smuggling seeds to Mauritius. The trees flourish only in a tropical maritime climate and are now grown in Indonesia, Madagascar, Tanzania, Sri Lanka, Malaysia and Grenada.

Cloves have a warm, strongly aromatic perfume and flavour. They can be quite bitter on their own, but the heat of cooking tempers their flavour, making them an uncommon spice in everyday cooking (though no kitchen should be without a jar of cloves). This spice is essential to many festive cakes and biscuits, and a clove-studded onion will add depth of flavour to broths for boiled meats.

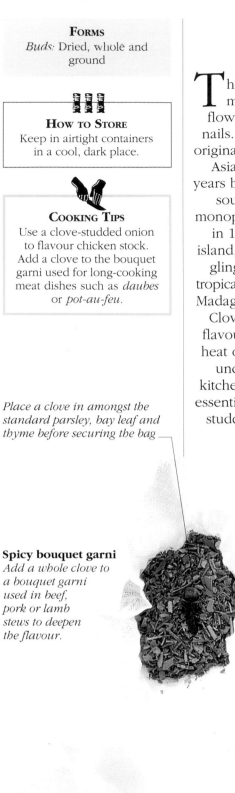

Place a clove in amongst the standard parsley, bay leaf and thyme before securing the bag

Spicy bouquet garni
Add a whole clove to a bouquet garni used in beef, pork or lamb stews to deepen the flavour.

Bouquet garni

Whole cloves

Clove-studded onion

Ground cloves

TASTES GOOD WITH/IN

Beef, lamb and pork stews, any dish made with ham, boiled bacon, tongue or other boiled meats, Christmas pudding, mincemeat, gingerbread, spiced cakes and breads, bread sauce, pickles, mulled wine, fruit cakes, marinades for game, chutneys and stewed fruit dishes.

COOK'S CHOICE
BAKED HAM WITH CLOVES

Serves 4

2–3 tbsp soft brown sugar
1 tsp Dijon mustard
4 tbsp milk or apple juice
1.5 kg (3 lb) whole cooked ham
Whole cloves for studding

Preheat the oven to 180°C (350°F, gas 4). In a bowl, combine the sugar, mustard and milk or apple juice, and stir to blend. Trim all but a 1 cm (¹/₂ in) layer of fat from the ham. Score the fat in a diamond pattern. Spread the sugar mixture over the ham, pressing well into the fat. Insert a clove in the crossed point of each diamond. Place the ham in a shallow roasting pan. Bake for 30 minutes, basting frequently; take care that the glaze does not scorch. Serve hot, with mustard and baked potatoes; or cold, accompanied by spiced fruits, chutneys and salad.

ASAFOETIDA

There is no concealing the fact that asafoetida, the resinous substance from two species of the giant fennel, has a dreadful stink. The repellent smell is caused by sulphur compounds present in the resin which, fortunately, disappear with cooking. A much used seasoning in Asian cuisine, asafoetida is especially popular for flavouring Indian vegetarian dishes. The larger species, *Ferula asafoetida,* can grow as high as 3.5 metres (12 ft), while *Ferula narthex* only reaches 2.5 metres (8 ft). The plants are native to Afghanistan and Iran, and the leaves and stalks are still eaten as a vegetable in these countries. The ancient Romans used the resin medicinally as well as for flavouring sauces and wine. Ground asafoetida is the most convenient form to buy; in order to appreciate the strong flavour, use in minute quantities. A tiny pinch is the right amount to use for any dish. The plant should not be confused with *Ferula communis,* which is often grown as a foliage plant and called giant common fennel. This is unrelated to garden fennel and is poisonous. Many other plants of the genus *Ferula* are believed to have medicinal properties and are used in Chinese herbal remedies.

OTHER NAMES
Devil's dung, stinking gum

FORMS
Resin: Fresh, dried, compound

COOKING TIPS
When adding to dishes, use *ground* in minute quantities. Rub a grill lightly with a piece of asafoetida before cooking meats.

Ground asafoetida

Chat masala *is an Indian spice blend made with ground asafoetida, mint, ginger, ajowan, cayenne, black salt, mango powder, cumin and dried pomegranate seeds*

TASTES GOOD WITH/IN
Fish, salt fish, vegetables and all pulse dishes. In very small quantities: chutneys, pickles, sauces.

COOK'S CHOICE
RICE WITH PINE NUTS AND MUSHROOMS

Serves 4

4 tbsp unsalted butter
125 g (4 oz) mushrooms, sliced
Salt
Freshly ground black pepper
30 g (1 oz) pine nuts
250 g (8 oz) long-grain rice, cooked
Small pinch of asafoetida
2 tbsp finely chopped parsley

The Romans stored asafoetida in jars with pine nuts and used a few crushed nuts to flavour dishes. This version of risotto is a modern-day setting for this ancient and pungent spice. Heat the butter in a frying pan, add the mushrooms and cook them over moderate heat until they are lightly browned. Season to taste. In a small frying pan, roast the pine nuts, shaking the pan until they are very lightly browned, 2–3 minutes. If necessary, reheat the rice to warm through. Fold the mushrooms, pine nuts, asafoetida and parsley into the rice and taste for seasoning. Serve immediately.

Compound
Specialist shops often sell asafoetida in this packaged form.

OTHER NAMES
Chinese anise, badian anise

FORMS
Dried: Whole, broken, ground and seeds

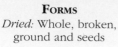

HOW TO STORE
This spice will stay fresh indefinitely if stored in an airtight container and kept away from light.

COOKING TIPS
For a spicy-sweet flavour, place a small piece in the cavity of a chicken or duck before roasting or braising, or add to pork, chicken or duck stews.

STAR ANISE

Star anise is the star-shaped fruit of a small evergreen tree native to China. The tree, which grows to a height of about 8 metres (26 ft), does not bear fruit until it is about 6 years old, but it can continue to bear fruit for up to one century. Its yellow flowers are followed by brown fruit which open, when ripe, into star shapes. Each point of the star contains a shiny brown seed which is less aromatic than the pod. Star anise is much used in Chinese and Vietnamese cooking, and it is an essential ingredient in Chinese five-spice powder. It is believed that an English sailor brought this spice to Europe at the end of the 16th century, but it has never been widely used as a culinary spice. It is similar in flavour to anise as it contains the same essential oil, anethole, but is slightly stronger. Medicinally, it is a stimulant and a diuretic, and an infusion is thought to relieve a sore throat. The essential oil is used to flavour liqueurs such as anisette.

Whole star anise

Seeds

Ground star anise

Broken star anise

Five-spice powder *is a blend of star anise, fagara, cassia, fennel seeds and cloves which is used throughout China and Vietnam*

Oriental-style dishes, especially pork, duck and chicken, stir-fried vegetables, long-simmered dishes also flavoured with soy sauce, fish and shellfish dishes, and pumpkin.

COOK'S CHOICE
ORIENTAL CHICKEN WINGS

Serves 4

16 chicken wings
4 tbsp dry sherry
250 ml (8 fl oz) chicken stock or water
2 tbsp soy sauce
1 star anise, broken
Salt

Place the chicken wings in a casserole and pour over the sherry. Let them stand for 30 minutes, turning from time to time. Add the stock or water, soy sauce, star anise and season to taste. Bring to a simmer and cook, covered, over moderate heat until the chicken is tender, about 45 minutes. Taste for seasoning. Serve as a starter, or with boiled rice as a main course.

JUNIPER

The fruit of a small evergreen shrub, juniper berries are purplish in colour when ripe and ready to pick. Too pungent to be eaten fresh, the flavour of the dried berry is aromatic and spicy with a slight overtone of pine. For culinary use, the berries must be crushed to release their full flavour. In cooking, juniper is used primarily with game where its powerful flavour marries well with the equally powerful flavour of venison, wild boar and wood pigeon. The potency of the berries varies by region, with juniper from southern Europe being the most flavoursome. Juniper is essential as a flavouring for gin and other liqueurs popular in Holland, Belgium and Germany. In folklore both the tree and its berries are associated with protection and safe-keeping. The Holy Family is said to have sheltered under the branches of a juniper tree when fleeing from King Herod, the Romans believed the tree protected them, and there are countless legends in which the juniper tree serves as a guardian.

Fresh berries

Juniper berries grow on the branches of this evergreen shrub

Dried berries

TASTES GOOD WITH/IN

Marinades for meat or game, infused in sauces, stuffings, pot roasts, pâtés, sausages, cabbage.

COOK'S CHOICE

VENISON STEAKS WITH JUNIPER SAUCE

Serves 4

4 tbsp unsalted butter
2 tbsp plain flour
500 ml (16 fl oz) beef stock
125 ml (4 fl oz) dry Madeira, such as Sercial
2 tsp ground juniper berries
Salt
Freshly ground black pepper
2 tbsp oil
4 venison tenderloin steaks, about 125 g (4 oz) each

Melt 3 tbsp of the butter in a saucepan. Stir in the flour and cook over very low heat for 2–3 minutes, stirring constantly. Off the heat, gradually stir in the beef stock until smooth. Stir in the Madeira and return to the heat. Add the juniper and continue to cook, stirring, until the mixture is slightly thickened, about 5 minutes. Season to taste; keep warm. In a frying pan, melt the remaining 1 tbsp butter and the oil over high heat, add the venison and cook, about 6 minutes for medium-rare. Season to taste, transfer to warmed dinner plates, pour over the sauce and serve with buttered vegetables.

FORMS
Mace: Whole, ground
Nutmeg: Whole, ground

AFFINITY WITH OTHER HERBS/SPICES
Cardamon, cinnamon, cloves, ginger, pepper

HOW TO STORE
Whole and ground: In airtight jars in a cool, dark place; *ground mace* keeps better than most spices.

MACE AND NUTMEG

Records of the use of mace and nutmeg go back to the first century A.D. when Pliny described a tree bearing a nut with two separate flavours. Indeed, these two spices are distinct yet inseparable. The nutmeg is the hard kernel of the fruit of an evergreen tree native to the Moluccas, or Spice Islands. The fruit is split open to reveal the seed – nutmeg – which is wrapped in a bright red lacy covering – mace. Relatively unknown to the ancient civilizations of the West, both nutmeg and mace had long been used in India. The Arabs were the first to import these spices to the Western world, at the beginning of the Middle Ages, and it was not long before they were precious and sought after. Nutmeg was often carried in special containers of silver or wood, and the grater was attached, so the spice could always be at hand.

TASTES GOOD WITH/IN
Mace: Cakes, puddings, custards, desserts, soufflés, sauces, soups, poultry, fish.
Nutmeg: Baked or stewed fruit, custards, eggnog, punches, sauces, especially onion sauce and bread sauce, pasta, vegetables, especially spinach.

COOKING TIPS
Add freshly grated nutmeg at the end of cooking as heat diminishes the flavour. Boil vegetables such as cabbage, potato or cauliflower, mash with butter, salt and pepper, and stir in a pinch of freshly grated nutmeg.

The nutmeg is surrounded by lacy coverings, or aril, which is mace

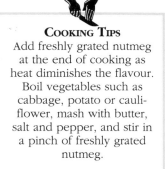

Nutmeg is oval-shaped with a wrinkled exterior and lies within the shell of the seed

Whole nutmeg

Ground nutmeg
Available pre-packaged, it is always better to grind your own supply as needed as it soon loses its flavour

Traditional graters *have a storage compartment so that freshly grated nutmeg is always at hand.*

COOKING WITH MACE AND NUTMEG

FUSILLI WITH MUSHROOMS AND NUTMEG

Serves 4

4 tbsp unsalted butter
2 medium onions, finely chopped
1 kg (2 lb) mushrooms, sliced
¼ tsp ground nutmeg
Salt
Freshly ground black pepper
250 ml (8 fl oz) double cream
500 g (1 lb) fusilli pasta
Freshly grated Parmesan cheese for serving

Heat the butter in a large, heavy saucepan, add the onions and cook over moderate heat until they are softened. Add the mushrooms and cook until they have given up all their liquid. Add the nutmeg and season to taste. Add the cream and cook just long enough to heat the mixture through. Cook the fusilli according to package instructions. Drain thoroughly. In a large bowl, toss together the pasta and sauce until blended. Serve immediately, with the Parmesan. This sauce is suitable for any type of pasta.

Essential oil
Primarily used for non-culinary purposes, a drop or two of nutmeg oil added to hot drinks at bedtime increases their sedative effects.

In the kitchen, these are versatile spices with uses in both sweet and savoury dishes. Nutmeg has a warm flavour and an affinity for rich foods; this is not entirely a coincidence as it is also an aid to digestion. In Italy, it is used to great effect in many filled pastas, either mixed with the stuffing or grated on top at the last minute. It is essential in béchamel sauce and many charcuterie mixtures. The flavour of mace – a combination of cinnamon and pepper is similar to that of nutmeg though much more subtle.

Mace blades
The colour of the blades is often a clue to the derivation of the spice. Orange-red blades tend to be Indonesian; orange-yellow blades are more likely to come from Grenada.

The two forms of mace
Mace is impossible to grate and most homeground mace is coarse in texture because it is difficult to grind finely. Use a coffee grinder in preference to a mortar and pestle.

Ground mace

Coarse ground mace

NUTMEG CAKE WITH LEMON-MACE SAUCE

Serves 6

Butter for preparing the tin
250 g (8 oz) plain flour, sifted
150 g (5 oz) caster sugar
200 g (7 oz) brown sugar
250 g (8 oz) unsalted butter, at room temperature
1 tsp bicarbonate of soda
1 tsp grated nutmeg
1 egg
250 ml (8 fl oz) soured cream
90 g (3 oz) chopped walnuts
150 g (5 oz) honey
Salt
1½ tbsp cornflour
2 tbsp lemon juice
1 tsp grated lemon zest
2 tbsp unsalted butter
Pinch of ground mace

Preheat the oven to 180°C (350°F, gas 4); butter a 23 cm (9 in) cake tin. In a bowl, combine the flour, caster sugar and brown sugar. Add the butter and cut with a pastry blender until it forms coarse crumbs. (Alternatively, blend in a food processor.) Press half of this mixture into the cake tin. To the remaining half, add the soda, nutmeg, egg and soured cream and mix to blend. Pour this on top of the crumbs in the tin and sprinkle with the walnuts. Place in the oven and bake until the sides of the cake come away from the tin, 30–40 minutes. Cool slightly in the tin placed on a cake rack, then turn out. For the sauce, combine the honey and a pinch of salt in a saucepan and heat gently to melt. Dissolve the cornflour in the lemon juice and add to the honey, along with 250 ml (8 fl oz) water. Bring gently to the boil, stirring constantly, until thick. Boil for 1 minute. Remove from the heat and stir in the lemon zest, butter and mace. Slice the cake while warm, place on plates, pour over the sauce and serve.

NIGELLA

(see page 75)
(see page 79)

The pretty plant, love-in-a-mist, with feathery foliage and attractive blue flowers, is a very close relative of nigella and the two are often called by the same name. It is nigella, however, whose edible seeds are used in cooking. The culinary nigella plant is native to western Asia, the Middle East and southern Europe, though today it is grown primarily in India, where it is used extensively in the cuisine of all regions. It is a familiar ingredient in the many spice mixtures of the area, and is frequently found sprinkled on breads including those of Turkey and other Middle-Eastern countries. A hardy annual growing to about 60 cm (2 ft) in height, its seeds must be gathered before they are ripe, otherwise the pods will burst and the seeds will be lost. They are very small and black in colour with a lightly aromatic, peppery flavour, and look rather like onion seed with which they are often confused. This spice seems to attract confusion; in France it is sometimes, inaccurately, called *quatre-épices* (see page 75) and in India *kala jeeras* which is black cumin (see page 79). It can be purchased in speciality grocery stores under its Indian name, *kalonji*.

OTHER NAMES
Devil-in-the-bush, *kalonji*, love-in-a-mist

FORMS
Dried seeds: Whole and ground

HOW TO STORE
In airtight containers kept in a cool, dark place.

COOKING TIPS
In Western dishes, use nigella as a pepper substitute; the taste will be slightly more spicy and bitter. To bring out the most flavour, dry roast the *seeds* in a frying pan before use. Add to buttered vegetables, such as cabbage or courgettes to give them an exotic flavour and pleasant, crunchy texture. Rub *seeds* into steaks before grilling or frying.

Panch phoran *is an Indian spice mixture which combines the seeds of cumin, fennel, mustard, fenugreek and nigella; it is used to flavour pulses and vegetables*

Nigella seeds

Ground nigella

Similarly to pepper, nigella seeds can be ground using a pepper or coffee grinder, and added directly to food

TASTES GOOD WITH/IN

Vegetables, pulses, breads, yogurt, cottage cheese, salads, especially cucumber and yogurt salad, lamb and poultry casseroles, pickles and chutneys.

COOK'S CHOICE
SPICY CUCUMBER SALAD

Serves 2–4

1 cucumber, finely diced
Salt
250 g (8 oz) thick yogurt, preferably Greek yogurt
¹/2 tsp nigella seeds
1 tbsp finely chopped fresh mint leaves
Crisp lettuce leaves for garnish

Place the cucumber in a shallow bowl and season to taste. Add the yogurt, nigella and mint and toss to blend. Serve lightly chilled, on plates garnished with lettuce leaves. If preparing in advance, do not toss with the yogurt, nigella and mint until ready to serve or the cucumber will dilute the dressing.

POPPY SEEDS

OTHER NAMES
Maw seed

FORMS
Seeds: Whole and ground

HOW TO STORE
In airtight containers kept in a cool, dark place.

COOKING TIPS
Use poppy seed oil when a very light, delicate oil is needed for a salad dressing. Known as *huile d'oeillette* in France, it must be from the first cold-pressing which produces a clear, odourless oil with a slight almond flavour. Further pressings produce an oil which is used in artist's paints, soaps and ointments. It is important not to confuse the oil from an artist's supply shop with the culinary oil. Light toasting of the seeds will improve flavour.

This is the seed of the opium poppy whose botanical name means "sleep-bearing." Native to the Middle East, this large annual plant has handsome pink, white or lilac flowers. The minute slate-blue kidney-shaped seeds have a nutty flavour and a crunchy texture. The spice consists of the ripe seeds, while the medicinal derivatives – opium, morphine and codeine – come from alkaloids in the sap of unripe seed pods. The ripe seeds are used widely in the cooking and baking of central and northern Europe, the Middle East, India, and some areas of North America. Most of the seeds in Europe are the slate-blue variety, but there are also yellow seeds used in India and brown seeds used in Turkey. Opium was valued for its medicinal properties by the ancient Egyptians, and not an abused narcotic until the 19th century when opium smoking became fashionable, especially in China and among European artists and writers. As a precaution, many countries prohibit cultivation of the opium poppy without a permit.

TASTES GOOD WITH/IN

Breads, biscuits, cakes, pastries, salads, especially coleslaw, cream-based dressings, curries, sauces for meat and fish, egg noodles, or sprinkled on vegetables as a garnish.

COOK'S CHOICE
POPPY SEED FILLING

Makes about 350 g (12 oz)

125 g (4 oz) sugar
125 ml (4 fl oz) milk or water
125 g (4 oz) poppy seeds
75 g (2 ½ oz) sultanas, coarsely chopped
2 tbsp clear honey
Grated zest of 1 lemon

In a small saucepan, combine the sugar and milk or water, and bring to a simmer over moderate heat. Cook, stirring constantly, for 5 minutes. Add the poppy seeds, sultanas, honey and lemon zest, bring to a simmer, and cook for a further 3 minutes, stirring constantly. The mixture should be thick. Cool before using as a filling for cakes and pastries.

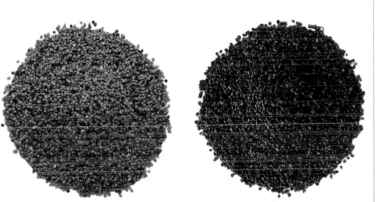

Brown seeds *are usually Turkish in origin*

Slate-blue seeds *are most common in Europe*

Yellow seeds

Poppy seed paste *is made from roasted, ground poppy seeds mixed with poppy seed oil and is used in a variety of Turkish dishes and pastries*

Ground poppy seeds

Ripe seed head *has a ribbed outer casing and is crowned with a stigma; inside are several chambers containing hundreds of seeds*

ALLSPICE

OTHER NAMES
Jamaica pepper, myrtle pepper

FORMS
Berries: Whole, ground

HOW TO STORE
In airtight containers kept in a cool, dark place.

COOKING TIPS
An all-round spice, this enhances the flavours of most other spices. Add to pickles, savoury preserves or chutneys, or use to impart a warm flavour to baked goods or mulled drinks. Add *whole* berries to the peppermill.

Although allspice is a native of the New World, unknown elsewhere until it was introduced into Europe by the Spaniards in the 16th century, it is now used in cuisines the world over. One of the myrtles, the tree is handsome and very aromatic. It grows to a considerable height and has small white flowers. Allspice berries are the size of large peppercorns; they are green when unripe, at which time they are harvested and sun-dried. They turn brown when dry and are then ready for use. The name "allspice" describes its flavour, which is a combination of nutmeg, cinnamon and cloves with slight peppery overtones. The best berries come from Jamaica, which produces most of the world's supply. The cultivated trees grow in what is called an allspice walk, and when they are flowering, the air is filled with perfume from the aromatic bark, leaves, flowers, and later, the berries. The West Indian Arawak and Carib tribes used allspice, and it is more than likely that it was used in Aztec and Mayan kitchens. For the best flavour, grind a few berries in a mortar and pestle; the taste will be fresher than the ready ground spice.

TASTES GOOD WITH/IN
Pickling spice mixtures, marinades for fish, shellfish, meats, game and poultry, all charcuterie, especially ham, vegetables, rice, cakes, pies, puddings, relishes and chutneys.

COOK'S CHOICE
PRAWNS WITH ALLSPICE

Serves 4

1 litre (1 3/4 pt) lager
1/2 tsp salt
1 tsp lightly crushed allspice berries
500 g (1 lb) large, frozen, cooked prawns, defrosted

In a large saucepan combine the lager, salt and allspice berries and bring to a simmer. Cover and simmer for 5 minutes. Remove from the heat. Add the prawns and leave to infuse in the liquid as it cools. Drain, and serve as an hors d'oeuvre, or as a first course with a tomato coulis or a vinaigrette dressing.

Ground allspice

Allspice is a versatile spice which can be used in both sweet and savoury dishes. It is best to grind berries as needed rather than buy the ground version

A pepper grinder
can be used in place of a mortar and pestle when a fresh supply of the ground spice is required

Allspice and peppercorns
For a flavoursome pepper alternative, combine equal amounts of allspice with dried green, black and white peppercorns

Whole allspice berries
are pea-sized and have a roughly textured surface in which most of the flavour lies

ANISE

OTHER NAMES

Aniseed, sweet cumin

FORMS

Seeds: Dried *Leaves*: Fresh

HOW TO STORE

Leaves: Can be stored, briefly, in plastic bags in the refrigerator.
Seeds: Keep in airtight containers in a cool, dark place. Do not keep too long as the flavour does not persist over long periods, even when correctly stored.

Small creamy-white flowers appear in summer followed by seeds

One of the oldest spices, anise is a botanical relative of dill, fennel, caraway and cumin. The plant grows to a height of about 60 cm (2 ft) with leaves similar to coriander and clusters of yellow-white flowers. Native to the Middle East, it is now grown in southern Russia, Turkey, India, and many parts of Europe, where it is a popular spice for flavouring alcoholic drinks. In France, *pastis* is the catch-all name for the many brands of anise-flavoured drinks quite popular in cafés in the south, where they are served in glasses, over ice, with a pitcher of water. *Ouzo* is a favourite anise aperitif in Greece, while *arrack* is the drink of the eastern Mediterranean countries. Anisette, anise-flavoured liqueur, is widely popular, especially in Spain, both as a drink and in cooking. Pastis is also used in cooking, most often added to fish soups or snail butter, but lobster and other seafoods are also greatly enhanced by the flavour of anise. An infusion of anise seeds sweetened with honey can be taken to aid digestion.

Pale brown, ribbed and fuzzy, the seeds are the most flavoursome part of the plant

Anise seeds

Anise-flavoured drinks
such as Pernod, Ricard and Sambuco are popular as aperitifs, and they can also be used to great effect in cookery

Ground anise *loses its flavour and aroma rapidly so buy in small quantities or grind whole seeds with a mortar and pestle*

TASTES GOOD WITH/IN

Sweets, cakes, biscuits, breads, fish and shellfish, tomato-based sauces, vegetable dishes, sweet and savoury mixtures with nuts and dried fruit, especially figs and chestnuts.

COOKING TIPS

For the best flavour, the *seeds* should always be bought whole, not ground, in small quantities for grinding as needed; the seeds are easily ground in a mortar. Young *leaves* can be added, sparingly, to green salads, cooked vegetables, fish soups or stews, and fruit salads.

COOK'S CHOICE
ANISE FRITTERS

Makes 10–12

1 tbsp sugar
¼ tsp salt
2 tbsp anise seeds
175 g (6 oz) plain flour
1 large egg
Oil for deep frying
Sugar for coating

In a large saucepan, combine 250 ml (8 fl oz) water with the sugar, salt and anise seeds and bring to the boil. Add the flour all at once and beat with a wooden spoon until smooth. Off the heat, add the egg and beat until thoroughly incorporated. In a deep fryer, heat the oil to 190°C (375°F) on a frying thermometer. Force the mixture through a pastry bag fitted with a large tip (or use a large funnel) and fry in long strips in the oil until golden. Drain on paper towels, cut into 7 cm (3 in) pieces and coat with sugar while still warm. Serve immediately.

PEPPER

FORMS
Fresh: Whole *Dried:* Whole, crushed, ground
Processed: Pickled whole

HOW TO STORE
Dried: Black and white peppercorns should be kept in a cool, dark place in an airtight container.
Ground: Should also be stored in an airtight container away from light, though the keeping time of ground spices is generally shorter than that of whole.
Fresh: Can be kept in an airtight container in the refrigerator.
Processed: In tins and jars, will keep indefinitely.

Invaluable in the kitchen, pepper is quite rightly known as the king of spices. This spice, which plays an important role in cuisines the world over, is the berry of the plant *Piper nigrum*. India is the world's foremost producer, but it is also cultivated in Indonesia, Malaysia and Brazil. Pepper production accounts for one-quarter of the global spice trade, with America being the single largest importer. Records of its use go back as far as the 4th century B.C., when its Sanskrit name was *pippali*. Like salt, it was a precious spice, and its value was increased by the Roman Empire's demand. The Arabs grew rich furnishing the Romans with pepper, and ancient Roman grocers often blended juniper berries in with peppercorns to stretch the product and increase their profits. There was even a time when pepper was worth its weight in gold. Pepper probably changed the course of history, being the single most important factor in the European search for sea routes to the East. This quest for pepper dominated the spice trade for centuries, and without it, the colonial empires of modern history might not have existed. The glorious past of this simple berry may have long since faded, but for the cook, pepper remains a vital and ever-present spice.

COOKING TIPS
The *ground* form of pepper fades in a relatively short period of time, so it is best to use *whole* peppercorns and grind as needed. Always pepper at the end of cooking time for the maximum flavour. As ground pepper quickly loses its flavour in long-cooking dishes, use whole peppercorns tied in a muslin bag for easy removal. Take care when cooking dishes, such as peppered steak, which require a great deal of pepper to be cooked over a high heat. The effect is similar to that of chilli, and the pepper smoke will irritate the nose, eyes and respiratory tract. Be sure the kitchen is properly ventilated before proceeding with the dish.

Black peppercorns *are green fruits that have been sun-dried after fermenting*

The green berries can be added to duck dishes and creamy sauces

White peppercorns *are the dried insides of ripe berries that have been soaked in water and the outer skin rubbed off*

Pepper berries are harvested from their vines in spring and summer

Ground black pepper

Fresh unripe peppercorns

Ground white pepper

Fresh green pepper-corns *can be difficult to obtain; crush lightly for soups, stews, butters and sauces*

Mixed peppercorns *are especially attractive in glass pepper mills for use at the table*

Dried green pepper-corns *can be rehydrated to use in stocks, soups, or casseroles; crush before using dry*

Pink peppercorns *should be used sparingly as their flavour is less delicate, but their colour will enhance any finished dish*

Pickled green peppercorns *should be rinsed before using in pâtés, flavoured butters or sauces*

TYPES OF PEPPER

FAGARA

Unrelated to pepper, fagara is the dried berry of a Chinese variety of a small prickly ash tree. Also known as Sichuan pepper, these berries have a spicy, woody aroma with a tingly taste. Fagara is essential in Chinese five-spice powder, along with star anise, cloves, fennel and cassia. Before use, the berries should be dry roasted in a cast-iron frying pan, until smoking, then ground.

The pepper plant is native to the equatorial forests of India, and the berries from the Malabar Coast are held to be the finest. It is a perennial vine which takes about eight years to reach maturity and, in good conditions, it will continue to bear fruit for up to 20 years. Green pep-percorns are harvested while still unripe. Their flavour is somewhat milder and fruitier, but not entirely without spice. Sun-dried green peppercorns are more commonly known as black peppercorns. For white pepper, the same berries are left on the plant until fully ripe and red in colour. They are then soaked and peeled to expose the inner white corns, which are then dried. The flavour is slightly less piquant than that of black pepper. Tree-ripened red peppercorns are rarely found outside their country of origin. The almost ripe, soft pink berries of a South American tree, *Schinus terebinthifolius*, are known as pink pepper-corns, though they are not a true pepper. They have a slightly resinous flavour and their culinary value is primarily visual; they offer a stunning contrast when combined with whole green, black and white peppercorns. Use sparingly as pink peppercorns can be toxic in great quantity.

SANSHO

Sometimes called Japanese pepper, this spice is not a true pepper. It is a table spice, usually sprinkled on cooked foods, and it is only available ground. Another use for sansho is in *shichimi*, or Japanese seven-spice mixture, which combines sansho, seaweed, chilli, orange peel, poppy seeds and white and black sesame seeds. This is often sprinkled over noodles or into soups.

BLACK AND WHITE PEPPER

There are many different types of black and white peppercorns with varying flavours; much depends on where they are grown. Singapore black pepper, grown on the Malay peninsula, has a particular taste due to the local method of drying. The rather large berries are spread to dry on suspended mats with a herb fire smouldering beneath. The smoke both dries and flavours the berries, making them one of the most aromatic peppers available. Alleppey and Tellicherry peppers are both grown on the Malabar coast of India. These have a flavour which is clean, aromatic and slightly less pungent than other black peppers.

White pepper from Leghorn, in Italy, is a fine pepper which is produced in limited quantities. Decorticated white pepper is a very high-grade pepper manufactured in England. Especially large, fragrant berries are imported and, after soaking, several layers are removed as opposed to the single layer which comes off for ordinary white pepper. This results in white pepper with a refined flavour.

White peppercorns come from ripe red berries which are soaked after harvesting to facilitate removal of the red skin; these have the advantage of being less visible in delicate sauces

Black peppercorns are obtained from unripe green berries which are left to ferment for several days before drying; the flavour is pungent and aromatic

COOKING WITH PEPPER

From East to West, pepper is appreciated for its warm aroma and spicy flavour, which adds depth and balance to many dishes. It lends vigour to meats like pork and beef, picks up the delicate flavour of eggs, and enhances the subtle flavour of seafood. Whole peppercorns are as much a delight to the eye as to the palate; slices of black-specked peppered salami are much more appetizing than plain, and uniform liver pâtés get a lift from the addition of pretty green peppercorns. Apicius, the Roman author of the first cookery book, recommended adding pepper to enliven the flavour of dull, boiled foods, and also to enhance the flavour of some sweet dishes. Indeed, pepper still finds its way into sweet fruit preparations, especially those made with pears or strawberries. Green peppercorns can be stirred into mayonnaise for seafood or egg salads, or added to simple cream-based sauces served with pan-fried meats, such as duck breast or veal. They also feature in many charcuterie items. White peppercorns are hotter than black, but they lack perfume and flavour. Use alone when a peppery flavour is desired but black specks are not, for example in white or cream sauces, egg dishes, light cream soups, savoury custards or mayonnaise. The best way to use pepper remains the age-old standard: a few turns of the mill just before serving.

Black peppercorns

Coriander seeds

Cardamom

Allspice

Berber spice mixture

Ginger

Chillies

Ajowan

Cinnamon

SUMAC

HOW TO STORE

Keep in an airtight container away from light. The flavour will remain intact for several months in the *whole* berry, though it fades more quickly in the *ground* form.

COOKING TIPS

Seeds can be soaked in water. Allow 100 g (3 ½ oz) seeds for 350 ml (12 fl oz) water and soak for 30 minutes. Strain through a muslin-lined sieve and squeeze to extract the flavour. Proceed with the recipe or use liquid in dressings or marinades.

With leaves that turn a beautiful red in autumn, sumac is a highly decorative bush. It grows wild throughout the Middle East, and while gardeners in the West regard it solely as ornamental, cooks from Lebanon, Syria, Turkey and Iran esteem the spikes of bright red berries it bears. The berries are a deep, brick red when dried, and are used, whole or ground, in a large number of dishes. They have a fruity sourness and were used by the Romans before lemons reached Europe. The berries have a pleasantly sour and rather astringent flavour, but without the sharpness of either vinegar or lemon juice. Mixed with yogurt and herbs, they make a light and refreshing sauce. The Lebanese and Syrians sprinkle sumac on fish; the Iraqis and Turks add it to salads; and the Iranians and Georgians season kebabs with it. Now an uncommon spice in European cookery, sumac can be bought, usually ground, from shops which stock Middle Eastern products. Several other members of the sumac family, prevalent in North America, are poisonous. These include poison ivies and poison oaks, which produce an oil that causes intense skin irritation.

TASTES GOOD WITH/IN

Seafood, vegetable salads, stuffings, rice, pulses, poultry and mixed meat dishes such as meatballs, kebabs and stews.

COOK'S CHOICE
ONION SALAD

Serves 4

*1 large, sweet onion, about
250 g (8 oz), thinly sliced
Salt
1 tsp ground sumac*

Place the onion in a bowl with iced water to cover and let stand for 15 minutes. Drain thoroughly and pat dry. In a salad bowl, combine the onion, salt to taste and sumac, and toss to blend. Let stand for 15 minutes. Serve immediately or refrigerate until needed.

Sumac berries *are not uniform in colour; they can vary from brick to brown- or purple-red depending on their origin*

Ground sumac *will keep its flavour for several weeks if kept in an airtight jar*

Sumac seeds *are small and brown and found in the middle of the berries*

Soaking berries
If berries are used whole they must be cracked and then soaked in water for 20 minutes. Afterwards they are pressed well to extract all the juice. This can then be used as part of the cooking liquid.

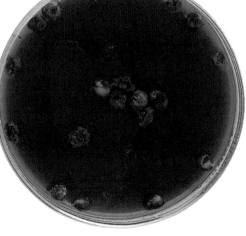

Zahtar *is a Middle Eastern spice blend combining sumac, roasted sesame seeds and ground thyme*

This aromatic mixture can be sprinkled on meatballs or vegetables; mixed with olive oil, it can be brushed over bread before baking

SESAME SEEDS

OTHER NAMES
Benne

FORMS
Seds: Whole, ground

HOW TO STORE
Keep in airtight containers in a cool, dark place.

COOKING TIPS
The somewhat bland flavour of the *seeds* can be enhanced by dry roasting in a frying pan before use. Use roasted sesame seeds as a garnish for dishes flavoured with sesame oil. For example, parboil vegetables, such as green beans, sauté in a little sesame oil and sprinkle with roasted sesame seeds.

There is some confusion over the origin of the sesame plant. Some authorities say it originated in Africa, others say India. It has been known and used in China for about 2,000 years but is still regarded as a foreign plant. A tall, straight-growing annual, it has deeply veined, ovate leaves and white or pink flowers. There are several varieties – white, brown or black – which burst out of the seed capsules when they are ripe. Because of this tendency to scatter, sesame seeds destined for the spice rack are harvested while still green, unripe and neatly contained within the pod. The seed, although small, is quite rich, containing 50 per cent oil which is extracted for culinary use. With a versatile nutty flavour, sesame is popular in many countries and with many types of food, both sweet and savoury. A paste made from untoasted white seeds, known as tahina, is used in Middle Eastern cookery; while a similar paste made from toasted seeds is used in Asia. Another Middle Eastern sesame seed product, Halva, is sweet and a variation of this is made in India.

White seeds

Tahina is a thick paste made from ground sesame seeds; it is most often added to sauces and dips that accompany Middle Eastern-style kebabs and sandwiches, and it can be used to flavour vegetable and fruit dishes

Brown seeds

Black seeds

Halva

Sesame oil

TASTES GOOD WITH/IN

Bread, rolls, cakes and biscuits, vegetables, especially green beans, rice, meat, noodles.

COOK'S CHOICE
COLD SESAME NOODLES

Serves 4

3 tbsp soy sauce
3 tbsp rice vinegar
1 tsp sugar
3 tbsp Asian sesame paste
3 tbsp sesame oil
1 tsp chilli oil, or to taste
1 tbsp freshly grated ginger
Salt
500 g (1 lb) Oriental noodles
3–4 tbsp roasted sesame seeds
Chopped spring onions for garnish

In a large bowl, combine the soy sauce, vinegar and sugar and stir to dissolve. Add the sesame paste, sesame oil, chilli oil and ginger and stir to blend. Bring a large pan of water to the boil; add salt then the noodles and cook until just tender. (Cooking time depends on the type of noodle; follow package instructions.) Drain the noodles, add to the sesame sauce and toss to coat the noodles. Serve chilled or at room temperature. Sprinkle with the roasted sesame seeds and spring onions before serving.

SALT

FORMS
Rock salt: Crystal, fine
Sea salt: Crystal, fine

HOW TO STORE

All salt should be stored in a dry place to prevent it from solidifying or caking; under proper conditions it will keep indefinitely. Do not store salt in silver salt shakers or salt-cellars because the chlorine in the salt reacts with the silver, causing a green discoloration. A traditional salt-cellar which keeps out light is the most convenient method for keeping salt fresh and dry, and the most attractive way of keeping it handy in the kitchen.

Few are the recipes which do not include salt. It is an essential ingredient in both simple everyday cooking, and in the finest of *haute cuisine*. The role of salt is threefold: it seasons food, it preserves food and it provides sodium and chloride which are nutrients necessary to the body's fluid balance and muscle and nerve activity. Always a highly-prized commodity, it was once commonly taxed by governments – just as alcohol and tobacco are taxed today – and this provided a reliable source of revenue. We read the Old Testament, that precious salt was used as an offering to God, and the Romans valued it so highly that their soldiers were given a salt allowance. The English word *salary* is derived from the Latin *salarium*, or salt money.

A certain amount of controversy surrounds the culinary uses of salt. Research has revealed a link between high levels of salt consumption and high blood pressure, increasing the risk of stroke and heart disease. While a diet high in processed foods makes salt intake difficult to control, if used moderately with fresh ingredients, salt can be a healthy source of nutrients.

COOKING TIP

When cooking in a microwave oven, salt can toughen meat and "burn" vegetables, so season after microwaving.

MONOSODIUM GLUTAMATE

Most commonly known as MSG, monosodium glutamate is the sodium salt of glutamic acid, which is an amino acid also found in mushrooms. MSG has no flavour of its own, but it does enhance the flavour of other foods. Originally extracted from seaweed or wheat gluten, it was first discovered in the Orient, where it remains a popular flavour enhancer. While MSG cannot be tasted, its presence can be felt by those who are sensitive to it; unpleasant sensations of pressure behind the eyes and forehead are often provoked. The largest concentrations of glutamic acid occurring naturally in the body are found in nervous tissue, so it is thought that the symptoms of MSG syndrome are merely a temporary excess of the acid. But this theory has not been confirmed. MSG is used extensively in the cuisines of Japan, China and Vietnam.

Coarse salt

Fine salt

Black salt, *also called sauchal, adds its rich flavour to many dishes from Northern India*

Monosodium glutamate

SALT FROM THE EARTH

Sodium chloride, or salt, is present in the Earth and has been since its formation. Rock salt occurs in underground deposits as seams of impacted salt. The salt is extracted, boiled down and crystallized to varying degrees of fineness. At its best, many regard it as the finest flavoured of all salts, though there are those who claim sea salt to be superior; this debate is surely a matter of taste. Coarse or crystal rock salt can be used in the kitchen or on the table, though it is usually placed in a salt mill for table use. Table salt is finely ground rock salt, and it is the most widely used type. It can also contain magnesium carbonate or other chemical anti-caking agents to provide an easy flow. Because of these additives, table salt is considered the least flavoursome by discerning cooks. In North America, "rock salt" refers to freezing salt for ice cream machines and is inedible.

Refined table salt *is often treated to make it more free-flowing*

Crystal rock salt *is mined only from deposits safe for human consumption*

Coarse rock salt *can be used for curing foods; rubbing meats and fish with it is an ancient technique*

Fine sea salt *dissolves quickly and is most suitable for table use*

English sea salt *should be used sparingly as it is very flavoursome*

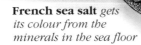

French sea salt *gets its colour from the minerals in the sea floor*

SALT FROM THE SEA

All of the world's salt deposits are of marine origin; salt mines are simply markers for the areas where water once flowed. Sea salt is obtained either naturally by sun and wind evaporation, or artificially from water evaporation pans. Unlike rock salt, it contains only 34 per cent sodium chloride and is rich in trace elements. There are several types available. English sea salt comes primarily from Maldon, in Essex. It has a very "salty" taste and can be distinguished by its flake form. Brittany sea salt from France has a grey colour characteristic of the sea floor beneath the salt marshes. With a delicate flavour, it is an exceptional salt for both kitchen and table. *Fleur de sel*, which translates literally as "flower of salt," from the salt marshes in Guérande is very rare and said to form only when the wind blows from the east. It is harvested manually, using traditional wooden scoops, from June to September.

COOKING WITH SALT

Salt is a basic flavour. In fact, "saltiness" is one of the four categories which make up the range of flavours discernible by human taste buds. And while salt is undoubtedly the most common kitchen ingredient, it is also the most easily abused; a pinch too much or too little can make or break the taste of a dish. The most important thing to remember when using salt is that it is not added as a flavouring in its own right, but as an enhancement to the overall flavour of the dish. This is why a lack of it results in bland food; salt is the background against which other flavours are displayed. When salt is added to a dish depends on many factors. Since salt raises the boiling point of water, it should be added after the boil to reduce cooking time. Consider the way in which salt interacts with ingredients. Salt draws moisture out of food, therefore, do not add prior to cooking beef, for example, as it will drain away the flavoursome juices. Sometimes, however, this effect is desirable. For example, when sautéing onions to soften but not to brown, the addition of salt at the beginning draws the moisture out of the onions and into the pan. This little bit of added humidity lessens the harshness of the heat, allowing the onions to cook without browning. Always bear in mind the salt content of the other ingredients in a dish, as foods such as cheese, bacon and ham are already salty. Mastering the use of salt in cooking is the mark of a great chef, as it takes a great deal of experience to develop a sense for the proper dose.

COOKING TIPS

- In sweet mixtures, salt helps to develop flavour; this is why most batters and doughs often call for a pinch of salt.
- Salt balances the action of yeast and is an integral part of bread making. Thus, follow recipes exactly as the ingredients are calculated carefully and quantities of yeast must be adjusted in low- or no-salt breads.
- A pinch of salt can be added to lightly beaten egg whites when preparing meringues; the salt "relaxes" the protein, making it easier to whisk the whites into stiff peaks.
- Always salt the water for boiling vegetables; this enhances their natural flavour and diminishes the need to add salt at the table. Also, salting at this stage prevents the nutritious mineral salts present in the vegetables from dissolving into the cooking water.

SALT AS A COOKING AGENT

Gravad lax, a traditional Swedish dish, is an example of a simple dry-salted dish which can be prepared at home. Serve with rye or whole-grain bread, and mayonnaise flavoured with chopped fresh dill or mustard-dill sauce (see page 63).

Be sure to choose very fresh salmon and ensure that constant refrigeration is maintained. Signs of poorly salted salmon are salt crystals on the surface, discoloration and a stringy texture. Do not keep longer than two days.

1 Grind together 6 tbsp salt, 6 tbsp sugar and 2 tbsp black peppercorns in a mortar and pestle.

2 Sprinkle half the mixture evenly over one fillet of a 1 kg (2 lb) salmon. Cover with a layer of chopped fresh dill.

3 Cover the dill with the remaining salt mixture and place the second salmon fillet on top so that the skin side is uppermost.

4 Wrap in cling film and weight with a heavy casserole or kitchen weights. Place in the coldest part of the refrigerator for 24–36 hours.

PRESERVING WITH SALT

Salted anchovies   **Preserved lemons**

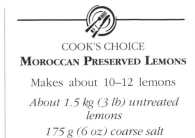

COOK'S CHOICE
SALT COD WITH EGGS

Serves 6

250 g (8 oz) salt cod fillets
2 tbsp cornflour
450 ml (3/4 pt) milk
75 g (2 1/2 oz) butter
1 medium onion, grated
2 medium tomatoes, peeled,
seeded, and chopped
2 tbsp capers, drained
Salt
Freshly ground black pepper
Unsalted butter for ramekins
6 eggs
Freshly grated Parmesan
cheese

One day before preparing the dish, soak the cod in cold water to cover for at least 12 hours, changing the water several times. Drain and rinse the fish. Place in a saucepan and add cold water to cover. Bring just to a simmer over moderate heat, cover and remove from the heat. Leave for 10 minutes, or until it flakes easily when tested with a fork. Drain, remove the bones and skin, flake the fish and set aside. In a bowl, mix the cornflour with a little of the milk until blended. Add the remaining milk and pour into a saucepan. Add 15 g (1/2 oz) butter and cook, stirring, over moderate heat until the mixture is smooth and lightly thickened. In another saucepan, melt the remaining 60 g (2 oz) butter. Add the onion and cook until soft, about 3 minutes. Add the tomatoes and cook until the mixture is thick. Stir in the milk mixture and the capers. Fold in the cod and add a little salt if necessary. Season generously with pepper. Preheat the oven to 200°C (400°F, gas 6). Butter six small ramekins and break 1 egg into each. Pour the cod mixture over the eggs and sprinkle each ramekin with Parmesan cheese. Bake until the egg is set and the top is browned, about 8 minutes. Serve immediately with crusty bread.

B efore every kitchen was equipped with a refrigerator, salt was one of the principal means of food preservation. The ancient Romans were the first to use this method, salting olives, seafood and cheese; and while less popular, preservation with salt is still widely used today. Salt preserves by acting upon the bacteria present in foods. By drawing out the moisture, salt limits the humid environment which fosters these micro organisms. In some cases, salt inhibits bacterial growth; in others, it stops it entirely.

Saltpetre is not sodium chloride, but a potassium salt, potassium nitrate. It is used in small quantities with salt in the preservation of meat and fish, and it is saltpetre which gives many of these foods their characteristic pink colour.

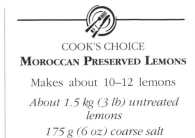

COOK'S CHOICE
MOROCCAN PRESERVED LEMONS

Makes about 10–12 lemons

About 1.5 kg (3 lb) untreated
lemons
175 g (6 oz) coarse salt

Cut the lemons in quarters without slicing all the way through; they should remain attached at the stem end. Sprinkle the salt inside the lemons, on the flesh. Place the lemons in a sterilized clamp-top jar, push them down and weight. Store in a cool, dark place for about 1 month. The peel and the fruit can be used together, whole or chopped, and served with Middle Eastern rice, meat or fish dishes. The juice can be used as a flavouring for grain or vegetable salads.

COOKING TIPS
Add sparingly when reducing as the salt does not evaporate and the flavour can become too concentrated. Do not salt meat before cooking as the salt draws out all the flavoursome juices, but fish fillets will benefit from a bit of salt during refrigeration prior to cooking.

DRY-SALTING AND BRINING

Rubbing coarse salt over the surface of food prior to storage is known as dry-salting. Brining, which involves soaking ingredients in a salt solution, is the method most often used for large cuts of meat or fish. Both methods are equally effective, but brining is best suited to bulky ingredients, as dry-salting would not penetrate deeply enough to hamper bacterial growth. For very large cuts of meat, the brining solution is often injected into the centre as a safeguard.

Sauerkraut
Widely used in the cuisines of Eastern Europe, this is the classic example of an ingredient preserved by brining.

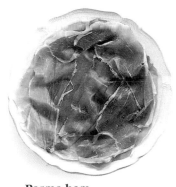

Parma ham
This is the Italian version of salt-cured ham. There are other types, but this is the most widely available.

HERB AND SPICE SALTS

A variety of flavoured salts is a useful addition to any kitchen cupboard. Many commercial seasoning blends are available; sometimes they are labelled as salt though they may also be labelled as seasoning. These seasoning mixtures contain varying quantities of salt, and sometimes none at all, so always check before using to avoid oversalting. When prepared at home, herb and spice salt mixtures can add a new dimension to an old standard or spice-up an otherwise ordinary dish. Celery salt with tomato juice is classic, but flavoured salts have many uses: rub into meat or fish before roasting or grilling, use to season vegetables and sauces, dust over home-made crisps or add to soft cheese for a simple canapé spread. If making in large batches to keep on hand, use free-running table salt. Seasoned salts are also used in many Asian cuisines. *Gomashio* is a Japanese blend of black sesame seeds and salt. To prepare, allow three parts black sesame seeds to one part coarse salt. Dry roast the seeds, cool and then pound together in a mortar and pestle. A similar Chinese spiced salt mixture consists of equal parts of dry roasted fagara (see page 95) and coarse salt pounded together.

1 *Combine all the ingredients in a mortar and crush with a pestle until combined.*

2 *Spoon into airtight containers for storage.*

Garlic salt *can be bought pre-packaged or made in a mortar by pounding a clove with a few tablespoons of salt*

Celery salt

Seasoned salts
Home-made seasoned salts are ideal for sprinkling over meat, poultry and fish before grilling.

Herb salt

TAMARIND

COOKING TIPS
It is worth searching for tamarind *concentrate* which is a sticky dark paste without seeds or fibrous, broken pods. This is the most convenient form as only a small amount is ever needed for most dishes. Alternatively, soak the *fresh* pulp in water for a souring agent that can be used like vinegar and lemon juice. Pour 100 ml (3 ½ oz) hot water over 6 peeled pods and leave for 30 minutes. Strain into a bowl, cover and refrigerate. Keep for up to 1 week.

The exact origin of the tamarind tree is not known. The tree may have originated in tropical East Africa, or in southern Asia. It has been cultivated in India for many centuries and was probably introduced into Europe in the 15th century. The Spanish *Conquistadores* took it to the West Indies and Mexico in the 17th century, and it has remained a popular ingredient in the cuisines of the islands and the South American mainland. An evergreen with light green, oval-shaped leaves, it has red-veined yellow flowers which ripen into dark brown pods. Tamarind is characterized by a sour, fruity flavour and a pleasant aroma. It is useful where a gentle sourness is needed, and it so enhances the flavour of fish and poultry dishes. Though its primary importance is in the kitchen, both red and yellow dyes are derived from the leaves. It is also used in many commercial products, most notably in Worcestershire sauce.

TASTES GOOD WITH/IN
Indian curries, fruit drinks, vegetable stews, desserts, jams and jellies, hot and sour soup, chutneys, rice, lentils, seafood, especially prawns, meat and chicken dishes.

COOK'S CHOICE
TAMARIND WATER

Makes 3 litres (5 pt)

125 g (4 oz) tamarind concentrate

3 litres (5 pt) cold water

Sugar

Combine the tamarind concentrate with water in a large jug and leave to stand in a cool place for about 4 hours, or until the pulp has softened. Stir from time to time. Strain through a fine sieve and sweeten to taste. Serve chilled. Alternatively, reduce the amount of soaking water and serve the drink over ice cubes.

The brown pods can reach a length of 10 cm (4 in) and are picked when fully ripe and cracked

The shells are brittle and house a fleshy pulp, which can contain as many as 10 seeds

Tamarind pods

Tamarind seeds

Tamarind block

Tamarind concentrate

FENUGREEK

HOW TO STORE
Keep in airtight containers in a cool, dark place.

COOKING TIPS
Fenugreek is so strongly aromatic that the whole plant gives off a spicy odour. The *seeds* however, are very disagreeable and bitter in their raw state, and they should always be lightly roasted before use. A heavy iron frying pan is ideal for dry roasting the seeds, which then have a pleasant aroma and flavour.

A sturdy annual whose Latin name means "Greek hay," fenugreek is native to western Asia though it has been cultivated in Mediterranean regions since ancient times. Although this spice is associated primarily with Indian cookery, it has been used in the West for medicinal purposes and as cattle fodder. The ancient Egyptians used a paste made from ground fenugreek which was plastered on the body to reduce fever; today it is used in the manufacture of some oral contraceptives. In cooking, the seeds must be dry roasted before use to remove their bitter flavour, though over-roasting will leave them just as unpleasant. Ground fenugreek is an essential ingredient in curry powders and it is also used for pickling. In parts of Africa, the seeds are soaked and prepared like pulses. The seeds can also be sprouted and added to green salads where they add a crunchy texture and a slightly bitter flavour.

TASTES GOOD WITH/IN

Seeds: Indian curries of all kinds, Egyptian and Ethiopian breads, the Ethiopian spice mix, Berber, stews and to coat fried foods. *Sprouted seeds*: Salads. *Dried leaves*: Boiled root vegetables.

COOK'S CHOICE
POTATOES WITH FENUGREEK

Serves 4

500 g (1 lb) new potatoes
Salt
75 g (2 ½ oz) unsalted butter
175 g (6 oz) fresh fenugreek leaves, finely chopped, or 2 tbsp dried fenugreek leaves
½ tsp curry powder
½ tsp mango powder (optional)
Freshly ground black pepper

Cook the potatoes in boiling, salted water until just tender, 10–15 minutes. Drain and pat dry. Melt the butter in a large pan. Add the potatoes and fenugreek leaves and cook gently until golden, 5–10 minutes. Sprinkle on the curry, and mango powder if using, and cook for a further 5 minutes; stir often for an even golden brown colour. Season to taste. Serve either hot or at room temperature.

Golden-brown with a deep furrow on one side, they are smooth and hard

Fenugreek seeds

Ground fenugreek

Crushed fenugreek

Hard to grind, fenugreek seeds are best pounded in a mortar after roasting

Fresh leaves *have few culinary uses but sprouted leaves may be tossed into salads and the plant can be eaten as a vegetable*

Dried leaves *known also as methi, are often combined with root vegetables in Indian and Middle Eastern dishes*

VANILLA

The pod of a climbing orchid, vanilla originated in southern Mexico. When the Spaniards conquered Mexico, the Aztecs were already flavouring their hot chocolate with vanilla, a practice the world has since copied. It was the Aztecs who developed the technique of curing the pods by repeatedly sweating and drying them to develop the white crystalline vanillin, without which the pods have no flavour. The best pods are supple but tough, dark brown in colour and covered with a frosting of aromatic crystals. Because it is an expensive spice, there is a great deal of false vanilla on the market, much of it chemical. Synthetic vanilla can be recognized by its coarse aroma and unpleasant after-taste. The best vanilla comes from the state of Veracruz in Mexico and, where it grows, the air is richly scented. It is also grown in Madagascar, Central America, Puerto Rico, Réunion, and other areas with a suitable climate.

HOW TO STORE
Whole pods: Can be stored in glass jars with tightly fitting lids, kept in a cool, dark place.
Essence and extract: These are best stored in a cool, dark place, or in the refrigerator.

Pods *are dark brown, narrow, long, wrinkled, waxy and supple*

The flesh gives off a rich, mellow, perfumed tobacco-like aroma

COOKING TIPS
Vanilla is expensive but it is best to buy *whole pods* as they are more flavoursome and can be used sparingly; they can also be used more than once. After splitting a whole pod to scrape out the seeds for use in a recipe, leave the pod to dry for several days. Place the dried pod in a sealed jar of sugar. Keep topped-up with fresh sugar, which will take on the delicate vanilla aroma; add more pods to maintain a steady supply of flavour. Alternatively, split the pods, extract the seeds, place them in a bowl and pour over some boiling milk. Sweeten to taste and allow the mixture to stand for 15 minutes. Use in rice puddings, or in any sweet recipe calling for milk.

Vanilla pods should be plump and tender; avoid those which are brittle and dry

Vanilla sugar

Vanilla essence *is very concentrated and should be used sparingly*

TASTES GOOD WITH/IN
Chocolate, coffee, puddings, custards, ice cream, fruit desserts; in small quantities, with savoury dishes such as those made with veal and lobster.

COOK'S CHOICE
VANILLA GRANOLA

Makes about 1 kg (2 lb)

250 g (8 oz) porridge oats
250 g (8 oz) barley flakes
125 g (4 oz) flaked almonds
60 g (2 oz) wholemeal flour
125 g (4 oz) dried apricots, chopped
1 vanilla pod, split
125 ml (4 fl oz) honey
125 ml (4 fl oz) sunflower oil

Preheat the oven to 190°C (375°F, gas 5). Combine the oats, barley, almonds, flour and apricots. Scrape out the vanilla seeds. Whisk together the vanilla seeds, honey, oil and 125 ml (4 fl oz) water. Stir in the dry ingredients. Spread in a tin and bake, stirring often, until golden, 30-45 minutes. Cool. Place in an airtight jar, add the vanilla pod. Leave for 1 week before using.

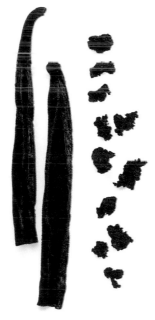

Split pods with seeds

GINGER

OTHER NAMES

Ginger root, green ginger

FORMS

Fresh: Whole *Dried:* Slices and ground *Processed:* Preserved in syrup, crystallized and pickled

HOW TO STORE

Fresh: Rhizomes are best refrigerated, wrapped in paper towels, in tightly closed plastic bags where they will keep for several weeks.
Dried: Should be stored in airtight containers kept in a cool, dark place.
Pickled: Should be refrigerated in its container.
Preserved: Should be stored in its container and kept in a cool, dark place.

The underground rhizome of an attractive flowering plant, ginger is used extensively in the cuisines of Asia where it is second in importance only to salt. It has been cultivated in tropical Asia for over 3,000 years, though its exact origins are unknown. Ginger was also used in the Middle East and southern Europe well before Roman times. The Portuguese introduced it into Africa, the Spanish took it to the West Indies, and by the 16th century, the Spaniards had a flourishing Jamaican ginger trade with continental Europe. With a clean, fresh, spicy flavour, ginger is appreciated in many dishes both sweet and savoury, though it is in the Orient that ginger is used to its full potential. There are many forms: fresh, dried, pickled, preserved in syrup and crystallized. In Chinese cookery, fresh is preferred to the dried, both for flavour and texture. Chopped, crushed, or sliced into matchsticks, it is used to season innumerable meat, fish and vegetable dishes. Pink pickled ginger, called *gari* in Japan, is the familiar condiment for sushi. The Japanese also have a special tool, an *oroshigane*, which is reserved for grating fresh ginger.

Knobbly, off-white or buff-coloured and branched, the rhizome should feel firm

Fresh ginger

Dried ginger

TASTES GOOD WITH/IN

Curries, soy sauce, meat and poultry stews, chutneys and pickles, vegetables, soups, fish and cheese dishes, stewed and baked fruit, cakes, puddings, biscuits, sweet breads, drinks and mulled wine.

COOKING TIPS

Always have some *fresh* ginger in the refrigerator and buy a fine grater of the kind (sold in Japanese shops) made especially for grating ginger. Grate the ginger and squeeze out the juice, which will lift any fish or shellfish dish out of the ordinary. Add to soups, marinades and stews, especially those made with beef, just before serving.

Fresh grated ginger
With a sharp knife, peel away the rough outer skin only as far as the ginger to be grated.

Mainly used for desserts and other sweet dishes, it imparts a rich and warming flavour

Ground ginger

Pickled ginger

Preserved ginger

Crystallized ginger

CRYSTALLIZING GINGER

Peel and thinly slice 500 g (1 lb) fresh ginger. Place in a saucepan, add water to cover and cook gently until tender, about 30 minutes. Drain. Weigh and place in a saucepan with an equal amount of sugar and 3 tbsp water. Bring to the boil, stirring often, until the ginger is transparent and the liquid is almost evaporated. Reduce the heat and cook, stirring constantly, until almost dry. Toss in sugar to coat. Store in an airtight jar for up to 3 months.

COOKING WITH GINGER

The uses for ginger in the Western kitchen are many. It adds a clean, fresh bite to seafood, picks up the flavour of dull foods, and cuts the fattiness of rich meats such as duck or pork. In marinades, ginger has an affinity for citrus fruit, garlic, soy sauce and onions. When choosing fresh rhizomes, weight and firm flesh are a sign of freshness. Length is a sign of maturity, and mature rhizomes will be hotter and more fibrous. For grated ginger, the fibres are not problematic though they can be for slicing. Fresh ginger will keep for about one week in a cool place. In the refrigerator, it will keep for a few weeks wrapped in paper towels to absorb moisture and placed inside a plastic bag. Dried ground ginger tastes nothing like fresh and the two are not interchangeable in recipes; ground ginger is best in sweet dishes such as breads, biscuits and puddings. It also has a wonderful affinity for baked rhubarb and apples.

COOK'S CHOICE
GINGERBREAD BISCUITS

Makes about 30–40 biscuits

150 g (5 oz) honey
90 g (3 oz) soft brown sugar
30 g (1 oz) unsalted butter
375 g (13 oz) flour, sifted
2 tsp ground ginger
Pinch of ground cinnamon
Pinch of ground cloves
Pinch of ground cardamom
1 egg yolk
1 tsp bicarbonate of soda

In a pan, combine the honey, sugar and butter over low heat and stir to dissolve. Leave to cool. Preheat the oven to 160°C (325°F; gas 3). In a bowl, combine two-thirds of the flour, the spices, the egg yolk and the honey mixture, and stir to blend. Dissolve the bicarbonate of soda in 1 tbsp tepid water and add to the mixture. Slowly knead in the remaining flour, as needed, to obtain a firm dough. Roll out 1 cm (1/2 in) thick and cut out shapes. Place on a greased baking sheet and bake for 10–12 minutes. Cool on a rack.

Gingerbread biscuit

FLAVOURS OF THE WORLD

THE MIDDLE EAST

J ust as the Middle East has always been a melting pot of different cultures, so too is its cuisine a rich mix of flavours. It is a combination of gleaming fruit and vegetables eaten almost straight from the fields, and long-stewing, slow-baking dishes featuring lamb, yogurt, beans and spices, mopped up either by rice or by the region's characteristic flat discs of bread. To walk down any Middle Eastern street at dusk is to breathe in the scent of gently grilling meat, with different fragrances vying for attention like traders in the *souk*, or marketplace.

In the many countries that make up the area known as the Middle East – Egypt, Syria, Iran, Iraq, Lebanon, Jordan, Saudi Arabia, Yemen, Kuwait and Israel – the style of cooking is not affected by fashion or new fads. A deeply rooted respect for traditional values is mirrored in dishes that have a history stretching back many centuries, to the time when they were devised by Persian princes, Palestinian farmers or Bedouin nomads scratching a living from the desert.

TRADITIONAL INGREDIENTS

Aubergines
Allspice*
Basil*
Burghul
Caraway*
Cassia*
Cardamom*
Chillies*
Chick peas
Cinnamon*
Cloves*
Coriander*
Cumin*
Dill*
Fennel*
Fenugreek*
Figs
Garlic*
Ginger*
Honey*
Lemon*
Marjoram*
Mint*
Olives*
Orange flower water*
Parsley*
Phyllo pastry
Pine nuts
Pomegranates
Rosemary*
Saffron*
Sesame seeds*
Sumac*
Tahina*
Thyme*
Turmeric*
Yogurt*
Zahtar*
Zhug

(*see Index)

INFLUENCES

It was in the "Fertile Crescent," formed by Iraq, the Levant and Egypt, that humans first became farmers rather than hunters, some 12,000 years ago. Wheat, barley, pistachio nuts, pomegranates and figs flourished alongside flocks of sheep and goats. And while the Middle East influenced the rest of the world's eating habits, the rest of the world has had little effect in return. All the main culinary influences and traditions have come from countries, or empires, that are or were found within the region.

Around A.D. 700, invading Arabs flooded out from what is now Saudi Arabia, bringing with them the gospel of Muhammad and a desert diet in which goat's or sheep's milk was substituted for water, and nuts and dates for fresh vegetables and fruits. By the 10th century, when Baghdad had become the administrative, cultural and culinary centre of this empire, a more sophisticated court cuisine evolved. This essentially set the style for Middle Eastern food, marrying more simple Arab dishes with more complex Persian creations (using rice, duck, almonds and fresh fruits) as well as the many oriental spices – cumin, cardamom, coriander, fenugreek, turmeric and ginger – which Arab traders were transporting to all corners of their sprawling empire.

Four centuries later, the luxury-loving sultans of Turkey's Ottoman Empire added new layers to this already very colourful confection of foods. They introduced sweet, sticky pastries, such as honey-drenched *baklava* and *kadayif*, as well as the thick, sweet coffee that is still popular today. This is ground from a mixture high in mocha beans (named after the Yemeni port Al Mokha), flavoured with ground cardamom pods and is drunk from small cups, in vast quantities, throughout the region.

FLAVOURINGS

In the prolific use of spices, Middle Eastern chefs come second only to their Indian counterparts in enthusiasm. Among the most commonly used are aniseed, caraway, clove, coriander, cumin, ginger, nutmeg, sesame seed and allspice. Likewise, the markets of the Middle East are thick with the scent of kitchen herbs: basil, coriander, dill, fennel, marjoram, mint, parsley, rosemary, sage and thyme. In addition, each country has its own preferred seasoning blend. *Zahtar*, for example, is a blend of powdered marjoram leaves, thyme, roasted sesame seeds and the sour red berries of the sumac tree, and it is widely used by the Jordanians. *Zhug* is a lip-tingling Yemeni paste, made of ground cardamom, cumin, garlic and chillies, which is often added to soups and stews for extra bite.

Tahina paste, made from oil and sesame seeds, forms an integral part of many dips and dishes. Nuts feature prominently in Middle Eastern cookery; almonds are favoured in Iran, pine nuts in the Levant and walnuts and hazelnuts in Iraq. Olives and olive oil are to be found in every domestic kitchen, as are jars of pickled vegetables, called *torshi*; the most well known is made from turnips, coloured pink with beetroots.

The smoky flavour of charcoal grilling is imparted to meats, poultry and fish. For sweets and desserts, honey is often used in place of sugar, and many are also delicately imbued with the perfume of orange flower and rose water.

OTHER INGREDIENTS

Lamb is the dominant meat, due largely to the predominance of the Muslim and Jewish religions, which forbid the eating of pork. It is often cubed and grilled over charcoal (*kebabs*), or minced with herbs and spices and turned into meatballs (*koftas*), or stewed with spices and then yogurt for the Bedouin dish, *laban ummo*. Lamb also forms the basis of the Iranian national dish *chelow kebab*, in which lamb kebabs are served on a bed of crusted rice and accompanied by a generous portion of butter and raw egg yolk. Goat and camel meat is also widely eaten across the Middle East, as is chicken which, along with turkey, forms the main source of meat in Israel.

Whereas a meal without meat is conceivable, a meal without bread is unthinkable. Most Arab bread is made from wheat that has been lightly leavened and shaped to a hollow flat round, forming a pocket that is perfect for stuffing. Cracked wheat, *burghul*, is served either as a bread accompaniment or substitute. Rice is used in the same way. It was introduced to the area by the Persians, who had adopted it from their Indian neighbours. Rice with cardamoms, cloves, cumin and cassia is still an Iranian speciality (*polo*).

Aubergines are commonly used, as a guest in stews and as a host for stuffings of rice, meat and nuts, or simply sliced, salted and fried. Courgettes, okra, olives, cucumbers, tomatoes and vine leaves come close behind. Brown fava beans, seasoned with garlic, onion, lemon juice and cumin, form the Egyptian national dish, *ful medames*, which is eaten and enjoyed throughout the country, in luxury restaurants, at roadside stands and even on the breakfast table.

Fish tends to decrease in importance away from the various Middle Eastern coastlines, where fresh-caught mullet, swordfish and sardines are often charcoal-grilled, after being marinated in olive oil, lemon juice and onion. *Gefilte* fish – white fish fillets minced with eggs, breadcrumbs and onions – is an Israeli favourite.

MEALS

Early morning in the Middle East sees a bustle of activity outside most bakeries, as people come to buy still-warm bread for their breakfast, to eat with eggs, fresh fruit and vegetables, honey, nuts and yogurt.

Coffee is drunk throughout the day, at home, at work, in restaurants and coffee houses that also provide a bubbling hookah, or hubble-bubble pipe. Only in Iran is black tea, with large sugar lumps, a more popular drink than coffee.

Lunchtime brings with it a selection of small dishes, known collectively as *mezze*, usually featuring pitta bread in abundance with hummus, yogurt, rissoles, tabbouleh, assorted vegetable salads, stuffed vine leaves, taramasalata and a variety of dips.

The evening meal is generally the largest of the day. In traditional households, it is eaten in two shifts; first the men, then the women and children. Before eating, a jug filled with soapy water is passed round, and all diners wash their hands before their first mouthful. The food is served in communal dishes, and it is customary to eat with the fingers – preferably just the thumb and first two fingers, though all five are allowed for more fiddly foods. In order to show that they have finished, satisfied diners lean back and lick their fingers. Sweet pastries or puddings are not usually served after a meal, except when entertaining.

The Arab tradition of hospitality pervades the households of the Middle East. Shame is attached to the host who does not extend a surfeit of food towards the guest, and equally to the guest who does not pay fulsome tribute to his host.

Many culinary customs are dictated by religion. For example, alcohol is proscribed by the Koran. Nevertheless, some fine wines are made in the Lebanon, as well as in Egypt and Israel.

MENU GUIDE

Tabbouleh
A salad of chopped parsley, tomatoes, onions, burghul, lemon juice and olive oil

Hummus bi Tahina
Puréed chick peas blended with tahina paste

Moutabal
Smoked, puréed aubergines with tahina paste

Felafel (Israel)
Ground deep-fried chick pea balls, served in pitta bread

Ful Medames (Egypt)
Brown beans tossed in a cold dressing of lemon, garlic, cumin, onion and oil

Kibbeh
(Syria and Lebanon)
Minced meat, burghul, and onions, usually deep-fried

Labaneya (Egypt)
Spinach soup with yogurt

Sambousek (Lebanon)
Phyllo pastries filled with meat, onion and pine nuts

Kofta Mabrouma (Syria)
Baked rolls of minced meat with a filling of pine nuts

Samak Masguf (Iraq)
Charcoal-grilled fish with a tomato and curry sauce

Khouzi (Saudi Arabia)
Whole roast lamb

Faisanjan (Iran)
Duck or chicken in walnut sauce flavoured with pomegranate juice

Khoresh (Iran)
Lamb in thick sweet-and-sour sauce

Kadayif
Shredded pastry dough cake stuffed with honey syrup and chopped nuts

Ma'amoul
(Syria and Lebanon)
Nut- or date-filled pastries

GREECE AND TURKEY

From the whitewashed walls and blue skies of the Greek islands to the bare plains and citadel towns of eastern Turkey is a distance of some 1100 km (700 miles). It is a journey which crosses not only the Aegean Sea, but also from a Christian land to a Muslim, from Europe to Asia. Centuries of differences divide the two nations, and yet in their cooking they are united. In common they have one thing: a hot, often harsh climate, making for land which does not yield readily to the plough. Not here the lush meadows of Northern Europe, but dry, baking hillsides on which flourish not tall pines but hardy, hunched olive trees and herds of goats. The cuisine reflects the landscape: a rugged, peasant fare of bread, tomatoes, olives and aubergines, enlivened by grilled meat and, in Turkey, by skilful, deployment of spices. A few European dishes have found their way into Greece, and Russian influence is apparent in Turkey's Black Sea region, but by and large, this is a cuisine which has its gaze very firmly fixed towards the East.

TRADITIONAL INGREDIENTS

Allspice*
Aubergines
Burghul wheat
Chillies*
Chicken
Chick peas
Cinnamon*
Cumin*
Dill*
Fennel*
Feta cheese
Figs
Garlic*
Grapes
Honey*
Lamb
Lemons*
Marjoram*
Mint*
Octopus
Olive oil*
Olives*
Oregano*
Onions*
Parsley*
Peppers
Phyllo pastry
Pine nuts
Pistachios*
Pitta bread
Rose water*
Rice
Saffron*
Sardines
Spinach
Sunflower seeds
Tomatoes*
Vine leaves*
Watermelon
White haricot beans
Yogurt*

(*see Index)

INFLUENCES

As far back as the 5th century B.C., Greece had a reputation for cooking every bit as distinguished as it enjoyed in the fields of art, politics and literature. The early Greek writers Philoxenus and Archestratus wrote whole treatises on the art of cookery. We know from them and others that bread, goat's cheese, wine, olives, beans, fish, fruit, honey and pine nuts formed the basis of an early Athenian's diet. Five centuries later, when Greek power had waned, it was still every Roman nobleman's ambition to employ a Greek chef in his household.

The greatest outside influence on Greek cooking came with the invasion of the Ottoman Turks in the 15th Century. Previous occupation by the Venetians had introduced pasta to the region, but the Turks came bearing an altogether spicier, fruitier cuisine, heavily influenced by Persian cooking, but also comprising a rich variety of dishes devised by the court chefs of the Ottoman capital Constantinople (modern-day Istanbul). These were rich confections of tomatoes, olive oil, aubergines and meats, along with syrupy sweetmeats that bore luxurious, at times lascivious, names such as "girl's breasts" and "ladies' navels".

For nearly four centuries, the Ottoman sultans ruled Greece, and throughout this period the two nation's cuisines became inextricably intertwined. Today, many dishes not only share the same ingredients but also the same names.

FLAVOURINGS

Green and fruity-tasting olive oil lies at the heart of almost all Turkish and Greek cuisine. It serves as a dressing, a marinade, a flavouring and a cooking fuel.

Garlic is another flavouring that is intrinsic to both regions; combined with olive oil it forms the basis for the Greek sauce *skorthalia* and its Turkish counterpart *tarator* (with the addition of walnuts); both sauces are used to accompany otherwise plainly cooked fish and vegetables.

Lemon is another constantly recurring flavour; its sharpness is used to balance the richness of olive oil in the two savoury dips which are synonymous with this area, and which even share the same name in both languages: *hummus* (olive oil, sesame seed paste, puréed chick peas and lemon juice) and *taramasalata* (puréed smoked cod's roe, olive oil and lemon juice).

In Greece, lemon juice is an almost mandatory ingredient in salad dressings; along with eggs, it forms the principal ingredient of the Greek sauce *avgolemono*, used to flavour soups and stews, and to bring zest to fish and vegetable dishes.

Herbs such as dill, mint, parsley, marjoram and oregano flourish in the temperate Greek climate, while spices are more a Turkish phenomenon. Most commonly used are allspice, cinnamon and cumin, which are mixed in with minced meat to make *kofta*, or rissoles. These, like many Turkish dishes, have a distinctive, spicy-sweet character.

OTHER INGREDIENTS

Patterns of meat consumption are dictated by both cultural and geographical factors. In Muslim Turkey, for example, pork is forbidden on religious grounds; in Christian Greece it tends to be eaten only on festival and feast days. As for beef, the general lack of green pastures makes the rearing of cattle impractical. Lamb is therefore the prevailing meat, and it forms the starting point for large numbers of Greek and Turkish dishes.

Both countries have long coastlines, and their seas harbour rich supplies of fish and seafood. Prawns, lobster, red mullet and tuna are often served, plainly grilled, with a light seasoning of oil and lemon juice; squid and octopus are stewed in a red wine and tomato sauce or deep-fried in batter (as are whitebait and cuttlefish).

The most common vegetables of the region are aubergines, tomatoes, onions, peppers, white haricot beans, olives and vine leaves. The bulbous-shaped, purplish-black aubergine loves olive oil and soaks it up like blotting paper; aubergines are simmered, stewed, deep-fried or else stuffed with tomatoes, peppers, onions and garlic, as in the famous Turkish dish *imam bayildi* which means "the priest fainted" (from pleasure, tradition has it).

Flattened, oval-shaped, lightly leavened pitta bread is the staple of both countries, and is usually served warm. A popular variation in Turkey is *semit*, a crisp ring of white bread covered in sesame seeds.

Water-thin, flaky phyllo pastry is used in both countries to make *baklava*, a popular sweetmeat filled with nuts and spices and drenched in honey syrup. Phyllo pastry also forms the outer casing for the many different Turkish *boreks*, pastry parcels filled with mixtures of melted cheese, spinach or minced meat.

Rice is mainly used for stuffing vegetables, but it also forms the basis for the Turkish *pilavs* – dishes in which the rice is cooked along with the other ingredients: chicken, minced lamb, green peppers, tomatoes and even plain roasted wheat grain. In south-eastern Turkey, cracked wheat (burghul) is used instead of rice.

Goat's or sheep's yogurt is to be found everywhere. Combined with thick Greek honey it becomes a popular dessert; diluted with iced water and salt it becomes the refreshing Turkish drink *ayran*. The other most common dairy product is cheese, eaten in melted form in both countries, but more commonly in solid form in Greece; no Greek salad is complete without some crumbled chunks of *feta*, goat's cheese.

MEALS

The Greeks generally eat three meals a day: first, a light breakfast of bread, goat cheese, olives and tomatoes, then at midday their main meal, and in the evening a lighter collection of snacks.

The Turks, on the other hand, favour four visits to the table, with two main meals (breakfast and dinner) and two lighter snacks (at lunchtime and last thing at night).

In both countries, a selection of appetizers (*mezze*) usually forms the bulk of the lighter meals. These may be as simple or complicated as required, ranging from cubes of salty goat cheese, slices of tomato drizzled with olive oil and a bowl of plump, black olives, to selections of savoury dips, stuffed vegetables, oil-soaked haricot beans and spicy meatballs. In Turkey, soup (*chorba*) will often be the starter for a main meal, even at breakfast.

Strong Turkish coffee (known as Greek coffee in Greece) is always served at the end of the meal. In Greece, guests may also be offered preserved fruits or spoonfuls of sweet jam dissolved in water. Other sweets include *baklava* and *kadayif*, syrup-soaked pastries filled with rich mixtures of honey and nuts.

The instinct of extending hospitality towards strangers is deeply ingrained in both the Turks and the Greeks. In remote rural areas, travellers are likely to be invited not just to have dinner but also to stay the night in a local family's home. Failure to accept can cause deep offence.

In traditional Turkish homes, food is eaten with the fingers; only the thumb, the index and the middle finger are used and damp flannels sprinkled with toilet water are passed round at frequent intervals.

In the restaurants of both countries, meals are taken at a leisurely pace, and diners are usually invited into the kitchens to inspect the food before making their choice.

MENU GUIDE

Mezze
A selection of hot and cold appetizers

Hummus
Chick peas puréed with olive oil and lemon juice

Taramasalata
Cod's roe blended with olive oil and lemon juice

Tzatziki (Greece)
Çaçik (Turkey)
Yogurt with cucumber, mint and garlic

Borek (Turkey)
Pastries stuffed with spinach, cheese or minced meat

Fasoulia (Turkey)
Beans cooked in tomato sauce

Skorthalia (Greece)
Tarator (Turkey)
Creamy garlic paste

Avgolemono Soup (Greece)
Chicken soup flavoured with rice and lemon juice

Imam Bayildi (Turkey)
Aubergine stuffed with onion, tomatoes and garlic

Kleftico (Greece)
Slow-roasted lamb on the bone flavoured with spices

Moussaka (Greece)
Layers of baked vegetables and minced lamb covered in a light cheese sauce

Chicken Guvech (Turkey)
Chicken cooked with green peppers, onions and tomatoes

Gharithes Yiouvetsi (Turkey)
Prawns baked in a special tomato sauce with feta cheese

Pilav (Turkey)
Rice cooked with meat, vegetables or wheat grain

Halva (Turkey)
Hard, biscuit-like fudge, made with nuts

Rahat Loukoum (Turkey)
Turkish delight

EUROPE

E urope is the world's dairy. In no other continent are milk, butter and cheese produced so plentifully and used so prolifically. And together with onions, bread and potatoes, they make up the superstructure of European cookery, at the pinnacle of which stand the rich varieties of meat and fish that prosper in this largely temperate zone. The focal point of any European meal is the main course, be it a leg of roast lamb, a bubbling beef stew or a tureen of steaming seafood; starters and puddings play a secondary role. While there is much diversity, the three-course-meal pattern prevails, as does the use of knives, forks and spoons. Trade, wars and migration have consistently blurred the region's physical and political boundaries, but throughout the process, the different European peoples have largely succeeded in preserving their own languages, their own cultures – and their own foods.

TRADITIONAL INGREDIENTS

Asparagus
Bay leaf*
Beetroot
Butter*
Cabbage
Caraway*
Cherries
Chocolate*
Cinnamon*
Cream*
Dill*
Dried fish*
Game
Garlic*
Herring
Mushrooms*
Mustard*
Nutmeg*
Offal
Olive oil*
Onions*
Parsley*
Pasta
Peppers
Potatoes
Rabbit
Sage*
Sausage
Smoked fish
Tarragon*
Thyme*
Tomatoes*
Wine
Vinegar*
Yogurt*

(*see Index)

MEDITERRANEAN EUROPE

United by a common, near-landlocked sea, the countries that comprise Mediterranean Europe – Spain, Portugal, Italy and Southern France – have for many centuries enjoyed a circular interchange of trade, people and foods. Merchants have always plied these waters, beginning with the Phoenicians, then the Greeks, the Romans, the Venetians and countless others. Although they use largely the same ingredients, all the countries have retained their own clearly defined cuisines. Pasta remains inviolably Italian, sherry and ham Spanish, port and spicy sausages Portuguese, and wine and herbs French.

With such a long coastline, fish and seafood play a key role. By contrast, beef cattle like neither the high summer temperatures nor the lack of lush pastures; Mediterranean cookery thus tends to revolve round the hardy pig and chicken.

Rarely does a meal in the Mediterranean pass without olive oil having played a part. Sprinkled over fresh green salad and tossed with vinegar, quickly fried with silvery sardines, or long-stewed with meat and bubbling tomatoes, olive oil spreads its fruity, delicate flavour throughout the region's food. Add some sunshine and you have the unmistakable aroma that characterizes dishes from this region.

More often than not, olive oil works in partnership with garlic, suffusing dishes with a flavour that varies in strength from lightly perfumed to fiercely pungent. Garlic also forms the principal ingredient (along with eggs and olive oil) of the French mayonnaise *aïoli*, which in Spain becomes *alioli*, minus the eggs but plus herbs. In Italy they eat pasta with nothing but garlic and olive oil (*aglio e olio*), and in Portugal, chefs pack garlic cloves into *açorda de alhos*, a substantial bread soup.

Alcohol is often used to flavour Mediterranean dishes: the wine bottle is never far from the French or Italian cook's grasp, while Spanish and Portuguese chefs tend to use sherry more often.

Herbs are widely used in French and Italian cooking, principally basil, tarragon, parsley, sage, thyme, marjoram and bay leaves. The pounding of basil, Parmesan cheese, pine nuts and olive oil produces a tasty, concentrated paste called *pesto* in Italy (used as a sauce for pasta) and *pistou* in France, where it lends its individual personality to a vegetable and vermicelli soup (*soupe au pistou*). In Spain, parsley has a higher profile than elsewhere in the Mediterranean, forming the principal ingredient of *salsa verde*, the piquant green sauce (with olive oil, garlic and shallots) which accompanies boiled meat or fish dishes. The Portuguese have a fondness for fresh coriander in their soups, fish stews and vegetable dishes.

Many Mediterranean dishes contain saffron, either in thin, silky threads or (more commonly) in powder form. It appears in the French seafood soup *bouillabaisse*, in Italian *risotto alla milanese* and in Spanish *paella*, spreading aroma and a yellow hue. However, the cuisines of Spain and Portugal place more emphasis on spices than do those of France and Italy, with the most popular being paprika, chillies, cinnamon, nutmeg, cloves and saffron.

Garlic

Pork is the most common meat of the region and from it comes cured ham, popular throughout the Mediterranean. This is ham which has been salted, then hung and dried for several months; it is served in near-translucent slices. In Italy, the most famous kind is Parma ham, in France it is *jambon de Bayonne* (slightly smoked). The Spanish version is *jamon serrano* and the Portuguese *presunto*. Numerous varieties of pork sausage are also to be found.

From the sea comes a multitude of ingredients: red mullet, anchovies, sardines, sea bass, hake, sole, monkfish, mussels, scallops, squid, cuttlefish, lobster, crayfish, clams and prawns. Fish stews are prevalent throughout the region: *caldeirada* (Portugal), *zarzuela de pescado* (Spain), *brodetto* (Italy) and *bouillabaisse* (France).

As well as being a primary ingredient, fish is also used as flavouring. A tuna mayonnaise sauce accompanies cold slices of poached veal in the Italian dish, *vitello tonnato*. Likewise, anchovies are pounded into a paste with olive oil and garlic, to become the tangy fish sauce called *anchoïade* in France and *bagna cauda* in Italy.

A visit to any Mediterranean market demonstrates the region's abundance of fresh vegetables. Tomatoes are the basis for the well-known Spanish soup *gazpacho*, enhanced with raw peppers and cucumber. Onions contribute much to Mediterranean cuisine; chopped and lightly sautéed in olive oil, they are called *refogado* in Spain and *sofrito* in Portugal, and act as a base for many stews and sauces.

Bread is the automatic accompaniment to any meal, be it the French baguette or the Italian olive oil-based *ciabatta*. Rice is most common in Spain and Italy. For Italian risottos, the native Arborio rice is labouriously stirred in simmering stock, often with small pieces of meat, fish or vegetables, until the liquid is absorbed and the rice cooked to a soft consistency. The paella dishes of Spain are similar, though usually on a larger scale. Portuguese cuisine has similar rice dishes to those of Spain while rice often accompanies the *daubes* (stews) of Southern France.

In Italy there are supposedly 200 different shapes and types of pasta, the country's celebrated staple. Pasta is made from durum wheat, and comes in many forms: long, thin straws (*spaghetti*), flat noodles (*tagliatelle*) and squat tubes (*rigatoni*), among many other configurations. Popular sauces include *bolognese* (minced beef, onions, tomatoes, wine and herbs), *carbonara* (eggs, cream and bacon) and *vongole* (tomatoes, onions and clams). Other unique Italian staples include the much-loved pizza.

In Italy, egg yolks whisked with sugar and Marsala and served warm is *zabaglione*. In France, it is called *sabayon*. The flan (baked caramel custard) is probably one of Spain's most popular dessert offerings.

As well as a wide variety of eating cheeses, France and Italy boast a large range of cooking cheeses. Most notable of these is Italy's hard, pungent Parmesan, often sprinkled on pasta dishes, and the softer, chewier *mozzarella*, which is a frequent topping for pizzas made outside Italy. The most widely eaten Spanish cheese is the firm-textured *manchego*, while *queijo da serra*, made from ewe's milk, is the most popular Portuguese cheese.

French olives

MENU GUIDE

Tortilla Espanola
Spanish omelette

Caldo Verde (Portugal)
Cabbage and potato soup

Vitello Tonnato (Italy)
Cold veal in a tuna sauce

Mejillones en Salsa Verde
(Spain)
Mussels in green parsley sauce

Rinones al Jerez (Spain)
Kidneys in sherry sauce

Lomo a la Naranja (Spain)
Loin of pork with oranges

Osso Buco (Italy)
Braised veal shin

Calamares en su Tinta
(Spain)
Squid cooked in its own ink

Brandade de Morue
(France)
*Salt-cod purée with olive oil
and croûtons*

Risotto alla Milanese (Italy)
Creamy rice with saffron

**Arroz de Bacalhau com
Coentros** (Portugal)
Salt cod with coriander

**Chanfana à moda da
Bairrada** (Portugal)
Kid or lamb in red wine

Daube de Boeuf Provençale
(France)
*Long-simmered beef stew with
wine, herbs and garlic*

Granita all' Arancia (Italy)
Orange water ice

Tiramisù (Italy)
*Sponge with mascarpone and
Marsala*

Flan de Huevos (Spain)
Sweet egg custard

Clafoutis aux Cerises
(France)
*Cherries baked in a custard
batter*

Arroz Doce (Portugal)
Rice pudding

THE BRITISH ISLES

Britain has absorbed many culinary influences over the centuries. Early invaders included the Romans, from whose festive bread, *siminellus,* descends the Easter Simnel cake (with almond paste and dried fruit); the Vikings brought with them a fondness for pickled and smoked fish, and the Normans for dairy products. In addition, the British have always been great travellers and traders, with a love of spices and condiments. The influence of the British presence in India can still be seen, for example, in chutneys and pickles, as well as in the breakfast dish kedgeree (rice, fish, eggs and spices, from the Indian dish *khichri*) and mulligatawny soup (spicy meat and vegetable broth). Peasant cooking remains a strong tradition, with one-pot dishes such as Lancashire hotpot (lamb), Welsh *cawl* (bacon and beef or lamb) and Irish Stew (mutton). Suet figures prominently either as an extra (beef stew and dumplings) or more substantial savoury (steak and kidney pudding) or sweet (spotted dick, jam roly-poly) pudding. Roasts are very British, especially when served with roast potatoes and Yorkshire pudding (batter baked in hot beef fat). Sauces include horseradish sauce for beef, mint sauce for lamb, and apple sauce for pork.

Fish has always been popular, whether fish and chips or regional dishes such as the Cornish Stargazey Pie (mackerel under pastry crust with the heads visible around the edges), as well as shellfish such as oysters, mussels and cockles. Afternoon tea is an institution, with sweet breads (scones, crumpets and muffins), spread with homemade preserves and sometimes cream, and cakes such as Bakewell tart, Eccles cakes, gingerbread and flapjacks.

NORTHERN EUROPE

A characteristic peculiar to most North European nations is that they have not been subjected to the same deluge of invasions as the more southerly parts of Europe. They have invaded one another, but unlike Italy (invaded by Ottoman Turks) and Spain (occupied by North African Moors), who have been substantially influenced by the cooking of their incursors, Northern European cuisine has remained relatively insular.

Amid the many different national cuisines, two distinct styles stand out. The first belongs to mainland Europe, covering northern France, Belgium, Holland, Germany, Austria and Switzerland. This can be categorized as a predominantly meat-based diet, with emphasis on the taste of the basic ingredients rather than on added flavourings. The second style belongs to Scandinavia; a lighter, predominantly fish-based cuisine that is similarly concerned with the freshness and quality of raw materials.

In mainland Northern Europe, the moderate climate and generally fertile countryside provide an environment ideal for the rearing of beef and dairy cattle, as well as sheep and pigs. Historically, meat has always been of sufficiently good quality not to need great embellishment from spices and herbs. More problematic has been the storage of meat after slaughter, which is why the predominant tastes – salting, marinating and smoking – are all methods of prolonging storage as well.

After salt and pepper, the most common condiment is mustard, a blending of mustard seeds, vinegar, water and salt, with the optional addition of herbs and spices. Particularly popular in Germany, along with horseradish (*Meerrettich*), mustard is used to accompany the vast range of Northern European charcuterie. In northern France, herbs are an important flavouring; the combination of bay leaf, thyme and parsley, known as bouquet garni, is the flavour base for many stocks and stews. Tarragon is seen as the natural partner of chicken, and it features frequently in French mustards and vinegars.

Meats of all kinds are eaten throughout mainland Northern Europe: beef, rabbit and chicken are common; duck, lamb and game birds are enjoyed mainly in Germany and France. Germany is the capital of pork: boiled knuckle and smoked loin; thick, grilled chops served with mustard, plain roast leg served with cabbage. Pork's relatives, ham (*Schinken*) and bacon (*Speck*), also abound in Germany; the most famous ham is a smoked variety from Westphalia, traditionally served with slices of buttered bread and glasses of *Steinlagen* (juniper flavoured brandy). Bacon is served plain or added to stews such as *Blundhuhn*, a combination of broad beans, bacon, fresh vegetables, apples and pears. The variety of German *Würste*, or sausages, is immense; among the better known are *Leberwurst* (liver sausage), Brunswick *Mettwurst* (smoked pork sausage), *Weisswurst* (a white veal and herb sausage from Munich) and the famous Frankfurter, traditionally served in a roll with mustard. Austria, Belgium, Holland and Switzerland share a similar enthusiasm for sausages. France leans towards pâtés and *rillettes* (potted meats) which are rich, spreadable mixtures made from pork, though some are blended with goose.

Beef is eaten in all regions. *Tafelspitz* is an Austrian and German speciality where beef is braised and served with freshly grated horseradish. *Vlaamse karbonaden* is a Flemish dish in which beef is simmered in a rich beer broth. Veal is most commonly associated with Austrian cuisine, thanks to the celebrated *Wiener Schnitzel* in which thin veal escalopes are coated with breadcrumbs and then pan-fried.

As well as fish from the North Sea and the Atlantic (cod, herring, mackerel), seafood is in plentiful supply off the coasts of Brittany and Normandy. A classic French dish is *moules marinière*, mussels steamed with shallots and wine; the Belgians serve their mussels with fried potatoes. In addition, the rivers of the area yield freshwater carp, pike and trout.

Bread is the staple of mainland Northern Europe, travelling the full range of flavours and colours, from dark brown German rye bread (*Pumpernickel*) to the crisply baked white sticks of French bread known as baguettes. Rice features in Dutch cooking in the form of the dish *rijsstafel*, imported from Holland's erstwhile colony of Indonesia; it is a feast of meat, fish and egg dishes all served with rice.

Throughout the area, potatoes are the almost automatic accompaniment to all main dishes. Sliced and deep fried, they appear as *pommes frites* in Belgium and France; simmered in herb-infused milk then baked

Scandinavian cured salmon

Waterzooi (Belgium)
Fish soup with white wine

Svenska Köttbullar
Swedish meatballs

Königsberger Klopse
(Germany)
Meatballs in caper sauce

Leberknodel (Germany)
*Liver, bacon and potato
dumpling*

Sole Normande (France)
*Sole and mussels in creamy
cider sauce*

Kalakukko (Finland)
*Rye bread layered with fish
and pork, and baked*

Dillkött (Sweden)
Veal in dill sauce

Karjalanpaisti (Finland)
Beef, pork and mutton stew

Rösti (Germany)
*Fried potato cake with onion
and butter*

Poulet à la Normande
(France)
*Chicken cooked in Calvados
sauce with sautéed
apples*

Frikadeller (Denmark)
Veal and pork meatballs

Rote Grutze (Germany)
*A mould of summer fruits
served with milk or custard
sauce*

Sachertorte (Austria)
*Chocolate sponge covered
with apricot jam and
chocolate icing*

Stekta Äpplen med Sirap
(Sweden)
*Baked apples with golden
syrup*

Oeufs à la Neige (France)
*Poached meringues served
with custard sauce*

Rødgrod med Fløde
(Denmark)
Summer fruits with cream

with cream they become the golden brown *gratins* of France; formed into a crisp pan-fried potato cake, they become *Rösti* in Germany and Switzerland.

Apples are used in sweet and savoury dishes such as the German speciality *Himmel und Erde* (Heaven and Earth), which is a purée of apples and potatoes topped with grilled black pudding. Normandy apples feature in many tarts and other desserts.

Fruits are also used to fill the many cakes and confections enjoyed in North European coffee houses. In Germany, *Schwarzwälder Kirschtorte* (Black Forest Gâteau) is a rich mixture of chocolate sponge, cherries, lashings of whipped cream and grated chocolate. Austria is renowned for its *Tortes* (cakes), such as *Sachertorte* (chocolate sponge filled with apricot jam and covered with chocolate icing) and *Strudel*, made of thin pastry wrapped round a spiced fruit filling. The chocolate of Belgium and Switzerland is legendary, as are the spiced biscuits, cakes and buns of Holland; the best known are *Speculaas*, biscuits which are made into windmill shapes and flavoured with a mixture of ground sweet spices and almonds.

Dairy produce plays a vital part in the cuisine. Milk and butter (from France and Holland) are widely used in both sweet and savoury recipes. Cheeses come in many hundreds of regional varieties. France is noted for its soft, rich cheeses; other countries are associated with harder cheeses: *Gouda* and *Edam* (Holland), *Gruyère* and *Emmental* (Switzerland). The most famous Swiss dish is fondue, which revolves around a large pot of bubbling, melted cheese, sometimes flavoured with kirsch or white wine, into which squares of bread can be dipped.

By contrast, the foods of Scandinavia tend to be lighter and altogether more fish-orientated. This is due to the long, icy winters that turn dairy pastures into snowfields.

Mackerel, plaice, cod, haddock and halibut from the sea and carp, pike and trout from the rivers, are eaten widely. Salmon is often sliced thinly and marinated raw in salt, dill and spices for *gravad lax*. Herrings are a more workaday alternative: they are smoked, cured or marinated, and eaten on their own or mixed into salads. In Finland they are even combined with meat in the dish *forshmak* (salted herrings and chopped lamb). Other Finnish dishes are just as wholehearted: *karjalanpaisti* is a stew of beef, pork and mutton; while reindeer meat is dried, smoked or roasted and served with cranberries.

Dairy products feature in Scandinavia as well. Soured cream sprinkled with sugar is a traditional Norwegian breakfast, and it is also a frequent ingredient in other fish and vegetable dishes traditional to the region. Milk and sour milk are popular beverages. The best known cheeses of the area are *Samso* and *Danablu* (Danish blue).

Potatoes are another indispensable ingredient particularly in Denmark. Here, they are cooked and puréed, made into salads, sliced and fried, or boiled in their jackets and then peeled and rolled in sweet caramel to give a crunchy coating.

Berries of all sorts thrive in Scandinavia, including rowanberries and cloudberries; from these are made soups, fruit compotes and desserts such as Swedish *jortrontårta* (cloudberry tarts). Denmark is famous for its fruit-filled pastries, its rich confections containing apples and raisins, filled with spiced custard and sprinkled with chopped nuts and cinnamon.

RUSSIA

Spanning a range of climates from Arctic to sub-tropical, and a spread of cultures from European to Central Asian, Russia has naturally absorbed many styles of cooking. From the North, the Swedes brought smoked herring and soured cream (*smetana*). From the Middle East came aubergines and mutton. From Germany came salted cabbage and the tradition of combining meat with fruit.

Root vegetables are the workhorses of Russian soups. Cabbage, carrots, parsnips and potatoes are all used in the making of *shchi*, the hearty cabbage soup; *rassolnik* soup contains sorrel, cucumber, onion and celery; *borshch* is a thick, purple broth of beetroot, potatoes, carrots, onions and cabbage. Breads are the most common staple; white sourdough bread (*balabouchki*), nearly-black rye bread (*krouchenik*) and others with onion, cheese and sesame-seed flavourings. Flaky buckwheat (*kasha*) is also served as a soaker-up of stews and sauces. Pastry-encased salmon (*koulibiak*) is a court dish that has emigrated to the West, unlike the large range of pastries and puddings which rarely appear outside Russia. These include *krendiel* (sweet brioches), *gozhnaki* (walnut and honey cakes) and *kulich*, a sweet bread made with cinnamon, nutmeg, cardamom and candied fruit peel often served with *pashka* (sweetened cottage cheese pudding).

The main meal of the day is lunch, which consists of *zakuski* (a selection of hors d'oeuvres), soup, main course, then fruit or pastries. Vodka, plain or flavoured (pepper, lemon, caraway seed) may be drunk, but an alternative is *kvass*, a kind of beer often flavoured with fruit.

EASTERN EUROPE

For centuries, the countries of Eastern Europe have been pawns in the hands of larger empires: Roman, Austro-Hungarian, Ottoman and Russian. Armies of countless different rulers have rampaged back and forth across the plains of Hungary, Poland, Czechoslovakia, and through the hills and valleys of Yugoslavia, Romania and Bulgaria.

To be sure, the victorious forces left their mark upon the cooking of those countries. To this day, Turkish pastries are eaten in those parts where the Ottomans held sway, while Viennese-style cakes and strudels are still served in regions which were once ruled by the Austrian Hapsburgs. But at the same time as adopting the cuisines of their conquerors, the cooks of Eastern Europe have remained loyal to their traditional dishes and methods of cooking.

Skewered spicy sausages, for example, are to be found throughout Eastern Europe. In Yugoslavia they are called *cevapcici*, and are made of beef, lamb or pork. In Bulgaria, *kebabche* are a similar mixture of veal and pork, and in Romania *mititei* (known as *mici*) are made of beef.

The longevity of many Balkan mountain-dwellers is traditionally ascribed to their yogurt-based diet. Certainly yogurt appears

Assorted breads

with a large number of dishes throughout the area, as does soured cream. The Hungarian speciality *hortobagyi palacsinta* consists of pancakes filled with minced meat, onions and paprika, surrounded by soured cream. The Poles serve a thick soured-cream sauce with salted herrings (*sledzie w smietanie*), and the Czech dish *svickova* (baked spicy beef and vegetables) is not complete without a pool of soured cream beside it.

Salting and smoking are the most common means of flavouring and preserving. For example, shredded cabbage is stored in barrels of salted water throughout the winter and the Polish kabanos sausage is slowly smoked over juniper wood.

The taste of garlic leaps out of many cold meats and salamis, as well as from the cold Bulgarian *tarator* soup, in which it is combined with yogurt, cucumber and pounded walnuts. Dill, sorrel and fennel add their distinctive flavours to soups and stews. Paprika (crushed, dried, sweet red pepper) has become synonymous with Hungarian cooking, and is the central flavouring of *goulash*, the thick beef, onion, potato and tomato stew that is the country's well-known national dish.

Hardship has for centuries stalked this part of the world, with the result that East European chefs have long since developed an expertise in making a little meat stretch a long way. Thus, there is a profusion of different soups and vegetable-dominated stews found in each country. *Kapismak* is the classic Polish soup, filled with cabbage, celery and bacon. *Gyuvech* (*ghiveciu* in Romania) is the name of a hearty, Polish vegetable stew which usually includes peppers, beans, aubergines and whatever meat is to hand.

Pork, followed by beef, is the most popular meat, especially in Czechoslovakia, where the specialities are roast pork (*veprova pecene*), pairs of pork sausage (*parky*), and sumptuous Prague ham, often baked in a thick bread crust. Lamb and suckling pig are served whole, but only on special occasions; chicken is more readily available. Country dwellers often have an advantage over the urban population in their access to game: wild boar from the Polish plains, and venison, hare and quail from the mountains of Romanian Transylvania.

Apart from Baltic herring, East Europeans mainly have to content themselves with freshwater fish – trout, carp, and the celebrated *fogas* (pike-perch), from Hungary's huge Lake Balaton.

Of all the vegetables, cabbage is the most popular, being used both to bulk out soups and stews and also to provide the "wrapper" for a rice, meat and sauerkraut stuffing. This combination appears under different names: *tölltött kaposzta* (Hungary), *sarma* (Yugoslavia), *sarmi* (Bulgaria) and *sarmale* (Romania). In other words, stuffed cabbage, which is well-known in many countries.

Thick, hearty breads further supplement the cuisine. These come in many different forms. Romanians have *mamaliga*, which is a firmer version of Italian *polenta*. Bulgaria has a range of breads made with butter, cheese and yogurt, which are dipped before each mouthful in a spicy, tarragon-tasting powder called *kubritsa*. Dumplings – *knedliky* in Czechoslovakia, *csipetke* in Hungary – appear as a matter of course in many dishes.

Buckwheat, a flaky, somewhat soapy-tasting staple, is widely eaten and is very popular in Poland. Pasta also features in some cuisines: Hungarian chefs use *tarhonya*, small pasta grains that are boiled then cooked with chopped onions; Yugoslavian pasta is particularly common on the Dalmatian coast (as is risotto), and the Polish dish *lazanki* can claim direct descendancy from lasagne, having been introduced in the 16th century by the King of Poland's young Italian bride.

All countries in this region have a well-developed pastry repertoire, of which the most elevated is Poland's. The tastiest creations of the Polish pastry chef include light *paczki* doughnuts filled with rose-petal jam, deep-fried *faworki* (made with flour, cream and rum) and little rectangular *mazurki* (pastry bases with a marzipan and chocolate topping). There is also a range of fluffy *babka* sponges, of which the most famous is the raisin-dotted *babka wielkanocna*, which is traditionally made at Easter.

MEALS

Breakfast in mainland Europe often consists of a variety of cold meats, cheeses and breads. In Belgium, Austria, Holland, Switzerland and Germany, hot coffee or chocolate is served. The two main meals of the day are interchangeable according to taste, but the larger tends to be at the end of the day's work, in the evening.

Breakfast is a light meal in Denmark, Finland and Sweden, usually just fresh bread and coffee. In Norway, where, in summer, daylight comes very early, it can be an enormous affair: fish, cold meats, fresh bread, hot waffles, cheese and eggs, washed down with hot chocolate, milk or coffee. Lunch may consist of a hot vegetable soup and open sandwiches, called *smorrebrod* in Denmark and *violeipä* in Finland. Supper is another soup and a main dish. All countries have their versions of Sweden's famous *smörgåsbord*, which is a buffet meal of hot and cold dishes such as herrings, cold meats, pâtés, salads, cheeses and hot, meat-filled vols-aux-vents. Smörgåsbord is served in restaurants and homes, at lunchtime or as a evening meal.

Breakfast in Spain and Portugal is a brisk downing of coffee or chocolate and a pastry, or simply some toast. In Spain, a post-siesta snack (*merienda*) is usually eaten between 5:30 and 7 p.m., with dinner eaten as late as 11 p.m. The Portuguese take their evening meal much earlier (between 7 and 8 p.m.); dinners in both countries are variations on the lunchtime menu.

In Italy and southern France, buttered bread and strong coffee start the day, with lunch or dinner the larger meal according to taste and circumstances. In both countries fruit frequently takes the place of dessert, and in France cheese precedes the sweet course. The Sunday afternoon meal is a tradition in France: families gather round a well-laden table, often spending the rest of the day there, lingering over the multiple main courses followed often by salad, cheese, dessert, coffee, and possibly a cognac or armagnac.

East European tradition does not frown on the early morning downing of a vodka or fruit brandy before venturing out into the winter sub-zero surroundings. This may also be accompanied by a steaming hot bowl of soup (*chorba*), filled to the brim with cabbage, beans and small pieces of meat. City dwellers favour less hearty dawn fare – a mixture of cheese, bread, hard-boiled eggs and salami is more typical – but in the middle of the day, both rural and urban populations alike pause to enjoy the main hot meal of the day. The evening meal is usually a cold version of lunch, with warmth added by one of the region's many strong alcoholic distillations.

MENU GUIDE

Tarator (Bulgaria)
Cold garlic and walnut-flavoured yogurt soup

Caviar (Russia and Poland)
Salted sturgeon eggs

Rassolnik (Russia)
Sorrel and cucumber soup

Crni Rizoto (Yugoslavia)
Squid ink risotto

Hortobagyi Palacsinta
(Hungary)
Minced meat, onion and paprika pancake

Sledzie w Smietanie
(Poland)
Salted herrings and soured cream

Szeged halaszle (Hungary)
Goulash-style fish soup

Pui Cimpulugean (Romania)
Chicken stuffed with bacon, sausage, vegetables and garlic

Pirozhki (Russia)
Hot savoury pastries

Blinis (Russia)
Small, buckwheat pancakes, often served with caviar

Hideg Fogas (Hungary)
Pike-perch in mayonnaise

Koulibiak (Russia)
Salmon baked in pastry

Cholent
(Poland and Russia)
Beef baked with onions, buckwheat and potatoes

Mamaliga (Romania)
Polenta bread

Lazanki (Poland)
Pasta squares baked with ham, mushrooms and cabbage

Paczki (Poland)
Light doughnuts filled with rose petal jam

Sharlotka (Russia)
Charlotte Russe—sponge cake with custard and fruit purée

NORTH AFRICA

Like their Middle Eastern neighbours, the North Africans enjoy a daily cuisine that originated many centuries ago and many hundreds of miles away. They inherited the Persian penchant for combining meat and fruit, and have fallen willing victims to the Turkish sultans' weakness for sweetmeats. Even today, in the smartest Tangier or Tunis hotel, North Africans are still roasting lamb in the same way that Arabian desert nomads did a thousand years ago.

But as well as absorbing the foods and flavourings of other peoples, the North Africans also have developed their own highly individual cuisine. This is a cuisine in which a chef might use twenty-five spices in a dish, or just one; a cuisine in which one national dish – *bstilla*, or pigeon pie – contains as many as fifty carefully constructed layers of delicately spiced stuffing and another – couscous – is the embodiment of peasant rough-and-readiness. It is a distinctive mixture of forceful, spice-driven main dishes and delicate little nut and date desserts. Like the land that has shaped it, the cuisine of North Africa is a juxtaposition of the wild and the lush, the barren and the fertile.

INFLUENCES

Two thousand years ago, the land mass that is modern-day Morocco, Algeria, Tunisia and Libya was just one country, known as the Maghreb. It was home to the Berbers, a pale-skinned, blue-eyed race who, for many centuries had pursued a nomadic life within its vast and arid interior.

Having a long coastline, the Maghreb was open to any seaborne invaders or colonizers, and the first to arrive in numbers were the Phoenician traders from northwest Syria, in the first millennium B.C.. The Phoenicians made many long sea journeys and required meat that was both easy to preserve and to store; their solution was a dried sausage. This became the direct ancestor of the spicy North African *merguez*. After the Phoenicians came the Carthaginians, who introduced durum wheat and its by-product, semolina, which the resourceful Berbers adapted for couscous, now the staple of the area as a whole.

In the 7th century A.D., the invading Arab armies brought spices and the word of the prophet Muhammad. Seven centuries later, the sweet-toothed Turkish Ottomans established a pastry repertoire that the North Africans have since elevated to a high state of refinement.

In 1715, European merchants and colonizers took over, following the Ottoman demise in North Africa. The Italians left their mark with pasta, the French with their language and the British with tea, which they successfully encouraged the local inhabitants to mix with the traditional mint brew, thereby creating *chai bi naa'naa*, the mint tea that is now universally popular throughout the Maghreb region.

FLAVOURINGS

Tastes vary among the different peoples of the Maghreb. The Moroccans like rich, full flavours (particularly saffron), the Algerians favour less spicy dishes, and the Tunisians find food bland without some chilli- or ginger-generated heat.

Chefs express their own preferences in the range of spices they choose to put in their *ras-el-hanout*. Meaning literally "top of the shop," ras-el-hanout is a mixture of up to twenty-five different spices and flavourings, which may include cardamom, cassia, mace, chillies, cloves, cumin, fenugreek, nutmeg, lavender and dried roses.

Another distinctively North African flavour is *chermoula*, a powerful purée of onion, garlic, coriander, chillies, chilli powder, paprika, salt, pepper and saffron. Gentler, more aromatic flavouring comes from the Moroccan spice mixture *la kama*, a blend of black pepper, turmeric, ginger, cumin and nutmeg, often used to bring soups and stews to life. Tunisian *harissa* is a fiery paste (see page 71) often served with couscous, and *tabil* is another Tunisian chilli-based paste made with garlic, fresh coriander and caraway seeds.

Main course dishes will often come with pickled lemons, which serve as part relish, part vegetable.

OTHER INGREDIENTS

As in most Muslim countries, lamb and mutton are the most common meats and feature in many regional dishes. Merguez sausages are made of coarsely-chopped mutton, garlic and ras-el-hanout. *Meshwi* is

Ras-el-hanout

spit-roasted lamb and *choua* is steamed lamb with cumin. Rabbit and goat are also eaten, and poultry is the basis for many dishes, including *tajines*, which are slow-cooking stews, usually featuring fruit (dates or prunes) and honey. These dishes get their name from the tajine pot in which they are cooked; this is a round earthenware dish, sometimes ornately painted, topped by a tall, conical lid that looks like a witch's hat.

Wheat, rather than rice, is the main staple throughout the Maghreb. Northern Arabs eat the flat, round discs of lightly leavened Arabic bread, of which *kesra* is a tasty

variant, spiced with sesame and aniseed. Couscous, also a wheat product, is made of tiny semolina pellets. In many parts of the area, couscous made in the traditional manner is subjected to a delicate ritual that alternates steaming and hand-fluffing.

Local bakers are particularly skilled in the making of thin, near-transparent pastry, known as *malsouga* in Tunisia. This pastry is used not only for *bstilla* but also for the colourful range of brown, red and gold pastries that are to be found stacked up beneath the fluorescent lights of North Africa's countless cake shops.

In those parts of the Maghreb that are not desert, vegetables abound. The most common are courgettes, peppers, broad beans, carrots, turnips, aubergines, celery, leeks, onions and chick peas. These usually form the vegetable content of the chicken or lamb stew that is served in a flavoursome broth alongside mounds of couscous.

As well as the soil, the sea is a rich source of food: mullet, hake, sea bass and pilchards are the commonest catch. Chermoula paste is often used with fish, either as a marinade or as a flavour enhancer in fish soups.

MEALS

Many North Africans begin the day with soup, often *harira* (lamb) and lentil broth, flavoured with saffron and la kama.

Before eating, all diners ritually wash their hands in water that is passed round the table in a jug. For special occasions, the meal might start with pigeon pie, continue with a chicken dish and feature couscous as its centrepiece. This is cooked in a special, two-tiered casserole called a *couscousière*. Meat and vegetables are simmered in the lower level, sending steam up into the upper compartment, which contains the couscous. Before serving, the couscous is mounded on a platter and a hollow is made in the centre. The cooked meat and vegetables are placed inside and harissa is served on the side. Couscous is eaten with the fingers, the grains being rolled into balls and occasionally anointed with the broth in which the meat and vegetables have been cooked. Dessert usually consists of pastries, fruit, or a sweet semolina confection washed down by mint tea.

Harira (Morocco)
Lamb and lentil broth

Merguez
Spicy sausages

Brik à l'Oeuf (Tunisia)
Seasoned tuna and egg wrapped in thin pastry sheets and lightly fried

Chakchouka (Tunisia)
North African ratatouille made with brown sugar, often topped with beaten egg

Couscous
Semolina with meat and a vegetable stew in broth

Djej M'Ahmar
Chicken stuffed with couscous

Salata Mcshwiya (Tunisia)
Salad made with tuna, egg and vegetables

Bstilla (Morocco)
Minced pigeon pie

Djej Tajine (Morocco)
Chicken stewed with prunes and honey

Arnhab Chermoula (Morocco)
Roast marinated rabbit

Zaytun Meshwi (Tunisia)
Olive-dotted beef balls

Dolma Gara (Algeria)
Stuffed courgettes

Tajine Malsouka
Meat, bean and egg stew flavoured with saffron and cinnamon encased in phyllo pastry

Limon Makboos
Pickled lemons

Mahancha (Morocco)
Thin almond-stuffed pastries

Righaif (Morocco)
Honey and sesame pancakes

Ghoriba (Tunisia)
Light pastry balls

Chai Bi Naa'naa
Mint tea

AFRICA

Like the continent itself, African cooking can be described in only one word: "big." Bulging across the centre of the globe, this vast land contains a riotous array of nationalities, cultures and religions. Its climate, too, touches all ends of the meteorological spectrum: while the Kalahari Desert in the south might not see rain for years, Mount Cameroon, looming large in the west, has the world's second highest rainfall.

But for all Africa's diversity, its chefs are united by hardship: much of the soil is lacking in vital nutrients and many areas are subject to savage droughts. And where food is available, the equipment with which to cook is frequently primitive. Accordingly, the disparate strands of African cuisine are brought together by a thread of inventiveness. From the Sahara to the Cape, meals are characterized by tastiness, heartiness and a determination to nourish and sustain against often inhospitable conditions.

TRADITIONAL INGREDIENTS

Atokiko (ground mango stone)
Avocados
Bananas
Bitter-leaf
Black-eye peas
Camel butter
Cardamom*
Cassava
Chillies*
Cloves*
Coconut*
Coriander*
Cinnamon*
Curry powder*
Dates
Dried fish*
Egusi (melon seeds)
Fenugreek*
Garden-egg (aubergine)
Gari
Garlic*
Ginger*
Lemon*
Mangos
Maize
Millet
Nutmeg*
Ochroe (okra)
Palm oil
Pawpaw (papaya)
Peanuts*
Plantains
Rice
Sorghum
Sweet potatoes
Tomatoes*
Yams

(*see Index)

INFLUENCES

A thousand years before the birth of Christ, powerful African kingdoms were exchanging gold, slaves and ivory for the produce of India, China, Greece and the Middle East. But of all these trading partners, it was Arab merchants who left the strongest imprint. From the north, their camel trains plodded across the Sahara bearing salt, spices and herbs. From the east, their *dhows* came laden with mint, saffron, coriander, cloves and cinnamon. Nor was it just foodstuffs that arrived. The Arabs also brought the Islamic religion, and today the annual fast-feast cycle of Ramadan and Lebaran is observed by large numbers of African Muslims.

It was not until the 15th century that Portuguese explorers brought sub-Saharan Africa into direct contact with Europe. From this nation of seafarers came imports such as citrus fruits, chilli, corn, pineapple and tomato. Today, in their former colonies of Angola and Mozambique, the stamp of Iberian cuisine lingers in the crusty rolls eaten for breakfast, and in dishes such as kid cooked in Madeira wine.

The Portuguese were just the tip of a massive colonial iceberg that melted over Africa in succeeding centuries. And where each European nation deposited its settlers, it also deposited its cuisine. In West Africa, the French instilled an appreciation of snails. In Kenya, the British introduced the genteel delights of strawberries, raspberries and asparagus. And South Africa felt the sticky bite of the Dutch sweet tooth: coconut, sweet

potato and creamy cinnamon custard tarts abound, as do delights such as *koeksusters*, sweet plaits of dough that are deep-fried and then dipped in a sugary syrup coating.

With the Europeans came their indentured labourers, who added their own exotic tang to African menus. Throughout East and South Africa, pilau rice, curry and samosas remain as an edible legacy of Britain's Indian Empire. Dutch trading vessels left behind Malaysian slaves to long-lasting culinary effect. *Sosatie*, for example, is the name of a South African speciality made of cubed, spiked mutton served with spicy sauce, which derives directly from the Malay word *sesate*, meaning "meat on a skewer."

FLAVOURINGS

There is no smoke without fire in the African kitchen. And as stoves are lit throughout the continent, so cooks reach for their chillies. Of the many varieties to hand, the most common are the plump, bombastic Scotch Bonnet, and a fierce imp called pilli-pilli. A volcanically hot, but compulsive sauce, called *periperi*, is used almost universally as a condiment. Chilli combines again with ginger, black pepper, cardamom, ajowan and other spices in the mouth-tingling Ethiopian spice mixture, *berber* (see page 97).

Not all African flavourings are such palate-busters. Palm oil, for example, plays a prominent part in West African cooking, lending a pungent flavour and striking red-gold hue to every dish it touches. One such confection is *joloff* rice, originally from Sierra Leone, but now a festive dish enjoyed throughout West Africa, which combines chicken marinated in lemon with rice, in a sauce of palm oil, chillies and tomatoes. The palm oil turns the rice a deep orange, and the finished dish is garnished with onion rings and tomatoes.

Elsewhere, the most common cooking oil comes from peanuts, which also provide a rich and versatile source of protein. All over the continent they are roasted as snacks or used as a flavouring in the cooking pot. Versions of peanut stew – chicken simmered in a sauce thick with peanuts – can be found in almost every country. Little balls of pounded peanut paste are a popular and nutritious snack.

In the tropical regions, coconuts are a prominent ingredient, and their flesh can be grated into stews as a flavoursome thickener, or deep-fried in strips for succulent snacks. The milk, meanwhile, makes a rich stock for cooking rice, beans, sweet potatoes and other vegetables.

OTHER INGREDIENTS

Spices may give spirit, but it is starches that keep body and soul together. And nowhere is this truer than in Africa. Whether grain, pulse or root, these basic foodstuffs provide nourishment, bulk and a neutral complement to the fiery seasonings that are used throughout the continent.

These staples vary with Africa's climate. Where there is plenty of rainfall, as in West and Central Africa, rice reigns supreme. Elsewhere, corn and drought-resistant millet and sorghum come into their own. In South Africa, for example, corn is pounded into a standard filler described aptly as "stiff porridge" or baked into loaves of a hearty bread known as *mielie*. In Ethiopia, millet flour is turned into a sour flatbread, known as *ingera*, which is as vital to everyday eating as the *baguette* is in France. Any of these grains can be made into dumplings that are wrapped in banana leaves and steamed.

Roots such as cassava, yam and sweet potato appear on every menu. And though foreign in origin, they have been given a robust versatility to match the nature of African cooking. They can be boiled or

mashed, cut into chunks and splashed into stews, or sweetened with sugar, sprinkled with cinnamon and baked, or pounded with palm oil and made into a deep orange "bread." Plantains – small cooking bananas – are another versatile food that can be roasted, chipped, boiled, mashed, fried or fermented, for use in a wide range of sweet or savoury dishes.

Africa also has its own unique taste sensations. Where else, for example, might one make an omelette for twelve out of a single egg – ostrich offerings weigh in at approximately 1.5 kg (3 lb) apiece – or battle one's way through a giant Achatina landsnail? In what other continent might one spoon through a bowl of crocodile or snake stew? And on what other menu might a diner dither between fried locusts or white ants?

MEALS

A typical African meal consists of just one course, usually a thick stew – short on meat, long on oil, brimming with vegetables and bursting with spicy flavours – plus one of the substantial, starchy puddings or dumplings used as a tasty utensil to scoop up the juicy morsels. Desserts, meanwhile, come as nature provides them, in the form of fresh fruits such as pineapple, grenadilla, passion fruit or mango.

In Senegal, Christmas is marked by the lemony aroma of *yassa*, a dish in which chicken is marinated in garlic, cloves, chilli and lemon juice before being fried in palm oil and simmered in a lemon sauce. It is accompanied by rice on a large platter. Diners sit in a circle around the platter and eat with their hands.

And in those few places where the European influence still prevails, mealtimes carve the day into the orderly European trinity of breakfast, lunch and dinner. Even then, the tastes of Africa are evident. A typical South African breakfast might start with a fresh papaya before progressing to bacon and eggs; a lunchtime barbecue might include skewers of wild game, or spicy *boerewors* sausages, as well as regular hamburgers; and dinner might consist of *bobotie*, Africa's answer to England's cottage pie – curried minced meat and flaked almonds topped with savoury custard.

MENU GUIDE

Egusi (Nigeria)
Soup flavoured with melon seed, spinach, dried shrimp and palm oil

Tatale (Ghana)
Plantain cake

Nkui (Cameroon)
Okra and corn soup

Akkras (West Africa)
Black-eye pea fritters

Dovi (Zimbabwe)
Chicken and peanut stew

Doro Wat (Ethiopia)
Chicken and hard-boiled eggs in a chilli sauce

Matoke Ngege (Uganda)
Plantain and fish stew

Paleva (Sierra Leone)
Beef and melon seed stew

Joloff Rice (West Africa)
Spicy chicken and rice dish

Ndizi Na Nyama (Tanzania)
Meat stew with plantain and coconut

Yassa (Senegal)
Chicken simmered in a pungent lemon sauce

Bobotie (South Africa)
Curried minced meat and almond pie, covered with a savoury custard

Pondu (Zaire)
Cassava leaf with palm oil, aubergines and dried fish

Dioumbre (Ivory Coast)
Mutton stew flavoured with okra and palm oil

Sosaties
(Zimbabwe and South Africa)
Spicy mutton kebabs

Foofoo (West Africa)
A stiff pudding of mashed yam or plantain

Ugali (East Africa)
A stiff pudding of maize flour

Bassi Salté (Senegal)
Couscous-like dish made from millet

CARIBBEAN

Stamp and Go, Run Down, Dip and Fall Back – the dishes themselves tell the story of Caribbean cooking. Posted across the Gulf of Mexico like happy-go-lucky sentinels, the islands of the Caribbean offer an adamantly exuberant cuisine. On to Amerindian origins have been added European, African and Asian influences. The whole has then been stirred, seasoned and served up in a unique compote of creativity.

Caribbean chefs make the most of a rich natural bounty. The fertile soil sprouts a profusion of tropical produce, while creeks, lakes and rivers combine with the sea to provide a superabundance of fish and shellfish. Each nation has its own speciality – saltfish and ackee in Jamaica, *colombo* in Martinique, *jug-jug* in Barbados, to mention just some – but thanks to culinary island-hopping, every dish appears in different guises throughout the region. The result is a cuisine that, like the islands themselves, is hot, colourful, and decidedly eclectic.

TRADITIONAL INGREDIENTS

Ackee
Allspice*
Annatto*
Arrowroot
Bananas
Beans
Breadfruit
Calabash (gourd)
Calabaza (pumpkin)
Callaloo
Cassareep
Cassava
Chayote
Chillies*
Cinnamon*
Cloves*
Coconut*
Coriander*
Curry powder*
Ginger*
Limes*
Mangos
Molasses*
Mushrooms*
Nutmeg*
Okra
Pigeon peas
Plantains
Saffron*
Sweet potatoes
Tamarind*
Thyme*
Vanilla*

(*see Index)

126

INFLUENCES

In 1492, Christopher Columbus stumbled across a remarkably beautiful archipelago stretching between North and South America. He was two oceans and two continents away from his ultimate goal of India, nevertheless he dubbed his discovery the West Indies, and claimed for Spain as many islands as he could find.

The lands Columbus discovered were inhabited by two peoples, the Arawak and Carib Indians, who subsisted mainly off farming and fishing. The mainstay of their diet, however, was provided by nourishing roots such as cassava and sweet potatoes – a legacy that lingers to this day.

It was not long before the West Indies were swamped by Spanish settlers, who brought with them such staples as bananas, mangos and coconuts. But the most devastating import was sugar cane. It grew well, and before long, Britain, France and Holland were vying with Spain for a slice of the sweet Caribbean pie.

Islands were seized, fought over and exchanged according to the vagaries of European politics. Today, the cooking of each island reflects the outcome of those distant power struggles. French technique and Caribbean flavours merge in the cooking of Martinique and Guadeloupe. The presence of Holland is unmistakeable in Curaçao's *Keshy Yena coe Cabaron*, a scooped-out Edam cheese stuffed with prawns. And *jug-jug*, a traditional Christmas dish from Barbados, is comprised of minced beef, pork, pigeon peas and millet – no more than a homesick haggis from Scotland.

But above all, it is the flavours of Africa that dominate Caribbean cooking. Okra, yam, pigeon peas, plantain, *taro* (a tuber that is similar in appearance to yam), *dasheen*, a relative of taro that closely resembles swede in texture, and its leaves which are called *callaloo*; all are staples that owe their origins to Africa.

Through the centuries, this culinary melting pot was enriched by the arrival of other immigrants: Jews fleeing the Spanish Inquisition, Britons leaving the newly-independent United States, merchants from Lebanon and Syria, and, after the abolition of slavery, indentured labourers brought from India and China to work the land.

FLAVOURINGS

The chilli, in all its diverse manifestations, is the undisputed queen of the Caribbean kitchen. Every island – and possibly every household – has its particular version of hot pepper sauce, coloured red with tomatoes or golden with turmeric. It can be made with just onion and chilli or a number of additional spices and flavourings.

Other flavourings are gentler to the tongue. The native spice annatto (see page 60), for example, has long been prized for the delicate flavour and strong red colour it imparts to food.

Pepper sauce

Allspice, from the small round berries of a tree indigenous to Jamaica, is another valued ingredient, as is coconut milk. A flavouring peculiar to the Caribbean is *cassareep*. It is made from the juice of the cassava root that is boiled with sugar, cinnamon and cloves until thick.

Curry powders are common throughout the region, reaching an apogee of complexity in Trinidad. And marinating, known as "seasoning-up," is a much-used cooking method on English-speaking islands. A typical seasoning-up may include chopped chives, oregano, celery leaves, grated onion, crushed garlic, mashed chillies, ground cloves and lime juice. The resulting mixture is liberally rubbed over meats, poultry or fish before stewing or barbecuing.

OTHER INGREDIENTS

Being islanders, it is hardly surprising that West Indian chefs make extensive use of seafood. Every conceivable kind of marine creature graces the Caribbean table – parrot fish, flying fish, red snapper, land crab, scampi and conch. The list is endless – as are the different methods of cooking. Seafood is marinated in lime juice and then skewered on kebabs; slowly baked with herbs and garlic; simmered in a tamarind and coconut sauce; fried in a seasoning of crushed ginger, garlic and thyme; and stewed with pumpkin or curried with green mangos and potatoes.

The Caribbean abounds with tropical fruit and vegetables, almost all of which are put to excellent and imaginative use. Stuffed dishes are particularly popular – breadfruit with saltfish, green papaya with spicy meat and pumpkin with prawns. The cooking banana is a prime example of tropical versatility. The large green plantain, for instance, can be used unripe, ripe or over-ripe, in sweet or savoury dishes. It can be boiled, mashed, roasted, fried, chopped or simply served as it is. Banana leaves, meanwhile, impart a delicate flavour when wrapped around cornmeal and meat parcels, otherwise known as Conkies in Barbados and Tie-a-Leaf in Jamaica.

Starchy roots such as yam, cassava and sweet potato provide filling bulk in an equally versatile manner. They also cater for the sweet-toothed diner when transformed into delicious cakes, puddings or pies, and flavoured with rum, molasses, coconut, raisins, nutmeg and cinnamon.

MEALS

A popular start to the Caribbean day is cassava bread fried in butter, but heartier dishes are also common. The traditional Jamaican breakfast is saltfish and ackee – a fruit that appears aptly like scrambled egg. On the English-speaking islands, a brunch might consist of Pudding and Souse – blood sausage and the lime-marinated meat of pig's head, tongue and trotters.

A typical family meal consists of a big, one-pot dish packed with vegetables, pulses, meat or fish, cooked in a spicy sauce and served with slightly flattened cornmeal dumplings bobbing on top. This will be accompanied by *foo-foo* (pounded plantains) or hot buttered cornbread. Alternatively, a drier main course will be eaten with some starch such as boiled cassava or yam, foo-foo, rice and peas, cornmeal and okra, or *bakes* (fried biscuits) and a vegetable such as spiced aubergine, mushy pumpkin or stewed okra. Dessert is usually fruit based, making good use of local produce for puddings, custards and ice cream.

SOUTH AMERICA

Spain's *Conquistadores* never found El Dorado, the fabled city of gold, when they stormed into South America during the 16th century. But they did discover something just as valuable – an array of exotic foods that literally doubled the contents of the world's larders, and changed global eating patterns almost overnight.

The resulting cuisine is an amalgam of New World ingredients and Old World cooking that varies from country to country. Brazil, for example, boasts an exuberant mix of African, Portuguese, and Guarani Indian flavours. In the Andean states of Peru and Ecuador, indigenous ingredients such as chillies and potatoes prevail. The rolling grasslands of Argentina provide beef in abundance, and Chile's lengthy coastline is an unparalleled source of seafood.

TRADITIONAL INGREDIENTS

Almonds*
Annatto*
Bananas
Black-eyed peas
Black haricot beans
Brazil nuts*
Cashews*
Cassava
Chick peas
Chillies*
Cloves*
Cinnamon*
Coconut*
Coriander*
Corn
Cuy (guinea pigs)
Erizos (giant sea urchins)
Hearts of palm
Lima beans
Mangos*
Mustard*
Nutmeg*
Okra
Olives*
Oranges*
Papayas
Parsley*
Peanuts*
Plantains
Pineapple
Pine nuts
Pumpkin
Rice
Salt cod
Seafood
Sugar cane
Sweet potatoes
Tomatoes*
Walnuts*

(*see Index)

INFLUENCES

Rome's viaducts were still just a gleam in the architect's eye when the Incas were channelling hillside torrents into massive irrigation channels, up to two kilometres (1.2 miles) long, to link the disparate valleys of their empire. They were fine agriculturalists, and the fruits of their labour crammed the marketplaces of imposing stone cities perched atop Peru's mountains. But these were no common marketplaces. South American civilization had grown up in complete isolation and its cuisine was accordingly different from any to be found elsewhere in the world. The farmers of the Andean hillsides, for example, were pioneers in potato cultivation. Millennia before the rest of the world learnt the art of freeze-drying, they were pounding their potatoes into pulp that was alternately frozen by night and thawed by day until it formed a dehydrated, rock-hard lump that could be either stored for the future or ground into flour for immediate use.

The potato was just one of the culinary surprises that greeted the Portuguese and Spanish invaders when they colonized South America during the 16th century. Some of the others included sweet corn, chillies, tomatoes, beans and guinea pigs.

Foodwise, the newcomers gave almost as good as they got. The introduction of cattle brought beef, butter, cheese and milk into the kitchen. Wheat, rice and sugar cane were further welcome imports. The Iberians also passed on the secrets they had learnt during 800 years of Arab occupation. Egg and sugar rice cakes, puddings and Portuguese desserts became popular in Brazil, the vast, pot-bellied land that Portugal had claimed for its own.

Slave labour that was brought over from the African continent added another layer of foreign flavour: more chillies, along with okra, palm oil, ginger and melon seeds.

When the floodgates of European colonialism burst open during the late 19th and early 20th centuries, further settlers arrived, bringing with them their own culinary customs and preferences. The resulting blend is a cuisine that varies from region to region, but is uniquely South American in its rumbustious vigour.

FLAVOURINGS

Despite the many different peoples that have settled in South America over the years, it is the old, indigenous flavours that still dominate. The exceptions are rice, to which all of South America took with enthusiasm, and parsley and coriander leaves, which were adopted as the favourite herbs.

Peruvian cooking is notable for its lavish use of chillies, not only in food preparation but also in freshly made sauces that appear on the table at every meal. A Peruvian market, even today, is filled with piles of red, orange, yellow and green chillies that come in a multitude of varying shapes, sizes and degrees of hotness.

Another typically Peruvian ingredient is the native corn, available in many colours including purple. When simmered in water, this releases a beautiful colour and a flowery, lemon-like perfume, providing an ideal liquid base for desserts that are thickened with cornflour, or jellied.

In the northern countries, chefs infuse annatto seeds in their cooking oil to impart a light, delicate flavour and warm orange colour to meat and poultry dishes.

In Colombia, coconut milk figures prominently as a cooking liquid. Sauces are thickened with nuts, and it is common to find meat cooked with the many indigenous tropical fruits. Nuts, too, are commonplace in Brazil. These include not only "Brazils," named after the country itself, but also peanuts, a reminder that, until divided by the earth's shifting crust, South America and West Africa were once joined together.

Food from Brazil is also marked by the bright orange colour of palm oil – an African import – and by the imaginative use of cassava. A vital staple for the native Guarani Indians, cassava root is ground to a meal that is toasted and sprinkled over dishes in the manner of Parmesan cheese, and imparts a distinctive, nutty taste.

OTHER INGREDIENTS

Of the many other items in South American kitchens, perhaps the most common is the potato. By the time the Spaniards arrived in Peru, the Incas had already developed over a hundred different varieties of potato, white, yellow, black or purple in colour, and in numerous sizes and flavours. One of Peru's most notable potato creations is *causa a la chiclayana*. This hearty and attractive dish consists of potatoes served with a sauce of ground walnuts, cheese, chillies, onions and garlic, and garnished with sliced ears of corn, fried fish or prawns, hard-boiled eggs, cassava root and black olives.

But potatoes are not all South America has to offer. Along both seaboards – the Pacific especially – there is an abundance of magnificent shellfish: abalone, scallops, conch, lobsters and clams. In Chile, for example, a local dish to look out for is *erizos al matico* – giant sea urchins cooked with chopped onions, lemon juice and seasonings. This is usually served as a first course, but is robust enough to provide the bulk of a light luncheon.

Across the Andes, in Argentina, it is beef that rules the roost. *Matambre*, which literally means "kill hunger," is a dish that comprises thinly sliced and pounded steaks, rolled around a mixture of spinach, carrots and hard-boiled egg, and braised in a rich beef stock. In Uruguay, the same dish is served filled only with spinach. A bit further inland, minced beef figures in *so'o-yosopy*, a robust Paraguayan soup with sweet peppers and chillies.

MEALS

Breakfast in South America consists for the most part of fruit or fruit juice, bread rolls, and tea, coffee or chocolate. Lunch begins with nibbly appetizers, proceeds to soup, then a main course of fish, meat or poultry, with vegetables and either rice or potatoes, and usually ends with fruit and coffee. Dinner is much the same, but possibly with the addition of a separate fish course.

What exactly is eaten depends, of course, on where exactly the eater is. Each country has its own preferences. While salads are a common starter in any part of the continent, Ecuadoreans are more likely to enjoy a plate of cooked vegetables – the high altitude means that water will boil at a lower temperature than normal, making the cook's task that much easier.

The cuisine varies not only from country to country but also, within the Andes nations (Peru, Venezuela, Colombia, Ecuador and Chile), it alters between highlands and lowlands. In Colombia, for example, a popular lowland dish is *sábalo guisado con coco* (shad fillets in coconut milk), while highland specialities include *ajiaco de pollo bogotano* – a chicken stew that uses two different types of potato and fresh corn. In the mountains of Ecuador, a first course of potato cakes, *llapingachos*, is served with tomato, avocado slices and lettuce. On the coast, the same cakes appear fried in oil, seasoned with annatto, and arrayed alongside fried plantains and a peanut sauce.

From the German settlers came the art of making fine beers, and the French gave the continent both vines and wine-making skills. Coffee can be found everywhere, usually served very strong in a demi-tasse cup, with a little hot milk.

Empanadas Salteñas (Bolivia)
Small meat pies

Aguacates Rellenos
(Ecuador)
Avocados stuffed with chopped ham, hard-boiled eggs and mayonnaise

Ajiaco de Pollo Bogotano
(Colombia)
Chicken stew with two kinds of potato and fresh corn

Llapingachos (Ecuador)
Annatto-coloured potato cakes served with fried plantain and peanut sauce

Ají de Gallina (Peru)
Chicken in chilli sauce

Sopa Paraguaya (Paraguay)
Corn bread made with two kinds of cheese

Feijoada Completa (Brazil)
Meat with black beans served with orange salad, kale, toasted cassava, rice, and chilli and lime sauce

Pabellón Caraqueño
(Venezuela)
Thin beef steaks with rice, black beans and plantains

Carbonada Criolla
(Argentina)
Meat and vegetable stew with peaches and pears

Pudim de Bacalhau com Ovos (Brazil)
Baked eggs topped with salt cod in tomato sauce

Pichones con Salsa de Camarones (Peru)
Pigeons in shrimp sauce

Porotos Granados (Chile)
Beans with corn and pumpkin

Budín de Yuca (Guatemala)
Cassava-root soufflé

Torta de Zapallo (Ecuador)
Sweet pumpkin cake with cheddar-style cheese

Manjar Blanco (Chile)
Milk pudding

129

MEXICO

The cuisine of Mexico was born at the point of a musket, blending the dishes of the native peoples with those of their Spanish conquerors, and its fiery flavours linger like smoke from the encounter. From the ancient Aztec and Mayan civilizations come the basic foodstuffs such as sweet corn, chillies and tomatoes. Onto these has been grafted the Spanish love of sweets, marinades and sauces. It is a hearty, peasant kitchen relying on the region's profusion of fresh vegetables, and dominated by the *tortilla*, a round pancake of unleavened maize flour that is as much a plate as a food. But the flavours are not without subtlety or variety. There are, for example, some 50 species of bean and over 140 different types of chilli pepper, each of which has its own distinctive taste and appearance.

TRADITIONAL INGREDIENTS

Acitrón (candied cactus)
Allspice*
Annatto*
Avocados
Banana leaves*
Beans
Cactus paddles (nopales)
Chayote (squash)
Chillies*
Chocolate*
Cinnamon*
Coconut*
Corn husks*
Epazote (herb)
Guavas
Hominy (corn)
Jerusalem artichokes
Jicama (root vegetable)
Lemon*
Lime*
Masa harina
Mushrooms*
Oregano*
Onions*
Papayas
Pine nuts
Plantains
Prickly pear cactus
Pumpkin
Pumpkin seeds
Sweet corn
Sunflower seeds
Squash blossoms
Tamarind*
Tomatoes*
Tomatillos
Tortillas
Vanilla*

(*see Index)

INFLUENCES

Like their South American neighbours, the Mexicans had climbed a long way up the culinary ladder before the Spaniards came. It was here, around 7000 B.C., that sweet corn was first cultivated, as was the avocado. And shortly after, local tables were graced by the indigenous turkey, Muscovy ducks, venison, quails, pigeons and a host of fish and shellfish. It was here, too, that chocolate was born.

These foods, along with potatoes, chillies, squash, tomatoes and beans, formed the staple diet of the area when the Spanish over-ran the Aztec and Mayan civilizations in the early 16th century.

These *Conquistadores* brought with them all the produce of Europe and, thanks to their trade links, exotic food-stuffs such as rice from India. One popular import was citrus fruit, which allowed coastal dwellers to develop *seviche*, which is the technique of marinating fish in citrus juice until it is "cooked" by the acidity (see page 174). Equally liked was pork, not least because it introduced lard to what had previously been a virtually fat-free diet. Foods that might once have been simply steamed in banana leaves or corn husks could now be fried or roasted.

It was not until the 19th century that Mexico finally regained its independence, but by that time, the cuisine had solidified into a decidedly colonial whole.

Mexico's proximity to North America brought it bad news and good. Their neighbours seized large tracts of land, but at the same time took to their new subjects' food with uninhibited relish. And while America gave Mexican cooking no new ingredients, it gave it an unmistakable enthusiasm. It was *norte americanos* who gave the name of *burritos*, "little donkeys," to the dish of wheat tortillas stuffed with almost every conceivable filling. It was they, too, who came up with the idea of turning tortillas into deep-fried *taco* shells, ready to be filled with whatever ingredients came to hand. And, curiously, chewing gum originated not in America but from Mexico's *chicle*, made from the sticky sap of the *zapote* (sapodilla) tree.

FLAVOURINGS

Chillies, onions and pumpkin seeds are among the flavourings most commonly used in Mexican cooking. Close on their heels comes the tart green *tomatillo* (husk tomato) which is used nowhere else in the world. Mexican dishes themselves are not necessarily spicy, and often the chillies are made into an on-the-table sauce that can be heaped on as liked. Nor is there a monotony of chilli flavour, thanks to the many varieties of capsicum on offer. One popular type is the *poblano*, a hot, dark green pepper that forms the main ingredient in *chiles rellenos* – poblano chillies stuffed with either cheese or spiced meat and deep-fried in a golden batter.

Salsa cruda and *salsa verde*, two of the most popular sauce-like relishes, combine chillies and tomatoes to telling effect. Salsa cruda is simply tomato, chilli and onions. Salsa verde follows the same recipe but substitutes green tomatillos for the tomatoes. Another popular relish is *guacamole*, made of pounded avocados flavoured according to taste with tomatoes, chillies, onions, garlic and coriander leaves. This is served as an accompaniment to many dishes, to be spooned onto food or simply scooped up with a piping hot tortilla.

Coriander – always the leaves and only rarely the seeds – is immensely popular, figuring in numerous dishes, as does the indigenous *epazote*, a pungent smelling herb essential to the cooking of black haricot beans. Annatto is used a great deal in the southern region of Yucatán, and the juice of lemons and limes is squeezed into many dishes as a finishing touch.

Chocolate is perhaps the area's most famous contribution to global cuisine, and it features distinctively in Mexico's national dish, *mole poblano* – turkey steeped in a rich sauce thickened with nuts and seeds and flavoured with tomatoes, chillies and bitter chocolate.

OTHER INGREDIENTS

As this region was the birthplace of maize, it is little wonder that its cooks make extensive use of this corn. Whole kernels (hominy) are cooked into hearty soups called *pozole*. Kernels are ground into a coarse flour (*masa harina*) for the making of *tamales*, meat or vegetable filled packets that are steamed in corn husks or banana leaves. And in the tortilla, finely ground corn becomes not so much an ingredient as an integral part of everyday life.

However, it is fresh fruit and vegetables that distinguish this cuisine. Thanks to the region's diverse topography, almost any edible plant can be grown somewhere, at some time of the year. The selection is enormous, ranging from avocados to mangos to prickly-pear cactus paddles.

Poultry and beef abound. These are usually stewed or grilled, as in *carne asada a la Tampigueña*, the ubiquitous restaurant dish found throughout the country. This combines thinly sliced steaks served with an assortment of accompaniments: beans, tortillas, salsa, guacamole, cheese and fresh onion slices. Pork, however, is the most succulent of the meats used and it finds its

way into many traditional preparations such as spicy *chorizo* sausages, minced stuffings for peppers and stews.

Seafood is also an important item in the kitchens of Mexico. And little wonder, considering that the Mexican coastline is over 9,000 km (6,000 miles) long. It is said that the Aztec emperor Montezuma had fresh fish delivered to him daily by relays of messengers travelling barefoot from the Gulf to his capital of Tenochtitlán. Today, the seas provide coastal markets with an abundance of produce – such as red snapper, grouper and shellfish – while rivers and lakes supply tasty freshwater fish including catfish, trout and bass. Giant prawns, shark and ray are amongst the many exotic species to be tasted, usually grilled with pepper and garlic.

MEALS

The Mexican day starts with *desayuno*, first breakfast, and consists of coffee or, more rarely, chocolate, and the sweet breads and pastries inherited from Spain. A second breakfast, *almuerzo*, comes at around midday and usually comprises a more substantial dish such as *huevos rancheros*, (country-style eggs) with *frijoles refritos* (mashed, fried beans) and a fresh chilli sauce.

The high point of the day is *comida*, a sturdy afternoon meal served anytime between 2:00 and 5:30 p.m. The first course is usually a light soup such as consommé, followed by *sopa seca*, a "dry soup", which is actually a rice or pasta dish. Then comes a main course of fish, poultry or meat with a salad or vegetables. After this comes a separate course of beans – usually pinto – served in a small bowl in their own thick cooking liquid. The whole might be accompanied by tortillas or fresh *bolillos*, the Mexican equivalent of *petit pain*. To round off the meal there is fruit, either fresh or stewed, or perhaps *flan*, caramel custard.

The Mexican day ends on a relatively subdued note. *Merienda*, a light supper, is served later in the evening, and consists of bread, jam, blind (unfilled) tamales, and possibly some sliced, boiled ham.

On special occasions, such as birthdays and weddings, eating might extend into the night, with *ceña*, a late dinner held most commonly in a restaurant.

MENU GUIDE

Sopa de Lima
Lime soup

Guacamole
Mashed avocado with chopped onion, chillies, fresh coriander and chopped tomatoes

Pozole Verde
Hominy soup with chicken, pork and ground pumpkin seeds

Esquites
Sweet corn kernels with onions, mushrooms and peppers

Calabacitas
Courgettes cooked with onion, garlic, tomatoes and chillies

Hongos Guisudos
Mushrooms with garlic, chopped epazote, chillies and lime juice

Ensalada de Jícama
Jicama salad with oranges in a lime, coriander and chilli dressing

Quesadillas Fritas
Corn tortilla turnovers filled with cheese

Frijoles Charros
Beans simmered with bacon and roasted chillies

Mole Poblano de Guajolote
Turkey in sauce of tomatoes flavoured with chillies, pepper, cinnamon and bitter chocolate

Pescado Adobado en Hojas de Maîz
Chilli-marinated fish cooked in corn husks

Pescado a la Veracruzana
Fish with tomatoes, capers, olives and chillies

Tamales de Dulce
Sweet tamales filled with candied fruit

Flan
Vanilla custard with a caramel sauce

NORTH AMERICA

North America is an enormous expanse blessed with a wealth of natural resources; the vast wheat fields of its prairies have been called the bread basket of the world. The United States boasts the world's largest cattle industry and its lakes, rivers and thousands of miles of coastline offer an unrivalled bounty of fish and shellfish. The North American climate encourages a diverse range of foodstuffs that encompass the lush citrus groves and mangos grown in Florida, the carefully cultivated salad greens from California, the corn and wheat of the midwestern states and Canada, and the salmon, oysters and berries from the colder Pacific Northwest.

This diversity of ingredients is fully matched by a variety of cooking styles that has been carried, over the generations, to the New World. Since North America's "discovery," nearly every nation in the world has seen some of its members emigrate to it, adding another layer of culture and tradition to the expanding weave of the continent's fabric. All the recipes they brought with them were adapted to the indigenous ingredients, producing a unique cuisine. And like its culture, this is a cuisine that is constantly changing and adapting, ever open to new influences and ingredients.

AMERICAN REGIONAL STYLES

New England and The Northeast When the first British settlers arrived here, they found a native population skilled in exploiting the wealth of indigenous food-producing animals and plants. Squirrel, deer and bear filled the woods; wild turkey, pigeon and quail abounded; a profusion of fish and shellfish stocked the lakes and ocean, and squash, corn and berries were there for the harvesting and picking.

These early settlers used ground cornmeal in place of wheat flour for breads and puddings, and maple syrup that came from the heavily wooded areas of New Hampshire and Vermont, as a flavouring. Maple syrup is still used as a topping for breakfast pancakes and waffles, and to glaze baked ham. It was these hardy New Englanders that were responsible, too, for another traditional favourite – Boston baked beans.

The first British settlers also brought with them a fashion for pies. These could be both savoury – filled with meat, fish or poultry – or sweet, stuffed with the berries and fruit that grew in such abundance. As every housewife was able to produce a version of apple pie, this dish became, and remains, one of the great icons of American culture.

In the 1750's, many German immigrants arrived in the farmlands of Pennsylvania. Now known as the Pennsylvania Dutch, a corruption of *Deutsch*, they brought a liking for sausages and hams, and a knowledge of pickling and preserving techniques. These cured goods and condiments are still part of their traditional cuisine, as well as being appreciated throughout the country.

Also of German origin are the many yeast-dough coffee cakes, or festive specialities, such as stollen and lebkuchen, which remain firm favourites.

Many Scandinavians settled in the area now known as the Midwest and brought the tradition of smorgasbord, as well as meals that feature a variety of dairy products.

The South The colonies of Virginia were blessed with a gentle climate and the inhabitants were able to enjoy a lavish lifestyle famed for its generous hospitality. An enduring speciality of the area is Smithfield ham. With a distinctive flavour of hickory smoke, this is still cured in the small town of that name, to the same recipe the colonists used.

The Spaniards introduced livestock, such as pigs, to many parts of the South and it was not long before pork featured prominently in the local cuisine. Bacon, ham and pork sausages still feature in the traditional Southern breakfast, served with grits (corn that has been dried and ground, and then cooked into a porridge-like dish) and hash brown or home-fried potatoes. Ham hocks and collard greens is a standard, as is ham with red-eye gravy.

French, Spanish and African culinary traditions came together in the more southerly states of Mississippi and Louisiana, and

TRADITIONAL INGREDIENTS

Apples
Avocados
Beef
Black-eyed peas
Blueberries
Catfish
Chillies*
Chocolate chips*
Clams
Cinnamon*
Crab
Cranberries
Crayfish
Cumin*
Dill*
Filé powder*
Ginger*
Ketchup*
Lima beans
Maple syrup*
Molasses*
Monterey Jack cheese
Okra
Oysters
Peanuts
Pecans*
Pumpkin
Rock Cornish Hens
Salsa*
Sarsaparilla*
Sourdough bread
Soured cream*
Squash
Sweet corn
Sweet potatoes
Turkey
Wax beans
Wild rice

*see Index

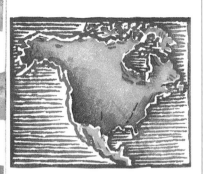

produced Creole cooking. The centre is New Orleans, and the cooking has something of the sophistication of that city, being often imaginative and highly flavoured. Popular Creole dishes include *calas*, a breakfast favourite of deep-fried sweet and spicy rice balls; and *bisques*, which are rich, thick seafood soups.

Cajun, too, has its origins in the cuisine of France. It was brought to the bayous of Louisiana by the Acadians, French settlers who were expelled from Nova Scotia in the middle of the 18th century. It has since mixed with the Spanish, African and Native American cuisines of the South and is often very spicy. *Jambalaya* (a dish of rice, pork, sausage, ham, shrimp and crayfish, seasoned with chilli or cayenne pepper), and *gumbo* (a highly seasoned soup or stew thickened with okra and a variety of meats, seafood and vegetables) are two well-known traditional Cajun dishes.

The East Coast By the 19th century, immigration had increased to a new level and New York City became the main port of entry for most émigrés arriving in America. Jewish families from Eastern Europe joined the Irish, Italians, Hungarians and Germans that were flocking to a new life.

A great many of these new Americans settled in New York City itself, and today the cuisine of every nationality of the world can be found in this city. Its multitude of delicatessens serve many dishes with an Eastern European flavour, and there is also a bustling Chinatown and some of the finest Italian food to be found on that side of the Atlantic.

The Southwest In the early days, many settlers pushed West, attracted by the promise of owning their own land, and the vast uninhabited plains were soon taken over by farmers and cattle and sheep ranchers.

Texas and the neighbouring desert states of Arizona and New Mexico have produced a style of cooking known as Tex-Mex, which is characterized by chilli-spiced flavours and an unmistakable south-of-the-border influence. This region is home to the popular dish of *chili con carne*, which has since travelled all over America to be adapted to local tastes, being served either alone or with rice or on hot dogs. Other dishes that are enthusiastically eaten from coast to coast include *tacos*, crisp cornmeal *tortillas* (pancakes) filled with seasoned minced meat and salads, and *burritos* (wheat flour tortillas rolled around a bean, meat, poultry or vegetable filling with cheese and a fiery

sauce). Many Tex-Mex dishes are flavoured liberally with fresh coriander, known locally as *cilantro*. *Salsa*, a spicy uncooked tomato relish, is another local speciality adopted from neighbouring Mexico, as is the avocado dip, *guacamole*.

The West Coast In sunny California, weather has had the biggest influence on cooking styles. Almost constant sunshine and lavish irrigation produce a wealth of fresh fruit and vegetables. Artichokes, avocados, citrus fruit, dates and melon thrive in the south of the state, and vineyards in the north provide grapes for local wine producers. San Francisco has a thriving Chinese community descended from the immigrant labour brought in to build the railways, and Peking duck is as much at home here as in the East. Another Chinese legacy is *chow-chow*, a vegetable relish coloured with turmeric.

In the Pacific Northwest, salmon, clams, crabs and oysters are abundant and among the finest in the country. Oregon is apple and pear growing country, while Washington State produces peaches, and the area is justly famous for its fruit pies. Washington's coast was settled predominantly by the English, and steak and kidney pie and Christmas pudding are still local favourites.

Blueberry muffins

MENU GUIDE

BLT
Bacon, lettuce and tomato sandwich

Chowder
Hearty soup with seafood, chicken or vegetables

Oysters Rockefeller
Baked oysters with a spinach, bacon and cheese topping

Hash Browns
Fried grated potato cakes

Muffins
Individual cake-like sweet breads made without yeast

Buffalo-Style Chicken Wings
Grilled chicken wings coated with a spicy chilli sauce

Eggs Benedict
English muffins topped with poached eggs, Canadian bacon and hollandaise

Reuben Sandwich
Grilled corned beef and Swiss cheese sandwich with sauerkraut, on rye bread

Caesar Salad
Cos lettuce with a piquant dressing and Parmesan cheese

Cioppino
Mixed seafood stew

Hangtown Fry
Fried eggs, oysters and bacon

Surf n' Turf
Lobster tail with filet mignon

Baked Alaska
Meringue-topped sponge cake and ice cream

Fruit Cobbler
Deep-dish fruit pie with a thick, scone-like topping

Shoofly Pie
Spiced molasses and brown sugar pie

Devil's Food Cake
A two-layer chocolate cake with a chocolate fudge filling and icing

CORNUCOPIA OF CORN

Sweet corn has been a regular feature of American meals since before the Pilgrims arrived. Native Americans used this indigenous crop as a staple, and many of their recipes are recognizable in modern-day dishes.

Cornmeal Available white or yellow, this is much like polenta; it was favoured by colonial cooks over the more expensive wheat flour.

Cornbread A savoury bread made with cornmeal, often used for turkey stuffing. When baked in cast-iron moulds shaped like corn cobs, it becomes corn pones.

Corn Chowder Milk-based soup with salt pork, potatoes and fresh sweet corn.

Corn Fritters Pan-fried patties of sweet corn in a light milk and egg batter.

Hush Puppies Deep-fried cornmeal dumplings, most popular in the South.

Indian Pudding Cornmeal dessert with milk and molasses; colonists called this "hasty pudding," a name which is still used in some areas.

Grits Ground dried sweet corn; it is popular in the South, with butter and sugar, as a breakfast item.

Spoon Bread Baked custard-like cornmeal.

Succotash A native American dish combining sweet corn kernels and lima beans.

Tortillas Flat, thin unleavened bread made from cornmeal; essential in Tex-Mex cooking.

Traditional cast-iron corn pone pan
Corn pones are small cornbread rolls baked in a pan like this, which moulds them into a corn-cob-like shape.

OTHER INGREDIENTS

The influence of the longhorn breed of cattle on American eating habits cannot be overestimated. This hardy animal, able to withstand cattle drives over great distances, produced beef that no longer had to be corned or preserved in salt. In addition, the opening of the railways brought fresh beef to a vast new market and soon steak houses were opening in all cities. Until the late 1980's, when health concerns about animal fats came to the fore, beef dominated the American diet, and roast beef, pot roast, steak and hamburger were standard fare in both homes and restaurants.

To go with the beef, tomato ketchup and mustard became the two essential condiments found in all American homes. The preferred mustard is somewhat milder than its European counterpart and is always smooth rather than whole-grain.

Sourdough bread was a speciality of the early pioneers, especially the gold prospectors who set out from San Francisco for Alaska and, having no yeast, were forced to find a substitute. For the dough, a mixture of flour, water and sugar is left to stand until it begins to ferment and smell sour; this is then used as the starter to make the bread rise.

What was born out of necessity, is now considered a local delicacy, and in Alaska scores of different breads are made with sourdough as the starter.

Another traditional bread that has become all-American is the Jewish bagel. This is a round bun, with a hole in the middle, which may have a poppy seed, onion or garlic topping. It is often eaten with smoked salmon and soft cheese for Sunday breakfast, or used for sandwiches.

Crayfish, or crawfish, are small lobster-like freshwater crustaceans, which were part of the diet of the Native Americans and remain an American speciality, especially in Louisiana. In this state, they are cooked in pies, gumbos and stews, or simply boiled and eaten with the fingers.

One of the native fruits noted by Captain James Cook in the late 18th century was the blueberry. Blueberries are now cultivated in most cool northerly regions, especially New England, and are popular eaten raw with cream, cooked in waffles and pancakes, or baked in muffins and pies.

The heritage of American food has been strongly influenced by the German immigrants. The ubiquitous ground beef patty served in a bun takes its name from the city of Hamburg, and hot dogs derive from Frankfurt sausages. The fruit and vegetable preserves that originated with the Pennsylvania Dutch travelled West with the early pioneers, as did their fruit butters and chicken pot pies. Many Pennsylvania Dutch recipes remain an integral part of the American cuisine, including *scrapple*, a porridge and pork dish served for breakfast. It is said that they can also be credited with putting the hole in the middle of the ever-popular doughnut.

Another dish that has been successfully co-opted by Americans of all regions and ethnic backgrounds is the pizza. This flat pie made from a yeast dough and topped with various cheeses, vegetables, meats and seasonings is now one of the most popular of all American meals.

Bakers' brick ovens were used in the pizza parlours that the Italian immigrants opened in New York City in the early part of the 20th century, and they are still essential to making a true pizza. Today, most major cities have gourmet pizza restaurants where the traditional mozzarella and tomato toppings have been replaced with more innovative items such as goat cheese, sun-dried tomatoes or smoked chicken.

Americans are also well-known for their outstanding range of desserts. Cheesecake – hot, cold, baked, no-bake, flavoured, fruit or cream-topped – is found throughout the country. The most traditional is made in a deep tin and has a crust of crushed graham crackers, a popular sweet biscuit.

Ice cream, the ubiquitous and crowd-pleasing treat, is eaten out of a bowl, in cones, between wafers, on waffles, pancakes and cakes, in sodas and coffee, in and on pies, and baked under meringue. New flavours are constantly being developed and its pride of place as America's favourite dessert is still unchallenged.

MEALS

Big meals and snacking throughout the day are two ways to sum up American eating habits. The only consistent feature about American meals is that portions are generous in both homes and restaurants, and there is a strong tradition of hospitality.

Breakfast can be anything from freshly squeezed orange juice, cereal and toast, to pancakes or waffles served with sausages, maple syrup and butter. Coffee is universally drunk at breakfast, and throughout the day, in preference to tea. Lunch is usually the lightest meal of the day, with salads and sandwiches being the most popular meal choice in delicatessens or sandwich bars, or as items taken from home to the school or the place of work.

American dinners tend to be early in the evening, anywhere between 6 and 7 p.m., and will usually consist of a main course and a simple dessert. Meat loaf, mashed potatoes and boiled carrots, followed by ice cream, might be a classic example. Small leavened and shortened rolls, called biscuits, might be served with the meat course, to be buttered or eaten with the gravy. These do not resemble British biscuits, but are more like unsweetened scones. Milk, juice, soft drinks or coffee are the most common beverages in homes. Wine is generally reserved for restaurant outings, though with a reputable wine industry of its own, more and more Americans are drinking wine with their meals at home.

Brunch is an American invention that combines breakfast with lunch. Today it is a popular choice on many hotel and restaurant menus at weekends. Reading the Sunday papers over brunch has become a ritual for many Americans and the menu might include sliced meats, bagels and lox (smoked salmon), pancakes, and Eggs Benedict, along with coffee, orange juice or even cocktails.

Americans enjoy eating out of doors when they entertain, and picnics, clambakes, barbecues and tailgate parties (food served from the back of a large estate car) are indulged in, when weather permits.

Americans also eat out a great deal and so-called fast-food chains populate every high street. A wide variety of food is on offer including burgers, pizza, chicken pieces, Mexican specialities, and spare ribs, almost all served with French fried potatoes, milk shakes or soft drinks. Some chains specialize in pancakes, doughnuts, ice cream, or frozen yogurt with dozens of toppings.

Another American innovation is the "drive-thru" fast-food restaurant. Without ever leaving the car, diners can order from one point, then drive round and pick up their meal at another.

Thanksgiving, the fourth Thursday in November, is the most important family feast of the American calendar and its traditional menu celebrates the first harvest festival of the earliest European settlers. The occasion is memorialized in a meal consisting of roast turkey with cornbread or oyster stuffing, giblet gravy, cranberry sauce, candied sweet potatoes, and pumpkin or pecan pie.

CANADA

The cooking of Canada, like that of its neighbour the United States, reflects the mixed heritage of its many settlers. It most resembles the cuisine of the northern American states as they share many of the same foods, and there was often a flow of population between the two countries. The oldest and most traditional dishes are those of the first French settlers of Quebec, who came primarily from Normandy and Brittany. Among the traditional pies are the pork *tourtière* served on Christmas Eve; *cipâte* or *cipaille*, layers of pastry interleaved with a filling of game, poultry, pork and vegetables; *cipâte aux bleuets*, a three-crust blueberry pie. *Pâté chinois* is simply an unusual name for a universal favourite: shepherd's pie. Seafood is a staple part of the diet in the coastal regions, and the chowders, stews and hashes are simple and sustaining. The crabs and scallops found around Prince Edward Island in the east and Vancouver Island in the west are noted for their quality. From the Northwest comes the Arctic char, a fish of the salmon family with an exquisitely delicate flavour. The eastern province of New Brunswick is famous for its delicately flavoured fiddlehead ferns. Among the foods native to the country is wild rice, also called Indian rice or Canadian rice. This is not a true rice, but the grain of a tall aquatic grass, which is now cultivated extensively. It is usually boiled and served with butter, but sliced almonds, fresh herbs, or sautéed mushrooms or onions may be added. The Saskatoon berry is another native, something like the blueberry, but with its own unique flavour, and the tiny pinchberry makes a wonderfully tart jelly to serve with the abundance of game.

INDIA

From time immemorial, India has been renowned as the source of exotic spices. Its cuisine is famed for its variety and infinitely subtle blends of aromatic spices and seasonings, which flavour meat, pulses and vegetables. The word "curry" does not do justice to the sheer range of Indian dishes, which reflects the diversity of geography, culture and religion that this vast country has to offer. What does not vary is the care and sophistication with which food is prepared and cooked, and the value that is attached to its excellence and flavour. From the rich meat-based dishes of the North to the simple pulse-based diet of the South, food is a way of life, with many religious and social rituals surrounding it, and throughout the whole country it is a source of great enjoyment and celebration.

TRADITIONAL INGREDIENTS

Almonds*
Amchoor (mango powder)
Asafoetida*
Basmati rice
Buttermilk*
Cardamom*
Chick pea flour
Chillies*
Cinnamon*
Coconut*
Coriander*
Cumin*
Curry leaves
Dried fish
Fennel seed*
Fenugreek*
Garam masala*
Ghee*
Ginger*
Lentils
Limes*
Mangos
Mung beans
Mustard seeds*
Nigella*
Onions*
Panch phoran*
Pistachios*
Saffron*
Sesame seeds*
Split peas
Tamarind*
Tomatoes*
Turmeric*
Yogurt*

(*see Index)

REGIONAL STYLES

Northern India It is the food of northern India that has become familiar to millions, for this is the common cuisine of Indian restaurants all over the world. It is a cuisine that was profoundly influenced by the Moguls, Muslim conquerors of India and its rulers. The Mogul Empire was founded in 1526 by Baber, and lasted until 1857. Starting from Delhi, their seat of power, their cooking style radiated outwards to be adopted and adapted through much of the region. Their food had its roots in the Middle East, a legacy that can be traced back through dishes such as the Persian *pullaos*, saffron-perfumed combinations of rice and meat; and kebabs, grilled skewered meat, perhaps minced with ground spices, or with lentils (*shami*). Another famous Mogul dish is *biryani*, the great festive casserole of tender meat and rice imbued with the fragrance of saffron and other spices. Another is *murgh masala*, a stuffed chicken marinated in spices and yogurt then roasted. Among sweets is *zafrani chawal*, sweetened rice with saffron and nuts, and *gajar halwa* (carrot halva). One of the great Mogul centres was Lucknow, the royal city, which was renowned for the luxuriance of its courtly life. Vast banquets were often held, the chefs striving each time to excede past triumphs and astound the guests with their inventiveness.

Food in the Muslim-influenced north of India is meat based, although for the large population of Hindus the cow is sacred, making beef a meat that is never touched.

Goat is the most commonly used meat in all regions, though lamb and chicken are also consumed, and there is a whole variety of ways to prepare them.

Unique to the state of Punjab is the famous *tandoori* style of cooking. The most well-known dish is tandoori chicken: the meat is marinated in seasonings and yogurt and then cooked at very high temperature in the traditional clay oven, called a tandoor. This results in a succulent combination of moist, fragrant meat on the inside with a flavoursome spicy coating on the outside. Other delicious northern dishes include *kormas*, meats cooked in rich creamy sauces with yogurt and fruit, or nuts and saffron, and *koftas*, which are spicy meatballs, served alone or with a sauce.

While oil is more commonly used in southern India, *ghee* (clarified butter) is the preferred cooking fat in the cooler northern climes. Spices are put to milder use here, *garam masala* (see page 79) is a typical blend of spices designed to warm the body, unlike the fierce blends more commonly used in the south. The great wheat-growing plains of the Punjab produce the flour from which *roti* (bread) – the essential component of every meal in Northern India – is made. The most common, everyday bread is *chapati*, a flat, unleavened circular bread that is cooked on a griddle and then transferred to live charcoal and charred. Its purpose is twofold: it is a starchy accompaniment and an edible utensil for scooping up the rich and delectable sauces. Other kinds of roti include *naan* – a luxurious leavened dough that is slapped on the inside of the tandoor and baked – and *paratha*, a crispy, fried bread that is rolled out and folded into fine layers, often stuffed with vegetables or *kheema*, minced meat.

Southern India From Bengal in the west, Gujarat in the east and Tamil Nadu on the most southern tip of the peninsula, the southern half of India incorporates a vast culinary repertoire. At the heart of this predominantly vegetarian cuisine is the use of grains and pulses, as always combined with skilfully blended spices. However, there are deservedly celebrated exceptions.

Goa, once colonized by the Portuguese, has a cuisine that is strongly influenced by the Europeans, with many meat-based dishes that blend East and West to exotic effect. Although there are many dishes that use meat, a style of cuisine more typical of the north, the taste is unmistakeably southern, with widespread use of flavourings such as coconut milk, tamarind, chillies, cinnamon, curry leaves and peanuts.

Chillies, ginger, garlic and coconut are the characteristic flavourings of much of the region, and their uses vary according to custom and geography. The style of cooking alters subtly further south. Oil, not ghee, is a staple ingredient and steaming is a common cooking method, producing such snacks as *dhoklas* (steamed lentil cakes, found in Gujarat) and *idlis* (fermented steamed rice cakes, popular in Kerala.)

Rice, such as the fragrant basmati variety that grows on the foothills of the Himalayas in the north, accompanies every dish. It is a vital component of each meal, used to absorb the spicy, liquid vegetable and pulse curries that are commonly eaten. Another ubiquitous dish is *dhal*, a blend of pulses and spices that offers a valuable source of protein in this predominantly vegetarian region. While dhal is the word for split peas, the term is applied to all pulse dishes of this type. Among the most common are those made from Egyptian lentils (*masoor*), black-eyed peas (*Ihobia*) and mung beans (*moongs*). Lentils are also an important ingredient, with such dishes as *sambar* (lentils with vegetables) and *rasam* (lentils with garlic) that are prepared daily, being seasoned with different spices to give them variety. *Dhansak* is a dish that combines meat with lentils and is served with brown rice; *dosas* are lentil and rice pancakes. Another characteristic of the south is the use of small amounts of roasted or fried split peas to impart a nutty flavour to dishes.

Very spicy food helps the body to perspire and thus lose heat, making it popular in this warm region. The fiery *vindaloo* – a Goan dish in which spices soaked in wine and vinegar are added to meat is perhaps the most well-known example.

The magnificent exotic fruits that flourish in this hot climate add a rich dimension to the diet; red bananas are eaten as a nutritious snack, and mangos may be pulped into juice and mixed with milk and nuts to provide a delicious and refreshing drink. Another use for the abundant supply of bananas involves banana leaves, which can be used as plates.

In the most southerly states, freshly roasted and ground coffee is the popular drink, while further north the natively grown teas, such as Assam, are preferred.

Different areas do use different ingredients. Buttermilk, for example, is a vital part of Gujarati cooking, as are ginger, chillies and coconut. In Maharashtra, a primarily agricultural area with a long coastline, fish is a common ingredient, its flavour enhanced by the coconuts from the palm groves that cover much of the state.

From here comes "Bombay Duck," which is not of the quacking variety at all. It is actually the name given to dried fish, which is a popular seasoning. It comes from a fish that is native to the waters around Bombay, whose local name is *bommaloe macchli*. After being caught, these fish are filleted and hung on frames to dry. In its dried form, bombay duck can be added to curries, or pickled, or served as a snack with aperitifs.

In the fertile coastal strip that comprises the state of Kerala, coconut-scented fish dishes are prevalent, and the availability of coconuts, also grown here in great quantity, has given rise to the use of coconut oil in the local cuisine.

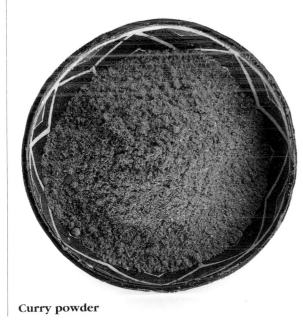

Curry powder

Bhajia
Vegetables or fish deep-fried in a batter of rice and chick pea flour

Samosas
Triangular crispy pastries with a spicy meat or vegetable filling

Pakoras
Vegetable fritters

Poppadums
Crispy, fried wafers made from split peas

Poriyal
Cauliflower with chillies and mustard seeds

Koftas
Spicy meatballs

Mattar Paneer
Peas with fried cheese

Dosas
Rice pancakes with a spicy potato filling

Rhogan Josh
Lamb braised in a yogurt sauce with chillies and saffron

Murgh Tikka Masala
Chicken pieces marinated in yogurt and spices and baked in a clay oven

Tandoori Murgh
Chicken coated with spices and cooked in a clay oven

Tarka Dhal
Spiced green lentils

Lassi
Yogurt drink, either sweet or savoury

Kacchi Biryani
Rice pilaf with meat and spices

Naan
Leavened bread baked in a clay oven

Kulfi
Ice cream flavoured with cardamon and nuts

CHUTNEYS

Few Indian meals are served without the traditional fruit or vegetable chutneys. Unlike Western chutneys, they are not cooked, but are more like relish salads and are notable for their fresh flavours. They can be mild or very hot.

Sesame chutney *Often served at breakfast, this combines sesame seeds with coriander leaves, mint, chillies and tamarind.*

Tomato chutney *A sweet-and-sour chutney made from tomatoes flavoured with ginger, chillies and often the spice mixture panch phoran (see page 90).*

Coconut chutney *Eaten in the south, this combines chick peas, flavoured with freshly grated coconut, and ground spices.*

Raita *This is a mild yogurt mixture, usually made with cucumber, which is meant to offset the heat of curries.*

Ginger relish *A commonly eaten spicy mixture of ginger, garlic, green chillies and coconut which is said to aid digestion.*

Mango chutney *A sweet fruit chutney to enhance the flavour of meat dishes.*

Coriander chutney *This is a very popular chutney, made daily in many homes, blending fresh coriander with oil, mustard seeds and asafoetida, eaten in small quantities with meals or served as a dip.*

Lime pickle *A delicious, tangy, strong pickle in which the limes are marinated in spices and oil for several days until soft.*

Onion relish *A simple side dish of raw onions, finely sliced and tossed with lemon juice and paprika.*

FLAVOURINGS

Most dishes are seasoned by blending a combination of whole or freshly ground spices. The combinations are infinite, with each cook having a personal preference, though the basic principle is to make the masala so that no one flavour dominates the mixture.

There is a whole philosophy attached to the use of spices, which has been handed down through the generations and, which subconsciously at least, every Indian cook applies. This goes beyond simply the flavour they impart, important though this is. Spices are considered to have medicinal properties: garlic, for instance, is good for the circulation of the blood; turmeric is an antiseptic and is often sprinkled on fish before frying. Asafoetida is a pungent resin, derived from the rhizomes of a species of fennel, which helps the digestion; it is often combined with difficult-to-digest pulses. Ginger is another digestive that is often paired with lentils and other pulses.

Garam masala means "warm blend of spices" and these are usually highly aromatic, made with spices that are believed to warm the body. For this reason, they are traditional in the more temperate regions of the north.

Masalas can be wet or dry. The latter type, more typical of the north, usually includes bay leaf, cardamom, cinnamon, ginger, mace and nutmeg; all of which are considered warm spices. They are blended with ghee or sprinkled over a dish just before serving to add fresh aroma and flavour. The wet masalas of the south may contain freshly ground chillies, ginger or onions, particularly in the hotter blends, which help the body to lose heat.

Another classic combination of spices is *panch phoran*, a Bengali blend of whole spices – cumin, fennel, nigella, fenugreek and *radhuni* seeds (or black mustard) – customarily used to flavour lentil and vegetarian preparations. *Tarka* is a combination of hot oil and spices, such as chillies and cumin seeds, which is often used to add interest to simple dhal dishes.

Cumin, available in white or black varieties, is one of the most commonly used spices throughout India. Other popular spices and seasonings include coriander

Tamarind

seeds, which are ground and used in meat and vegetable dishes; mango powder, made from dried mango fruit, which is used to impart a sour tang; tamarind, made from the pulp of pods soaked in hot water, also sour in flavour; and curry leaves, from the curry tree, which flourish in many home gardens in the south.

Saffron and turmeric are favoured throughout the country. Turmeric has a pungent flavour and imparts a characteristic yellow colour to foods. Much more precious is saffron, the golden spice made from dried stamens of a type of crocus found in Kashmir, most often used to imbue rice dishes with a subtle fragrance and colour.

Fresh flavourings are used too. Hot green chillies give a special spicy tang to many dishes and fragrant fresh coriander leaves are used both as a flavouring and a garnish. In southern Indian cuisine, fresh grated coconut and coconut milk are added to many dishes, lending a sweet delicate flavour to fish and vegetable stews, and salads.

Apart from spices, other ingredients also influence the flavour, varying in their use from region to region. There are many kinds of oils that add another dimension of flavour to the ingredients they are cooked with. In southern India, groundnut oil is widely used, giving a nutty flavour. In the coastal areas, where coconuts grow in abundance, coconut oil is used along with coconut milk to give the distinctive flavour of the south. In Bengal, a state criss-crossed by waterways, fish is widely available and much consumed. Mustard oil is used here, imparting characteristic flavour to the regional cuisine. In Kashmir, it is sesame oil that gives a distinctive flavour to the local cuisine. Ghee, which is butter clarified to the point where it contains no milk solids, is used instead of the oil found in many northern dishes, and has a special nutty flavour of its own.

Thick, creamy buffalo-milk yogurt (*dahi*) is made daily in most kitchens. It is the basis of the classic yogurt, mint and cucumber salad, *raita*, which is served alongside main dishes. The yogurt adds richness to sauces and tones down the fire of spices, resulting in a creamy sauce such as the kind found in the meat or fish kormas. Dahi is also used for making *lassi*, a refreshing, cooling drink which can be either sweet or savoury. Sometimes the seasonings are simply salt and black pepper (*lassi namkeen*); but rose water, sugar and fruit can also be used.

Chenna is a kind of soft cheese made in the home for use in sweet and savoury dishes. For example in the sweets *rasgulla* and *sandesh*, or the savoury *mattar paneer* (cheese with peas). Chenna is made by adding vinegar and water to milk and bringing it to the boil before straining the milk through cheesecloth.

The cheese forms the basis of many other sweets, for which Bengal is a particularly famous centre. Other ingredients commonly used in sweets are pistachio nuts, almonds, raisins and coconut. Rice is combined with milk – in *zafrant chawal*, and in rice pudding made with rice and milk, like that familiar to many British children – and yogurt, which can be combined with saffron and sugar to make a creamy dessert. Flavourings, apart from sugar, of course, are cardamom pods and rose water, which give a delicate fragrance to the sweetmeats.

Rather than being made in the home, sweets are generally bought from market stalls. Sweets have always been bought in the bazaars, and they hold a special importance in all occasions of celebration or religious festival. *Halwas* of every kind, based on milk and then sweetened and flavoured with coconut, almond or pistachio, are sold in numerous shops by the professional sweet-makers, the *Halwais*.

MEALS

Traditionally, food in India is not eaten with a knife and fork: custom dictates that the right hand be used to pick up food, with the help of the rice or bread that is always served with it. Northern Indians use their fingertips, but the less formal manners that prevail in the south permit the use of the whole hand. It is utterly taboo to use the left hand for eating, as it is considered unclean.

An ordinary meal consists of a rice dish, (or bread in the north), a lentil dish, a vegetable, a meat and a chutney. There are no courses, and even the dessert, if there is one, is served at the same time as the other dishes. Food is served in small dishes that are placed on a *thali*, a round metal tray given to each guest. Women serve the guests and the men of the household, and all sit on small mats on the floor.

In the south, the customary replacement for the thali is a banana leaf. The leaves are also used at formal events, such as wedding banquets, when a slice of lime will be salted and placed on a tender, young banana leaf and served as a condiment.

Religious customs also dictate etiquette in the dining room. A purifying ritual that dates from 1500 B.C., the Vedic period of Hinduism in southern India, is traditionally carried out on the rice that accompanies each meal. This involves a ceremony of combining rice with ghee. Rice is considered the most important ingredient in the meal and will be served with each course. In an Orthodox Hindu household, the guests will not be allowed in the kitchen as this is considered unclean. Orthodox families will not eat out in public for the same reason. Other religious restrictions include separate dining quarters for men and women, and the prohibition of alcoholic drinks.

SWEETS

Made by special sweet-makers, the Halwais, Indian sweets are eaten as an afternoon or evening snack, often accompanied by a savoury titbit. They are also essential at all religious and festive occasions.

Burfi *A sugary, fudge-like sweetmeat with a crumbly texture, sometimes called Indian fudge. Plain burfi is light brown; bright green pistachio-flavoured burfi is called pista, and almond-flavoured burfi, called badam, is a deep brown.*

Halwa *A distant relative of Middle Eastern halva, this can be made with nuts or vegetables. Habshi halwa is made with pistachios, cashews and almonds; gajar halwa, made from carrots, is orange.*

Jalebi *Crisp, orange squiggles of batter that are deep fried and then immersed in a syrup flavoured with saffron.*

Laddu *These are bright yellow balls made from ground almonds, pistachios and chick pea flour.*

Sindhi halwa *This is cut into squares or diamonds from a large two-coloured slab; the green layer is flavoured with pistachios and the yellow layer with almonds.*

Assortment of sweets

JAPAN

Clear, light, simple and neat – such is the meaning of the word *sappari,* which defines the cooking of Japan, renowned for its attention to preparation and presentation. Appearance is as carefully considered as flavour, for it is believed that food is eaten with the eyes as well as the mouth. Harmony and balance are all-important, so alongside the emphasis on presentation goes a disdain of excess.

While a Japanese meal is meant to be beautiful, it should also include a measure of modesty. Central to this idea is the effort to respect true, unadorned flavours. Thus, a Japanese cook will always endeavour to bring out the natural qualities of an ingredient, in the belief that separate flavours should be shown in relief rather than blended to a whole. Today, these culinary traditions coexist with an invasion of Western food. Steak bars and hamburger joints are popular for outings, though most meals prepared at home remain essentially Japanese.

TRADITIONAL INGREDIENTS

Aubergines
Bamboo shoots
Brown rice
Buckwheat noodles
Burdock
Chestnuts*
Chinese cabbage
Chrysanthemum leaves
Cloud ear mushrooms*
Dashi
Dried bonito flakes*
Dry mustard*
Fish paste
Garlic*
Gingko nuts
Ginger*
Lotus root
Matsutake mushrooms
Mirin
Mooli*
Miso*
Persimmons
Plums
Red beans
Rice wine vinegar*
Sake
Sansho*
Seafood
Seaweed*
Sesame seeds*
Seven-spice seasoning*
Shiitake mushrooms*
Soy sauce*
Sweet potatoes
Taro
Tofu
Watercress
Wasabi*
Wheat noodles

(*see Index)

INFLUENCES

Invasions and colonialism are two primary factors that shape the way a nation eats, and Japan has had little of either. During the 6th century, however, Japan did absorb many ideas from neighbouring China. The system of imperial rule and the religion of Buddhism were two of China's most important contributions, along with tea, which is arguably the national beverage.

All of Japan's ports were closed to foreigners between 1600 and 1868, consequently, Europeans had little opportunity for culinary exchange. The exception is tempura, the well-known dish of batter-coated, deep-fried foods, which was introduced by the Portuguese in the 16th century.

The tenets that shaped Japanese cuisine were laid down by Zen Buddhist monks. Every meal is designed to include a total of five dishes, each prepared in one of five ways: raw, simmered, steamed, grilled and fried. Each meal should include five flavours: bitter, salty, sweet, spicy and sour. Red, green, yellow, black and white are the requisite five colours.

A reverence for nature is inherent in both Zen Buddhism and the native Japanese religion, Shinto, and seasonality is therefore of utmost importance in the cuisine. Springtime delicacies include cherry-blossom rice in April and fragrant green *shincha*, or new tea, which appears in May. The moon is assigned to the month of September, when shimmering white dishes, such as abalone steamed over cucumbers or simmered bamboo shoots may be served. The mandarin oranges of winter, symbol of the sun, are the traditional offering of the New Year.

The natural resources of this volcanic land are limited, and this has shaped the Japanese diet around crops such as rice and soy beans, and the abundance of seaweed and fish from the surrounding oceans.

FLAVOURINGS

Of all the Asian cuisines, Japan's is the most spice-free. Peppercorns are used today, though they are not traditional, leaving *wasabi* (see page 166), *sansho* (see page 95) and dried chilli peppers to do most of the seasoning. Even so, these are added quite sparingly. Sansho berries have a similar taste to black peppercorns, and wasabi is best known as the fiery green paste that accompanies sushi. *Kinome* leaves come from the same tree that bears sansho berries. They have a pleasing minty fragrance and are used mainly as a garnish.

There is one uniquely Japanese flavour and this belongs to *dashi*, an all-purpose stock that is made from *konbu*, or kelp, and dried bonito flakes. It is mandatory for all soups and simmered dishes, and it manages to find its way into many other dishes via marinades, dipping sauces and dressings. *Dashi no moto* is the instant version, and it serves much the same purpose in Japan as stock cubes do in the West.

Along with tea, the Chinese left their legacy of soy sauce to the Japanese. Known as *shoyu*, Japanese soy sauce is less salty and somewhat sweeter than the Chinese version as it contains more wheat. True *tamari* is a rich, high-quality, wheat-free Japanese soy sauce, which is very rare even in Japan. In the West, many shops sell a dark-coloured liquid that is labelled tamari, regardless of its actual quality.

Sesame seeds, both white and black, are a staple, but as with most Japanese seasonings, they are used more as a condiment than as a flavouring that is cooked with the food. *Gomashio* is a mixture of salt and black sesame seeds, often placed on the table for sprinkling over rice and raw vegetables. Sesame oil lends its distinctive taste to the finest tempura oils.

For sweetness in marinades and dipping sauces, the Japanese prefer their sweetened rice wine, *mirin*, to sugar.

OTHER INGREDIENTS

With little land suitable for agriculture and livestock, the Japanese make good use of the products that they do have in abundance: soy beans, rice, seaweed and fish.

Miso (see page 188) is fermented soy paste, available in colours ranging from chocolate brown to red to creamy white. When combined with dashi, it is made into a soup, *misoshiru*, which can be consumed at any time of the day, and sometimes several times a day. *Tofu* is soy bean curd, which can be simmered, steamed, grilled or fried.

Sushi

Sushi is the meeting place for some important ingredients. Here, rice flavoured with Japanese vinegar that is sweetened with sugar is topped with raw fish, and sometimes rolled in thin sheets of *nori*, a kind of seaweed. Kelp and *wakame* (see page 220) are two other types of seaweed that figure prominently in Japanese cuisine, being used in salads and soups or as wrappers.

The Japanese are renowned for their *kobe* and *matsuzaka* beef. The cows are reared on a diet high in beer, and are massaged to ensure even distribution of the fat. This beef is not an item for everyday eating, and seafood is actually the mainstay of the diet. Dark-fleshed oily fish are highly prized, as is freshness. Tuna, mackerel and salmon are popular, as are squid and octopus. Blowfish are considered a delicacy, though the liver is poisonous and consumption can be fatal. A restaurant must employ a licensed chef in order to serve it.

The Japanese are also devoted noodle-eaters. Wheat noodles, *udon*, are the preferred type in the south, while buckwheat noodles, *soba*, are eaten from Tokyo to all points north.

MEALS

Rice sprinkled with nori flakes and miso soup is common breakfast fare; the miso is mixed using chopsticks and the broth is then sipped from the bowl. Lunch is a light meal, often just a bowl of noodles, or a *bento* box. This is a multi-compartment lunch box filled with a variety of cold dishes that is either bought on the way to work or delivered to the workplace.

The main meal of the day is in the evening. Traditionally, this meal consists of a simmered dish, a salad and one fried, grilled or steamed dish served with rice and a soup. All the courses are served simultaneously on a low table and they are eaten in no particular order.

More formal meals usually begin with an appetizer course accompanied by small ceramic cups of *sake*, wine made from fermented rice. The main meal will include many dishes that combine colours, flavours, textures and cooking methods. A bowl of rice, some pickles and green tea will be served to conclude the meal.

MENU GUIDE

Nimono
Fish or vegetables simmered in soy sauce broth, served as an accompaniment

Umeboshi
Tangy, salty pickle of under-ripe apricots or plums

Dengaku
Skewered food coated with sweet miso paste

Kamaboko
Fish paste cakes

Misoshiru
Miso soup with tofu

Natto
Fermented soy beans, often served with raw quail eggs and soy sauce

Sushi
Vinegared rice with vegetables and raw fish sometimes wrapped in nori seaweed

Sashimi
Finely sliced raw fish

Oden
Stew with fish cakes, potatoes, carrots and seaweed

Tempura
Seafood and vegetables dipped in a feather-light batter and deep-fried

Teppanyaki
Slivers of beef and fish cooked at the table on a hotplate

Tonkatsu
Breadcrumbed and deep-fried loin of pork served with sweet soy sauce

Kushi Yakitori
Skewers of chicken, vegetables or seafood basted with soy sauce

Sukiyaki
One-pot dish of thinly sliced beef and vegetables cooked at the table

O-cha
Green tea served at the end of the meal

KOREA

Bounded by the Sea of Japan on one side and the Yellow Sea on the other, the mountainous peninsula of Korea has been historically overshadowed by China and Japan. Centuries of invasion – both cultural and military – have ensured that its kitchens are rich with their influence. Chinese principles, for example, form the basis of Korean cooking, but a modern chef is also likely to be an expert at preparing Japanese specialities such as teriyaki and sushi.

Korea possesses an ancient cuisine with its own distinctive food. The national pickle dish, *kimchi*, is held in such reverence that Seoul boasts a museum devoted entirely to its 160 different varieties. From Seoul, too, comes a strong tradition of elaborate and highly decorative dishes developed over the years in the royal kitchens. But no amount of pomp can disguise the robust flavours and natural ingredients used in the dishes that typify a home-cooked Korean meal.

TRADITIONAL INGREDIENTS

Abalone
Adzuki beans
Agar agar*
Aubergines
Barley
Bean curd
Bean sprouts
Chestnuts*
Chillies*
Chinese cabbage
Coriander leaves*
Garlic*
Ginger*
Gingko nuts
Ginseng
Mung beans
Mushrooms*
Noodles
Pickled fish
Rice
Rice vinegar*
Rice wine
Seaweed*
Sesame oil*
Sesame seeds*
Soy bean paste
Soy sauce*
Spring onions*
Sweet potatoes
Watercress

(*see Index)

INFLUENCES

Almost every nation in the Orient seems to have invaded Korea, at some point or another. As early as 100 B.C., Chinese colonies were sprouting up along the peninsula and, shortly after, the ancient Korean kingdom of Silla was calling itself – with some pride – "Little China." In the 13th century A.D., Genghis Khan's Mongol hordes swept over the land. And right up until World War II, Japan's warlords were a constant menace.

With each invasion, Korean cooking gained a new and valuable input. From China and Japan came the principle of five flavours (sweet, sour, hot, salty and bitter) as did the practice of emphasizing preparation time over cooking time. And it was from its southerly cousin, too, that Korea gained the *sot*, a version of the Chinese wok. Even the unruly Mongols left their mark on Korean cooking. The most eye-catching reminder of their presence remains the table-top grill, shaped like the crown of a steppe-horseman's hat, that is still used today.

Amidst all the commotion, however, Korea retained its sense of identity. When Buddhism spread from China during the 5th century A.D., the Koreans steadfastly refused to embrace its vegetarian principles. Instead, they clung – as they still do – to their traditional diet of grilled red meat. And the higher up the social ladder, the more jealously did they guard their culinary traditions. Even a century ago, the table-top dish of *shinsollo* – combining seafood, chicken, meat, eggs,

vegetables and nuts, all cooked apart then brought together for braising in a flavoursome broth – was one that could only be enjoyed by royalty.

It is geography, however, that has probably had the greatest influence on Korean cooking. The surrounding seas offer almost limitless supplies of seafood and edible seaweed, the flat plains of the south are perfect for rice cultivation, and the mountains that cover most of the peninsula provide a variety of vegetables, herbs and roots. In addition, the region's severe winters mean that, traditionally, food has had to be dried or pickled for storage, to be eaten during the harsh months.

FLAVOURINGS

Korean cooking makes generous use of a few simple flavourings, most notably garlic, ginger, spring onions, toasted sesame seeds and sesame oil. Other important flavourings are soy sauce, bean paste, rice vinegar and chillies – the latter being a hallmark of the southern chef. Fermented soy beans and red chillies are combined in the popular flavouring *kochujang*, which is a hot, thick, dark paste. This is made in spring and then stored in large stone jars so that it can be used throughout the year.

Further long-life flavouring is provided by *kimchi*. This is a spicy vegetable pickle that is served at every meal from breakfast to dinner. As well as being an ubiquitous condiment, kimchi also plays a prominent role in soups, stir-fries and stews. There are endless versions of kimchi, which can be made with Chinese leaf, radish, cucumber, Chinese turnip, onion, chilli, garlic and ginger. Kimchi is prepared in the autumn and almost every household has a large vat in which the ingredients are left to ferment, growing ever more potent by the week.

A widely appreciated item in Korea's daily fare is the native red ginseng, which is eaten as much for its flavour as for its reputed medicinal properties. Fresh ginseng root is eaten raw with honey or cooked in a vinegar sauce. Some restaurants specialize in *samgyae tang*, which is a steamed chicken stuffed with glutinous rice and ginseng. This dish is attributed with restorative properties.

A uniquely Korean flavour comes from the *gingko*. At 200 million years old, this is the world's most ancient genus of tree and its soft, yellow nuts are used to garnish a variety of festive dishes.

OTHER INGREDIENTS

As in most other parts of Asia, the basic Korean foodstuff is rice. It is usually of the sticky, medium-grain variety, and in per-capita terms, annual rice consumption in Korea is among the world's highest.

A symbol of longevity, noodles are also popular fare. Noodle stands are a familiar site on city streets and a bowl of noodles will often be the lunchtime meal. Wheat flour and buckwheat vermicelli can be found, as well as the near-transparent noodles made from sweet potato or mung beans.

Other staples include barley, which, when roasted, makes up Korea's national drink *poricha* – a barley tea that is drunk hot, lukewarm or cold – and mung beans, which have a number of uses, most notably as an ingredient in *pindaettok*, a unique dish comprising a thick pancake of ground mung beans topped with vegetables and meat, which is often called "Korean pizza."

From the many miles of coastline comes a plentiful supply of fish and seafood. The Koreans, however, are keen carnivores, regarding a meatless meal as slightly second-rate, thus seafood is often used to flavour meat dishes rather than as an ingredient in its own right. Pork and chicken are widely

used in dishes such as *yukhoe*, but beef is the favourite, essential in the Korean version of steak tartare, and *pulgogi*, marinated strips of meat cooked at the table.

MEALS

Korean meals are eaten at a low table in the Chinese manner, with the dishes served all at once and eaten with chopsticks and spoons. Breakfast and lunch – both served with the inevitable kimchi – are usually light, with the substantial meal being reserved for the evening.

The trademark of a Korean meal is variety. A simple family dinner might include some 20 bowls containing an array of tempting tidbits. At least one (if not many more) will contain kimchi. Soup is another essential, as are *namul*, salad accompaniments of raw or steamed vegetables. And while pride of place may be given to a centrepiece such as pulgogi, the true essence of Korean cuisine is that no particular taste should predominate. Every flavour is balanced by another to produce a harmonic combination, evidence of the Japanese influence.

Given the emphasis on the whole, it is unsurprising that Korean meals rarely include a separate dessert course, and when a sweet course is served, it usually takes the form of fresh fruit. More often than not, the evening's intake concludes with poricha – maybe enhanced with a little ginseng – or a glass of sweet-potato liqueur called *soju*.

The Koreans are avid feasters, particularly on the occasion of a person's first or sixty-first birthday. Sixty is traditionally considered the average life-span, so to have survived a year over is an achievement to be fêted with a grand banquet.

Table-top assembly and cooking are popular, as witnessed by one dish *kujolpan*, or Nine Heavenly Varieties, where nine different fillings are arranged in the separate compartments of a black lacquered tray. The fillings – which may include shredded vegetables, strips of meat and omelette – surround a central stack of pancakes. Each diner fills a thin pancake, choosing any or all of the fillings, then rolls it up and dips it in a sauce made of ground roasted sesame seeds, chopped spring onions, rice vinegar and soy sauce.

MENU GUIDE

Kongkuk
Soy bean sprout soup

Twoenjang-Tchigae
Soy bean paste soup

Kimchi
Korean pickled vegetables

Ttok
Rice cakes in chilli sauce

Kimbap
Vinegared rice with vegetables and eggs rolled up in sheets of nori seaweed

Miyokguk
Seaweed soup

Minarinamul
Steamed watercress salad with soy sauce and sesame oil dressing

Kajinamul
Steamed aubergine salad

Kulwigim
Deep-fried oysters

Pajon
Spring onion pancake

Pindaettok
A thick pancake made of mung beans and topped with marinated meat, spring onions and chillies

Tubu-Tchigae
Bean curd stew with garlic, ginger and vegetables

Chongol
Strips of beef, sliced vegetables and bean curd cooked at the table in a large pot of simmering broth

Pibimbap
One-dish meal of rice with beef, vegetable and a raw egg

Naengmyon
Buckwheat noodles in broth, served cold

Pulgogi
Grilled marinated beef strips

Kalbi-Tchim
Spare ribs braised in soy sauce with spices

CHINA

A Chinese kitchen is the place where gastronomy, medicine and religion meet. For many centuries, the people of China have seen food as promoting a physical and spiritual well-being that goes far beyond merely filling the stomach. Of primary importance is the quality of the ingredients – vegetables must be market-fresh, meat newly slaughtered. Harmony of flavours and textures is also important, both within a dish and within a meal.

This preoccupation stems from Taoism, an ancient Chinese religion, which teaches that the world consists of two complementary principles: Yin (negative) and Yang (positive). Taoism also advocates living off the land, which is one reason why a Chinese meal contains more vegetables than meat. A more practical reason is that only seven per cent of land in China is suitable for agriculture; barely enough to support humans, let alone animals. The Chinese farmer has always sought to get as many harvests as possible from the same soil in the same year, and to grow plants that serve more than one purpose: the soy bean, for example, produces oil, sauce, paste and bean curd. Meat, therefore, has always been a symbol of prosperity and security – the Chinese pictogram for a house represents a roof with a pig underneath it.

TRADITIONAL INGREDIENTS

Adzuki beans
Bamboo shoots
Bean curd (tofu)
Bean sauce (black and brown)
Bean sprouts
Beef
Chicken
Chillies*
Chinese cabbage
Cinnamon*
Coriander*
Duck
Fagara*
Five-spice powder*
Garlic*
Ginger*
Hoisin*
Lamb
Lobster
Lotus root
Lychees
Miso*
Noodles
Oyster sauce*
Pork
Prawns
Rice
Rice wine
Rock sugar*
Scallops
Sea bass
Seaweed*
Sesame seeds*
Soy sauce*
Spring onions*
Star anise*
Water chestnuts
Winter melon

(*see Index)

REGIONAL STYLES

China's vastness, and the diversity of its terrain and climate, have made for several different and distinctive regional styles of cooking.

Cantonese is the type of Chinese cuisine that is most familiar to Westerners, due to the large numbers of people who have left Southeast China over the past century and started up restaurants abroad.

Peking or Northern cuisine is found in the largest area of China, and incorporates many Mongolian dishes. Sichuan and Shanghai styles are generally spicier than those of other regions and are found in the eastern and western regions.

Cantonese This style of cooking has its historical origins in the south-eastern city of Canton (modern-day Guangzhou), but its most dramatic expression is to be found in prosperous Hong Kong (Zhu Jiang). A subtropical climate prevails throughout the area, with heavy rainfall from May to September. The Pearl River delta thus abounds in green vegetables and tropical fruit – particularly lychees, peaches, oranges and bananas. The coastal waters and the region's multitudinous rocky inlets are richly stocked with fish and many other kinds of seafood (crabs, scallops, clams, crayfish and lobsters). Rice is harvested up to three times a year, and is grown alongside other staples such as wheat, sweet potatoes and taro root. Nature's output is augmented with countless fish farms plus intensive pig and poultry units.

For natural ingredients, then, Cantonese chefs have a stock unsurpassed in any other part of China. This explains why of all the regional cuisines, Cantonese is the least obtrusive and – if not properly executed – the most bland. The chef's priority is to bring out the full flavour of each ingredient, rather than to mask or adorn it with others.

As in all Chinese cookery, herbs and spices are few in number and modest in application. Most prominent are coriander, ginger, garlic, chillies, cloves, tangerine peel, sesame seeds and star anise, a pervasive, liquorice-like spice. An alternative is five-spice powder (see page 86).

Chefs in this part of China make widespread use of dried ingredients, such as mushrooms (see page 161) and dried fish (see page 189) and of soy bean sauces and pastes. Particularly popular is black bean sauce, a thin, salty liquid made of fermented black soy beans that have been puréed and mixed with garlic and star anise.

The classic Cantonese method of cooking is stir-frying. This involves heating a small amount of oil in a wok, which is designed to focus the heat in the centre of the pan, allowing for a short cooking time. This method grew out of a shortage of fuel; a quick burst of cooking used up less wood or coal on the fire. Out of necessity, the Cantonese have developed an art.

With such a short cooking time, the secret of success lies in preparation. The ingredients must be chopped to uniform sizes, so that they cook evenly; for this, Chinese chefs use large, heavy cleavers. These cleavers have an unwieldy look, but in the hands of an expert, they can slice spring onions into tiny, silken threads.

Steaming is also a popular Cantonese method of cooking, particularly for fish. A typical southeast Chinese dish is steamed whole sea bass, which has been placed in a bamboo steaming basket above a pan of boiling water and then anointed with oil containing lightly cooked slithers of spring onion and ginger. Here the stronger-tasting flavourings blend surprisingly well with the delicate fish, as in another Cantonese speciality, steamed scallops in black bean sauce. Chefs pride themselves on being able to mix contrasting flavours and still retain the distinctive taste of each, without allowing any to dominate. Cantonese pickled vegetables, for example, are preserved in a mixture of salt, sugar and vinegar, while in the sauce for Cantonese sweet-and-sour pork, onions and green peppers go hand-in-hand with pineapple and cherries.

Finally, mention should be made of the delicious Cantonese roast duck. This is stuffed with spring onions and bean paste, then glazed with a honey and vinegar marinade and has a flavour deliciously suspended between sweet and sharp.

Pekingese Centred on the Chinese capital Peking (now Beijing), this robust and hearty style of cooking is to be found throughout the north of the country. In contrast with the lush southeastern deltas of Canton, this is rugged territory, incorporating large tracts of sandy wilderness and the rocky Mongolian steppe that borders Russia. A harsh climate operates throughout the year, careering from intense heat in summer to extreme cold in winter, while in spring, Beijing is peppered by violent dust storms that rise up from the surrounding desert.

Leafy vegetables do not grow here in huge quantities; cucumber, celery and white Tientsin cabbage are the most readily available. Rice, too, is not easy to cultivate in this climate. Instead, wheat, corn, millet, peanuts and soy beans are the staple crops. Where southerners would eat rice, therefore, northern Chinese will eat steamed breads, buns and noodles (made from wheat flour, egg and water). Noodles are a symbol of longevity; noodle cakes are given as birthday presents, and the recipient will try to eat as many as possible in order to ensure a long life. In the shorter term, inhabitants of Beijing and other northern provinces keep out the cold by stocking up on boiled and sautéed dumplings (*chiao-tzu*), filled with shrimp and pork.

A sizeable Muslim population exists in northern China, which means that pork is much less commonly eaten than in other parts of the country. Beef has never been a universally popular dish; the Chinese farmer has been traditionally reluctant to eat his ox, considering it of more lasting use to him as a general beast of burden than as dinner.

Lamb is therefore the dominant meat, the most spectacular manifestation of this being Mongolian lamb firepot. For this dish, the meat is cut into thin, almost transparent ribbons: a skilled chef will be able to get as many as 10 servings out of a 500 g (1 lb) joint. The diners then use chopsticks to transfer the lamb pieces into the hotpot, which is a heated, fondue-like container, made of copper and filled with boiling water. After only a few seconds the meat is done, and it is eaten with thinly sliced raw leeks or spring onions and coriander leaves, and accompanied by spicy red bean curd and sesame paste sauce. When the boiling water has turned to lamb broth, noodles and cabbage are added and the soup is eaten.

Cantonese wonton soup

DRIED INGREDIENTS

Dried ingredients play a crucial but often unseen part in Chinese cuisine. They are used to add flavour, texture and colour; often they impart an intenser taste than if they were used fresh.

Abalone

Sea Slug Pre-cooked and sliced, requiring several days soaking before use.

Agar-Agar Vegetable gelatine made from seaweed used in both sweet and savoury dishes.

Bird's Nest Swallows' nests lined with hardened, re-gurgitated seaweed. Highly prized and highly expensive.

Wind-Dried Sausages Made of pork or duck.

Dried Jellyfish

Dried Mushrooms Mainly to add texture, although the delicate cloud ear mushroom is eaten on its own when reconstituted.

Cloud ear mushrooms

Hair vegetable A type of dried seaweed.

Dried Oysters For saltiness.

Dried Red Dates For sweetness.

Dried Scallops

Dried Shrimps

Golden Needles Bitter, dried buds of the tiger lily.

Shark's Fin Sun-dried fins from more than one type of shark. Chinese gourmets say it adds a matchless quality of flavour to a soup.

Less rough-and-ready is northern China's most famous dish, Peking duck. For this, only hand-reared, specially fattened ducks are used. First, boiling water is poured over the bird followed by honey. Then the duck is hung in a windy place for 24 hours, to dry the skin to a parchment-like consistency, before being roasted on a wire rack placed in the middle of an oven. The crisp, shiny red-brown duck is then shredded off the bones with two forks and served with small, paper-thin Mandarin pancakes. The correct procedure is to smear the pancake with *hoisin* sauce (often known as plum or barbecue sauce), place one or two duck pieces on top, follow with a few shreds of spring onion and some cucumber matchsticks, and finally roll the pancake up and eat it with your hands.

Another typical Pekingese dish is fish in wine sauce. Large pieces of fish are deep-fried in vegetable oil for a minute and then removed before being plunged into a sauce of wine, stock, spring onions and ginger and brought back to the boil. Pickled Tientsin cabbage, similar in shape to a cos lettuce, is also typical of the region. For dessert, pancakes filled with a sweet red paste made from aduki beans are popular.

Sichuan The terrain of the Sichuan province (formerly Szechwan), and of neighbouring Hunan, is characterized by steep mountains and deep river gorges, once home to many a giant panda. Summers here are humid and rainy, and winters are far milder than in Beijing, which lies some 1600 kilometres (1000 miles) to the northeast. Agriculture continues all year round; rice, wheat, rapeseed, corn, bamboo shoots and citrus fruits are the most common crops. Chillies and Sichuan peppercorns, or *fagara* (see page 95), are also prominent in this cuisine, giving the food its characteristic hot taste.

Typical Sichuan-style flavourings are exemplified in the salty, yellow bean sauce, made of pickled yellow soy beans, and in chilli bean paste, which is a tingling hot mixture of garlic, dried chillies, fermented black beans and mixed spices.

In the West, Sichuanese cooking tends to be regarded as hot and spicy, but there is more to it than just heat. The best chefs aim to make each mouthful a mingling of many layers of flavour. They use chillies to stimulate the tastebuds, then apply salty, sweet and vinegary ingredients to provide a series of different tastes. Curing, pickling and marinating thus play a prominent part. In most Sichuan homes, a bitter-tasting pickle,

made from mustard greens in salt with chillies and garlic, is used throughout the year to add a characteristic flavour to simmered, braised and stir-fried dishes. One such dish is Sichuan cabbage with pork, which is made by first boiling pork, then deep-frying it and finally steaming it with pickled cabbage, ginger, chillies, spring onions, black beans and rock sugar.

The most picturesque name for a Sichuan dish is Ants Climbing a Tree. This tasty dish combines rather characterless "cellophane" noodles (made from ground mung beans) with minced pork that has been marinated in wine, flour and soy sauce and then stir-fried in a sizzling garlic sauce. The Sichuanese imagine the little minced pork pieces as ants clinging to a noodle tree. Their sense of humour is also at work in a series of "fish-fragrant" meat or vegetable dishes that are so called because the flavourings – a pervasive mixture of chilli paste, garlic, ginger and spring onion – are the same as those traditionally used in cooking fish.

One of the most complex Sichuanese dishes is smoked duck, which requires four different cooking processes. First, it is marinated in peppercorns, sage, ginger and sugar. Then it is boiled in stock. Next, it is smoked over a mixture of tea leaves, sugar, bay leaves and five-spice powder, and finally it is chopped and deep-fried.

Poultry features prominently in the cuisine of this landlocked area, and chicken provides a suitably blank canvas on which to paint the vivid taste pictures that are *Kung Pao* chicken (hot, sweet and sour, made with chillies, ginger and peanuts) and *Pang Pang* chicken: plain, poached breasts, shredded and served cold with cucumbers, but covered at the last minute with a dressing made mainly from sesame paste, soy sauce, vinegar and chilli oil.

Shanghai A fourth, but less clearly defined style of cuisine operates on China's eastern extremities, centring on Shanghai and the Yangtze (Chang Jiang) delta, midway between Beijing and Guangzhou. Rivers and ponds dot the area, which is rich in wheat, rice, fish and seafood. Shanghai crabs are famously tender, and the silver carp of nearby Hangzhou lake are considered to be the tastiest freshwater fish in China. The chefs of Shanghai are renowned for the red-braising method of cooking. This involves cooking meat, poultry and fish, slowly and gently, in a mixture of thick, dark soy sauce and rice wine, then raising the heat to thicken the sauce.

MEALS

The classic composition of a Chinese family meal is one soup dish, one rice dish and four meat, fish or vegetable dishes. The soup comes first, then all the dishes are put on the table at the same time.

Eating at home is very much a communal affair. The table is round, and the dishes are all placed in the centre so that everyone is within equal stretching distance. The basic eating equipment is one small bowl (with a saucer underneath for bones), plus a pair of wooden or plastic chopsticks. Although hard for novices to master, in skilled hands these slender implements live up to their name of *faai jee* – "nimble little boys."

It is proper to first make a bed of rice in the bowl, and then intermittently reach out with chopsticks to detach those parts of the main dishes that look most appealing. Good manners dictate that food from communal dishes should be placed at least momentarily on the rice before they are transferred to the mouth.

The correct way to eat rice in China is to bring the bowl up to the lower lip and carry little portions into the mouth with chopsticks. Spilling rice is thought to bring bad luck, and children who refuse to eat their last mouthful are told that for every grain they leave, a pockmark will grow on the face of the person they shall marry.

Every Chinese home is believed to have its own kitchen god, who in the last week of every year is called up to heaven to report on the behaviour of each member of the household. While the god is away, the family try to encourage a favourable report by smearing sticky sweetmeats onto his picture, which usually hangs above the stove. The kitchen god's return to earth marks the beginning of the Chinese New Year (early February); he is welcomed back with firecrackers and small, doughy cakes filled with black bean paste (*jien duy*).

At family meals, dessert usually consists of fruit, served with a mug of tea from a large pot that will have been simmering throughout the day. The tea is kept hot in the mug by a lid: from a very early age Chinese children learn how, with just one hand, to lift the mug to their lips, pull back the lid, let the tea into their mouth and then replace the lid. Tea is drunk without milk or sugar.

Particular favourites are jasmine tea, a green brew made fragrant with jasmine petals; oolong, a fruity, spicy tea grown in the Fujian province, and lapsang souchong, which has a strong smoky flavour (see page 268).

Many Chinese teas are thought to have intestinal-clearing, medicinal properties. The same applies to *congee*, a thin, glutinous rice soup that is traditionally eaten for breakfast, and into which is thrown whatever ingredients are to hand: perhaps soy beans, preserved eggs, pickles, dried fish, or water chestnuts.

At official banquets, the dishes are usually served one at a time, starting with tea, nuts and fruit, then moving on to small, cold delicacies (pickled cabbage, marinated mushrooms) then the hot dishes (a stir-fry, a soup, Peking duck) and finally a whole fish. Toasts are drunk in Chinese beer and strong *mao tai* wine, made from wheat and sorghum, a millet-like cereal.

Stricter rules apply at domestic dinner parties. Of great concern to everyone is the ticklish business of who sits where. There is one fixed rule, and it dictates that the host and hostess should always sit with their backs to the door, and the guest or guests of honour should sit directly opposite them. Thereafter, it is up to the other guests to sort out among themselves the relative order of social importance, which is done with much polite gesturing as the guests invite each other to proceed ahead into the dining room. The desired result is that the least important guests end up sitting next to the host and hostess.

DIM SUM

Dim sum means "touch the heart," and it is the phrase used to refer to the small snack dishes that the Chinese consume in great quantities in the middle of the day. Originally devised by teahouse owners in the Sung Dynasty (A.D. 960-1279), these little delicacies can often be difficult and time-consuming to make. Specialist dim sum chefs usually take over the whole restaurant kitchen, handing over to general chefs for the evening, when dim sum will not be on the menu.

Har Gow *Minced shrimp, covered with a thin, pasta-like transparent skin, made of wheat starch.*

Paper-wrapped Prawns *A deep-fried mixture of minced prawns, pork fat, ham and bamboo shoots, wrapped in rice paper.*

Siu Mai *A mixture of chopped pork, shrimps, mushrooms, spring onions, bamboo shoots, carrot and ginger, wrapped in little wheat starch skins that are shaped like party crackers without tails*

Char Siu *Cantonese red-roasted pork, marinated in soy sauce, rice wine, honey, sugar and garlic.*

Char Siu Bao *A heavy, doughy dumpling, the size of a tennis ball, stuffed with red-roasted pork.*

A selection of dim sum

VIETNAM

A land of swollen rivers and lush green paddy-fields, Vietnam has a climate which ranges from monsoon tropical to cool and temperate. The result is a mixture of rampant vegetation and ordered, crop-rich farmlands. Green is the dominant colour of Vietnamese cooking, in which the fragrance of indigenous herbs and vegetables neither gives way to the forcefulness of the Indian spices employed nor overpowers the more understated flavours that characterize its Chinese-style dishes. The outcome is a cuisine that gracefully blends the gentle and the vigorous.

TRADITIONAL INGREDIENTS

Aniseed*
Bamboo shoots
Basil*
Banana leaves*
Bean sprouts
Black bean sauce
Chillies*
Coconut*
Coriander*
Curry leaves
Duck
Dill*
Eel
Five-spice powder*
Frogs' legs
Galangal*
Garlic*
Lemon grass*
Limes*
Mint*
Mushrooms*
Mooli*
Noodles
Nuoc mam (fish sauce)*
Jellyfish
Palm sugar
Papayas
Peanuts
Prawns
Rice
Rice paper
Rice vinegar*
Sesame oil*
Sesame seeds*
Shallots*
Spring onions*
Star anise*
Tamarind*

(*see Index)

INFLUENCES

A thousand years of Chinese occupation, throughout the first millennium A.D., left a culinary mark on Vietnam that remains to this day. This is evident in its cooking methods (stir-frying and steaming), implements (bowl and chopsticks) and even its ingredients (soy sauce and noodles). On a deeper level, too, Vietnamese chefs have inherited the Chinese culinary principle of seeking to balance contrasting flavours and textures within a meal. This legacy is particularly noticeable in northern Vietnam, which is still inhabited by a large Chinese population. Here, food tends to be milder than elsewhere in the country.

The French have also had a long relationship with Vietnam, first as traders, then as colonists. It was they who introduced the crusty *baguette*, European vegetables such as asparagus and green beans, pâté and even frog's legs. The Gallic influence is at its most evident in the cities of southern Vietnam, where restaurants serve dishes such as French beans with crushed garlic and chilli, and frog's legs with chilli and lemon grass.

FLAVOURINGS

The generous use of herbs such as dill, lemon grass, coriander, mint and basil distinguishes Vietnamese cuisine from that of its Southeast Asian neighbours. Feathery dill is sprinkled over *canh chua ca*, a hot, sour fish soup comprised of white fish, fish sauce, chillies and lemon juice. It also features prominently in the powerful-tasting *cha ca*. To make this dish, the chef first marinates fish in a tangy mixture of citrus juice, tamarind, turmeric, shrimp paste and galangal. The fish is then charcoal grilled, reheated at table in fish sauce and finally coated with a thick layer of dill and spring onions before serving.

Lemon grass (*xa*) imparts its powerful lemony aroma and flavour to many salads, soups, and meat and fish dishes, such as *ga xao xa* (stir-fried chicken with lemon grass) and *thit bo xao xa ot* (grilled beef and lemon grass) . The Vietnamese also love to mix their herbs. Mint, coriander leaves and basil are piled onto cooked or marinated fish or meat that are then topped with finely-cut vegetables. These thick, aromatic clusters are placed on paper-thin rice pancakes or crisp lettuce leaves, rolled into neat little parcels and then dipped into a variety of salty, sweet and sour sauces.

The basis for many of these sauces is *nuoc mam,* or fish sauce. This is made by leaving layers of fish and salt in large, wooden barrels to ferment for several months beneath fierce sunshine. The result is a clear, pungent, fish-flavoured liquid, deep amber in colour. The addition of lime or lemon juice, wine vinegar, hot chillies, garlic and sugar features in another, still tangier, sauce called *nuoc cham.* As well as serving as a dip, nuoc cham is also used to provide an extra flavour dimension to soups, stir-fries, meat and vegetable dishes.

Peanuts are frequently called upon by the Vietnamese cook; roasted and crushed, they serve as a garnish, or else they are combined with nuoc mam, garlic, chilli, lime juice and coconut milk to make a deliciously smooth satay sauce called *dau phong rang.* Traditionally, this accompanies eel fried with lemon grass, but it is also employed alongside many meat and fish dishes. Sesame oil gives a nutty flavour to sauces, such as black bean sauce (black beans, garlic, fish sauce, sugar, vinegar, chilli, stock, sesame oil and seeds), while sesame seeds impart a nutty texture to finely sliced, charcoal-grilled beef. Spring onions, an ingredient of many Vietnamese dishes are used raw, or lightly cooked, to add last-minute bite to soups, spring rolls or stir-fries. Shallots are either stewed in casseroles, or deep fried into crisp flakes and used as a palate-stimulating garnish.

INGREDIENTS

Rice appears at the Vietnamese meal table in many different manifestations. In its simplest form, it is plainly boiled to provide bulk accompaniment to soups, stews and curries; alternatively, rice is made into fine noodles and then deep-fried or steamed. Ground rice is made into thin pancakes that are steamed and then stuffed with any number of different fillings. A favourite is *banh cuou*: pancakes filled with cooked pork and vegetables, topped with crispy fried shallots and dipped into a spicy, sweet sauce. Finally, rice flour is the basis for the transparently-thin wrappings for *cha gio* (spring rolls).

Widespread use is also made of glutinous rice, which is a starchier, stickier variety than its long-grained counterpart. It is particularly good in desserts; a Vietnamese speciality is glutinous rice soaked in coconut milk and then steamed inside banana leaves.

Pork is enjoyed throughout the country, and is frequently incorporated with the bounty of seafood. It is combined with crab for pancake and spring roll fillings, and with noodles and dried prawns for *mi quang*, a frequently-served soup.

Chicken is a popular ingredient, either roasted with five-spice powder (*ngu vi huong*) or stir-fried with fragrant stalks of lemon grass. Beef is the central ingredient of *pho*, which is a well-known Vietnamese meat and noodle soup. It is made with fine shreds of raw beef that are combined with mint, spring onions and coriander leaves and then sprinkled over a bed of noodles. Steaming hot aromatic meat stock, flavoured with ginger and star anise, is then poured over all the ingredients, partially cooking the raw

beef. Additional flavourings that are hot (red chilli), salty (fish sauce) and sour (lime juice) are added in various quantities and combinations to suit individual palates.

As for vegetables: lettuce, white radishes, potatoes, asparagus, broccoli, carrots, artichokes, cucumber, cauliflower, courgettes and aubergines are all used in varying degrees throughout the country. They are served raw or else stir-fried for the shortest time possible to preserve colour, flavour and texture. Vegetables are often cooked with a minimal amount of pork and seafood, bestowing a gentle hint of flavour.

Fruit abounds in Vietnam, particularly in the humid south, and it is almost always eaten plain. Oranges, coconuts, lychees, star fruit, mangos, bananas, custard apples, pomelos, guavas and water melons are the most popular, and are often combined to make sumptuous fruit salads.

MEALS

Traditionally, breakfast is a steaming bowl of pho, either home-made or bought from a favourite street vendor. Only a minority of Vietnamese prefer a Western-style breakfast of buttered bread with coffee or tea.

The Vietnamese lunch consists of rice, a clear soup and a selection of light meat, fish and vegetable dishes that are served with a full spectrum of dipping and flavouring sauces. The evening meal is usually similar to lunch but, being the largest meal of the day, consists of many more dishes.

On Sundays, the main meal is generally much more elaborate. Favourite dishes are scallops and crispy-fried, shredded seaweed, grilled pork balls with a sweet peanut sauce or the traditional do-it-yourself dish *ta pli lu*. This involves diners being provided with a large platter of raw ingredients – chicken, beef, prawns, squid and fresh vegetables – which are then cooked at table in a pot of simmering, aromatic stock. Delicately scented jasmine tea provides a gentle and refreshing end to the meal.

Meals are eaten at a shin-high wooden table called a divan; diners generally sit on the floor to eat. Fresh fruits, rather than sweet baked confections, are the usual way to finish a meal. If alcohol accompanies the meal it will almost invariably be rice wine.

MENU GUIDE

Pho
Rice noodles in broth with shredded beef or chicken

Canh Thit Nau Cua
Crab and pork soup

Cha Gio
Spring rolls

Bahn Tom
Prawn pâté served on toast

Canh Chua Ca
Sour-and-hot fish soup

Ga Xao Xa Ot
Chicken with lemon grass

Ca Hap
Steamed sea bass

Ca Loc Hap
Fish steamed in coconut milk and ginger

Goi Dua Lco
Pork, squid and peanut salad

Thit Ga Chien Gung
Chicken with ginger

Cha Ca
Monkfish and dill

Suon Chien
Barbecued spare ribs

Kho
Fish or meat cooked in lemon grass and fish sauce

Ca Tim Nuong
Aubergines cooked with lime

Bau Xao
Courgettes with prawns and pork

Banh Chuoi
Banana cake

Chuoi Va Thom Chien Gion
Deep-fried apple and banana slices

Chuoi Dua
Bananas in coconut milk

Hoa Qua Tuoi
Iced fruit salad

Dau Xanh Vung
Mung bean cakes coated in sesame seeds

THAILAND

Within their culinary arsenal, Thai chefs have an array of flavours that range from the gentle to the explosive, from the shudderingly sour to the syrupy sweet, and colours ranging from the leafiest green to the spiciest red. Thailand is blessed with a climate that is neither too wet nor too dry; the result is a land that nurtures meat and vegetables in tropical abundance, and seas and rivers that yield a shining harvest of fish and seafood. Confident in its own well-stocked larder, Thailand has felt free to look outside its borders for inspiration. Thai cooking has embraced Indian spices, Chinese cooking methods, and that most unmistakably Pacific of flavours, the coconut. Yet it has borrowed piecemeal rather than wholesale, never subordinating its own self to overseas influences, always making the newcomers play a Thai tune and retaining the indigenous cuisine. Thus, where the Chinese might steam fish plain, the Thais will add lemon grass; where an Indian curry might be flavoured with only two spices, a Thai curry may contain many, along with herbs, fish sauce and coconut milk. However, the real measure of Thai culinary skill lies not in the number of ingredients it employs, but in the artistry with which they are used.

TRADITIONAL INGREDIENTS

Basil*
Bean curd
Beef (nua)
Chicken (kai)
Chilli sauce* (sriracha)
Chillies*
Coconut*
Coriander*
Cumin*
Curry paste*
Fish sauce*
Galangal*
Garlic*
Ginger*
Kaffir limes
Kapee (shrimp paste)
Krachai
Lemon grass*
Limes*
Mint*
Mushrooms*
Noodles
Oyster sauce*
Palm sugar
Peanuts
Pork
Prawns
Rice
Sesame seeds*
Shallots*
Shrimp paste
Soy sauce*
Spring onions*
Star anise*
Sugar*
Sweet corn
Tamarind*
Taro
Turmeric*

(*see Index)

INFLUENCES

Geographically, Thailand stands closer to China than India, but its cuisine has adopted much from its more far-flung neighbours. From China, the Thais borrowed the wok, stir-frying and steaming. What they chose not to take up was the Chinese practice of thickening sauces with cornflour; consequently, Thai stir-fry dishes have always been lighter and more delicate than their Chinese counterparts. Similarly, Thailand adopted curries from India, but invested them with three distinctly Thai characteristics. Firstly, Thai curries are based on curry pastes, made from the pounding of wet herbs and spices, whereas Indian curries are generally flavoured with curry powders, produced by the pounding of dry herbs and spices. Secondly, the Thais slice their main curry ingredients (meat, fish or vegetables) into fine slivers rather than chunks. And thirdly, instead of using dairy products, such as ghee (clarified butter), Thai chefs employ coconut milk; this is produced by soaking grated coconut flesh in water and then filtering off the thick liquid that results (see page 179).

Strangely enough, it was Europeans who introduced the ingredient which has come to epitomize Thai cooking: the chilli pepper. Portuguese traders are credited with bringing this fiery addition to Eastern cuisines; perhaps to compensate, they also brought with them the soothing egg custard, original ancestor of the coconut custard, *sung kha ya*, which is so popular throughout Thailand today.

FLAVOURINGS

Ten varieties of the world's hottest chillies are grown in Thailand. The strongest of these is the tiny bird's-eye chilli; its innocuous size (1 cm; 1/2 in) conceals its prodigious capacity for searing the mouth. Chillies are put to a plethora of uses. When they are paired with *nam pla* (a thin, salty fish sauce), *kapee* (shrimp paste), garlic, coriander and citrus juice, *nam prik* is born. This liquid acts as condiment, sauce, dip and seasoning throughout Thai cooking. *Prik nam som* (chillies in rice vinegar) and *prik pon* (red chilli powder) are other popular chilli-based condiments.

Thai garlic, with smaller cloves and pinker skin than its Western relation, is used in vast numbers of Thai dishes; in addition, when crisply fried, it is used as a garnish, and when pickled in rice vinegar, salt and sugar it becomes the condiment *kratiem dong* (pickled garlic).

The sour flavour of tamarind, the citrus flavour of lime juice, lemon grass, and Kaffir lime leaves, plus the heated flavour of Thailand's three types of ginger – root ginger, greater galangal, and *krachai* – add up to an insistent perfume that pervades all Thai cooking. Chefs often combine this lively package of flavours with coconut milk, in order to create the sparring between tingling piquancy and creamy sweetness that typifies the nation's cuisine. This phenomenon manifests itself most noticeably in the many red and green curry paste dishes such as *kiaw wan goong* (green prawn curry) and *kaeng pet kai* (red chicken curry). The colour of the pastes depends on the colour of the chillies used, and usual constituents of a curry paste (see page 81) include chillies (red or green), lemon grass, shallots, garlic, galangal, coriander, cumin, white pepper, shrimp paste and kaffir lime skin or leaves.

Coriander and mint leaves act as ornament and ingredient. Another prominent taste is basil, which imparts its fragrance throughout stir-fries, curries and soups, as well as appearing shredded in salads.

OTHER INGREDIENTS

The invitation to a meal in Thailand is *kin khao*, which translates as "come and eat rice." There are two main kinds: long-grain, or fragrant rice, which is the dietary mainstay of southern Thailand, and the shorter-grained glutinous rice that is the main-course choice of northern Thailand, as well as the basis for desserts throughout the country. Glutinous rice is more compact, and much more manageable, than the long-grained variety.

Rice noodles are also eaten throughout the country, arriving at the table in a number of different dishes. When stir-fried, they appear in the national favourite *pad thai*, along with dried shrimp, roasted peanuts, lemon juice, fish sauce, bean sprouts, spring onions, chilli, preserved turnips, coriander leaves and sugar. When boiled, they luxuriate in soups such as *suki gai*, made with chicken, soy sauce, fish sauce, sugar, egg, red bean curd, pickled garlic, stock, chilli powder, lemon juice, celery and Chinese leaves. When deep-fried to a crispy consistency, they are the centrepiece of the famous dish *mee krop*, alongside garlic, shallots, chilli and pork.

Thailand's elongated coastline and its numerous rivers harbour a variety of fish and shellfish, which are prepared in a multitude of ways. They may be minced into fish balls, stuffed, curried or steamed with pickled plums and garlic. Grilled lobster with chilli and garlic is a fine example of balancing delicate shellfish with hot chillies.

Pork plays a versatile role, often being combined with seafood in dishes such as *bu ja* (steamed crab with garlic, coriander and chilli). Chicken and beef also appear in stir-fried vegetable dishes, as well as in curries such as *kaeng mussaman*. This combines beef, coconut milk, fish sauce, tamarind, potatoes, peanuts and onions, in Mussaman curry paste, which differs from other Thai curry pastes in containing cinnamon, cloves, star anise and cardamom.

MEALS

Rice porridge is the traditional Thai way to begin the day, eaten with pickled radishes or other preserved vegetables, and perhaps enlivened by some minced pork plus a few chillies. Lunch is generally bought in from one of the multitude of street traders, who throng the pavements of every Thai town, and who even make midday house calls in the more remote villages. The fare they peddle around lunchtime is usually noodle-based, perhaps a noodle soup, dotted with fragments of chicken, green beans and bean sprouts. It might also be a fried noodle dish, sparingly strewn with a few meat and vegetable pieces but lavishly stimulated by a mixture of sauces that will include sugar, fish sauce, fresh roasted peanuts and crushed dried chillies.

The evening meal is the most copious. There are many courses, which are all served simultaneously. Dessert, if served, usually comprises one liquid sweet dish, probably perfumed with coconut cream, and one dry sweet dish, perhaps based on sweetened bean paste. Fruit provides Thai meals with a refreshing climax.

Food is often garnished with exquisitely cut vegetables. Tomatoes are carved into the shape of roses, carrots into lotus petals, spring onions into lillies and ginger into tiny crabs, which are usually accurate right down to their claws.

MENU GUIDE

Poh Piah Tod
Spring rolls

Kha Nom Jeen
Thai-style dumplings

Suki Kai
Chicken, vegetable and bean curd soup

Yam Nua Saweo
Cucumber filled with beef

Tom Yum Kung
Hot and sour prawn soup

Pad Thai
Stir-fried noodles with shredded meat and vegetables

Tod Mun Pla
Fish cakes

Hoy Op
Steamed mussels with basil and lemon grass

Laab Nua
Spicy minced beef salad

Kaeng Pet Dang Mhoo
Red pork curry

Kiaw Wan Goong
Green prawn curry

Yam Talay
Hot and sour fish salad

Pla Kung
Prawns and lemon grass

Satay
Barbecued skewered meat

Homok Talay
Seafood and coconut bouillabaisse

Mee Krop
Sweet crispy noodles

Khanom Maw Gaeng
Baked custard

Ta-Kho
Coconut milk with glutinous rice

Kruay Khaek
Fried banana

Met Kanoon
Sweet mung-bean dessert

SOUTH PACIFIC

Acombination of rain, heat and humidity makes the South Pacific a greenhouse when it comes to food growing. Bunches of tropical fruits swell and bulge from their trees, leafy vegetables sprout densely from the ground, and rice stalks wave in their multitudes from the watery fields that dot the land.

Water is never far away, either in the form of a rice field, a river or the sea. Fish and seafood abound, as do the number of ways to cook them: boiling in coconut milk, stewing in vinegar, frying in soy or fish sauce, or dousing with fiery dips and relishes. The chefs of the South Pacific adapt their methods in order to express most eloquently the character of their main ingredients. With a treasury of herbs and spices, both indigenous and imported by many generations of seafarers, they have an almost unparalleled vocabulary of flavourings.

TRADITIONAL INGREDIENTS

Bananas
Banana leaves*
Basil*
Bay*
Buah keras/kemiri
Chillies*
Cinnamon*
Coconut*
Coriander*
Cumin*
Dried fish*
Fennel*
Fish sauce (patis)*
Galangal*
Garlic*
Ginger*
Hoisin*
Jackfruit
Kalamansi
Ketjap
Lemon grass*
Limes*
Lychees
Mangos
Noodles
Nutmeg*
Palm sugar
Papaya
Peanuts
Pineapples
Screwpine leaves
Shrimp paste (blachan/trasi)*
Soy bean paste (miso)*
Soy sauce*
Sweet potatoes
Tamarind*
Turmeric*
Yams

(*see Index)

MALAYSIA

Most Malaysians live on a long, tropical peninsula, which on its western shore borders the Strait of Malacca, a natural ocean corridor between the South China Sea and the Indian Ocean. The gentle coastline offers a natural landfall to seaborne traders, and in the 15th century A.D., merchants from China, India and the Middle East came in great numbers to the thriving seaport of Malacca (today Melaka).

Of these early visitors, it was the Arabs and Indians who left the most lasting imprint on the society by carrying over the Muslim religion. In terms of cuisine, however, all have had a profound influence.

Indian spices, such as cumin and turmeric, proliferate in Malaysian curries; *satay*, the Malaysian skewered meat dish, can trace its origins back to the Arab kebab; and dishes of Chinese extraction such as spring rolls and *char siu* (honey-basted pork) have, for centuries, been part of Malaysia's cooking heritage.

The Chinese influence is particularly strong in Singapore, the island republic that sits just south of Malaysia. In the 1820's many thousands of Chinese labourers flocked here to work on the construction of Singapore City. They intermarried with the indigenous Malay women and produced a clearly identifiable race of *Nonya,* or Straits Chinese, who practise a style of cooking that combines a Chinese regard for texture and balance with a Malaysian fondness for chillies and curries.

Coconut milk, or *lemak*, lies at the heart of Nonya cuisine, as it does with nearly all Malaysian food. This is not the raw juice of the coconut (which can be extracted by drilling a hole in the shell), but the strained product of warm water mixed with shredded or dried coconut flesh. Lemak is the main source of liquid in Malaysian curries, but it is most prominent in the ubiquitous *laksa lemak* (coconut soup) – a delicious brothy hotchpotch of prawns, lemon grass (*serai*), bean curd, garlic, onions, curry leaves and candlenuts, called *buah keras*, which are similar to macadamia nuts. It also features prominently in puddings, such as *serikaya*, coconut custard.

Coconut flesh, shredded or dried, is a common ingredient in *sambals*, which are little platefuls of paste, sometimes moist, sometimes dry, which are used as a relish or an extra source of flavouring. Combinations include chilli and shrimp, coconut and onion or pineapple and cucumber.

Sambals frequently contain a fish paste called *blachan*, which is a pounded-down combination of fermented shrimps and salt. It has a powerful odour but, when cooked, blachan imparts depth of flavour rather than unrestrained fishiness, surprisingly enough. Another common fish flavouring is *ikan bilis*, tiny dried fish, which are crumbled into soups and sauces to add an extra layer of taste. Soy sauce and hoisin (see page 242) are also used, though more often with dishes of Chinese rather than native Malaysian origin.

Powerful herbs and spices are used in abundance: lemon grass, coriander, garlic, cumin, chilli, turmeric, curry leaves, ginger and its woodier, pine-scented relative galangal, being among the best known.

Sweetness is supplied by brown palm sugar (*gula melaka*), and juice from the lime, lemon and crushed tamarind pod (*asam*) add tartness. Malaysian cooks often employ the long, thin leaves of the screw-pine tree, pandanus leaves, which lend foods a nutty flavour and a green colouring.

With a large Muslim population, and a significant Hindu one as well, the eating of beef and pork is limited. Only chicken is acceptable by the population as a whole. Chinese tradition, by contrast, imposes no such limits. Throughout Malaysia, fish and seafood are plentiful, particularly prawns, mackerel, pomfret and snapper.

Peanuts give flavour and substance to the traditional satay sauce. Aubergines, bean sprouts, gourds and Chinese cabbage are the other predominant vegetables, while the long list of fruits includes rambutans, lychees, bananas, pineapples, limes and star fruit.

Noodles (*mee*) are a popular snack, but rice is the daily staple of Malaysian life. There are two main types: the long-grain rice that is familiar in the West, and glutinous rice. The latter is starchier and stickier and comes in two colours: white and black. It is very often cooked inside a serving-sized container of plaited palm or banana leaves, which gives it a delicate flavour.

Satay and peanut sauce

INDONESIA

Indonesia is an ocean jigsaw, a collection of some 13,600 islands, of which the three best known are Java, Sumatra and Bali.

Between the 7th and 12th centuries A.D., many islands owed allegiance to the Southeast Asian Hindu-Buddhist empire of Srivijaya. But when its power waned in the 13th century, islanders began to adopt the Islamic religion that arrived with the Muslim seafarers and this then spread to many points along their trading routes. Today, 90 per cent of Indonesians are Muslim, though there is also a sizeable Hindu population on the island of Bali.

Indonesia shares many dishes and flavours with her Muslim neighbour Malaysia. Peanuts are the dominant taste. They feature in the conventional Indonesian dipping sauce for satay and in the sauce for the national dish *gado gado,* a cold salad of cooked vegetables served with prawn crackers, *(krupuk udang)* and slightly bitter little crisps called *emping,* which are made from the fried kernels of the nut from the giant melinjo tree.

Coconut milk, *santen,* is used in a large number of dishes, such as *ayam opur* (chicken cooked in coconut milk) and beef *rendang,* in which the meat is slowly cooked in spice-enhanced coconut milk. In some dishes, santen appears in the form of a thick sauce. While in others (rendang, for example), it is cooked until it is completely absorbed into the other ingredients.

As in Malaysia, sauces and pastes feature prominently. *Ketjap* (from which the word "ketchup" indirectly derives) is the Indonesian soy sauce. The two main types are *ketjap manis* (sweet, thick and treacly) and *ketjap asin* (lighter and saltier). Both kinds are used in the making of sambals – spicy, ground herb and spice mixtures that serve as both in-the-dish seasonings and on-the-table condiments. Examples are *sambal ketjap* made with crushed chillies, garlic, ketjap manis and juice from the Kaffir lime; and the all-purpose *sambal goreng,* which combines coconut milk, bay leaves, lime leaves, garlic, cumin, red chillies, galangal or *laos* (lenkuas in Malaysia) and *trasi,* the salted, fermented fish paste that is the Indonesian equivalent of Malaysia's blachan (see page 189).

MENU GUIDE

Acar/Achara
Pickled vegetable relish

Nasi Goreng (Indonesia)
Mixed fried rice

Char Kway Teo (Malaysia)
Stir fried noodles with meat and prawns

Martabak (Indonesia)
Minced meat pancakes

Char Siu
(Malaysia and Indonesia)
Chinese honey-basted roast pork

Dinuguan (Philippines)
Pork stewed in pig blood

Ikan Lemak (Malaysia)
Sweet-and-sour fish

Guinataan (Philippines)
Any dish cooked in coconut milk

Gado Gado (Indonesia)
Cold vegetable salad with peanut sauce and crackers

Pork Gulai (Malaysia)
Nonya dish of pork cooked in coconut milk

Chicken Relleno
(Philippines)
Stuffed chicken

Rendang (Indonesia)
Spicy beef and coconut milk curry

Kari-Kari (Philippines)
Beef or oxtail stew in peanut gravy

Nasi Kuning (Indonesia)
Festive dish of yellow rice

Lechon (Philippines)
Whole roast pig

Tahu Telur (Malaysia)
Bean curd omelette

Sinigang (Philippines)
Sour broth with tomatoes and acidic fruit

Lemper (Indonesia)
Chicken pieces encased in glutinous rice

MENU GUIDE

Lontong
(Malaysia and Indonesia)
*Cold, compressed boiled rice,
cooked in banana leaf
containers*

Singapore Laksa
*Mixed seafood soup with rice
vermicelli*

Pancit (Philippines)
*Noodles cooked in garlic and
onions, with shrimps and pork*

Ayam Opur (Indonesia)
*Chicken cooked in coconut
milk*

Adobado (Philippines)
*Pork and/or chicken stew
cooked adobo style – in
vinegar, garlic and soy sauce*

Laksa Lemak (Malaysia)
*Coconut milk soup with
prawns*

Satay
(Malaysia and Indonesia)
*Skewered beef, chicken or
turtle meat, served with peanut
sauce*

Paksiw Na Bangus
(Philippines)
Fish boiled in vinegar and salt

Gudeg (Indonesia)
Chicken with jackfruit

Chah Kangkung (Indonesia)
Stir-fried cabbage greens

Kilawin (Philippines)
*Fish raw-cooked in vinegar
and citrus juice*

Gula melaka (Malaysia)
*Coconut, sago and treacle
pudding*

Halo-Halo (Philippines)
*Sundae of dried and preserved
fruits mixed with ice shavings
and ice cream*

Serikaya
(Malaysia and Indonesia)
Coconut custard

Banana-cue (Philippines)
*Banana rolled in brown sugar
and barbecued*

Commonly used herbs and spices are lemon grass, cumin, coriander, *laos* powder, (dried and ground galangal), chillies and turmeric; the latter gives the yellow colouring to the feast-day rice dish, *nasi kuning*.

Because of the country's island make-up, great emphasis is placed on fish. Most frequently pulled from the sea are red snapper, sea bass, pomfret and the bony milkfish. Prawns of all sizes abound, as do mussels and squid. Of the many freshwater species, one of the most prized for its thick, white meat is the *gurami*.

As in Malaysia, the large Muslim population eschews the eating of pork. Only on the predominantly Hindu island of Bali does the pig feature to any great extent in the chef's plans. Lamb is viewed as a special-occasion ingredient, while beef (or water buffalo) is a more everyday meat, although it is not eaten by Hindus.

Fruits grow abundantly in this tropical climate; among them papaya, pineapples, mangosteen and several different types of banana, and in size they rise from little, crisp "rose-apples" (*jambu air)*, the size of a golf ball, to giant jackfruit (*nangka*). This is a boulder-sized fruit with fibrous yellow flesh inside its thick, rubbery-spiked skin. The jackfruit is a central ingredient in the traditional dish, *gudeg*.

Indonesians eat largely the same vegetables as Malaysians: Chinese cabbage, cucumbers, bean sprouts and *kacang panjang*, which are green beans that can grow up to one metre (3 ft) in length.

THE PHILIPPINES

Three hundred and fifty years of Spanish rule, which lasted from the 1550's to the 1890's, have left the Philippines not just with a Spanish name (after King Philip II of Spain) but also a culinary legacy of a large number of dishes and flavours that have the distinctive stamp of Spanish style.

The small, savoury snack dishes that make up the Filipino *merienda* buffet are the tapas of the South Pacific. *Arroz Valenciana* is a Filipino paella. The spicy chorizo sausage is a direct Spanish import, while other ingredients were imported from Spanish territories in the New World; corn, avocado, tomatoes, potatoes and coffee all came to

the Philippines via Mexico, which for many years administrated this island region on Spain's behalf.

The other major influence on Filipino cuisine came from the Chinese merchants who were trading in this area, some as early as the 10th century. Dishes such as spring rolls and *lomi* (sticky noodles with meat and seafood) were firmly established in the Philippines long before the first Spanish galleon was sighted.

There is a sharpness and a tartness running through most Filipino food. Frequent use is made of the juice from the *kalamansi*, which is a sour citrus fruit halfway between a lime and a lemon. Vinegar also plays a central part in two of the most common styles of cooking – *paksiw*, meat or fish slowly boiled in vinegar and salt; and *kilawin*, the practice of "cooking" fish by marinating it in vinegar and kalamansi juice, as in the South American dish *seviche*. In addition, vinegar is combined with garlic and soy sauce to make *adobado*, a tangy pork or chicken stew.

A thick, salty fish paste called *bagoong*, and its thinner, lighter by-product *patis* (fish sauce), provide extra body for soups and stews and also for the large number of dips and relishes known collectively as *sawsawan*. Both bagoong and patis are mixed with ingredients such as garlic, pounded red chillies, vinegar, onions, and tangy tamarind or kalamansi juice, to provide a collection of dishes that range in flavour from the sharp to the fiery.

A gentler source of flavouring is coconut milk. This forms the basis for the style of dish known as *guinataan*, in which a mixture of chicken, pork and vegetables is gently stewed until all of the liquid has been absorbed. The term "guinataan" can also be applied to sweet dishes, such as a combination of yams, tapioca, banana and jackfruit, again cooked in coconut milk.

The most frequently used spices are cloves cinnamon, ginger, star anise, turmeric and nutmeg. Herbs include rosemary, bay leaf, basil and dill. Chilli peppers, crushed, dried, sliced or fried, also make numerous appearances in Filipino dishes.

In a country made up of over 7,000 different islands, fish naturally play a part in the diet. Anchovies, sea bass, swordfish and milkfish are the most common, though stingray and abalone are also to be found.

Unlike their Southeast Asian neighbours, most Filipinos are not Muslim but Christian, and therefore can countenance eating pork.

This is witnessed in the well-known dish, *dinuguan*, a spicy stew of pork meat that has been cooked in pork blood. *Lechon* – whole roast pig – is reserved for feasts and special occasions: the guest of honour gets the meal under way by plucking off one of the cooked ears. Chicken and beef are also widely consumed, as is offal.

The Filipino staple is rice, both long-grain and glutinous. There is also a special purple rice, *pirurutung*, which is a decorative strain that is used only for puddings such as *puton bumbong*, a dish that is cooked in bamboo tubes and served with sugar and butter. Filipino cooking boasts a rich variety of dessert rice dishes, including the popular *pinipig*, which are individual cakes made of toasted glutinous and *champorado*, chocolate-flavoured sticky rice.

The favoured vegetables are gourds, Chinese cabbage, onions, white turnips, palm hearts and *kangkong*, a leafy swamp vegetable with a reputation for cheapness if not flavour. The fruits most commonly to be found on market stalls are bananas, guavas, pineapples, mangos, kalamansi, jackfruit, watermelons and *durian*, a large, spiky-shelled fruit with an overpowering smell (some would say downright unpleasant) and a consistency of soft cheese.

MEALS

Breakfast in Malaysia can be a filling affair, usually consisting of steamed buns or *nasi lemak*, a rich coconut milk porridge which can be sprinkled with dried fish (*ikan bilis*) and accompanied by anything from a hard-boiled egg and sambal, to a full-size fish curry. Lunch is generally a lighter meal, perhaps a selection of little Chinese dim sum dumplings, or else rice accompanied by a meat or vegetable dish, and washed down by scented Chinese tea.

The biggest meal of the day is dinner, which may consist of one rice dish and up to five fish, vegetable or meat dishes, all accompanied by sambals. Usually the food is put in the middle of the table and all the diners are invited to help themselves. The style of cutlery depends on the origin of the food; Chinese dishes will normally be eaten with chopsticks, and Malaysian dishes with either fingers (right hand only)

or a spoon and fork. Banana leaves usually play a part, either as rice containers, dinner plates or heat-retaining wrappers.

On special occasions, Malaysians will get out the steamboat – a charcoal-heated pot much like a Swiss fondue set. First, a bubbling stock is cooked up, then diners drop in pieces of meat, seafood, vegetables and fish, removing them when done.

The meal pattern in Indonesia is much the same. The standard breakfast is rice porridge (*bubur ayam*), which is a bowl of rice mixed with omelette and crumbled dried fish (*goreng teri*). Another popular first-thing-in-the-morning dish is *nasi goreng*, meaning literally "fried rice" that is mixed with whatever leftovers are to hand.

Lunch will consist of rice or noodles and a meat or vegetable dish, perhaps a chicken or beef satay that has been cooked at a roadside stall. Dinner is eaten at any time after 6:30 p.m., and if it is a special occasion, the fare will most likely be *nasi gerar* (the Dutch *rijstaffel* or "rice table"): a vast collection of rice, soup, fish, meat, vegetable and sambal dishes, selected so as to take the diners through the whole spectrum of tastes (spicy, bland, sweet and sour) and textures (crisp, soft, crunchy and chewy). Again, this is a serve-yourself meal eaten either with cutlery or with the fingers of the right hand; the left hand is considered unclean and should not be used, even to pass a dish to a neighbour. *Selamat makan* is the correct way to say *bon appétit* in Indonesia.

Filipinos also begin the day with rice, often fried with a hint of garlic and served along with salted, dried fish. At lunchtime, they may have *pancit* (noodles with pork and shrimps) or *lumpia*, which are the local version of spring rolls. Late afternoon is the time for merienda, a selection of small savoury dishes that can, in sufficient numbers, count as a full meal.

As in Malaysia and Indonesia, diners help themselves from communal plates, but in the Philippines it is much more common to eat with cutlery rather than with fingers.

Throughout all three countries, cooking implements are similar. The wok, either metal or earthenware, is the basic utensil. It is known as a *kwali* in Malaysia, a *wajan* in Indonesia, and in the Philippines it goes by the name of *carajay*.

Alcohol is never served to accompany meals in the two predominantly Muslim countries, and only infrequently in the Christian Philippines. Alternatives are tea, coffee, fruit juice and iced coconut milk.

British colonies for more than 200 years, both Australia and New Zealand combine heavy British-style dishes with a lighter, Oriental-style cuisine. Examples of the heavier dishes are Lamington cake (sponge covered with a thick layer of chocolate) and the Adelaide Floater, a meat pie surrounded by puréed tinned peas and topped with tomato sauce. Exponents of the lighter style borrow Southeast Asian flavourings such as lemon grass, coriander and ginger, and marry them with home-grown ingredients such as beef and green prawns. Roast meat plays an important part in the diet of both countries, particularly home-reared New Zealand lamb and Australian beef. A classic New Zealand dish is hogget, a whole roasted 1-year old lamb. Australians also have a festive lamb dish, called colonial goose, which is a rolled, stuffed shoulder of lamb. Another popular form of cooking is barbecuing, a method originally perfected by the Aborigines. Kangaroo, a gamey-tasting meat, is eaten in some parts of Australia, both roasted and braised. In New Zealand, venison is popular.

It is seafood, however, that is found in the greatest variety. Oysters, crayfish, prawns, red snapper and John Dory are common to both countries. In Australia, the tropical northern region is home to tasty Queensland mud-crabs and the estuary-dwelling barramundi fish.

Green vegetables grow in abundance in both countries, as do fruits both tropical and temperate, including apples, pears, peaches, kiwi fruit, passion fruit, custard apples and jackfruit. A selection of these make up the traditional filling for Pavlova, the famed meringue dessert that was invented in Australia.

VEGETABLE & FRUIT FLAVOURINGS

MUSHROOMS

Wild, cultivated or dried, the mushroom is a versatile and flavoursome ingredient. It is classified as a fungus, which is a plant that contains no chlorophyll and does not flower. The flavour of mushrooms, which is due to glutamic acid, is intensely savoury.

Mushrooms take well to most cooking methods: sautéeing, braising, baking and microwaving. They are even delicious uncooked. An all-purpose ingredient, mushrooms feature in cuisines around the world and can be used to enhance a wide variety of dishes.

CULTIVATED MUSHROOMS

Mushrooms which are grown commercially are called cultivated mushrooms. Cultivated varieties are the most readily available and the most versatile; they can be used as a flavouring, as an ingredient on their own or as a container for stuffings.

Button Mushrooms The most immature variety, these milky white mushrooms are harvested at a very early stage of development. The flavour has not had much time to mature, but they are good in salads – alone or in combination – where their fresh, crunchy texture is best displayed.

Cup Mushrooms A little further along in development, these mushrooms are available with the cups either closed or open. The closed type are barely distinguishable from button mushrooms in appearance though the taste is slightly stronger. Open-cup mushrooms have a speckled cap and exposed brownish gills on the underside. These are mature mushrooms with a fully developed flavour. They are delicious when filled with a savoury, herb-specked stuffing and baked.

Chestnut mushrooms

Fresh morel   **Dried shiitake**

Flat Mushrooms The most mature of all the common mushrooms, these also have the most intense flavour. Their fanned-out cap and exposed brown gills make them unattractive to many, but it would be a mistake to let their appearance interfere with their great flavouring potential.

Chestnut Mushrooms A dark brown variety of the cup mushroom, this type has a pleasant flavour which can be appreciated in dishes both cooked and raw.

Cultivated Wild Mushrooms Some popular varieties are now grown commercially and are more widely available:

Oyster mushrooms have a pleasing chewy texture and neutral flavour, making them ideal for a mixed mushroom sauté. However, they have a high moisture content and should be cooked just to warm. High heat will draw out all the liquid, and with it all the texture and flavour.

Shiitake mushrooms are an oriental variety now cultivated throughout Europe and North America. With a powerful and meaty flavour, these mushrooms lend themselves well to long cooking.

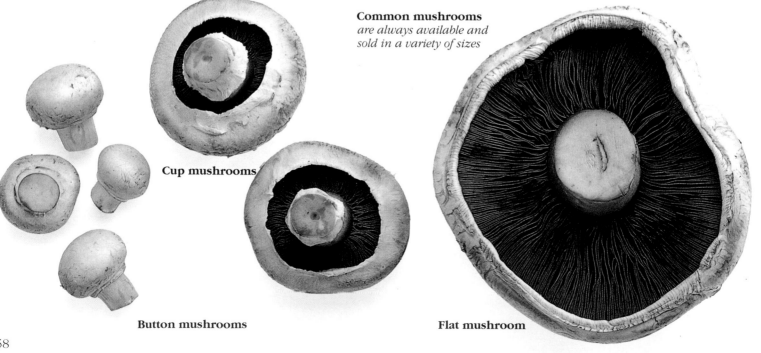

Common mushrooms *are always available and sold in a variety of sizes*

Cup mushrooms

Button mushrooms

Flat mushroom

WILD MUSHROOMS

In many European countries, mushroom gathering is a popular pastime and an extremely rewarding one as wild mushrooms are surely one of the most delicious woodland offerings. However, many mushrooms are poisonous, and the inexperienced gatherer should be wary. Never eat any mushroom garnered in the wild if it cannot be positively identified as safe for consumption. There are a number of books available to aid identifying non-poisonous edible mushrooms, although appearance varies from one area to another. For this reason, any suspicious mushrooms should be authenticated by an expert. Therefore, when in doubt, do not eat.

There are many wild mushrooms; the most common are described below.

Boletus Known as *cèpes* in French and *porcini* in Italian, these have a rich flavour and pleasing texture. Their taste improves with cooking.

Chanterelles Beautiful orange-yellow mushrooms, these are extremely tasty. They can be gently sautéed and served on their own. Grey chanterelles are known as *girolles*.

Boletus *are stout, fleshy mushrooms with a powerful, meaty flavour to match*

Chanterelles *are horn-shaped mushrooms of varying size with an orange-yellow colour*

Shiitake *can be eaten raw but their meaty flavour and unique texture is best appreciated when cooked*

Shiitake mushroom

Oyster mushrooms

Oyster mushrooms *lose their flavour when overcooked*

Horn of Plenty These are dark brown, almost black, mushrooms with a deep, rich flavour. They are less common, but easily recognizable in markets by their funnel-shaped stem. They offer a pleasing contrast when combined with other mushrooms.

Morels Considered to rival the truffle in flavour, these mushrooms are used in many European cuisines. The conical cap looks rather like a sponge with many small crevices. There are two types of morel: the lighter, or blond, morel is full of flavour, but the dark brown morel is considered by many to be superior.

Truffles The king of wild mushrooms, truffles have an incomparable flavour. Cost varies from year to year, and prices are prohibitively high. Wild truffles grow underground, around the roots of certain oak trees, and are gathered in the autumn with the aid of dogs or pigs trained to sniff them out. Black truffles, which look much like small lumps of coal, are the most common, but there is also a white Italian variety which is considered by many to be at the pinnacle of mushroom flavour.

Mushrooms in the Kitchen

A delicious mushroom dish starts with the selection of good quality ingredients. Loose mushrooms are always the best choice; plastic packaging suffocates the mushrooms, making them soggy. Only cultivated mushrooms will keep, and even then only for a short period. About three days in the vegetable compartment of the refrigerator is the maximum. Wild mushrooms are best used on the same day they are purchased.

Choosing and Storing

Avoid buying mushrooms which are wrinkled or soft to the touch; the caps should be smooth and firm or springy to the touch with no traces of moisture.

Although mushrooms are best purchased in small quantities for use as needed, they can be stored, unwashed, for about three days. Cover them with a damp cloth or place in a paper bag punctured for ventilation and refrigerate until needed.

Cooking with Mushrooms

Mushrooms are quite porous which makes cleaning them a delicate task. Cultivated mushrooms can be gently rinsed, but for salads it is best to trim the stems and wipe the caps with a paper towel to keep them crisp and dry. While it is common practice to peel mushrooms, this is not necessary unless the colour or texture of the cap is uninviting; be sure to reserve the trimmings for the stockpot. Wild mushrooms should never be rinsed or peeled. Simply trim off the thick, rough part of the stems and gently brush off any dirt with a soft brush.

COOK'S CHOICE
Duxelles

Makes about 500 g (1 lb)

1 small onion or shallot,
finely chopped
4 tbsp unsalted butter
500 g (1 lb) mushrooms,
finely chopped
2 garlic cloves, finely chopped
Salt
Freshly ground black pepper
2 tbsp chopped parsley

In a frying pan, combine the onion and butter and cook gently until soft. Add the mushrooms and garlic, and season to taste. Cook over low heat, stirring occasionally, until all the liquid has evaporated, about 20 minutes. Stir in the parsley. Add to rice dishes or stuffings, or serve with roast meats.

While most mushrooms are best when cooked, cultivated mushrooms work well in salads. Sliced button mushrooms are delicious when tossed with an olive oil and lemon juice dressing, topped with slivers of Parmesan cheese and sprinkled with fresh herbs, such as chervil or chives.

In many European countries, it is an autumn tradition to serve a mixture of wild mushrooms sautéed in butter as a starter. All wild mushrooms take well to this treatment. Heat butter or oil in a large frying pan and add the mushrooms. Cook over high heat until tender; cooking time depends on the variety. Chopped garlic or shallots can be added, but only in small quantities so as not to mask the delicate flavour of the mushrooms.

A small, supple brush is best for cleaning

Preparing Mushrooms

Slicing
Hold the mushroom by the stem and cut the cap into thin horizontal slices. Reserve the end slices for the stockpot.

Julienne
Cut into thin slices. Stack the slices and cut lengthwise into thin strips.

Chopping
Slice into thin julienne strips. With a small, sharp knife, cut across the julienne to obtain finely chopped mushrooms.

Dicing
Cut thick, crosswise slices; do not let them separate. Cut the same thickness across the existing slices for a thick dice.

DRIED MUSHROOMS

While the flavour of fresh mushrooms is incomparable, many varieties take well to drying. The taste of certain mushrooms, such as morels and boletus, is even more intense when dried. It is always useful to have a small packet of dried mushrooms on hand. Just a few dried mushrooms can greatly improve the flavour of almost any savoury dish, or stretch a small amount of stewed, fresh mushrooms.

Morels *are very expensive but reconstitute beautifully; 30 g (1 oz) is sufficient to flavour a recipe meant for 5–6 people*

Cloud ears *need reconstituting in several changes of warm water before use*

Shiitake *can be a bit tough when rehydrated but are successfully added to sauces and stews*

Boletus *are usually Italian in origin and will have been graded before being sliced and dried for packaging*

(see right)

In some recipes, generally stews or other long cooking dishes, dried mushrooms can be substituted for fresh. The general rule is to allow one part dried mushrooms for every eight parts fresh.

Morels These are the most expensive of the dried mushrooms, but only a few add quite a lot of flavour. When reconstituting (see right), be sure to stir occasionally to loosen any dirt or grit which may be lodged in the caps. Dried morels can be added to sauces or rice dishes, but they have a particular affinity with anything made with cream, eggs or butter. A creamy morel sauce is the classic accompaniment to chicken, and a few reconstituted dried morels, sautéed in butter, greatly enhance scrambled eggs.

Boletus Because these often have a spongy texture, many cooks prefer to use them dried. They are an excellent addition to risotto or pasta sauce, and porcini dust, which is available in many delicatessens, can be added to almost any savoury dish, with or without mushrooms.

Shiitake When dried, these have a smoky flavour, though they tend to be a bit tough when reconstituted. For best results, chop shiitake finely before adding to soups, stews or sauces.

Cloud ears These are another Asian variety, sometimes known as tree ears. While they add little in flavour, they are valued for their gelatinous, seaweed-like texture. This type is a common ingredient in Chinese soups and stir-fries.

RECONSTITUTING DRIED MUSHROOMS

Reconstituted dried mushrooms can be used in place of fresh in most recipes. Be sure to adjust the cooking time as dried mushrooms can be a bit tough and require additional simmering.

1 Soak the mushrooms for 15–30 minutes in warm water to cover. Strain through a lined sieve. The liquid can also be added to the dish.

2 Dry on paper towels and pat with another paper towel. They should be dry before use or they may dilute the flavour of the finished dish.

161

ONIONS

Finely chopped, sliced or whole, the onion is one of the most useful vegetable flavourings available to the cook. Native to Asia, it has been a kitchen ingredient for thousands of years. The ancient Egyptians preferred them raw, while the Greeks valued onions for what they believed were their curative powers. Since the Middle Ages, the onion has been a staple ingredient in all European cuisines. There are hundreds of onion types which vary in colour, size and flavour, and they are generally distinguished by their colour and the time of year they are available. Flavour depends on the climate where they are grown; the milder the climate, the sweeter the onion. Pungent when raw and sweet when cooked, onions can enhance just about any savoury dish.

TYPES OF ONIONS

Yellow Onions The most common onion, this type accounts for more than 75 per cent of the world's production. It is a strong-flavoured onion which keeps well and is best suited for long cooking in stews, soups or sauces. When adding to the stockpot, include the outer brown skin as this adds an attractive golden colour.

Sweet Onions Popular types include Spanish, Bermuda, Maui, Vidalia and Walla Walla. These are delicious when stuffed and baked, or coated and fried for onion rings. Sweet onions, thinly sliced and sautéed with sliced mushrooms and herbs, make a delicious accompaniment to grilled or pan-fried steaks. They can also be slowly simmered in wine and herbs and served with a pot roast.

Red Onions Also known as Italian red onion or purple onion, this type ranges in shape from round to oblong and has a pleasant sweetness. For maximum colour, these are best used raw, as cooking causes the colour to bleed, though the flavour does not suffer. For a delicious addition to sandwiches, thinly slice a red onion and marinate in vinegar mixed with salt, pepper and herbs.

Pickling Onions These tiny onions are harvested before they grow larger than 2.5 cm (1 in) in diameter. They have a papery skin which can be difficult to remove (see right). Ideal for pickling, these are delicious when served *glacés*, or glazed, as a vegetable or added whole to soups or stews.

Yellow onion is strong in taste and keeps well; it is available year round

Spring onions should have firm bulbs and green, unblemished stalks

Pickling onions are picked when the plant has just formed bulbs

Shallots

Dry onions *have a papery outer skin and should not show any signs of sprouting*

Red onions *have a vibrant fresh colour and sweet flavour; they are very attractive sliced thinly into rings and used raw as a garnish*

Shallots With a flavour more subtle than that of the onion and less pungent than that of garlic, these are the most refined members of the onion family. Shallots are indispensable for many classic French sauces such as *béarnaise* or *Bercy*. A fine wine vinegar infused with a shallot for several weeks makes a flavoursome dressing for salads. Roasted whole, shallots can also be served alongside roast meats or poultry. Finely chopped (see right), they can be mixed with a fine wine vinegar and seasonings and served alongside raw shellfish, such as oysters or mussels.

Spring Onions Also called salad onions or scallions, these long slender onions are merely immature yellow onion bulbs. Mild and sweet, they are best sliced and added raw to salads, soups or stir-fries. Larger spring onions, with a slightly more developed bulb, can withstand light cooking. The Welsh onion, also called a Japanese bunching onion, is a small bulb with six stems which resembles the spring onion. It can withstand slightly longer cooking and most resembles the leek in flavour.

CHOOSING AND STORING

Most onions are bought dry, with a papery outer skin. This skin, which protects them from moisture loss and light, is formed after harvesting, when they are left to dry. All that onions require for keeping, beyond this protective skin, is a cool, dark, well ventilated place. For maximum storage time, choose onions which are firm and have a crisp, dry skin. Avoid those which are

beginning to sprout or feel hollow as these will not keep; they may already be rotten on the inside. Once cut, the unused half can be wrapped in cling film and refrigerated, but most of the pungency will be gone after one day. Fresh onions can be stored, unwashed, in plastic bags in the refrigerator, where they will keep for about five days, but they are best bought in small quantities for use as needed.

PREPARING ONIONS

Avoid peeling or cutting onions ahead of time as they lose their flavour quite rapidly. It is best to reserve one chopping board for onions (and garlic) as the pungent flavour is easily picked up by more delicate foods.
To prepare an onion: Cut a slice off the top, leaving the root end intact. Peel off the skin and slice the onion in half lengthwise.
To chop an onion: Prepare as above. Place the onion, cut-side down, on a chopping board. With a sharp knife, cut horizontal slices from the top just to the root end but not through it. Cut a series of even, lengthwise slices from the top. Finally, cut the onion crosswise into a dice.
To slice an onion: Prepare as above. Place the onion, cut-side down, on a chopping board and cut thickly or thinly in vertical slices to obtain half-moons.
To cut onion rings: Peel the onion and slice just a bit off one round side to serve as a flat base. Place on a cutting board, cut side down. Hold the onion steady with one hand and cut downwards into thick or thin slices; separate into rings as required.

CHOPPING SHALLOTS AND ONIONS

1 Remove the outer skin with a small knife and separate the bulb into sections.

2 Place on a work surface and slice horizontally towards the root, leaving the end uncut.

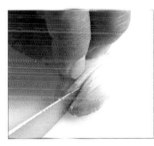

3 Repeat, slicing vertically, still leaving the root end intact and uncut.

4 Holding the root end, chop across to obtain a fine dice. Reserve the root end for stock.

PEELING PICKLING ONIONS

Tiny pickling onions can be difficult to peel. This simple method shows how to remove the skin by plunging the onions in hot water, which softens the skin so it can be slipped off. Once peeled, the onions can be "glazed" for serving alone as a vegetable or adding to stews. Place peeled onions in a small saucepan, add butter and cook gently until golden brown. Add salt, a pinch of sugar and water to cover. Cook over low heat in a covered saucepan until onions are tender.

Soaking
Place the onions in a bowl and add boiling water to cover. Soak for 2 minutes to soften without cooking.

Peeling
Drain the onions. When they are cool enough to handle, trim the root ends and peel away the skins.

GARLIC

One of the most controversial flavourings in the kitchen, garlic rarely leaves anyone indifferent. This distinctive ingredient is either loved or hated. A member of the lily family, garlic is thought to have originated in Central Asia. Each head, or bulb, of garlic is made up of several small cloves which are held together by an outer skin. There are many different varieties grown all over the world, varying in colour, size and flavour. The most common are the white-skinned, pink-skinned and purple-skinned; the latter is held to be the best. Elephant garlic is a giant variety and an ancestor of the modern-day leek. While the cloves are quite large, the flavour is very delicate. Garlic has many reputed medicinal properties, and it was once believed to repel evil spirits. But folklore aside, garlic remains a useful and flavoursome ingredient for the cook.

BUYING AND CHOOSING GARLIC

Garlic is available throughout the year but watch for the plump and succulent bulbs which appear in the shops at the end of spring. The delight of garlic enthusiasts, these are particularly delicious when roasted whole. The most important thing to look for when buying garlic is freshness. The head should be compact and firm to the touch, and it should not be sprouting. For maximum flavour, the peeled cloves should be white; avoid using any that are grey, yellow or stringy. Processed forms of dried garlic include flakes, powder and garlic salt. Garlic purée is also available in tubes and in jars. This is superior to the dried forms, but it is best to use fresh garlic whenever possible. The flavour of fresh garlic is incomparable, and the health benefits are diminished when it is dried.

Garlic powder

Garlic flakes

Pink garlic clove

Pink garlic head

Fresh garlic heads should be firm and compact

White garlic head

STORING GARLIC

Fresh garlic is at its best at the beginning of the season and should not be stored. Decorative, braided strings of garlic are available but these are not recommended for the restrained garlic user as the heads tend to dry out more quickly than they can be used. The most effective means of keeping garlic is in a cool, dry, well-ventilated place away from light. When stored properly, the bulbs should keep for several months.

COOKING WITH GARLIC

The odour of raw garlic tends to linger on kitchen work surfaces, although this can be circumvented by reserving one chopping board for use solely by members of the *Allium* genus (garlic, onions, shallots, etc.). With only one chopping board, the alternative solution is to wrap the garlic cloves in cling film before crushing. However, this method is not practical when chopping. A garlic press is also useful for keeping odours contained, though it can impart a metallic taste to the garlic. The best way to crush garlic is with a mortar and pestle; the cloves are thoroughly crushed, thereby releasing a maximum of flavour, and work surfaces stay odour-free.

Garlic's strong flavour, characteristic of all members of the *Allium* genus, comes from an oil released when a clove is cut. Chopping releases even more, and crushed garlic is the most potent of all. Like its relative the onion, the powerful flavour of garlic is easily subdued by cooking. Garlic cloves can be used whole, crushed or sliced. Quantity is really a matter of personal taste, though garlic should be used sparingly when

White garlic cloves

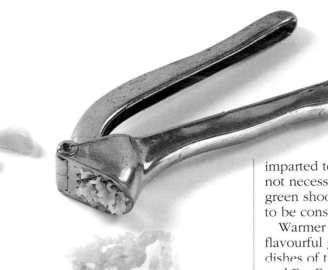

Garlic Press
To ensure that each batch of garlic contains only freshly pressed pieces, thoroughly wash and dry the press after each use. An old toothbrush, reserved especially for this purpose, is very handy.

COOK'S CHOICE
PRESERVED GARLIC

Makes about 60–70 cloves

6–7 whole garlic heads
About 500 ml (16 fl oz) extra-virgin olive oil
Sprigs of fresh thyme
1 bay leaf

Preheat the oven to 190°C (375°F; gas 5). Separate the garlic cloves but do not peel. Toss the garlic in oil just to coat. Wrap in foil and close securely. Roast until tender, 20–30 minutes. When cool enough to handle, place in a sterilized jar with a seal and add oil to cover generously. Add the thyme and bay and seal. Store in a cool, dark place for at least 1 month before using.

combined with delicate flavours because of its dominance. When frying garlic, never let it burn or it will impart a bitter taste to the dish. However, it can be allowed to colour slightly when used to enhance cooking oils, since the clove of garlic is discarded before the dish is served.

Whole heads of garlic can be rubbed with butter or oil and roasted alongside meat or poultry. Serve the roasted garlic cloves in their skins with the main dish, or discard the skins and mash or purée before adding to the sauce or gravy.

When using cooked or raw garlic as an ingredient in dishes that will be stored for several days, be sure to remove any small green shoots found in the centre of the cloves. These shoots have a slightly bitter taste which develops over time and can be imparted to the finished dish. However, it is not necessary to remove these very small green shoots from the cloves if the dish is to be consumed immediately.

Warmer regions tend to produce the most flavourful garlic, so it is no surprise that the dishes of the Mediterranean and the Middle and Far East use large quantities. One classic French recipe calls for forty cloves of garlic. These are roasted with a chicken and then puréed and incorporated into the sauce. The chicken takes on a subtle and delicious garlic perfume, and the sauce is just slightly sweet from having so many slowly roasted cloves of garlic in it.

The Italians use garlic to add a delicate flavour to spinach leaves. First, a crushed and peeled garlic clove is speared on the end of a fork, then olive oil is heated in a frying pan and the clove is rubbed around the pan for a few seconds. Finally, the spinach is added and stirred with the garlic fork. This gives a pleasant garlic taste without being too overpowering. This method is suitable for many other vegetables.

Garlic soup is a favourite in Spain. In this dish, garlic cloves are browned in olive oil until just golden, and then simmered in an earthenware pot with crushed pieces of fried bread, a pinch of paprika and beef stock. When the cloves are tender, an egg is cracked into individual soup bowls and the hot broth is poured over.

In Tunisia, a condiment called *tabil* is made by pounding together garlic, sweet red peppers, fresh chilli peppers, caraway seeds and fresh coriander; this paste is used to enhance the flavour of soups and stews.

Pickled garlic is a popular condiment in China and Thailand. Whole, peeled garlic cloves are preserved in sweet or tart vinegar. This pickle is delicious when added to Asian noodle dishes. It can also be served to accompany roast chicken or cold meats.

The simplest way to enjoy the flavour of garlic is with bread. For a strong garlic taste, blend together crushed garlic, salt and softened butter. Spread on French bread and brown under the grill. A less pungent version can be made with roasted garlic.

PREPARING GARLIC

Place the garlic cloves on the work surface. Lay the flat edge of a knife on top and push down to crush. The garlic will crack out of its skin, making it easier to peel. Alternatively, plunge the cloves into boiling water for 30 seconds. Drain, then peel when cool. Crush with the flat edge of a knife, then slice or chop as required.

A TOUCH OF GARLIC
Rub a crushed clove round the base of a fondue pot to impart a hint of garlic flavour to the ingredients. This is also ideal for ovenproof porcelain dishes and wooden salad bowls.

HORSERADISH, WASABI AND MOOLI

Roots with a peppery bite are an essential flavouring element in the kitchen. Some, like radishes, need no other embellishment; others are more often pounded or grated for sauces or other condiments. Horseradish and radish are members of the same botanical family and are native to Eastern Europe. Wasabi is another root, often called Japanese horseradish, though the two are not related. Fresh wasabi is rare outside Japan, but powder or paste can be bought at delicatessens. These roots are useful for stimulating the palate, which makes them ideal for hors d'oeuvres.

Horseradish Although the young, tender leaves of this plant can be eaten in salads, it is the root which is most often used. When buying fresh, choose firm roots without any blemishes and avoid those roots which are sprouting or slightly green as they may be bitter. To prepare fresh horseradish, peel the skin down to the flesh; peel only the amount necessary. Grate or shred in a food processor; using a hand grater can produce very strong fumes, causing burning and watering eyes. Grated fresh horseradish loses its pungency quickly, so only prepare in small quantities; it can also be frozen.

Dried horseradish flakes can be reconstituted and used as fresh, but, more commonly, horseradish is found in the form of a prepared sauce or relish.

Wasabi This root has a fierce aroma and a very biting taste. Sashimi, the Japanese dish of raw fish, is usually served with grated wasabi, or wasabi paste mixed with a soy dipping sauce. For sushi, wasabi paste is used for flavour and to help the fish adhere to the rice filling. Wasabi paste can be served with fish or meat dishes.

Grated horse-radish *should be obtained just prior to use; combine it with cream, mayonnaise or vinegar for a relish*

Horseradish sauce

Horseradish root *contains oils similar to mustard seed and has a powerful, painfully hot taste*

Wasabi powder

MIXING WASABI

Wasabi paste is available at Oriental shops, though it does not keep as well as the ground form. To prepare, mix equal quantities of powder and tepid water and stir to blend. Leave for at least 10 minutes to allow the flavour to develop. Serve with sushi or sashimi, or add in small quantities to barbecue sauces or mayonnaise-based salad dressings.

Wasabi paste

Mooli Also known as daikon or Japanese radish, this is simply a white, winter radish. It has a fresh, slightly peppery taste and a clean, crisp texture which makes it an ideal salad ingredient, although it can also be steamed or stir-fried. Available throughout the year, it is at the peak of its flavour during the winter months. Choose roots which are

firm to the touch and slightly shiny, and be sure to use within one week as mooli does not keep well.

In Japan, where mooli is most common, it is shredded or grated and served alongside raw fish dishes. Mixed with lemon juice or vinegar, it is used to accompany grilled fish. It is also sliced or cut into decorative shapes or carved for elaborate garnishes. The Chinese incorporate it into a sweet-and-sour pickle. In its pickled form, mooli is called *takuan* in Japan and *kimchi* in Korea. Slivered mooli can be used to enliven clear soups and stews and can be sprinkled over vegetable dishes. Shredded mooli is used also to tenderize octopus.

Red, White and Black Radish Salad

Serves 4

1 tbsp rice wine vinegar
1/2 tsp salt
2 tbsp soured cream
2 tsp clear honey
Freshly ground black pepper
6–8 large red radishes
1 small mooli, about 15 cm (6 in) long, peeled
1 small black radish
1 small red onion, finely chopped
2 spring onions, thinly sliced
Lettuce and snipped chives for garnish

In a small bowl, combine the vinegar and salt and stir to dissolve. Add the soured cream, honey and pepper to taste. Cover with cling film and refrigerate for 2–3 hours to allow the flavours to blend. Slice the red radishes and mooli crosswise into paper-thin slices. Peel most of the skin from the black radish, leaving several thin stripes for colour; slice thinly crosswise. Combine the radishes and onions and toss with the dressing. Serve on a bed of lettuce, garnished with chives. Use it as an unusual appetizer or salad accompaniment to an Oriental-style meal.

Peeled and sliced finely, the flesh is ideal combined with other vegetables

Mooli shapes

Pickled mooli

Whole fresh mooli *is milder than other radish types and is often found in Oriental food stores*

RADISHES

Radishes range in colour from white to red to black, and the varieties are numerous. The common red radish is delicious in salads but it can also be cooked. When stir-fried, red radishes turn a stunning aubergine colour and make an ideal accompaniment for roast meat. The black radish, with crisp, white flesh, is gaining popularity outside its native Eastern Europe. Its pungent flavour is best when eaten raw. The thick skin can be left on when thinly sliced, otherwise it is better peeled.

Black radish

Red radishes

OLIVES

The domesticated olive tree, *Olea europaea,* has flourished throughout the Mediterranean region since pre-historic times and produces one of the oldest known fruits. Olives, olive leaves and olive oil are all mentioned in ancient Greek and Roman writings, as well as in the Bible, and many olive motifs can be discerned on ancient Egyptian artifacts. A beautiful tree with silvery green leaves, the olive can continue growing for hundreds of years. It does not need rich, fertile soil and grows happily on stony, mountainous ground which is unsuitable for other crops. An evergreen, it flowers in springtime and produces berries which, depending on the weather, can be harvested from October throughout the winter.

Mediterranean countries are the major olive producers, with Spain and Italy providing more than 50 per cent of the crop, but the olive tree flourishes wherever a Mediterranean-type climate exists, and both California and Mexico have large olive-producing industries as well.

TYPES OF OLIVES

Most olives and olive oils come from either the *Sativa,* the most widely cultivated olive tree, or the *Oleaster,* the wild tree which still is confined primarily to its native Mediterranean region.

The difference between green and black olives is ripeness. Unripe olives are green, and fully ripe olives are black. Olives cannot be eaten straight from the branch; they must first be cured to remove their bitterness. There are two main curing methods: one for green olives, the other for black. Green olives must be soaked in a lye solution before brining, while black olives can be brined straight away.

Olives are generally cured whole, but they are often cracked to speed up the curing process as the bitter juices are more easily extracted from bruised fruit. Varieties such as the Spanish *manzanilla* and the

Green olives
are picked while they are still immature

Black olives
are fully ripened fruit that can be brined straight away

French *picholine* are better picked green, while others, such as the Greek *kalamata* and the tiny French *niçoise,* are best when harvested fully ripe.

Spain produces mostly green olives, which are often stoned and stuffed with various ingredients including almonds, pimientos, anchovies, capers or onions.

Italy produces mainly black olives such as the acidic *liguaria,* the mild *ponentine,* the wrinkled *gaeta* and the salty *lugano.*

California's most popular olive is the *sevillano,* which can be whole or cracked, and is usually salt-cured.

The Moroccans have a flavourful purple-mauve olive, which is picked when only half-ripe, and cracked before curing.

The most popular Greek olive is the deep purple *kalamata,* which is brine-cured. The plump, tasty black olives from Megara in Attiki are cured in salt.

French green olives

Spanish black olives

Greek green olives

Italian black olives

French black olives

Spanish green olives

Greek black olives

Italian green olives

Wooden olive scoop
Traditionally made from olive wood, this scoop has holes to serve up the olives without their brine or oil.

COOKING WITH OLIVES

The quintessential cocktail snack, olives have many other uses in the kitchen. Olives can decorate canapés, pizzas and buffet table presentations, and they feature in dishes such as *salade niçoise* and Greek-style salads. In Italy, France and North Africa, olives are paired with poultry, cooked slowly in meat stews or baked in breads.

Puréed olives, mixed with a little olive oil, are a useful condiment that adds an olive flavour without the inconvenience of the stone. The purée can be mixed into meat stews, vegetable casseroles and tomato-based sauces or rubbed on roasts before cooking. On its own, it is a light and flavoursome sauce for pasta, hot or cold.

Tapenade, the *provençal* black olive spread (see right), is the classic puréed olive mixture. Serve it accompanied by grilled French bread and chilled rosé wine.

FLAVOURING OLIVES

Olives packed in brine can be enhanced simply by storing them in olive oil. First, drain and rinse the olives well to remove all traces of brine. Then, put them in a sterilized jar and add olive oil to cover.

For more flavour, add herbs and spices to the oil. The process is the same as above, simply add the flavourings before pouring in the oil. For example, combine olive oil with a little red wine or balsamic vinegar. Put the olives in the jar, layer evenly with a few strips of lemon rind, a crushed garlic clove, some dried oregano and some lightly crushed peppercorns and pour over the oil and vinegar. Leave to mellow for one week before serving. Many herb and spice combinations are possible, but for an authentic taste, marry olives with flavours from their country of origin. Lemon peel and coriander seeds are good with Greek olives, while *herbes de Provence* (see page 51) enhance French olives, and garlic and black pepper with a few anchovies will set off any Spanish olives.

Olive bread *is made with both olive oil and chopped olives*

Makes about 300 g (10 oz)

150 g (5 oz) stoned black olives, preferably niçoise
8 anchovy fillets
60 g (2 oz) capers, drained
2–3 garlic cloves, peeled
125 ml (4 fl oz) extra-virgin olive oil
Freshly ground black pepper

Put the olives, anchovies, capers and garlic in a food processor and mix until just blended. With the machine running, slowly pour in the oil. (For a coarser mixture, whisk in the oil by hand.) Season with pepper to taste. Store in the refrigerator, tightly covered, for 2–3 days. Use this highly flavoured purée with toast, hard-boiled eggs, raw vegetables or pasta.

Tapenade on toast *makes a spicy snack and is a useful first course in an Italian meal*

STUFFING OLIVES

Olives with a flavoured butter stuffing make an attractive and delicious starter. For example, blend 125 g (4 oz) butter, 2 tbsp finely chopped anchovy fillets, a squeeze of lemon juice, and freshly ground black pepper.

1 *Place an olive in the stoning tool with the stalk end pointing up. Squeeze the handles together to extract.*

2 *Place the anchovy butter in a piping bag and carefully fill the centre of each olive with a rosette of flavoured butter.*

Mediterranean-style pizza *is dependent upon black, sun-cured niçoise olives for its distinctive taste*

TOMATOES

Both fruit and vegetable, the tomato is surely one of the most versatile flavouring ingredients. Brought from South America to Europe in the 16th century, the tomato was quickly integrated into the cuisines of the Mediterranean countries. The Northern Europeans, however, regarded the tomato with some caution, fearing it poisonous, and it was not until the 19th century that the tomato became an acceptable food in the northerly climes. Today, in the fruit and vegetable category, worldwide consumption of the tomato is second only to the potato. Tomatoes are at their peak of flavour when picked ripe off the vine, and can be grown successfully in gardens in a warm, sunny climate. Those less fortunate must content themselves with shop-bought tomatoes, often picked before maturity to prevent spoilage during transport.

When obtainable, the best way to enjoy the flavour of a fresh, ripe tomato is to serve it sliced as a salad, drizzled with a little olive oil and perhaps a scattering of fresh herbs. Long, slow cooking is the best way to appreciate less-than-ripe tomatoes. But whether sliced or whole, cooked or raw, alone or combined with other foods, the tomato has earned its place in cuisines around the world.

In many countries, tomato growers are cultivating varieties with an emphasis on taste rather than looks. There are also quite a few interesting hybrids, which range from round to long, and from green to yellow. The following types are widely available and serve all manner of culinary purposes.

Beefsteak Tomatoes An extra large variety of tomato with a firm texture, these are best for eating raw in salads and sandwiches. Their size also makes them an excellent choice for stuffing, both cooked and raw.

Plum Tomatoes Most popular in Italy, these elongated tomatoes are available fresh only in season. Their dense flesh, which has few seeds, and excellent flavour, make them particularly well suited for long cooking in sauces and stews.

Common Red Tomatoes Available all year round, these are at their most flavoursome during the summer. An all-purpose tomato, these are good for slicing into salads or sandwiches. After being peeled and seeded (see below), these can also be used for soups and sauces.

Cherry Tomatoes Small but packed with flavour, these can be added whole to salads or skewered for kebabs. Hollowed out and stuffed, they make a very attractive and delicious item for cocktail hors d'oeuvres or the buffet table. For a delicious accompaniment to grilled meats, sauté briefly in olive oil and sprinkle with fresh thyme.

Yellow Tomatoes Less acidic than red tomatoes, these also have a less pronounced flavour. Available in several shapes and sizes, they can be substituted for red tomatoes in any cold dish or combined with red tomatoes for an interesting contrast. Small pear-shaped yellow tomatoes make an attractive garnish when combined with other miniature vegetables.

Common red tomato *is an all-purpose fruit good for cooking and eating*

Plum tomato

PREPARING TOMATOES

1 Bring a pan of unsalted water to the boil. With a small knife, loosen a column of flesh around the core of the tomato and remove it.

2 Cut a small cross on the base. Immerse in a saucepan of boiling water. Lift out gently as soon as the skin starts to curl away.

3 As soon as the tomato is cool enough to handle, peel away the loosened skin with the tip of a small knife.

4 Cut the tomato in half and squeeze the halves to extract the seeds. Scrape away any remaining seeds with the tip of a knife.

Salad Tomatoes

Though tomatoes lend themselves admirably to any number of cooked dishes, their flavour is best appreciated in the raw state. Along with taste, they add colour and texture to salads, and as the various varieties attest, a size dimension.

Beefsteak tomatoes *are large and substantial; sliced into rings or chunks they provide meaty pieces*

Cherry tomatoes *are the midgets of the family and are used whole*

Yellow tomatoes *are valuable for providing visual appeal and are available in round and pear shapes*

COOK'S CHOICE
TOMATO SAUCE WITH HERBS

Makes about 1 litre
(1³/₄ pt)

2–3 tbsp extra-virgin olive oil
1 onion, chopped
Salt
Freshly ground black pepper
2 garlic cloves, chopped
2.5 kg (5 lb) tomatoes, peeled, seeded and cored
250 g (8 oz) fresh mixed herbs such as basil, oregano, thyme, marjoram, savory, parsley, rosemary, sage or bay leaf

In a saucepan, combine the oil and onions over low heat and cook until soft. Season to taste, add the remaining ingredients and 250 ml (8 fl oz) water. Bring to a simmer, then cover and cook gently over low heat for about 1 hour. Purée in a food processor fitted with a metal blade. Return to a clean pan and cook, uncovered, to reduce, about 1 hour. Taste for seasoning. Serve the sauce immediately or freeze. This makes an ideal accompaniment for a variety of pasta dishes or can be used to top a meatloaf.

TOMATO PRODUCTS

While tomatoes are available year round, they are not always at the peak of flavour. Tomato products, however, are an adequate substitute in cooked dishes. Canned plum tomatoes come either whole or chopped, and can be enhanced with paste or purée. Passata is a smooth, sieved sauce for use in hot or cold dishes. Sun-dried tomatoes have a strong, slightly smoky flavour. In small quantities they make an excellent addition to any cooked dish.

Chopped canned tomatoes

Sun-dried tomatoes

Tomato purée from a tube

Whole canned tomato

Canned tomato purée

Passata

CITRUS FRUIT

The cultivation of citrus fruits goes back at least 2,000 years. Originally from India and China, oranges and lemons gradually worked their way west. The ancient Greeks valued lemons both for their medicinal properties and their culinary contributions. Oranges were brought to Europe during the Crusades, and cultivation began in warm regions where the trees then flourished. In the 16th century, the Spanish took oranges with them to the New World, and groves were planted in temperate areas such as Florida, California, and many parts of South America. Centuries of cultivation and cross-breeding have resulted in many varieties and hybrids. In the kitchen, this diversity translates into an ingredient which lends its skin, flesh and juice to a variety of culinary preparations.

Valencia orange *is a sweet orange variety that is grown in many places round the world but not in Valencia, Spain*

Satsuma *is a Japanese seedless mandarin with a green tinge to its skin*

Clementines *are Algerian in origin and a cross between the bitter orange and tangerine*

Grapefruit *A yellow rind covers a white-fleshed fruit*

Limes

Mineola *are pip free grapefruit/tangerine crosses*

Lemons *have many uses in cooking; the juice, flesh and skin are valuable flavourings*

Ruby red grapefruit *produces an attractive juice but fewer seeds being present rather than a pink colour indicates sweetness*

The citrus family *This group of fruits is constantly being enlarged by the many hybrids developed for taste, lack of pips and ease of peeling. Citrus fruits add colour and flavour to many dishes both sweet and savoury*

Kumquats *are Eastern in origin but now grown mainly in Brazil; they are the smallest citrus fruits*

TYPES OF CITRUS FRUIT

Oranges The first cultivated oranges to flourish in Italy and Spain were, like their early ancestors, quite bitter. Available only for a short period in winter, the modern Seville orange is probably the closest in flavour to those early oranges. Seville oranges are much sought after for marmalades and sauces, where their tang acts as a foil to rich meats, such as goose or duck. Blood oranges, with a delightful tart-sweet flavour and mottled crimson-orange colour, are available only in season, which is generally in the winter months. Their red juice makes them invaluable for many preparations. Freshly squeezed, they produce an invigorating and beautiful breakfast drink, or a delicious addition to desserts and fruit salads. The skin of blood oranges may or may not be speckled with red – this depends on which side of the tree they grow. Nor does the skin colour necessarily reflect the colour of the flesh. Sweet oranges fall roughly into three categories: Jaffas are renowned for their juiciness, flavour and easy-to-remove peel; thin-skinned Valencia oranges are also full of juice, and navel oranges – easy to peel, juicy and virtually pip-free – can be distinguished by their navel-like growth at one end.

Mandarins This family of small, aromatic citrus fruits with easy-to-peel skins includes many varieties, such as satsumas and clementines. Satsumas are Japanese in origin. Less round than an orange, their light-coloured skin peels away very easily, making them a simple and delicious snack. Clementines – hybrids of the bitter orange and the tangerine – look much like small

Orange cups
Hollowed-out oranges make an excellent container for orange ice cream or sorbet.

oranges. Peeled, segmented mandarins are often canned in a sugar syrup, and they take well to jams and preserves. Their small segments make them ideal for fruit salads. Mincolas are a hybrid of the tangerine and grapefruit. Similar to oranges in appearance, they combine good flavour with the advantage of no pips. Tangelos are a commonly available fruit and are a cross between tangerines and other citrus fruit.

Pomelos These are the largest members of the citrus group with thick yellow-green skins and thick inner membranes. Not as juicy as the grapefruit, their flesh is very refreshing.

Grapefruits A newcomer to the citrus family, the grapefruit was developed from the pomelo during the 19th century. Grapefruits are quite large, with an aromatic skin and a sharp but not sour flavour. Pink grapefruits are much sweeter. The large Ugli (pronounced oo-gli) is a cross between a mandarin orange and grapefruit, but it most resembles the grapefruit in flavour. It is delicious sprinkled with sugar and baked. The Ugli can be used interchangeably with grapefruit in most recipes.

Lemons This citrus fruit is almost unpalatable when raw, but its kitchen uses are many. The juice, flesh and skin are valuable flavourings; the acidic juice can also be used as a cooking agent (see page 175). Segments and julienned peel can be used to garnish dishes, both sweet and savoury. The juice can be added to salad dressings or used to deglaze pans (see page 249).

Limes While this ingredient typifies the cuisines of tropical climates, it is not as valuable overall as the lemon. The juice can be used to flavour mousses, soufflés and drinks, and the peel can be candied for a garnish. Limes are good when used in combination with other citrus fruits.

KUMQUATS

The small golden kumquat is unique among citrus fruits. While most have a bitter skin, kumquats are more sweet on the outside than within. This olive-shaped fruit can be eaten whole, either raw or cooked. The heat of cooking releases the full aroma of the skin, making them a welcome addition to braised duck or pork dishes. Dipped into a sugar syrup (see page 194), kumquats make a refreshing dessert to follow a rich meal. They are ideal for candying or preserving in syrup.

USING CITRUS SKIN

When a recipe calls for the zest of a citrus fruit, it is referring to the colourful, outer part of the skin and not the inner white part, known as the pith.

Cutting julienne
Peel strips of zest with a vegetable peeler. Slice strips lengthwise into thin, julienne strips.

Zesting
Working from one end, hold zesting tool firmly against the fruit and pull down towards the other end

Drying skin
Cut the skin (peel) into strips and leave to dry. Use to flavour meat or fish stews, mulled drinks or sugar.

Citrus Fruit in the Kitchen

Aromatic zests, tart juices and fresh bright colour are the contributions of citrus fruit to the cook. Cuisines the world over make use of citrus fruits to season and enhance savoury dishes. Along with salt, freshly ground black pepper and olive oil, a squeeze of fresh lemon juice is often the only other seasoning required for grilled foods such as chicken or fish, or cooked vegetables such as broccoli or carrots. *Crêpes Suzette* and *tarte au citron* are well-loved citrus desserts from France, and North America has its Key lime pie. Candied citrus peel is an essential part of the traditional Italian Christmas cake, *panforte*. But whatever the recipe, an orange or a lemon in the fruit bowl will always offer the cook a world of flavouring and garnishing possibilities.

Choosing and Storing

Citrus fruits are available all year round, but the autumn and winter months provide the best quality and the biggest selection. When choosing, the same rules apply for all citrus fruits. Fresh, top-quality fruit should have a light sheen with no signs of bruising. The skin should be tight with an even grain. Avoid any fruit which is dry and shrivelled. Fruit which feels heavy for its size is a good sign of juicy flesh on the inside. Citrus fruits generally keep from three days to one week at room temperature, and anywhere from two weeks to one month in the refrigerator. As the peel is often called for in recipes, it is best to choose untreated or organically grown fruit. When in doubt, blanch the peel in boiling water for a minute or so to reduce the effects and bitter taste of pesticides or colouring agents. Chemical treatment only affects the skin and should not be able to penetrate through to the flesh.

Seviche

Raw fish marinated in citrus juice is called seviche. Fish should be very fresh, and many varieties can be used. Oily fish, such as mackerel and salmon, are delicious when paired with the tang of citrus juice.

Cooking with Citrus Fruit

Citrus fruits contain varying degrees of sugar and acid. However, while an acidic tang is characteristic, sugar predominates in most – oranges, tangerines and grapefruits, for example. The flesh can be appreciated in its natural state or use segments (see below) in a variety of preparations. The juice is both a seasoning and a cooking agent, and the zest offers a colourful and flavour-filled garnish.

Flesh A salad of grapefruit segments, avocados and smoked salmon makes an unusual and mouth-watering starter, as does a savoury salad of oranges, thinly sliced onions and olives, dressed with salt and extra-virgin olive oil. In sweet dishes, the acidic nature of citrus fruits is best tamed by poaching in a light syrup (see page 196). Serve poached orange segments or slices alongside a bitter chocolate mousse, and garnish with a sprinkling of

Preparing Citrus Fruit

Peeling zest
With a vegetable peeler, slice away the zest, taking care not to include the pith. If skin is treated, blanch before use.

Removing inner skin
Cut a slice from both ends. Slice downwards, taking care to remove all visible traces of skin and pith.

Cutting segments
Remove inner skin. Cut into a segment, separating flesh from membrane. Slice the other side and dislodge.

Slicing fruit
After removing inner skin, place the fruit on its side. With a sharp knife, cut downwards into thin slices.

candied julienne peel. Even tangy lemon segments can be used when poached; arrange them on top of a lemon curd tart and glaze with strained apricot preserves (see page 258) for a refreshing conclusion to a meal or tea-time treat.

Juice For a maximum of juice, it is best to use fruit at room temperature. Before juicing, roll the fruit, pressing down with the palm of your hand; this breaks some of the inner membranes, helping to extract as much juice as possible. Once squeezed, the uses for citrus juice are many.

Orange and grapefruit juice are almost universal breakfast items, and *citron pressé* is a classic summertime drink. Combine orange juice with garlic and freshly grated ginger and use as a marinade for grilled chicken. Or, prepare a stir-fry of pork tenderloin marinated in orange juice, soy sauce, crushed chillies and fresh garlic. Lemon juice can be combined with grated lemon zest, rosemary, garlic and olive oil for an all-purpose meat seasoning. A simple dressing of fresh lemon juice, olive oil, salt and black pepper can be used to season salads, poached or grilled fish, or steamed vegetables. Most fruit salads also benefit from a squeeze of fresh lemon juice; the sweetness of the fruit combines with the subtle acidity of the citrus juice, making for a more complex and delicious flavour.

The acidic nature of citrus fruit juice can be exploited for marinades and "raw cooking," and lemon and lime juice are used as a cooking agent in many Latin and South American countries. Known most commonly as *seviche*, fish is combined with citrus juice, chillies, onions and varying herbs and spices, and then left to "cook." After about five to six hours of marinating, the fish turns opaque – as it does when cooked by conventional heating methods – and is ready to eat. Marinating time depends on the type and quantity of fish. Citric acid also has a bleaching effect, which is useful with ingredients that discolour rapidly when sliced, such as apples, artichokes or celeriac, or when pristine whiteness is required of ingredients such as mushrooms.

Skin It is the zest which contains all the aromatic citrus oils. Like other vegetables and fruits, citrus fruits are often treated with chemical pesticides and dyes to enhance their natural colouring. While this rarely affects the fruit on the inside, it does affect the skin. Choose untreated citrus fruit when preparing recipes which call for the zest. If the fruit is treated, blanch zest before use. For easy removal, place the zest slices in a sieve or a muslin bag and immerse in boiling water for 1–2 minutes.

Grated lemon, lime or orange zest can be added to sauces or marinades for a hint of citrus tang. Thickly sliced zest can be dried and added to a bouquet garni or a jar of sugar. The flesh can also be scooped out, leaving a container for sorbet, ice cream, or fruit or vegetable salads.

The ideal garnish for ice creams, tarts and cakes, julienned citrus zest can be boiled in grenadine syrup for a splash of bright pink colour. Freshly grated lemon zest is useful for marinades and is essential in the classic Italian seasoning mixture *gremolada* (see page 44), which is sprinkled over braised veal shanks just before serving. It is also delicious combined with freshly ground pepper, salt, olive oil and Parmesan cheese for a simple pasta sauce.

CITRUS FRUIT GARNISHES

Sweet or savoury dishes flavoured with citrus fruit can be garnished with them too.

Place on top of food, or on plates for an attractive buffet presentation.

Double twist   **Segments**   **Multicolour julienne**   **Triple butterfly**

NUTS

In technical terms, a nut is a one-celled fruit encased in a dry shell. And while acorns, chestnuts and hazelnuts are true nuts, the term is also loosely applied to seeds or edible fruit kernels which are enclosed in a hard shell – almonds and cashews, for example. Nuts have been used as a source of food and oil for centuries. As early as 200 B.C., the Romans distributed sugar-coated almonds on special occasions. When the Spanish carried their culinary traditions to the Americas, they found the Aztecs already using peanuts and pecans. A predominant ingredient in the cuisines of the Middle East, nuts such as almonds and pistachios feature in both savoury sauces, such as Turkish *tarator* made with walnuts, and in many sweets, such as *baklava*. Peanuts and cashews are used in stir-fries throughout Indonesia and the Far East. In African cuisines, nuts are a staple, and hazelnuts and almonds enter into recipes for many European desserts and sweets. In many savoury dishes, nuts have an affinity with spicy curries and chillies; in sweet dishes, they go well with cinnamon, honey and chocolate.

TYPES OF NUTS

Almonds Related to the peach tree, the almond tree is a native of the eastern Mediterranean region and has been cultivated for thousands of years.
There are two types of almond – sweet and bitter – and the latter is often confused with apricot kernels. Often called Chinese almonds, apricot kernels have a flavour remarkably similar to sweet almonds, and they are used to flavour many products such as almond essence and almond-flavoured liqueurs. When raw, almonds can be toxic in large quantities and must be blanched or roasted beforehand. Sweet almonds are used whole or ground in cakes, pastries, butters, pralines, fillings and nougat. Chopped, diced, slivered and flaked, they are used for coating and garnishing. They also appear in many savoury dishes, especially those with chicken, fish and rice.
Brazil Nuts Not actually nuts, these seeds come from the tropical rain forests of Brazil. The edible part is one of two dozen seeds contained in a hard, brown

Cashews

Slivered nuts

Ground nuts

Walnuts *contain kernels that are hard to peel; the skin is usually left on for eating*

Hazelnuts

Pecans *feature in the cooking of the American South, and are found in cakes and pastries or stuffings for poultry*

Flaked nuts

Brazil nuts

Pistachios

Almonds

Chopped nuts

three-sided shell. Brazil nuts have a very high oil content which gives a richness to their slightly sweet flavour but also limits storage time. Large Brazil nuts can be grated into cake batters, or dipped in chocolate to serve as a sweet (see page 182).

Cashews The cashew tree is native to South America, but it now flourishes in many parts of Southeast Asia and India. Roasted, salted cashews are a popular cocktail item. In cookery, whole cashews feature prominently in Indian vegetarian dishes and Chinese stir-fries, and ground cashews are often used to thicken curries.

Hazelnuts Also known as cob-nuts or filberts, these are small, round, brown nuts. Their sweet, rich flavour lends itself well to all kinds of pastries. Freshly ground hazelnuts are an excellent addition to cake or biscuit batters, or they can be folded into meringues before baking. Chocolate and hazelnuts marry very well. In savoury dishes, chopped or flaked hazelnuts can be sprinkled over steamed or boiled vegetables. Hazelnut oil (see page 226) is very rich, and it makes an excellent addition to salad dressings or sauces, especially those served with veal or duck.

Pecans A type of hickory nut, these are native to the American south, though they are now cultivated in parts of Australia. The growing, harvesting, shelling and sorting of these nuts is a lengthy and complicated process, which accounts for their high cost. Pecans have a subtle, refined flavour; this is

surprising, considering that they have one of the highest fat contents of any vegetable food. Pecan pie is an American classic, and these nuts can also be used in cakes, ice creams and stuffings.

Pistachios Native to the Middle East, the green pistachio nut is sold in its shell, or shelled and blanched. Irresistible as a cocktail accompaniment, pistachios are also a versatile ingredient. Their vibrant green colour makes them an ideal garnish and a colourful addition to sausages, meat pâtés and other charcuterie items. Chopped pistachios are essential in Middle Eastern rice dishes, and in Greek, Turkish and Arabic pastries. They are used in all kinds of baking and make a delicious ice cream.

Walnuts The walnut tree is native to Asia, but it now grows in many other countries. French walnuts are held to be the finest, especially those which come from the Dordogne region in the southwest. The colour of a walnut shell reflects its quality; the lighter the colour the higher the grade. Popular as a snack, walnuts also make an excellent addition to fruit and vegetable salads, stuffings and a myriad of baked goods. Ground walnuts can be added to sweet pastry doughs and they also enter into many sauces from cuisines around the world: the Turkish *tarator*, the Mexican *chiles en nogada* and the Italian *sugo di noci*. Walnuts also produce a flavoursome and highly prized oil (see page 227), which makes an excellent salad dressing.

Peanuts are not a nut at all, but a pulse. They grow on long tendrils, just below the ground, which is why they are sometimes called groundnuts. Native to Brazil, peanuts are now grown in many temperate areas of the world. Peanut butter is a popular product in North America, where it is added to many baked goods, such as Peanut Butter Cookies and Peanut Butter Fudge, though it is most often combined with jam or jelly for children's sandwiches.

1 Place about 125 g (4 oz) blanched, lightly roasted fresh peanuts in a food processor and mix. Add 1–2 tbsp oil.

2 Process until the peanuts reach the desired consistency, either smooth or slightly crunchy. This will make about 60 g (2 oz) of peanut butter.

CHESTNUT PRODUCTS

Chestnuts are available bottled and canned, either whole or puréed. Sweetened chestnut purée topped with a dollop of crème fraîche (see page 235) is a French dessert classic known as *Mont Blanc*. It can also be used as a crêpe or sponge cake-filling. Dried whole chestnuts can be reconstituted by soaking.

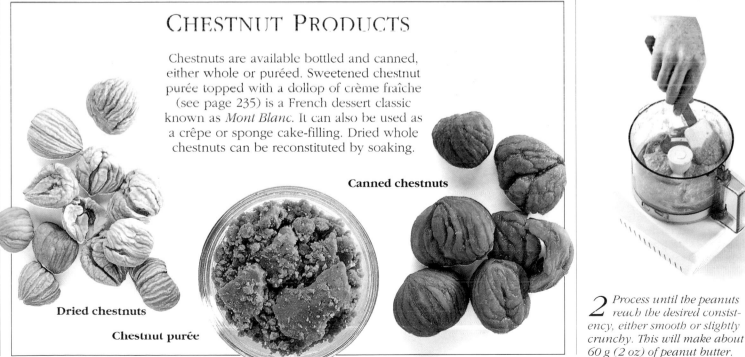

Dried chestnuts

Chestnut purée

Canned chestnuts

CHOCOLATE

The botanical name for the cocoa tree, *Theobroma cacao,* translates as "food of the gods," and few would disagree. When Hernán Cortés conquered Mexico in 1519, the Aztecs were already making a drink, called *chocolatl,* from the bean of this tree. In the centuries since then, the versatile cocoa bean has continued to provide pleasure as a drink, snack, sweet, savoury flavouring, simple garnish and elaborate decoration. Chocolate has a flavour that combines well with many others. Hazelnuts and almonds are a good match, as are spices such as cinnamon, nutmeg and cloves. Mint is a classic partner, as are raspberries and oranges, and vanilla enhances its flavour. Even coffee seems more satisfying and full-flavoured when accompanied by a chocolate. For added sophistication, chocolate desserts can be laced with brandy or other liqueurs.

PRODUCTION

The cocoa tree thrives in equatorial climates. Thus, the finest bean, *criollo,* comes from Central and South America and India. The largest crop comes from the *forastero* beans that are grown in Africa and Brazil. After harvesting, the beans are fermented to remove bitterness and develop the flavour content, and then dried. Roasting follows, which exposes the inner section, called the nib. Various bean nibs are blended to obtain the desired flavour and then ground to a paste that is more commonly known as *cocoa mass* – the heart of chocolate's flavour. This paste is enhanced with sugar, cocoa butter and flavourings, and passed through a series of rollers for blending. Thin, dry sheets of chocolate are obtained, but these must be "conched," a process developed by Rodolphe Lindt in 1879. Conching is a lengthy and costly procedure that enhances the texture and flavour. Inferior quality chocolate is made by replacing the cocoa butter with a synthetic substitute, and replacing the conching process by the addition of soy lecithin for smoothness.

STORING AND CHOOSING

Chocolate and cocoa powder should be stored in a cool, dry place. Chocolate should not be refrigerated; the temperature is too low and the environment too moist. Refrigeration also encourages sugar bloom, those greyish-white streaks which appear on the surface. Fat bloom is similar, though it is caused by improper heating during either manufacture or storage. Bloom is the result of temperature fluctuations and reflects improper storage. It will not affect the taste, but it is unsightly. Although costly, plain chocolate that has been manufactured with care is always the best choice for eating and cooking.

TYPES OF CHOCOLATE

Chocolate can be unsweetened, bittersweet and bitter, plain and milk. With the exception of white chocolate, eating and cooking chocolate are made from cocoa mass that is blended with cocoa butter, sugar and flavourings, and this is called cocoa solids.

The final taste of the chocolate does depend on the type, but the quality depends on several factors. Each type of bean has a particular taste, so individual bean types and the way in which they are blended have a direct impact on flavour. Equally important are the fermentation and roasting processes, as well as the method of manufacture.

Unsweetened Chocolate Also known as *baker's chocolate*, this type is cocoa solids without any additional sugar or flavourings. Used largely by manufacturers of chocolate products, it is bitter, grainy and troublesome to melt. It can be difficult for the home cook to obtain. In recipes that call for unsweetened chocolate, substitute 3 tablespoons unsweetened cocoa powder plus 1 tablespoon unsalted butter for each 30 g (1 oz) unsweetened chocolate.

Plain Chocolate Containing a minimum of 43 per cent cocoa solids, this type also includes bittersweet and bitter chocolate; the latter has the lowest sugar content. Recipes that call for plain chocolate will be most successful when made with a chocolate that contains a minimum of 50 per cent cocoa solids, though some chocolates can contain as much as 70 per cent.

Milk Chocolate As the name implies, this type contains milk along with the cocoa solids. It was developed in Switzerland in 1875. At that time, some of the cocoa solids were replaced with condensed milk, though nowadays it is made more frequently

Cocoa powder

Chocolate square

Chocolate chips

Chocolate shavings

Plain chocolate *made from quality beans, with a high percentage of cocoa solids, is the preferred type for cooking and eating*

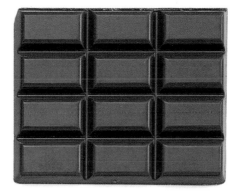

Milk chocolate *does not have enough cocoa solids to be used successfully in cooking and baking, except in specially adapted recipes*

Chocolate pieces *Manufacturers score their products in a variety of shapes and weights.*

with dried milk. When cooking it should not be used in place of plain chocolate as it has a lower percentage of cocoa solids and the flavour of the finished dish will suffer. Milk chocolate is more sensitive to heat and is often harder to work with.

Couverture Chocolate The high proportion of cocoa butter in this type ensures a glossy appearance and smooth texture in finished dishes. It is used primarily by professional confectioners to coat and dip chocolates, hence the French name, *couverture,* or covering. Because of its high cocoa butter content, it should be "tempered" before use. Tempering involves heating and cooling the chocolate, which allows it to retain its gloss after hardening. Melted chocolate is warmed up to 46°C (115°F) then spread thin on a work surface and stirred until it is almost cool enough to set, about 27°C (80°F). Then the

chocolate is scraped back into a bowl and heated until it reaches 32°C (90°F). Only couverture will give satisfactory results when tempered.

Cocoa Powder With only 18 per cent cocoa butter, this is less fatty than all other chocolates and is generally unsweetened. In 1882, C. J. Van Houten invented the cocoa press, which performs the task of extracting all the cocoa butter from the roasted beans. This produces dry cakes of cocoa which are then ground into powder. "Dutching" is another Van Houten innovation, developed later, which neutralizes cocoa's acid, making cocoa powder easier to dissolve.

Drinking Chocolate This is a sweetened product for use as a hot drink preparation. It should not be substituted for cocoa powder as the added sugar and flavourings will interfere with the recipe.

Cocoa butter

White chocolate

HOT CHOCOLATE

For most, hot milk flavoured with sweetened cocoa powder is a familiar and well-loved beverage. When made with whole milk and high quality cocoa powder, this can be a satisfying and delicious treat, however, the flavour and texture of hot chocolate made from melted chocolate is incomparable. Choose a plain chocolate with at least 50 per cent cocoa solids. Finely chop 250 g (8 oz) chocolate and melt. Bring 1 litre (1¾ pt) milk to the boil. Whisk half of the milk into the chocolate until frothy. Add sugar to taste. Over low heat, slowly add the remaining milk, whisking all the while. Serve warm with whipped cream. For a richer beverage, replace half of the milk with cream.

Hot chocolate

CHOCOLATE IN THE KITCHEN

Although chocolate is used primarily as a flavouring for sweet dishes, the taste of bitter chocolate blends well with many savoury dishes. In Spain and Italy, small amounts of chocolate are used with onion, garlic, tomatoes and spices in a sauce for meat and fish dishes. Ground dried chillies are combined with chocolate for the traditional Mexican *mole* sauce. Try adding a small square of plain chocolate to a meat or game stew at the last moment; it will reduce any bitterness, and the chocolate flavour will be only barely perceptible.

MELTING CHOCOLATE

Although a seemingly easy task, great care should be taken when melting chocolate. It burns very easily and this makes the flavour bitter, and if overheated, it becomes hard and granular. Be careful not to let any stray drops of water fall into the chocolate or it will "seize," or stiffen and solidify. Many recipes call for the addition of butter or oil when melting; this adds richness, without interfering with the melting process.

The most common method for melting is the *bain marie,* or water bath. A double boiler can be used, but a heat-proof bowl that fits snugly over a saucepan will also work. Place a small amount of water in the saucepan – do not allow the bowl to touch the water. Bring the water to the boil and remove from the heat. Place the chocolate in the bowl and return the pan to the heat, if necessary, stirring to melt. Do not cover; this will cause steam to condense on the lid, forming water droplets that will fall into the chocolate and make it seize. The microwave is ideal for melting chocolate. Break chocolate into pieces and place in a microwave-safe bowl. To melt 75 g (2½ oz) plain chocolate, cook on full power, uncovered, for 2–3 minutes, according to microwave output. Stir to melt completely; the chocolate will retain its shape until stirred.

Bain Marie
The gentle, even heat of simmering water facilitates even melting.

TOMATO AND CHOCOLATE SAUCE FOR GAME

Serves 6

3 thick bacon rashers, chopped

2 large tomatoes, peeled, seeded and chopped

2 large onions, sliced

2 carrots, chopped

2 garlic cloves, crushed

1 litre (1 ¾ pt) game stock

1 tbsp chopped fresh flat-leaf parsley

2 whole cloves

Pinch of freshly grated nutmeg

1 tbsp sherry vinegar, or red wine vinegar

Salt

Freshly ground black pepper

2–3 tsp grated bitter chocolate

250 ml (8 fl oz) dry sherry

In a saucepan, cook the bacon over moderate heat until brown. Drain off the excess fat and add the tomatoes, onions, carrots, garlic and stock. Stir in the parsley, cloves, nutmeg and vinegar, and season to taste. Bring to the boil, cover, and simmer for 45 minutes. Strain and return to a clean saucepan. Add the chocolate to taste and stir in the sherry. Simmer the sauce, uncovered, for 5–10 minutes; adjust the seasoning if necessary. Serve with roast game birds such as quail and partridge, or with braised hare.

COATING AND FONDUE

Firm fruit, such as pear slices, melon cubes, banana slices, strawberries or even starfruit, can be dipped in melted chocolate for a light and unusual sweet. Candied citrus peel works well, and chocolate-coated nuts, such as almonds or walnuts, are also delicious. Melt the chocolate (see left). Dip in the fruit or nuts, lift out quickly and turn round several times for an even coating. Hold upwards to set. Dry on greaseproof paper at room temperature and serve within the hour; do not refrigerate. For fondue, serve a variety of fruit and nuts with a bowl of melted chocolate, or arrange on skewers. Add a little melted butter to the chocolate, for a smoother consistency and richer flavour.

Dried fruit

Nuts

Fresh fruit

Dipping fruit
For coating, use bite-sized ingredients, such as berries and nuts.

DESSERT BASICS

BASIC CHOCOLATE SPONGE

Makes one 20 cm (8 in) cake

Melted butter for the cake tin
4 large eggs
125 g (4 oz) caster sugar
100 g (3 ½ oz) plain flour
30 g (1 oz) unsweetened cocoa powder
15 g (½ oz) unsalted butter, melted and cooled (optional)

Preheat the oven to 190°C (375°F; gas 5). Line the base of a round, 20 cm (8 in) cake tin with greaseproof paper and brush with the melted butter. Mix together the eggs and sugar in a heatproof bowl. Place over a low flame, or a double boiler, and whisk until just warm to the touch. Do not overheat or the eggs will cook and form lumps. Remove from the heat and beat with an electric mixer until light and fluffy, about 15 minutes. Meanwhile, sift together the flour and cocoa powder. With a spatula, fold the dry ingredients into the egg mixture in three batches. Fold gently but thoroughly; there should be no visible pockets of flour. Fold in the butter with the last batch, if using. Pour into the tin and bake until the cake just comes away from the sides of the tin, 30–40 minutes. Turn out onto a wire rack. When cool, slice the cake horizontally into thirds with a long, serrated knife and fill.

From a simple home-made sponge, to an elaborate glazed, filled and garnished dessert, chocolate cake is the perennial favourite of children and adults alike. The recipes given here are blueprints; they can be used together, as shown, or separately to add a bit of chocolate flavour to other desserts. For example, the sponge can be split and filled with raspberries and cream. Or, blend the chocolate batter with an ordinary batter for a marbled effect. The ganache can be flavoured with coffee, cinnamon or mint and used to fill a plain sponge or Swiss roll; it can also be used to fill a baked tart shell for an instant chocolate tart. The chocolate icing can be used to coat plain sponge cakes, or those flavoured with ground almonds or hazelnuts, or it can be served straight away as a warm dessert sauce.

The garnish can be simple, like a dusting of cocoa powder, or more elaborate, like chocolate leaves or coated nuts

Put the filled cake on a wire rack set on a baking sheet to catch drips when icing; left-over icing can be re-used

To obtain even layers, cut with a gentle sawing motion, turning the cake while slicing; a piece of cardboard will help transfer the layers as they are divided

When icing, use a palette-knife and spread an even layer that extends all the way to the edge of the cake

CHOCOLATE ICING

For one 20 cm (8 in) cake

350 g (12 oz) plain chocolate
125 g (4 oz) unsalted butter at room temperature

Finely chop the chocolate and place in a saucepan with 125 ml (4 fl oz) lukewarm water. Melt over low heat. Meanwhile, cut the butter into small pieces. Remove the chocolate from the heat and stir in the butter, a few bits at a time, until well blended. Pour over the cooled cake; use a palette-knife to help smooth the icing if necessary. Chill for at least 1 hour before garnishing and serving.

CHOCOLATE GANACHE FILLING

Makes about 250 ml (8 fl oz)

250 g (8 oz) plain chocolate
250 ml (8 fl oz) double cream

Chop the chocolate finely with a sharp knife; the smaller the bits, the more quickly and evenly the chocolate will melt. Place the chopped chocolate in a heatproof bowl. In a saucepan, bring the cream to the boil. Pour the boiling cream onto the chocolate and whisk constantly until smooth and thoroughly combined. Refrigerate until just set and cooled, about 1 hour. Beat the ganache with an electric mixer until it doubles in volume, about 10 minutes. When cool, refrigerate until needed. (The ganache can be made up to 1 week in advance if kept covered in the refrigerator. Warm slightly before beating.)

CHOCOLATE GARNISHES

Chocolate decorations always give a professional look to finished desserts. It is best to make more than are needed as they are fragile and can break when handled. Any remaining decorations can be stored in an airtight container in a cool place for several weeks.

Some of these decorations are very delicate and even the weather can affect them. Professional confectioners and bakers tend to work in environmentally-controlled areas. For best results at home, avoid working in excessively hot or humid conditions.

The simplest garnish is a dusting of cocoa powder: hold a sieve over the surface to be coated, then add some cocoa powder and tap the sides gently. Move the sieve as necessary to obtain a thin, even layer. For a more sophisticated decoration, hold a paper doily just above the surface to be dusted and proceed as before. A stencil design made out of cardboard can be used more than once. For example, a series of 2.5 cm (1 in) lines will result in a lovely striped pattern that can be used again and again.

Another simple, attractive garnish can be obtained with a sprinkling of grated chocolate. A hand-held grater is ideal. When grating, hold a chilled block of chocolate with a piece of foil to prevent the heat of your hand from melting it. A food processor fitted with a metal blade can be used when very fine shavings are desired. With the machine running, drop the chocolate pieces through the feed tube; be sure the chocolate is at least coarsely chopped beforehand or the blades may jam.

CHOCOLATE SCROLLS

To obtain long thin scrolls, first melt the chocolate and then pour it onto a board or work surface. Using a palette-knife, spread to an even thickness of about 3 mm ($^1/_8$ in). Allow the chocolate to cool for about 30 minutes. Place the edge of a long-bladed knife or palette-knife on the surface, pointing away from you at a 45° angle. Scrape off a thin layer of chocolate in long scrolls. Use a teaspoon instead of a knife to obtain short, rounded curls.

Small curls

CHOCOLATE CURLS

Small curls can be made using chocolate at room temperature. (The chocolate will splinter if it is too cold; soften it between the palms of your hands first.) Using a vegetable peeler, "shave" the chocolate lengthwise over a plate. If the chocolate is an awkward shape, make an even block by melting it with a little vegetable oil, about 1 tsp per 30 g (1 oz) of chocolate. Pour the mixture into a small rectangular tin or mould and refrigerate until set. Allow the block to soften to room temperature, then shave it in the same way.

Making scrolls
With a straight-edged knife or palette-knife, push the blade across the chocolate to form long, thin curls.

Long scrolls

Making curls
Slowly and firmly draw the blade of the vegetable peeler across the widest side of a chocolate block at room temperature.

PIPING CHOCOLATE

Confident cooks can pipe melted chocolate garnishes directly onto the surface of an iced cake. Novices may prefer to pipe onto greaseproof paper and then transfer the shapes to the cake when hardened. Two paper cones can be prepared from a 20 x 35 cm (8 x 14 in) piece of paper, cut in half diagonally. When the cones are made, melt the chocolate (see page 182). With a small spoon, fill one cone three-quarters full and pipe as shown right. Point cone upwards between piping shapes to prevent leakage.

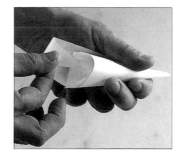

Making a paper cone
Fold the short side of a triangle over to the right-angled corner to form a cone. Wrap the long point around and tuck it inside the top.

Piping the chocolate
Place the design under greaseproof paper and then pipe chocolate over the outline. Do not force the chocolate; let it fall evenly from the tip.

Removing the shapes
When the shapes have set, lift off each with a palette-knife. Handle as little as possible as they will be fragile.

CHOCOLATE LEAVES

Any fresh non-poisonous leaf with distinct veins, such as rose, bay or lemon, can be used. Wash the leaves and pat dry with paper towels. With a pastry brush, small painting brush or small metal spatula, coat the underside of each leaf with melted chocolate. (This gives a more distinct pattern.) Leave a bit of the stem uncoated so that the leaf can be separated from the chocolate when set. Dry on wire racks and refrigerate until firm. Then, starting at the stem, with cool hands, carefully peel the chocolate away from the leaf.

Alternating dark, milk and white chocolate triangles makes a lively garnish

Shapes

Tri-colour leaves can turn a plain cake into something extremely decorative

Leaves

CHOCOLATE SHAPES

Pour melted chocolate onto a baking sheet lined with baking parchment or greaseproof paper, or onto an oiled work surface. Spread to an even thickness of 3 mm (1/8 in) and allow to cool for about 30 minutes; it can be refrigerated. Invert the chocolate layer onto another sheet of parchment or greaseproof paper and trim the edges. Using a ruler, trace lines for squares or diamonds and cut out. Squares can be cut diagonally in half to make triangles. Alternatively, use small pastry cutters to make other shapes, such as circles. Refrigerate until firm.

Making shapes
Using a small decorative cutter, press into the chocolate, then chill shapes until firm. Alternatively, use a ruler and a thin-bladed knife.

Making leaves
Coat the underside of non-poisonous leaves with melted chocolate and peel away the leaf when dry.

EXTRACTS ESSENCES & SWEETENERS

SAVOURY EXTRACTS AND FLAVOURINGS

Concentrated savoury extracts have been an essential flavouring in cookery for hundreds of years. In the East, they are based mainly on soy beans and fish, and are used for both flavour and colour. In the West, stocks are the best known and most widely used seasoning base. Intensely savoury reductions of liquid simmered with vegetables, meat or fish bones, and herbs, stocks can be prepared at home or shop-bought in the form of bouillon granules and dry stock cubes. Other concentrates include brewer's yeast, which is made from salt and the yeast by-product of beer and spirit distillation, and dried fish. But whether Eastern or Western, animal or mineral, what all of these products have in common is the ability to reinforce the flavour of foods.

Miso This flavouring of Japanese origin has been around for thousands of years. It is made by salting and fermenting soy beans together with a grain such as rice, barley or wheat, and a special mould, then ageing the resulting paste for several years.

Each region has its own traditional type of miso, ranging in colour from a light cream, to tawny brown, to deep chocolate. The flavour varies according to the type of grain, but it always has a wine-like pungency. Some versions are thick and smooth, others are more chunky.

Miso was originally intended as a preservative, and it is still used for many Japanese pickles, but along the way it has evolved into a very important seasoning, primarily in Japan and Korea. It is most often paired with Japanese soup stock, *dashi*, for miso soup. In Japan, this is traditional at breakfast, though it can be drunk at any time of day. It is also used to flavour sauces for salads, vegetables and bean curd, and in dips for tempura. When using miso in hot dishes, add just before serving; it should not be allowed to boil.

Skewered meat, fish and vegetables can be spread with plain miso and then grilled. *Denagaku*, a popular Japanese dish, is grilled bean curd coated in a sauce of miso blended with sake, dashi, sesame seeds, mirin, sugar, a few teaspoons of lemon juice, grated lemon rind, and thickened with beaten egg yolks.

Yellow miso, *shinshu*, is an all-purpose miso; red miso, *aka*, is a very salty version. White miso, *shiro*, made with two-thirds rice, is very smooth and sweet. It is used in pickles and as a topping for grilled meat. The strongly flavoured *hatcho miso* is most often eaten on its own, and barley miso, *mugi*, is dark with an earthy flavour.

Red miso
is very salty and should be used sparingly in stocks, soups and casseroles

Trasi *is a firm paste made from fermented shrimps; it is extremely pungent*

Yellow miso *is the all-purpose bean paste version, popular throughout Asia for enhancing the taste of many dishes*

Savoury Extracts
From East to West, savoury extracts and flavourings enhance the taste of many dishes.

Malt extract *provides the key note for several well-known milk drinks*

Meat extract *adds a salty, concentrated taste to many foods, from soups to drinks*

Yeast extract *is a blend of salt and brewer's yeast*

Beef stock cubes

Chicken stock cube

Bouillon granules

Fish Paste Made from salted and fermented prawns or shrimps, fish pastes are popular throughout Southeast Asia. Known as *trasi* in Indonesia, *blachan* in Malaysia and *kapee* in Thailand, these vary in appearance from a grey watery paste to crumbly brown blocks. Regardless of the form, they all have a very strong fishy taste and smell, and need to be used with care. Fish pastes are an acquired taste, so it is best to add them sparingly. When using in uncooked dishes, the block forms of fish paste must be cooked first. Cut off a piece and toast over a low gas flame, or place under the grill until roasted, then proceed with the recipe. European anchovy paste is a similar product, but it is no substitute for the pungent pastes of Southeast Asia. In Western kitchens, anchovy paste is used as a seasoning for minced meat mixtures, stews and sauces, or on its own as a spread for toast or crackers.

Meat Extract In the West, meat juices are concentrated into thick, commercially made pastes. Some, like Bovril, are mixed with vegetable extracts, flavourings and spices. Most often, these extracts are diluted with hot water for drinking, though they can also be used to impart a meaty flavour to soups, casseroles and gravies. They can also be enjoyed straight from the jar, as a spread for sandwiches and toast.

Stock Extract For convenience, meat and vegetable stock extracts are also available dried in cubes or freeze-dried into granules. Flavours include beef, pork, ham, lamb, fish and chicken, as well as pure vegetable. Both cubes and granules should be dissolved in hot water before use; they can be added directly to dishes that are high in liquid.

Yeast Extract First produced in the 19th century, this type of extract was developed by the French scientist, Pasteur, and the German chemist, Liebig. Even before the role of vitamins in daily nutrition was first discovered in 1912, yeast extracts, such as Marmite, were well-established health products. Yeast extracts are popular in Great Britain, Australia and North America as a spread for bread and toast.

Malt Extract Made from fermented barley, this extract has a distinctive sweetish flavour. It is used in Western kitchens for baking, and in malted milk.

COOK'S CHOICE
MISO SOUP

Serves 4–6

15 cm (6 in) square of konbu seaweed
3 tbsp bonito flakes
125 g (4 oz) red miso
125 g (4 oz) soft bean curd
2–3 spring onions, sliced

Wipe the seaweed with a damp paper towel and make several incisions with a knife. Bring 1200 ml (2 pt) water to the boil and add the seaweed. Cover, and leave for 10 minutes. Remove the seaweed and add 250 ml (8 fl oz) water. Return to the boil. Add the bonito shavings and stir. Strain the soup base and return to the pan (Alternatively, replace the seaweed and bonito flakes with concentrated *dashi*, available in Japanese groceries, and mix with the same total quantity of boiling water.) Stir in the miso. Cut the bean curd into small cubes and divide between warmed soup bowls. Add the spring onions to the soup, stir and pour over the bean curd in the bowls. Serve immediately.

DRIED SEAFOOD

Dried seafood has long been a staple ingredient in Chinese cuisine. Some, such as dried oysters, scallops *(conpoy)* and squid, must be soaked before use; the soaking liquid is also added to the dish, like dried mushrooms. Bonito flakes, or *katsuo-bushi*, are essential for *dashi*, Japanese soup stock.

Dried powdered shrimp

Dried scallops

Bonito flakes

Bonito flakes are dried, wood-like shavings that are obtained with a special tool, called katsuo-kezuri-ki

SWEET ESSENCES AND FLAVOURINGS

Essences are produced by extracting the essential flavours of a very wide range of plants, either by maceration or by distillation. The best liquid essences are made wholly from natural ingredients, however, good essences are expensive to produce. Some manufacturers may add cheap substitutes and synthetic flavours to their products. In the kitchen, essences are used to flavour desserts and baked goods, as well as savoury sauces and dressings. Flavourings are usually the dried form of an aromatic plant that has been ground to a fine powder. Sweet flavouring powders are used mainly in the manufacture of sweets and soft drinks.

Fruit and nut essences *such as lemon, strawberry, almond and hazelnut, are used primarily in baking and confectionery*

Strawberry essence

Hazelnut essence

Cola nuts *are dried and used in a variety of popular soft drinks; they contain a small amount of caffeine and so provide a mild stimulant*

Cola drink

Cola powder

Sarsaparilla *is made from the cord-like roots of the South American plant, smilax; the roots are dried and used to flavour a carbonated drink, once popular in America*

Liquorice roots *are dried and ground to a powder, or the bitter-sweet juices are extracted to make delicious black confectionery*

Liquorice root

Sarsaparilla powder

Sarsaparilla drink

Liquorice sweets

Herb extract *A few drops of a herb extract will reproduce a herb's flavour when it is not available fresh*

Fruit Essences Strawberries, raspberries and pomegranates are ideal for distilling into essences (or macerating into syrups) which keep well through the long winter months. Use these essences to flavour all kinds of food, from ice creams and sorbets, to tarts and cake fillings. They make an interesting addition to fresh fruit salads, and can also be used to enhance savoury dressings and sweet dessert sauces. These fruit flavourings are also used to give sweetness and flavour to many kinds of drinks, and they are a vital constituent of many classic cocktails.

Fruit Oils Extracted from the essential oils in the skins of citrus fruits, only a few drops of these are needed to infuse a dish. They are best to added to uncooked dishes, or at the end of cooking, as heat will diminish their flavouring potential.

Nut Essences These are a simple and flavoursome way to add interest to plain sponges, cakes, biscuits and tarts.

Vanilla Essence Widely available, it can be used in almost all kinds of baked goods to enhance their main flavour.

Herb Extracts Available in some speciality shops, only a few drops of these intensely concentrated extracts are needed to add extra layers of herbal flavouring to soups, stews and casseroles.

Liquorice This distinctive bitter-sweet flavour is a classic the world over. It is used mainly in confectionery items, such as bootlace sweets, English Pontefract-cakes and liquorice allsorts. Pieces of liquorice root can also be infused in hot water for a flavoursome and soothing tisane, and liquorice powder can be used to enliven fruit juices and dried fruit salads. Liquorice is also used in the production of some liqueurs, most notably Italian Sambuco.

Cola and Sarsaparilla Once prescribed as medicines, these flavourings were held to have revitalizing properties. Some soft drink manufacturers capitalized on the ostensible efficacy of these ingredients and included them in their products. Cola is now the basis for the most successful soft drinks.

FLAVOURING PASTRY CREAM
Blend together 125 g (4 oz) sugar, 60 g (2 oz) cornflour and 2 eggs. Pour on 600 ml (1 pt) boiling milk. Continue stirring over heat until the mixture thickens. Transfer to a bowl, stir in a few drops of a fruit or nut essence and leave to cool.

COOK'S CHOICE
GRAPEFRUIT AND GRENADINE SORBET
Serves 6

1 litre (1 ¾ pt) pink grapefruit juice
200 g (7 oz) caster sugar
2 tbsp grenadine
Cookie cups (see page 203)
Fresh mint for garnish

Combine the grapefruit juice, sugar and grenadine in a bowl; stir to dissolve the sugar. Freeze the mixture in a metal bowl. When the mixture has solidified, break into chunks and place in a food processor; meanwhile return the empty bowl to the freezer. Process the frozen chunks until the mixture is smooth. Return to the chilled bowl and freeze until set, 30–45 minutes. Serve scoops of the sorbet in cookie cups and garnish with the mint.

GRENADINE

Grenadine is a syrup made from the juice of the pomegranate. It is bright red in colour and has a sweet, fresh flavour. It is completely non-alcoholic, but plays an essential part in any good barman's repertoire.

No classic Daiquiri, for example, would be complete without it. Other cocktails flavoured with grenadine include Mary Pickford, with pineapple juice and maraschino, and Hollywood, made with fresh grapefruit juice and egg whites.

Grenadine is a natural colouring and is valued for its ability to tint cocktails as well as desserts and candied citrus peel. It looks particularly effective when added to sorbets, ice cream and fruit salads. Try it with grapefruit halves, or use in a salad dressing for avocado.

Do not confuse grenadine with pomegranate syrup, which is the unsweetened, boiled-down juice of sour pomegranate seeds. This syrup is used primarily in Middle Eastern cuisine, where its intensely concentrated flavour is used to enhance many dishes, most notably Iranian *faisinjan*. This dish combines duck or chicken in a sauce thickened with walnuts and perfumed with pomegranate syrup.

SIROP DE GRENADINE

LEJAY·LAGOUTE

Pomegranate seeds make an attractive garnish that can be sprinkled over ice cream, mousses or fruit salads

LIQUEURS, SPIRITS AND WINES

Almost any part of a plant – seeds, leaves, roots, fruit and kernels – can be macerated with or infused in alcohol to provide a spirited flavouring. Alcohol-based drinks, though normally imbibed straight from the glass, do have a useful range of culinary applications.

Wine adds richness to long-cooking dishes, while fruit and nut liqueurs can be added at the last minute or flambéed for a burst of flavour. Spirits and brandies work well in marinades and dessert coffees; they can also be poured over fruit or ice cream for a simple dessert.

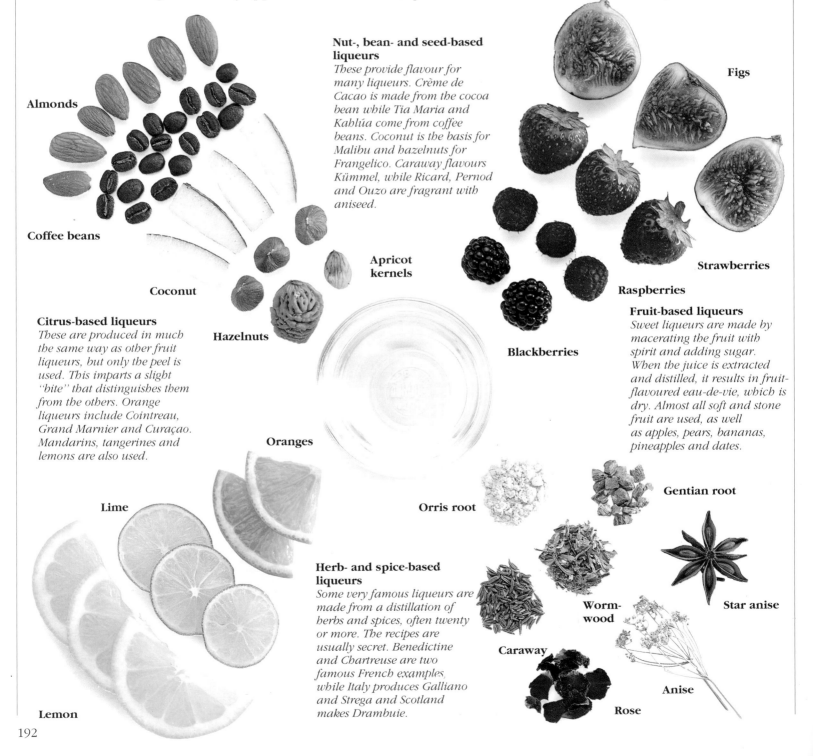

Almonds

Coffee beans

Coconut

Hazelnuts

Nut-, bean- and seed-based liqueurs
These provide flavour for many liqueurs. Crème de Cacao is made from the cocoa bean while Tia Maria and Kahlúa come from coffee beans. Coconut is the basis for Malibu and hazelnuts for Frangelico. Caraway flavours Kümmel, while Ricard, Pernod and Ouzo are fragrant with aniseed.

Apricot kernels

Figs

Strawberries

Raspberries

Blackberries

Fruit-based liqueurs
Sweet liqueurs are made by macerating the fruit with spirit and adding sugar. When the juice is extracted and distilled, it results in fruit-flavoured eau-de-vie, which is dry. Almost all soft and stone fruit are used, as well as apples, pears, bananas, pineapples and dates.

Citrus-based liqueurs
These are produced in much the same way as other fruit liqueurs, but only the peel is used. This imparts a slight "bite" that distinguishes them from the others. Orange liqueurs include Cointreau, Grand Marnier and Curaçao. Mandarins, tangerines and lemons are also used.

Oranges

Lime

Orris root

Gentian root

Wormwood

Star anise

Herb- and spice-based liqueurs
Some very famous liqueurs are made from a distillation of herbs and spices, often twenty or more. The recipes are usually secret. Benedictine and Chartreuse are two famous French examples, while Italy produces Galliano and Strega and Scotland makes Drambuie.

Caraway

Rose

Anise

Lemon

FORTIFIED WINES

Some wines, mainly port, sherry and Madeira, are fortified with an added dose of brandy. With the exception of fino sherries, these wines are sweet and they have a full flavour that can be used to give richness to winter casseroles, game sauces and even some fish dishes. Port is often added to duck dishes and pâtés. Madeira goes well with ham and other pork dishes, and sherry enhances soups and sauces, especially those that are poultry-based. Fortified wines are also used in sweet dishes such as creams and jellies, trifles, savarins and sugar syrups for poached fruit.

Port　　**Sherry**

Many pâtés are flavoured with port

All alcohol-based drinks can be used to flavour foods. The easiest way is to add the alcohol directly to the pan, either by de-glazing (see page 249) or by pouring into liquid preparations such as soups and stews. In order to impart a deep, mellow flavour rather than an overpowering dose of alcohol, be sure to boil the mixture for at least one minute to allow the alcohol to evaporate.

Recipes that do not include an alcoholic flavouring can be easily enhanced by one. When choosing an alcohol to partner a particular food, consider the drink's ingredients. Cherry-flavoured Kirsch is the obvious ally for any dish made with cherries. The strong juniper flavour of gin goes well in dishes made with game, and *calvados*, French apple brandy, can be used in apple dishes. Origins are another clue to successful flavour pairing. For example, add a splash of Italian red wine to pasta sauces, or an anise-flavoured liqueur from southern France to season fish or shellfish dishes.

Flambéing is the culinary technique most often associated with wines, spirits, liqueurs and brandies. When these are heated, their alcohol burns off, leaving behind only flavour. Table-side flambéing makes for a spectacular presentation, and in the kitchen, it adds an attractive golden brown appearance as well as helping to caramelize dishes that contain sugar. This technique is simple but precautions should be taken when flambéing in a home kitchen. Keep hair tied back and your face well away from the pan. Also, be sure there are no obstructing shelves or cabinets directly above the cooking area.

These alcohols can also be used as the base for quick and delicious desserts. Pineapple slices and Kirsch are traditional; orange Curaçao goes well with peaches, or splash some ginger wine on fresh melon. On a lighter note, fresh strawberries and raspberries are even more delicious floating in a crystal coupe of pink champagne.

Whipped cream is the ideal base for an alcoholic flavouring. Add a nut-flavoured liqueur to whipped cream for chocolate desserts, or use blackcurrant-flavoured Cassis and serve with fruit salads.

Many ice creams also take well to a dash of liqueur or brandy. Flavoursome matches include green apple sorbet with Calvados, rum-raisin ice cream with rum, or French vanilla with something rich – hazelnut Frangelico, almond-scented Amaretto or coffee-flavoured Kahlúa.

To a cup of after-dinner coffee, add a splash of brandy, crème de vanille, or whisky and cream for Irish coffee.

Angostura Bitters
Made in Trinidad, Angostura bitters rely on the bitter but aromatic bark of the Cusparia tree, plus a combination of dried fruit and spices. A few drops can be used to flavour spirits for cocktails and to enhance fruit salads, ice creams, savoury sauces and soups.

PRAWNS MARSEILLAISE
Serves 4

2 shallots, finely chopped
30 g (1 oz) unsalted butter
500 g (1 lb) large peeled prawns
125 ml (4 fl oz) dry white wine
1 tbsp anise-flavoured liqueur
125 ml (4 fl oz) fish stock
150 ml (¼ pt) double cream
Salt
Freshly ground black pepper

In a saucepan, combine the shallots and butter over low heat and cook until soft, about 1 minute. Add the prawns and continue to cook for a further 1 minute. Add the white wine and the anise-flavoured liqueur, cover and bring to the boil. Simmer for 30 seconds. Remove the prawns and keep warm. Add the fish stock and return to the boil. Cook rapidly until reduced by at least half. Add the cream and cook until thickened, about 5 minutes. Season to taste. Arrange the prawns on serving plates and pour the sauce over. Serve immediately.

SUGAR

Sugar is one of the oldest flavourings and condiments, and its use in Asia goes far back in recorded history. Its earliest form was as a liquid sugar extracted from sugar cane. Early Europeans relied on honey and fruit to sweeten their food. When they finally "discovered" sugar cane, they described it as a reed which produced honey without the aid of bees. Christopher Columbus introduced sugar cane to the West Indies, where it was, and continues to be, widely and successfully cultivated. In the 17th century, the increasing popularity of beverages such as coffee, tea and cocoa had a direct impact on the European demand for sugar, making sugar cane a precious commodity. But it was not until the 19th century that the sugar beet was considered as an alternative source; its sugar being identical in strength and quality. Today, sugar is obtained from both sugar beet and sugar cane, and is available in a variety of forms: raw, refined, brown, cubes and even flavoured sugars.

Sugar cane is a tropical plant grown mainly in plantations in the West Indies and South America. It is a perennial plant which grows to a height of 6 metres (20 ft). The cane is usually 2.5–5 cm (1–2 in) in diameter and closely resembles bamboo.

Sugar beet is grown as a field crop in temperate regions across Europe, from Britain to Turkey. Sugar is extracted from the swollen root which looks rather like a fat parsnip.

PRODUCTION

After harvest, sugar cane is taken to factories for processing. The canes are crushed and then fed through powerful rollers which extract the sugar juice. This juice is then mixed with a substance which draws out the

Made from a blend of refined and unrefined sugars and honey, this gives a distinctive flavour to braised pork and duck dishes

Chinese rock sugar

Demerara sugar

Golden granulated sugar

Light muscovado sugar

Dark muscovado sugar

Granulated sugar *has a medium-fine texture that makes it the best all-purpose sugar*

Caster sugar *is much finer than other sugar; it dissolves quickly and is generally used in baking*

Icing sugar *is the most finely textured of all sugars; it can be used for both sweetening foods and garnishing*

impurities. Next, the juice is thickened by evaporation, boiled in vacuum pans, then seeded with tiny sugar crystals which encourage crystallization.

When the appropriate crystal size has been obtained, the mixture is spun in high-speed centrifuge machines, rather like spin driers, which separate the raw sugar crystals from the syrup base. For white sugar, the crystals are separated from the molasses syrup, then they are refined further for colour and texture. Brown sugars are made from refined white crystals that are coated with a thin layer of molasses.

In sugar beet production, the root is sliced and then infused in hot water. Otherwise, processing is identical to that of sugar cane: the resultant liquid is purified, concentrated and seeded with sugar crystals. When the appropriate crystal size is obtained, the sugar is spun, washed and dried. Unlike cane sugar, the molasses by-product is used only in cattle feed.

TYPES OF SUGAR

Unrefined Sugar True unrefined sugars are brown in colour. This is due to the molasses syrup that is left on, instead of being refined out and added later. They can easily be distinguished from other brown-coloured sugars by their labels: only the country of origin is listed, not the ingredients.

HERB AND SPICE SUGARS

Sugar can be flavoured with flower petals, such as rose, lavender, or rose geranium, and spices such as cloves, aniseed, ginger, cinnamon, vanilla or cardamom pods. Use these sugars to add extra flavour to custard sauces, cakes and other baked goods. Make sure petals and spices are quite dry or the sugar will have lumps.

Molasses Sugar A dark unrefined sugar, this contains a high percentage of molasses, which is responsible for its strong flavour and sticky texture. *Barbados sugar* is one of the most widely available types of molasses sugar and is delicious in chutneys, fruit cakes, gingerbread and toffee.

Muscovado Sugar Light and dark muscovado sugars are not as strongly flavoured as molasses sugar. They can be used to add colour and a rich flavour to dried fruit puddings, spice cakes, biscuits, autumn fruit crumbles and baked apples. These sugars also add colour and sweetness to savoury dishes such as glazed ham, barbecue sauce and chutneys.

Soft Brown Sugar This is the description usually given to brown sugars refined from sugar cane, and they can also be described as light or dark. Colour and flavour will depend on the amount of molasses added. This type is well suited to baking.

Demerara Sugar True demerara came originally from Guyana. The distinctive large crystals are obtained by regulating the conditions under which the sugar syrup is spun. High-quality demerara should be slightly sticky with an aromatic flavour. It is particularly good in baked goods, such as biscuits, cakes and crumbles, and with hot beverages such as coffee and mulled wines.

Golden Granulated Sugar This is a dry, free-flowing sugar with a buttery taste. Its light golden crystals are made by a unique process which produces a very clear and brilliant juice for crystallization. This type is unsuitable for cakes and delicate pastries as it is difficult to blend into batters.

Granulated Sugar This is the sugar for everyday use in the kitchen and at the table. In savoury cooking, it is the best type to caramelize for added colour and depth of flavour, as is often done in Caribbean cuisine. This is also the best type to use for making flavoured sugars (see left).

Caster Sugar Granulated sugar is milled further to produce this fine sugar, which is ideal for use in sponge cakes, meringues, and any recipe where the coarser texture of granulated sugar might affect the texture of the finished dish.

Icing Sugar This is powdered granulated sugar. As its name implies, it is used mainly for icing and decoration, though it is also useful for delicate pastry preparations, such as tart crusts, which benefit from the absence of more coarsely textured sugars. Store in a cool, dry place, and always sift before use as this sugar is prone to lumps.

SPECIALITY SUGARS

Flavoured or coloured sugars can be used in place of ordinary sugar for drinks, or decorating cakes and pastries. Chocolate sugar can be stirred into *café au lait* and rainbow crystals make an attractive addition to the coffee tray. Swizzle sticks are also pretty alternatives to sugar cubes, but they are best used with coffee, tea and other hot drinks to ensure that the sugar dissolves.

Chocolate-flavoured sugar

Rainbow crystals

Coloured decorating sugar

Sugar swizzle stick

SUGAR IN THE KITCHEN

Although sugar is used mainly as a sweetener, it does have many other applications. It inhibits the growth of micro-organisms, making it useful for sweet preserves and chutneys, it is a yeast activator for breads, and a texture enhancer and flavouring for home baking. Sugar undergoes changes upon heating, which facilitate sweet making, and it is essential for pastries and baked goods, not only as flavouring but as decoration. Sugar is used for most decorative icings – from royal icing to butter cream – and it can be heated to the caramel stage and spun or moulded into a whole variety of patterns, shapes and sculptures. At its first stage of cooking, the syrup is ideal for poached fruits, sorbets and iced soufflés, and for preserving fruits in alcohol. For extra flavour, the sugar syrup may be infused with spices, such as vanilla and cardamom, or flavourings such as lemon peel.

Sugar syrups are simple mixtures of sugar and water and they have a variety of different uses in the kitchen. Differing strengths of syrup can be achieved by increasing or decreasing the quantity of sugar in a given amount of water.

Light syrups are used for poaching fruit, bottling apple slices or freezing delicate fruit such as melon and pineapple. Allow 125 g (4 oz) sugar to 600 ml (1 pt) water.

Medium syrups, for fruit sorbets and iced soufflés, are made with equal quantities of sugar and water. An even heavier syrup is needed for fondant icing or for bottling peaches. Allow about 600 g (1¼ lb) sugar to 500 ml (16 fl oz) water.

COOKING WITH SUGAR
Sugar syrup for sweets, pastries and poached fruit is made by boiling a mixture of sugar and water. Simple sugar syrups can be prepared in an ordinary saucepan, but for those which must be heated to high heats – as when making caramel – unlined copper pans should be used. To prevent any sugar that splatters from burning, use a pastry brush dipped in water to brush down the sides of the pan.

Sugar syrup will keep unrefrigerated for several days, or for several weeks if kept cold. For extra flavour, it can be infused with vanilla pods, star anise or citrus peel. Or, boil a handful of lime flowers in the water, strain and proceed with the syrup making, using the flavoured water. The result will be subtle yet delicious.

A sugar syrup changes its composition as it is boiled. The stages through which the sugar passes are known as thread, soft-ball, hard-ball, soft-crack and hard-crack. Each of these stages corresponds to a specific temperature and is used in the preparation of different kinds of pastries, sweets and even savoury dishes. Professionals often

Fudge

Marshmallows

Boiled sweet

Fruit drops

Peppermint fondants

Nougat

Humbugs

Toffees

Soft-ball 115°C (239°F)
Use for fondants, fudge and butter cream. Test by dropping into cold water. It should be able to hold a small ball shape.

Hard-ball 120°C (248°F)
Use for almond paste and Italian meringue. Test in cold water; it should roll into a larger, harder ball than soft-ball.

Soft-crack 125°C (257°F)
Use for caramels, toffee and boiled sweets. Test in cold water; it should be brittle, but still sticky on the fingers.

Hard-crack 146°C (295°F)
Use for almond brittle, glazed fruits and barley sugar. Test in cold water; it should be very brittle with no stickiness.

DECORATING WITH ICING

A sugar syrup heated to the soft-ball stage can be used to prepare a butter cream icing, which is ideal for cake decorating. To fill and coat a 23 cm (9 in) cake, combine 6 tbsp water and 100 g (3½ oz) sugar in a saucepan. Heat until the sugar dissolves, then boil until it reaches 115°C (239°F) on a sugar thermometer. In a large bowl, whisk together 4 egg yolks. With an electric mixer, slowly beat in the sugar syrup and continue beating until cool, 5–10 minutes. Cream 250 g (8 oz) unsalted butter and add to the syrup mixture in batches, beating constantly. Place in a piping bag and decorate.

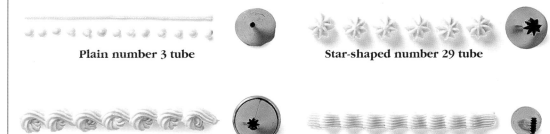

Plain number 3 tube

Star-shaped number 29 tube

Star-shaped number 5 tube

Ribbon number 22 tube

test the temperature with their fingers, keeping a bowl of ice water nearby, but the home cook will obtain the best results with a sugar thermometer. Always be sure to put the thermometer in the mixture when beginning to heat or it will break.

When the mixture reaches 177°C (350°F), the syrup starts to change colour. This is the beginning of the caramel stage and it is possible to judge it by eye without the thermometer. When the syrup is a tawny brown colour and just beginning to smoke, remove it from the heat and immediately place the pan in a shallow basin of cold water to stop the cooking. The unlined copper pans, which are imperative for caramel making, are great conductors of heat, so it is important to cool the pan down straight away or the caramel may burn, even off the heat.

Rolled and blown sugar decorations and sweets are made by highly skilled confectioners who have been trained to sculpt and mould scaldingly hot sugar syrups. They must work on heatproof surfaces, often under special lamps that maintain the heat necessary to retain the pliability of the sugar. This sugar is white, but colour can be added with food colouring. For blown sugar, a tube is inserted in the sugar mass. The confectioner then blows air into the sugar through the tube, much like blowing up a balloon.

For the home cook, icing sugar offers the most accessible form of sugar decoration. A very simple cake decoration is achieved by placing a stencil over the top of the cake and sprinkling with icing sugar. Paper doilies are handy for ready-made stencils, but patterns can also be cut out of ordinary cardboard. Decorate the cake or pastry just before serving and do not place the stencil directly on the surface of iced cakes.

Sugar-based icings (see above) can be used plain, or flavoured with chocolate, liqueurs or fruit purées. Beautiful and intricate decorations can be made with an assortment of piping bag tubes, or a simple cone made from greaseproof paper (see page 185) can be used for lettering or a lattice pattern.

COOK'S CHOICE
BUTTERSCOTCH

Makes about 250 g (8 oz)

Oil for greasing
100 g (3½ oz) caster sugar
100 g (3½ oz) unsalted butter
90 ml (3 fl oz) liquid glucose
150 ml (¼ pt) single cream

Grease a small square tin. In a saucepan, combine all the ingredients over very low heat. Stir until the sugar has dissolved. Raise the heat, bring to the boil and cook to 125°C (257°F). Pour at once into the prepared tin and score the surface into squares. When set, cut or break into squares as marked. Wrap in greaseproof paper and store in an airtight container.

COOK'S CHOICE
TOFFEE APPLES

Makes 12 apples

12 eating apples
12 wooden skewers
500 g (1 lb) caster sugar
125 g (4 oz) unsalted butter

Wash and dry the apples and push a large skewer into the centre of each. In a pan, combine the sugar, butter and 2 tbsp water. Cook gently until the sugar dissolves. Bring to the boil and heat to 125°C (257°F). Dip the apples into the hot toffee. Leave to set on greaseproof paper.

Sugar sieve
For icing sugar decorations, always use a sieve to sift out any lumps.

SYRUP

There are many different types of commercial syrups – golden syrup, molasses, maple syrup, corn syrup and treacle – and while their flavours and colours vary, they are all, essentially, liquid forms of sugar. Most syrups are by-products of cane and beet sugar refinement. They are made from the liquid that is left over after the sugar crystals have been removed, which is then reduced to obtain a thick syrup. Corn syrup is derived from sweet corn kernels and is relatively mild in flavour. It is sometimes mixed with molasses for added colour and flavour, and then it is known as dark corn syrup. Along with golden syrup, it is used in baking to flavour cakes and biscuits, and for sweets.

Molasses and maple syrup are popular sweeteners in North America, where they lend their distinctive flavours to many baked goods and some savoury sauces. Cane syrup tastes like molasses and is the result of simmering sugar cane juice until thick and golden-brown. Another molasses syrup, though a golden and tart one, is sorghum. This is extracted from the stalks of the sorghum plant and is widely used in the American south. Barley malt syrup, also known as malt extract, has a delicate flavour and is high in vitamins and iron. Nowadays, treacle is probably the least used sweetening syrup; many desserts, such as treacle pudding and treacle tart are, in fact, made with golden syrup.

Liquid sweeteners
Syrups are liquid forms of sugar and most are popular as toppings. Darker syrups tend to have stronger, more distinctive flavours while lighter syrups are more delicate. Mild varieties such as golden syrup and corn syrup can be used interchangeably.

Syrups vary in consistency and strength of flavour and this may affect the ways in which they are used in the kitchen. The following is a selection of some of the different types.
Molasses This is a very dark syrup which is produced during the manufacture of sugar cane. The Americans nicknamed the heavy molasses from the West Indies "black strap syrup", and this name is now applied locally to any type of dark syrup. Molasses is an unrefined syrup with a very thick texture and a strong taste that leans towards the bitter side of sweet. Once a common household item, today its use is confined primarily to speciality cakes and biscuits, and toffee.

Treacle A smoother syrup, this is made by blending molasses and refinery syrup. Although less bitter than molasses, the flavour is still distinctive. Treacle ranges in colour from light gold to black and is slightly thinner than molasses. It is most common in traditional English baked goods, such as Parkin and Ginger cakes, and it is essential for black treacle toffee.
Golden Syrup This is a very smooth, clear syrup with a bright, golden colour. The flavour is sweet and mild, and it is used in batters for flapjacks and other baked goods. Pour into cored apples with raisins for baking, or drizzle over the top of a steamed pudding. It is especially nice as a sweetener for porridge, and in Britain, it is traditionally served with pancakes on Shrove Tuesday.
Corn Syrup A rather runny, mild flavoured syrup, this is popular in America where it is used in all kinds of baking. It can also be used in barbecue sauces, jellies and sweet-and-sour dishes.
Maple Syrup Made from the sap of the black maple and sugar maple trees, both of which flourish in America and Canada, this is a thin, runny syrup which has a very distinctive flavour. Maple syrup is graded for quality; the lowest grades are often made from corn syrup which has simply been flavoured with maple syrup. Maple syrup is delicious poured over vanilla ice cream, hot crumpets and scones, French toast and American pancakes. In baking, it can be used to enhance the flavour of robust sweet breads and in any cake, biscuit or pie made with nuts. It can also be used in savoury preparations, such as glazed ham. Maple syrup also has a particular affinity with brussel sprouts.

Corn syrup

Molasses

Maple syrup

Black treacle

Golden syrup

HONEY

This sweet substance, made from the nectar of flowers, has been used in cooking since very ancient times. Neolithic man probably robbed beehives for his honey, but by the Bronze Age, domesticated bee-keeping was widespread. Ever since then, honey has been used as a sweetener and a preservative, as well as a flavour enhancer. Many Europeans used it to sweeten their wine or brewed it into an alcoholic drink. In the Middle East, it has long been used in sticky-sweet phyllo pastries. Honey's popularity has endured to the present day and its culinary uses range from sweet to savoury. The flavour and appearance are determined by the flower. Lavender honey is a deep gold with a perfumed flavour, while acacia honey is clear and pale with a delicate flavour.

Honey imparts its own distinctive flavour to the food with which it is cooked, so it is important to choose the right honey for the job. Ordinary commercial blends are fine when an unobtrusive honey flavour is desired, however, single-flower honeys have more personality and often more taste. Herb flowers, such as thyme and rosemary, produce aromatic and flavoursome honeys which stand out in any dish. Orange blossom and clover honeys are both delicately perfumed and mild.

Not only does honey add flavour, it also improves the keeping qualities of baked goods; it even gives a better texture to bread crusts. For baking, the more liquid honeys mix more easily into batters; warming the honey also facilitates blending. Straight from the jar, honey adds pleasant sweetness to cereals, toasted bread or scones, ice creams, yogurt and soft cheeses such as fromage frais. Fruit, such as apricots, peaches, pears and plums, are delicious when poached in a honey syrup consisting of one-third honey to two-thirds water.

In Europe, honey is traditionally used in baking, for example, in Dutch Honey Cake and German Christmas cookies. Many of the phyllo pastries from Greece and Turkey are soaked in a sweet, honey syrup.

Honey is also used in savoury cookery. Oven-roasted hams with a honey glaze are popular in many parts of Europe, and in America. Honey lends itself well to spicy barbecue sauces, and honey-flavoured vinegar makes a remarkable vinaigrette.

The Chinese use honey to baste roast pork and duck, and in Turkey, chicken is often cooked with honey and almonds.

To store, keep honey in a cool, dry place; refrigeration is not absolutely necessary as it will last for a very long time without deteriorating. In fact, many honeys will crystallize at low temperatures.

Nutritionally, honey is made up of fructose and glucose sugars, which are considered to be easier to digest than the sucrose of sugar beet or cane. Fructose is the sweetest of all sugars, so use less honey than sugar when substituting one for the other.

Honeycomb

English clover honey

French lavender honey

Greek Hymettus honey

Honeys range in appearance from light and clear to thick and opaque; the flavour depends on the flower from which it came

FRUIT PURÉES, ESSENCES AND SYRUPS

The seasonal appearance of fruit, often in copious quantities, has encouraged cooks to develop ways of capturing these flavours for future use. Preserving, bottling or concentrating fruit flavours into syrups are the traditional methods; freezing is a more recent development, but no less useful. The many and varied flavours of fruit are used in dessert and pudding recipes, jams and jellies, sweets, and a wide range of alcoholic and soft drinks. They also turn up in savoury dishes, mostly in chilled soups, or in sauces where their tartness acts as a foil to fatty meats such as duck or pork. Very often, the fruit is lightly processed to make better use of its flavour and texture. The fruit flesh may be pulped with the juice to make versatile purées or the two may be separated and the juice used alone.

Blackcurrant syrup

The most familiar type of fruit purée is made from apples. Apple purée turns up in traditional desserts from around the world: Normandy Apple Tart, Swedish Apple Cake, English Apple Charlotte, Austrian Apple Strudel and American Apple Pie. Sometimes the purée is plain, sometimes it is flavoured. Popular additions include lemon zest or juice, and spices such as cardamom, nutmeg and cinnamon. Apple and blackberry is a favourite combination in Britain.

Indeed, mixing fruit flavours allows for more complex and interesting tastes. In some European countries, gooseberry is traditionally cooked with elderflowers as the two coincide in season. Gooseberries are also very good mixed with strawberries, raspberries and oranges. Try orange and gooseberry cream in a choux ring, or fold puréed gooseberries into a raspberry fool. Apricot purée, thinned with fresh orange or lemon juice, makes a flavoursome sauce for steamed puddings, especially those made with banana. Herbs and spices can also be added. Rhubarb has an affinity with ginger, and a squeeze of lemon juice subdues rhubarb's bite. Plum with cardamom, or pears and raspberries with mint are just some of the possible flavour combinations.

Soft fruits are easily puréed for sauces and, while they are delicious on their own, they can also be combined. Try papaya with lime, blueberry with peach, strawberry with redcurrant, blueberries with blackberries, or raspberries with orange juice and serve with a plain chocolate cake. Enhance the flavour of the purée by adding a splash of kirsch, cassis or almond-flavoured liqueur. The same mixtures are delicious used as a base for ice creams and sorbets.

Fruit sauces are traditional with some savoury foods too. Apple sauce is served with roast pork and potato pancakes, redcurrant sauce can be served with lamb, cranberry sauce is a classic with turkey, and in England, gooseberry sauce is the traditional accompaniment to baked mackerel.

Other savoury sauces are made by adding both sugar and vinegar to the puréed fruit for a sweet-and-sour flavour. An American-style apricot glaze for barbecued spare ribs can be made in this way.

Fruit soups are very popular in Central and Northern Europe. These are sometimes based on apples, as in apple and celery soup, or carrot and apple soup; sometimes on cherries, as in the German chilled cherry soup with dumplings, or the Hungarian yogurt and sour cherry soup.

In Scandinavia, fruit purées are cooked with cereals for a dish which is a cross between porridge and soup. When seasoned with salt, it becomes a savoury supper dish; when sweetened with sugar or honey, it is served as a dessert.

Apricot purée

Fruit essence *is extracted from the skins of citrus fruit which contain the flavoursome essential oils. They dissipate in the heat of cooking, so use as a last-minute flavouring for sauces or custards*

Pear, *like other hard fruit, must be cooked before sieving*

Apple *is found in puréed form in many world-famous dishes*

Apricots *are commonly paired with banana*

Strawberries *are among the soft fruits that need no prior cooking*

Raspberries *must have their seeds filtered out before being puréed*

Cherries *are cooked as purées for warm and cold soups*

Kiwi fruit *may need sieving after puréeing to remove all the seeds*

Blackberries *produce more juice when cooked first*

Blueberries *need gentle cooking to soften their skins*

Rhubarb *lends itself to purées but benefits from a squeeze of lemon*

Mango *purée is easily obtained from ripe fruit*

FRUIT PURÉES

Thick fruit purées have always been used as fillings for pies and crêpes, and as a base for mousses and fools. Thinner purées can be used for both hot and cold sauces. The latter are often known as *coulis*, which is quite simply a French word that is applied to all sieved sauces, though the term was once reserved for savoury meat and fish sauces. Most fruit can be used for purées; soft fruit can be used uncooked, while firmer fruits usually need to be stewed first. While fresh fruit is always best, both frozen and dried fruits can also be used. Modern electric appliances, such as food processors and blenders, are quite handy for making coarse and medium purées, but a really smooth and delicate purée can only be obtained by hand-sieving through a fine, nylon mesh.

Soft fruits – strawberries, raspberries, loganberries, ripe peaches, mangoes, kiwi fruit, bananas, pineapple and melon – are prepared simply by hulling, peeling or removing the stones. The flesh is then forced through a nylon sieve, or puréed in a food processor or blender, and sweetened to taste. Sugar is standard, but honey has an affinity for many fruit flavours, especially peaches and apricots. It may be necessary to heat the honey slightly for easier blending.

Firmer soft fruits, such as redcurrants, blueberries and blackberries, may require gentle cooking to release all the juices or to soften the skins. Place the fruit in a non-reactive saucepan with very little water and place over a gentle heat. When warmed through, proceed as for other soft fruit. Hard fruit, such as apples, pears and rhubarb, must be cooked. Allow 2–3 tablespoons water to every 500 g (1 lb) fruit; slightly more water may be needed to cook pears. The advantage of pre-cooking is that it affords the opportunity to add an extra layer of flavour. For example, add a slice of fresh ginger, a star anise or a sprig of fresh thyme to the fruit. Remove before puréeing.

Some fruits have a tendency to discolour. Bananas and apples are prime examples; add lemon juice before cooking to preserve their colour. The ascorbic acid (vitamin C) in the juice inhibits the oxidation process and it also imparts a pleasant tang to the mixture. Speed will keep discoloration to a minimum, so peel mangoes, apples and pears as quickly as possible, and do not prepare them until the last minute. Alternatively, squeeze the juice of one lemon into a bowl of water and add the peeled fruit. This will keep it from discolouring, but it will also dilute the flavour.

FEATHERING

For a spider's web pattern, pipe a spiral of cream onto a fruit purée base. Draw a skewer across from the centre to the edge, then from the edge to the centre. Repeat round the plate. Hold the plate steady when serving or the design will be marred.

PURÉEING FRUIT

Purées can be fine or coarse; fine purées lend themselves to sauces or coulis while more substantial purées can be eaten as desserts, or relish accompaniments to cooked meats. Purées can be processed using electrical machines, hand-cranked food mills or by forcing through a sieve; and can be made with fresh, frozen or cooked fruits. Be sure to adjust the processing method to match the desired consistency. For example, a fine-mesh nylon sieve will result in a very fine purée. Also, some fruits, such as kiwi fruit, which can be processed in a mill or blender, may need further sieving to remove all the seeds.

A trio of textures
The many different textures of fruit result in a variety of different textured purées.

1 Fruits with a lot of seeds, such as raspberries, gooseberries and passion fruit, need to be forced through a sieve to remove the pips. If desired, add lemon juice to thin.

2 A food processor can be used for soft fruit, such as pineapple, to make a coarse purée, or for cooked fruit, such as apples, to make finer purée.

COOK'S CHOICE
FRUIT FOOL IN COOKIE CUPS

Serves 4–6

*500 g (1 lb) fruit purée, such as
gooseberry, rhubarb or apple*
Sugar to taste
250 ml (8 fl oz) double cream
*60 g (2 oz) unsalted butter,
softened*
60 g (2 oz) caster sugar
Vanilla essence
2 egg whites
60 g (2 oz) plain flour, sifted
Raspberry purée
Single cream for feathering

To prepare the fool, force the purée through a fine-mesh nylon sieve. Add sugar to taste and set aside. In a bowl, whip the double cream until it just begins to stiffen. Fold the purée into the cream until well blended. Chill until serving. For the cookie cups, preheat the oven to 190°C (375°F; gas 5). In a bowl, cream together the butter and sugar until light and fluffy. Add the vanilla, continue mixing and gradually add the egg whites. Gently mix in the flour. Line baking sheets with parchment. Take a teaspoon of the mixture and, with circular movements, smooth it out with the back of the spoon. Place in the oven and bake until just golden around the edges, 5-7 minutes. With a spatula, lift off and transfer the soft cookies to upturned glasses or bowls for a cupped shape. Work in small batches as the cookies cool and harden very quickly. To serve, coat the bottoms of dessert plates with raspberry purée and feather with the cream (see page 202). Fill the cookie cups with the fool, place in the centre of the purée and serve immediately.

Use fruit purées for flavour and colour

Once prepared, fruit purées have many uses. They can serve as the base for ice creams or sorbets, or they can be folded into yogurt for a simple but flavoursome dessert. Purées also make excellent dessert sauces. Rich chocolate desserts go well with a raspberry purée base. For an attractive presentation, simply place a spoonful on a dessert plate and tilt the plate, swirling the purée to coat. Place the cake or pastry in the centre of the purée. Use a single purée or combine them for more flavour and colour. Vanilla ice cream can be served on a plate that has been coated with strawberry purée to one side and kiwi purée to the other, and garnished with a sprinkling of fresh blueberries. Passion fruit purée has a wonderful flavour and a bright red pink colour; pair it with apricot purée and serve with Madeira cake.

Freezing is the best way to preserve the flavour of fruit purées for future use. To freeze, pack the purée in plastic containers, allowing some room for expansion, and cover with airtight lids.

Figs

Prunes

Apricots

DRIED FRUIT

Dried fruit can be used for purées. Use them alone, in combination, or with fresh fruit. For example, pair dried apricots with cranberries, or dried figs with pears. Spices, such as cinnamon and cloves, go well with the musky flavours of dried fruit. Purée as for fresh fruit, but it is best to soak overnight or simmer gently before using.

FRUIT SYRUPS

Syrups are clear, sweetened juices, the strongest of which used to be known as cordials. Most familiar as a flavouring for drinks, fruit syrups are a versatile ingredient which can also be used as a sauce for desserts, cakes and puddings. They are essential for fruit sundaes and ice cream sodas, and make a pleasant sugar syrup alternative for fruit salads. They can also be used to enhance mousses, ice creams and sweets. Use fruit syrups undiluted, or add water, soda, milk or drinking yogurt to make drinks such as shakes, sodas or fruit cups. Provided they are stored properly in a cool, dark place, syrups can be kept for up to one year; they can also be frozen. Fruit syrups can be shop-bought, but they are also easy to make at home, where the sugar content and flavour can be personalized.

Fruit juice can react with certain substances, so it is important to ensure that the pans and utensils used are not made of zinc, copper or iron. Once the juice has been extracted, work quickly to keep discoloration to a minimum. Fruit syrups must be made with fruit which is at its peak; under-ripe fruit has an unsatisfactory flavour and is not juicy enough. However, over-ripe fruit will give the juice a musty flavour, and mouldy fruit can affect the keeping qualities of the finished syrup.

The best fruits to choose are flavoursome, juicy berries, such as blackcurrants, blackberries, raspberries and loganberries. Other choices include strawberries, gooseberries, elderberries, apples and rosehips. Citrus fruits such as lemons, limes and kumquats, also make good syrups. For these, both the zest and the pulp can be used in combination for extra flavour.

FRUIT WATERS

Fruit waters are made by infusing fresh fruit with water and sugar for a refreshing drink. Puréed berry fruits work the best though any strong-flavoured fruit can be used. For 500 g (1 lb) fruit, add 600 ml (1 pt) water and 125 g (4 oz) sugar. Strain before serving. For firmer fruit, dice, place in a saucepan with the water and bring to the boil. Stir in the sugar, cool and strain. Citrus waters are made by adding the zest to boiling water. Cool, stir in the juice and sweeten to taste. Serve chilled, in tall glasses without ice, which would dilute the flavour. Garnish with fruit or mint sprigs.

Home-made syrups can be flavoured in many ways. Combine fruit, such as apple and blackberry, add herbs such as mint, sweet cicely and lemon thyme, or infuse with spices such as cardamom, whole vanilla pods and cinnamon sticks.

The pulp which remains after all the juice has been extracted can often be put to good use. Strawberry, gooseberry, apricot and apple pulp can be puréed and sieved to make a fruit fool or mousse. The pulp from berry fruit, such as raspberries and blackberries, is usually too full of pips to yield much purée, but it can be used for making fruit wine. The pulp from rosehips, however, cannot be re-used.

Some fruit syrups tend to lose their colour faster than others, though a little vegetable colouring may be added to give a more attractive appearance. The addition of lemon juice also helps preserve colour. Apple juice,

MAKING SYRUP

Any fruit can be used to make syrups, though berries are the easiest. Use alone, combine with other fruit or flavour with citrus peel, herbs or spices.

1 Prepare a purée (see page 202), then strain through a sieve lined with muslin. Gather the corners of the cloth together and twist tightly to force out the juice.

2 Add 500 g (1 lb) of sugar to every 300 ml (½ pt) of juice. Place over a low heat and stir to dissolve the sugar, then boil. Less sugar may be used, but it will reduce keeping time.

3 Lower the heat. With a spoon, skim off any scum. Dip a pastry brush in water and clean the sides of the pan to prevent burning. Cool before using.

Fruit syrups

Colourful and deliciously sweet syrups can be used to enhance a wide range of recipes. They make attractive toppings poured over scoops of ice cream; mixed into shakes and sodas they add colour and an extra taste dimension; stirred into fruit salads they increase the range of flavours.

Fruit salad with syrup

Strawberry milkshake

Blackcurrant soda

on the other hand, tends to darken with processing and this can be a problem for the home cook. Freezing fruit syrup helps to counteract the problem of fading colours. Instead of using bottles, pour the syrup into small plastic containers, leaving room at the top for expansion, then freeze. Ice-cube trays are also effective. Each cube will be sufficient to make one 250 ml (8 fl oz) drink. Freezing also solves the problems of sterilization for bottling, which is a lengthy and complicated process; unless the bottles are specially made, they tend to break in the preserving pans.

Despite the processing, most fruit syrups are a good source of vitamin C. This is particularly true of rosehip and blackcurrant syrups, which are delicious when mixed with orange or grapefruit juice for extra nutrition at the start of the day.

Fruit syrups are concentrated, so a little goes a long way. A couple of spoonfuls will flavour a sauce, and the same amount will make a refreshing drink diluted with water, white wine, drinking yogurt or soda. Fruit

syrups are the ideal edible gift as they can be made in large quantities. Use clear or coloured bottles for attractive presentation, and tie with pretty ribbons to decorate.

FRUIT JELLIES

Fruit jellies are another flavoursome use for fruit juice. Heat together 450 ml (³/₄ pt) juice, 90 g (3 oz) sugar and 4 tbsp liquid glucose, stirring until the sugar dissolves. Add 30 g (1 oz) powdered gelatine and stir to dissolve. Pour into a moistened tin, about 6 mm (¹/₄ in) deep. Leave to set in a cool place. To cut, use a sharp knife; dip the blade in hot water to make slicing easier. Alternatively, use cutters for festive shapes. Use single juices or combine a light and a dark coloured juice for layered jellies. Let the bottom layer set slightly before adding the top layer. Serve plain, or roll in caster sugar for a crunchy coating.

EDIBLE
LEAVES
& FLOWERS

FLOWERS

One of the most visually appealing ingredients available to the cook is undoubtedly a sprinkling of fresh, edible flowers. The culinary use of flowers dates back thousands of years; the first recorded mention was 140 years before the Christian era. In the Far and Middle East, rose and orange blossoms have always been used; in the Mediterranean region, stuffed courgette flowers have been deep-fried or braised as a starter for many years. Some flowers, such as lavender, rose, nasturtium, jasmine and orange blossom,

can lend their delicate flavour to sorbets, custards, jams and jellies, liqueurs, wines and teas. Other blossoms – cornflowers, geraniums, chrysanthemums and marigolds, for example – are rather dull in flavour but add a splash of colour, which has the effect of stimulating the palate.

When choosing flowers to use with or on foods, there are several important guidelines which should be followed. Firstly, be sure to use only edible blossoms, such as the flowers shown here. Ensure that the flowers selected have been grown without the help of pesticides or other chemical sprays. Flowers from the florist are quite often treated, so those from a reliable source, such as an untreated home garden, are best. Even if the flowers are being used as a decoration and not as an ingredient, any flower which comes into contact with food should be suitable for human consumption. If in doubt, check with a local horticultural society or poison control centre. All of the flowers shown are nontoxic and safe for culinary use.

If gathering flowers from the garden, they should be picked early in the day and in dry weather. Rinse quickly under gently running, cool water. Do not gather more than one day in advance as the blossoms wilt quickly. Before using in any preparation, remove the pistils, stamens and the white part at the base of the petals. This is called the "heel" and, where visible, it should be cut off as it will impart a bitter flavour to the finished dish.

Many flowers, such as lavender, hibiscus, heather and rose buds, can be dried for use out of season. One of the best uses for dried flowers is for flavouring sugars. Grind the dry petals, then mix 1 part petals to 4 parts sugar. Let the mixture sit for at least 1 month to allow the flavour to mellow before using.

Fresh flowers are preferable for flavouring butter. Wrap unsalted butter in muslin, place in a bowl of flower petals and leave overnight in a cool place to infuse the butter. To best enjoy the delicate flavour, spread on thin slices of bread and serve with flower jellies and jams.

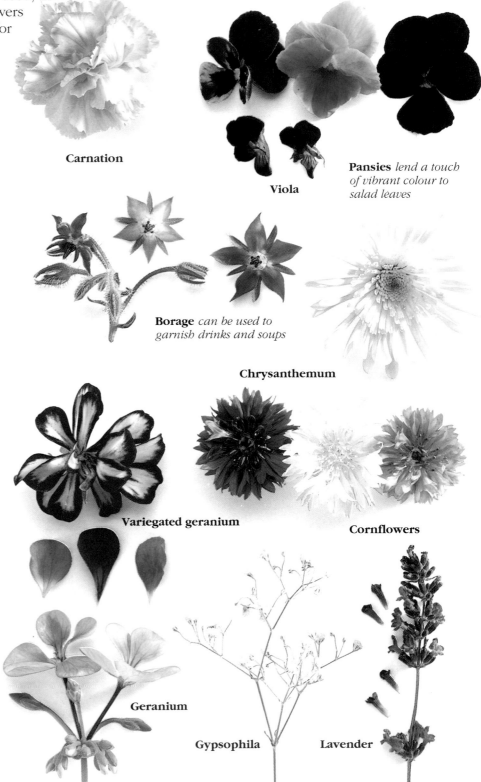

Carnation

Viola

Pansies *lend a touch of vibrant colour to salad leaves*

Borage *can be used to garnish drinks and soups*

Chrysanthemum

Variegated geranium

Cornflowers

Geranium

Gypsophila

Lavender

Marigolds *can be used in savoury dishes; chop finely and, with one or two leaves, add to omelettes, cream cheese, soufflés and vegetable terrines*

Nasturtiums *can be shredded and added to a risotto or mixed with olive oil to top a hot pasta*

Daylily (Hemerocallis) *can be floated in a soup tureen or punch bowl; some lilies are poisonous so check with a reference source before using*

Honeysuckle *is one of the more fragrant flowers that can be used to good effect to flavour cakes, sorbets and soft drinks*

Gladiolus *can be used to top cakes and gateaux and be served alongside ice creams*

Rose *has many uses with food both as a garnish in fresh and crystallized form and as an ingredient*

Wild roses

Freesia *is highly scented and makes a wonderful flavouring for sorbets if infused in a sugar syrup*

Sweet pea *makes a very attractive garnish for vegetable dishes*

FLOWERS IN THE KITCHEN

Edible blossoms are an unusual and colourful garnish that can be used to great effect in dishes both sweet and savoury. They impart a delicate flavour to sorbets, jams and salads, for example. Courgette flowers are even robust enough to be lightly fried, while dried flowers are a common ingredient in many spice mixtures.

A scattering of colourful petals and flowers is most striking when set against a background of lightly dressed salad greens. Be sure to use lettuces which match the flowers in texture and complement them in flavour. Delicate lettuces and salad herbs, such as lamb's lettuce and chervil, are best. Use a dressing which is light in vinegar or lemon juice. A highly acidic dressing will both discolour the petals and overwhelm their subtle flavour. Toss the leaves beforehand and arrange on individual plates; add the flowers just before serving for the most appealing and colourful appearance. Herb flowers, such as borage and chive, are ideal for salads, as are peppery nasturtium blossoms. Cornflowers, violas and marigolds are also useful for their colour. In sweet dishes, roses are the obvious choice, and they marry well with many fruits, especially cherries.

A selection of brightly coloured edible flowers can turn an ordinary salad into something eye-catching

Flowers in salads
Never add flowers to a salad before tossing as the dressing will spoil the colour and fresh appearance of the delicate flower petals.

Ras-el-hanout

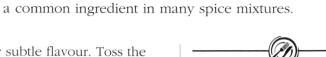

COOK'S CHOICE
STUFFED COURGETTE FLOWERS

Serves 4

12–14 courgette flowers
250 g (8 oz) ricotta cheese
4 tbsp freshly grated Parmesan cheese
1 small bunch fresh basil, chopped
Freshly grated nutmeg
1 egg, beaten
Salt
90 g (3 oz) plain flour, sifted
Vegetable oil for frying

Rinse the flowers and pat dry. In a bowl, combine the cheeses, basil, nutmeg and egg, and season to taste. Fill each flower with the cheese mixture and close, twisting the tip of the blossom to seal. In a bowl, whisk the flour with 250 ml (8 fl oz) water added gradually; it should resemble heavy cream. Heat the oil in a frying pan. Dip each flower into the batter and fry until golden, about 2–3 minutes each side. Drain on paper towels, sprinkle with salt and serve hot.

RAS-EL-HANOUT
Ras-el-hanout is a North African spice mixture which translates literally as "top of the shop." It is used to flavour rice, couscous and tajines, the slowly cooked stews common to Morocco and Tunisia. There is no one specific recipe; North African grocers often mix their own, so the combinations can vary. A typical blend could include peppercorns, cardamom, mace, galangal, nutmeg, allspice, cinnamon, ash berries, cloves, ginger, turmeric, nigella, lavender, rosebuds, Spanish fly, cassia and fennel seeds.

Rose petal ice cream is traditional in concept but very contemporary in terms of today's cuisine

500 ml (16 fl oz) milk

Petals from 1 large rose, or to taste, rinsed

8 egg yolks

125 g (4 oz) caster sugar

250 ml (8 fl oz) double cream, whipped

Red food colouring (optional)

Fresh or crystallized rose petals for garnish

Place the milk in a saucepan and bring to the boil. Add the rose petals, cover, and leave to infuse for 15 minutes. In a large, heatproof bowl, whisk together the egg yolks and the sugar until thick. Strain the rose petals out of the milk and then return the milk to boiling point. Pour a little of the hot milk onto the yolk mixture and whisk to blend, then pour it all into the saucepan of milk, lower the heat, and stir constantly with a wooden spoon until thick. Draw your finger across the back of the wooden spoon; if it leaves a clear mark, the mixture is cooked. Cool, then fold in the whipped cream and food colouring, if using. Churn in an ice cream machine according to manufacturer's instructions. Garnish with rose petals and serve immediately.

Candied violets *can be made at home or bought ready-made, and are the perfect decoration for many desserts*

Fresh rose petals are the ideal garnish for this refreshing dessert, but crystallized petals can be used to delicious effect, too

CRYSTALLIZING ROSE PETALS

The ideal dessert decoration, crystallized rose petals can be bought or made at home. Separate the petals and trim away any white parts. Be sure to work in a dry environment as they are very sensitive to humidity. Many other edible flowers can be crystallized, such as violets and borage.

1 Dissolve 60 g (2 oz) gum arabic (or edible gum) in 300 ml (½ pt) warmed rose water. Allow to cool.

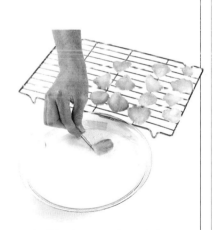

2 With tweezers, dip each petal into the rose water mixture and coat lightly and evenly. Shake the petal gently to remove excess liquid.

3 Dip the coated petals into sugar and place on greaseproof paper to dry. Store in an airtight container lined with greaseproof paper.

FLORAL WATERS AND CORDIALS

The use of floral waters in cookery dates from the Middle Ages. Orange blossom and rose were the most commonly used essences, which, along with elderflower, gained popularity in 17th-century England. Nowadays, floral waters are used primarily in the cuisines of India, the Middle East and Eastern Europe, where they flavour everything from meat stews, to pastries, to after-dinner coffees. Floral waters are available in speciality shops, but be sure to use only floral waters intended for cookery as some are destined for cosmetic use only.

ROSE WATER

In Turkey, rose water flavoured sweets such as Turkish delight, are traditionally served with coffee

A diluted form of attar of roses (pure rose oil), rose water is an ancient flavouring. Indeed, before the birth of Christ, Persia was exporting rose water as far afield as China. Once a favourite flavouring in Elizabethan England, rose water still reigns supreme in the highly-perfumed sweet dishes of India and the Middle East. In India, a festive creamed rice dish, known as *kheer,* is flavoured with cardamom and rose water, and decorated with silver leaf. In Turkey, rose water scents the sweetmeats served with the strong coffee: a heavy sugar syrup, fragrant with rose water, is thickened with cornflour and mastic to make *loukoum,* better known as Turkish delight. It may be used to soak the rich, sweet pastry known as *baklava.* Delicate rose-scented sorbets, ice creams, mousses and jellies make an unusual conclusion to a meal.

Try rose water sprinkled over fresh strawberries, or used to perfume sweetened whipped cream

Rose water

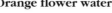

Orange flower water

ORANGE FLOWER WATER

A highly scented blancmange can be made with orange flower water

Distilled from orange blossoms, orange flower water is used to greatest effect to enhance oranges, or to add a delicate perfume of flowers to citrus fruit salads, sorbets and jellies. Like rose water, it is a powerful flavouring and should be used with restraint. As a culinary ingredient, it was most popular in Medieval times; orange-scented blancmange, still appreciated today, dates from this period. Today, it enjoys great popularity the Middle East where a soothing mixture of orange flower water and sugar is often given to children before bedtime. When this drink is prepared with boiling water, the infusion is called white coffee, and it makes a relaxing and digestive drink for all ages. To prepare, allow 1 teaspoon orange flower water per small cup and add boiling water to fill. Sweeten with sugar or, better still, with orange blossom honey. Although it is most commonly used to perfume puddings and pastries, a spoonful will also enhance salad dressings and stews.

To prepare simple cordials, sweeten shop-bought floral waters and blend with water, or use fresh or dried flowers to make a syrup (see below) and create more original beverages. Choose highly scented edible blossoms, as these will make for the most flavoursome syrups. Elderflowers, roses, violets, clove-scented pinks, primroses, lilacs and orange blossoms are all intensely perfumed and make delicious syrups.

In hot weather, cordials are more refreshing when diluted with chilled soda water or sparkling fruit juice, or they can be combined with sparkling or still wine for an unusual aperitif. In cold weather, teas or tisanes (see page 274) can be mixed with floral syrups for a warm and soothing drink, or combine syrups with hot mulled cider or wine, and wintery spices such as cloves and cinnamon sticks.

Floral syrups can also be used to flavour jellies, puddings, desserts, fresh fruit salads, ice creams and sorbets. A tablespoon or two of a floral syrup can also add a subtle difference to a salad dressing, barbecue sauce, marinade or dipping sauce.

COOK'S CHOICE
RATAFIA OF CARNATIONS

Makes 1 litre (1³/₄ pt)

250 g (8 oz) scented carnation petals
60 g (2 oz) caster sugar
1 clove
1 very small cinnamon stick
1 litre (1 ³/₄ pt) vodka or white eau-de-vie

Remove all flower heels, if any. Combine all the ingredients in a large bottle or glass jar. Seal and leave to infuse in a cool, dark place for at least 1 month, stirring occasionally. When the petals lose their colour, strain and rebottle the ratafia.

COOK'S CHOICE
CHERRY AND ROSE PETAL BRANDY

Makes 1 litre (1³/₄ pt)

750 g (1 ¹/₂ lb) sour cherries
250 g (8 oz) cherry leaves
500 g (1 lb) caster sugar
6 scented roses, petals only
60 g (2 oz) dried jasmine flowers
1 litre (1 ³/₄ pt) brandy

Pit the cherries; crack the stones. In a jar, combine the cherries, stones, leaves and sugar. Add the rose petals, jasmine flowers and brandy and stir. Seal. Infuse in a cool, dark place for at least 1 month. Strain into bottles and store in a dark place.

Floral syrups
Any edible blossom can be infused in a sugar syrup for use in unusual and refreshing drinks.

Floral cordials

COOK'S CHOICE
SUMMER PUNCH

Makes about 1 litre (1³/₄ pt)

1 orange, sliced
1 apple, sliced
1 tbsp orange flower water
1 tsp vanilla essence
1 litre (1 ³/₄ pt) sparkling water or tonic water
125 ml (4 fl oz) floral syrup, such as elderflower
Lemon and orange slices for garnish

In a large bowl or jug, combine the orange, apple, orange flower water and vanilla. Pour over the sparkling water or tonic water, cover and leave to infuse for at least 2 hours. Alternatively, refrigerate for slightly longer. Stir in the elderflower syrup. Serve over ice cubes, and garnish with the lemon and orange slices.

MAKING FLORAL SYRUP

For a basic syrup, place about 500 g (1 lb) flower petals (white heels removed) in a saucepan and add 600 ml (1 pt) water, or more if necessary to cover. Bring to the boil, cover, and infuse for 30 minutes. Strain and return to the pan with 350 g (12 oz) sugar, or to taste. Simmer for 10 minutes. Infuse the petals alone or create floral, fruit, herb and spice combinations: violets sweetened with honey, hawthorn or may blossoms with borage flowers, elderflowers and orange blossoms with dried apple.

WRAPPINGS

An often under-exploited technique, wrapping with leaves offers a means of presenting food in an attractive, flavoursome and easy-to-manage manner. *Dolmades*, the Greek dish of vine leaves stuffed with rice, is the classic example. Fragile ingredients, such as fish, which are easily broken during cooking or serving, can be wrapped in lettuce, spinach or vine leaves for reinforcement. This not only enhances the flavour, but it makes them easier to get from kitchen to table, and offers a stunning presentation. Large, tough leaves, such as lotus or corn husks, are ideal wrappers but they are inedible and must be discarded. Some edible leaves should be blanched to remove bitterness, or render them supple enough for wrapping. Do not limit the use of leaves to ingredients which must be held together: experiment with any filling that could benefit from a delicate infusion of leafy flavour.

Lettuce Leaves The long, outer leaves of cos lettuce make an excellent wrapping for steamed fish, served whole or in fillets. The more tender, pliable tips are well suited to the traditional Thai manner of serving spring rolls: a raw lettuce leaf is lined with fresh mint, the spring roll is placed on top, and the package is rolled up and dipped into a sweet-and-sour sauce.

Spinach Leaves With their assertive flavour and deep green colour, these are the ideal leafy green for wrapping. For an attractive presentation, line small, buttered ramekins with blanched spinach leaves and fill with a vegetable mousse. Bake in a water bath and turn out before serving.

Cabbage Leaves Particularly suitable for slow cooking, stuffed cabbage leaves is a classic dish in many countries. The leaves can be filled with meat or rice, or both, and served with a tomato-based sauce. For easier rolling, it is best to remove the tough central core before stuffing.

Vine Leaves A familiar and popular wrapping, these have a pleasant lemony tang and are suitable for many ingredients, such as fish or quail, and many cooking methods. Blanching before stuffing is imperative: fresh leaves need their slight bitterness subdued, and leaves packed in brine are very salty. Always adjust the seasoning accordingly when using preserved vine leaves.

Lettuce leaves

White cabbage leaves

Spinach leaves

Vine leaves

PAAN LEAVES
Throughout India, it is customary to offer a paan leaf bundle at the end of the meal as a breath freshner and an aid to digestion. The paan leaf is filled with a mixture of bitter, sweet and sour flavours, such as: betel nut, coconut, cardamom, aniseed, sugar balls and melon seeds. The leaf is secured with a clove.

MAKING STUFFED VINE LEAVES

Vine leaves stuffed with a savoury mixture – such as the cooked rice, sultana, onion, pine nut and parsley mixture shown here – are a classic. They can be served cold with Greek yogurt as a starter, or warm, with tomato sauce as a main course. The leaves should always be blanched before filling. Rice is essential, but try other ingredients: crushed tomatoes, chopped spring onions, mint, cumin and minced lamb.

1 Place a vine leaf, vein side up, on the work surface. Place a spoonful of filling at the base of the leaf, just above the stem.

2 Bring the leaf tips up alongside the filling, making the shape slightly more rectangular. Roll securely to make a tiny bundle.

3 Serve cold as a starter, or warm as a main dish. If filled with raw stuffing, simmer in a covered pan until tender, about 2 hours.

Lotus Leaves These are usually available dried, and are most familiar as a wrapping for steamed Chinese dumplings, or dim-sum. Only fresh, young leaves can be eaten raw.
Corn Husks Frequently used in Central and South America, these are employed for the sweet, nutty flavour they impart to food, but they are not edible.
Banana Leaves These enormous leaves can be up to 3 metres long (10 ft) and 60 cm wide (2 ft). They have a very delicate flavour, which is quickly absorbed by the ingredients they enclose. Banana leaves are a common feature of Asian and West Indian cuisine.

Banana leaves are used most commonly in dishes of Asian or West Indian origin where they protect barbecued, baked or steamed fish and poultry

Large enough to wrap most foods, banana leaves impart a delicate flavour to ingredients but are inedible

WRAPPING WITH CORN HUSKS

Parboil two sweet corn husks. Lay one husk on top of the other to form a cross. Place stuffing in the centre and, starting with the bottom husk, fold over to form a square. Secure with long, thin strips of corn husk. Remove husks before serving.

Dried corn husks

Dried lotus leaves

LETTUCES AND CHICORIES

In the past, spring heralded the arrival of leafy vegetables; nowadays, many varieties are available all year round. Edible leaves come in many forms and flavours: there are a great number of commercially grown types, including lettuces and chicories, and some wild varieties such as nettle and dandelion. Rich in vitamins A and C, leaves are best used immediately after gathering as both the flavour and nutritional value are quickly lost. When choosing, look for leaves which are glossy and firm, and avoid those which are limp, discoloured or blemished. If leaves are to be stored, clean and dry thoroughly, and keep in a cool, well-ventilated place. Before storing, remove all plastic wrapping as this tends to foster humidity and encourage rot. Whether destined for the salad bowl or the soup tureen, having a year-round supply of lettuces and chicories is a great advantage for any cook.

Lettuces and chicories provide a wide range of flavours, colours and textures. Their traditional place is in the salad bowl, but many types can also be cooked successfully. The more robust chicories are delicious when braised and served alongside roast meats or poultry. Or, try a leafy, lettuce chiffonade garnish (see page 47), which offers a more substantial alternative to the traditional chopped parsley or chives.

Loose-leaf Lettuce This type of lettuce is so-named because the heads are open with no core. The leaves are easily separated and this makes them a practical plant for the home vegetable patch. You need only pick the required number of leaves while the lettuce remains firmly planted, and this guarantees a lasting supply of garden-fresh leaves for the salad bowl.

These lettuces tend to have a more delicate flavour and texture, so for salads which are well balanced, combine these lettuces with more robust leaves. Among the increasing number of varieties are *Lollo Biondo*, a very bright green lettuce with a distinctive frilly edge, and *Lollo Rosso*, which is tinged with red. *Red Oak Leaf Lettuce*, also called *Feuille de Chêne*, has rich red leaves, a fine flavour and a pleasing texture, and mixes well with other salad leaves.

Round Lettuce *Butterhead* and *Batavia* are good examples of this type, which is characterized by a compact head, a solid core and soft, tender leaves. The darker, outer leaves provide a strong flavour; the paler, inner leaves are more delicate. Round lettuces are a universal favourite for the salad bowl.

Long Lettuce *Cos*, also called *Romaine*, is the classic long lettuce. It is robust, with a mild, almost nutty flavour. In salads, these dark green, flavourful leaves stand up well to powerful ingredients, such as anchovy or Parmesan, making Cos the best lettuce to use

Cos *combines a crisp texture with a mild taste; it is named after its place of origin, the Greek island of Kos*

Lollo rosso

Red oak leaf lettuce

Crispheart lettuce, *also called iceberg and Webb's Wonder, has a tightly packed firm head and a crunchy texture, if little taste*

Chicories *are a group of lettuces that provide a pleasant bitterness when mixed with milder leaves; they are also excellent when cooked in vegetable dishes.*

Curly endive *may be regarded as the prettiest member of the chicory family with its lacy head of white, yellow and green leaves*

Lollo biondo *is one of the newer varieties of lettuce and it has dense, ruffled leaves that form a compact bunch without a heart*

Radicchio

Batavia

Chicory *is one of the most versatile of all the chicories as it is well-suited to both salads and braising*

in Caesar salad. Slightly smaller varieties, such as *Little Gem*, have the added advantage of a storage period which is longer than most lettuces.

Chicories Many vegetables known as endives are members of the chicory family; consequently, much confusion arises. With their slighty bitter taste and sturdy texture, most of the chicories lend themselves well to both cooking and salads. The compact, spear-shaped shoots of *Chicory*, also called *Belgian Endive*, owe their pallor to cultivation: they are actually grown in sandy soil in the dark, much like mushrooms. Make sure that leaf tips are tinged with yellow; if turning green they are likely to be old. The leaves can be separated and chopped coarsely for use in salads, or left whole for baking or braising. To reduce bitterness when cooking, it is best to remove the central core. *Curly Endive*, or *Frisée*, fans out to display its sprawling, lacy leaves and it is delicious when combined with hot bacon, croûtons and a poached egg. *Escarole* is a chicory which looks like a cross between lettuce and curly endive. The flavour is quite bitter; for salads it should be torn into small pieces. It is delicious when braised in meat stock. *Radicchio*, a red-leaf variety of chicory, is favoured by the Italians. It has a glorious colour, which makes it a valuable contribution to any monotone green salad. The cup-shaped leaves offer a decorative container for hot or cold salads, and the heads can be sliced in halves or quarters and grilled.

LEAVES AND SALAD HERBS

Many of the leafy plants that grow wild in the Mediterranean region, such as lamb's lettuce and rocket, have been used in cookery since Roman times. These are now enjoying renewed popularity and are cultivated for year-round availability. Nasturtium leaves, with their distinctive peppery flavour, are also gaining favour, and they make a delicious addition to any green salad. Nettles and dandelion are among the most flavourful and easily obtained, provided that an untended field is accessible. Always make sure that leaves gathered in the wild have not been chemically treated with products unfit for human consumption. Also, avoid gathering plants growing close by the roadside where they are exposed to dirt and leaded petrol fumes. All of these leaves should be picked in the spring, while they are at their most tender and before the flowering varieties have begun to bloom.

Rocket (Arugula) Gathered by the ancient Romans, this was appreciated for its sharp peppery flavour. It is related to mustard and has fiddle-shaped leaves which look similar to radish tops. Rocket is one of the ingredients of *mesclun,* the traditional *Niçoise* mixture of tiny salad leaves. Quickly sautéed in olive oil, rocket can also be tossed with pasta and served hot.

Lamb's Lettuce (Corn Salad) There are several varieties of this small leaf which traditionally grew wild. The most common variety has long narrow leaves, while the marshland type has small, compact, rounded leaves. Ideal for salads, lamb's lettuce is delicious when tossed with a walnut oil dressing and served with diced beetroot and a sprinkling of shelled walnuts. It also marries well with sweet corn; tinned will do, but fresh baby corn, lightly blanched, is best.

Dandelions A nuisance to the gardener, dandelion leaves are the cook's delight. The most tender leaves appear in the spring, and the jagged, slightly bitter leaves make a

Leaves are long and spear shaped with a spicy bitterness

Lamb's lettuce

Watercress

Rocket is used to great effect in Italian cuisine, where it is added to salads, tossed with pasta or stirred into risottos

The pointed, spinach-like leaves contain oxalic acid, which gives sorrel its sour bite

Sorrel

delicious salad when young. Older leaves should be blanched or wilted with a hot dressing to tenderize before serving (see below). If gathered from a garden or un-tended field, be sure that the dandelions have not been treated with pesticides or other chemicals unfit for human consumption.

Nettle Only the young, tender tips are suitable for cooking; the stalks and lower leaves are not edible. Purée for soup or a vegetable accompaniment. Finely chopped nettles can also be added to a soft cheese, such as goat cheese or ricotta, and used as a filling for ravioli.

Sorrel The most acidic of all the edible leaves, this is very high in vitamin C, which accounts for its tart flavour. One or two torn leaves, tossed into a mixed salad, is all that is required to add a refreshing note. Likewise, only a small amount is required to impart sorrel's characteristic piquant flavour to a cooked dish. Like spinach, its volume dimin-ishes significantly when cooked, so raw quantities should be carefully calculated. Allow about 1 kg (2 lb) raw sorrel for each 500 g (1 lb) cooked.

Purslane Often considered to be no more than a weed, this plant has crisp, succulent leaves, which are actually quite delicious. It can be cooked like spinach and served with cream or butter, or added raw to salads.

Nasturtium The leaves of this plant can be used in a number of ways. With their slight peppery flavour, whole leaves are a welcome addition to green salads. Chopped or shred-ded, they can be blended into soft cheese for a sandwich filling, or added to scrambled eggs and omelettes.

Watercress In order to thrive, the shoots of this plant must grow in the cleanest of water, hence, most of the watercress available in stores is now cultivated. Delicious in a cream soup, watercress can also be chopped and added to butter and used to flavour meat or fish. Watercress is fragile and does not keep well; use within one day of purchase for maximum flavour.

Garden Cress Familiar as a garnish, this can also be combined with egg mayonnaise as a sandwich filling. Cress is easily grown at home (see page 62) or bought growing in small containers.

COOK'S CHOICE
NETTLE SOUP

Serves 4

500 g (1 lb) young nettle leaves, washed
4 shallots, finely chopped
2 tbsp unsalted butter
1 large potato, peeled and diced
Salt
Freshly ground black pepper
Double cream and croûtons for garnish

Separate one-third of the nettle leaves and chop finely. In a stockpot, combine the shallots and butter and cook over low heat until soft, about 5 minutes. Stir in the whole nettle leaves and cook for 1 minute. Add the potato and 1 litre (1¾ pt) of cold water and season to taste. Cover and simmer until the potato is cooked, about 20 minutes. Transfer to a food processor or food mill and purée, in two batches if necessary, until smooth. Taste for seasoning. Stir in the chopped nettles and the cream, sprinkle on the croûtons and serve immediately.

Nasturtium

Nettle

Purslane

Garden cress

Dandelion

WILTING LEAVES
The robust leaves of dande-lions can be tenderized by wilting with a hot dressing. Wash the leaves and place in a bowl. In a frying pan, cook diced bacon in olive oil until it browns, then sprinkle over the leaves. Deglaze the pan with wine vinegar (see page 249), pour over the leaves, season and toss.

SEAWEED

In the West, plants that grow in or around the sea have been acclaimed for their medicinal properties, to the detriment of their culinary possibilities. Ignored by the Ancient Greeks and Romans, Occidentals have subsequently had little enthusiasm for the number of edible sea vegetables that are native to their shores. But seaweed – rich in minerals, vitamins and protein – has long been a staple in the diets of most Asian populations. Seaweed has been harvested off the shores of Japan since the 17th century, and it is here that its many uses are appreciated. Most seaweed is available dried. It is easily reconstituted by soaking first in water, then boiling until softened. With a pleasantly subtle flavour and great visual appeal, seaweed can be adapted to a myriad of culinary preparations: from a seasoning for soups and poaching broths, to an ingredient in salads and stir-fries, to a setting agent in desserts.

Konbu Known also as giant sea kelp, this can be used raw, freshly cooked or dried. More than any other sea vegetable, it takes pride of place in the cuisine of Japan, though it features in many Korean dishes as well. It is the foundation for the numerous broths and stocks (*dashi*) that flavour so many Japanese dishes. When added to the cooking water of tough or hard ingredients, such as pulses, konbu strips impart not only flavour; they help to soften the ingredient, making it more digestible. Strips can also be plaited and deep-fried to make attractive basket-shaped containers. *Tororo konbu* are bleached, finely shaved strands, which become sticky when cooked. They can be used either in soups or as wrappers for parcels of rice. Konbu rolls are a traditional Japanese dish in which dried fish, usually herring, is rolled in sheets of konbu and then simmered in a flavoursome broth.

Nori Along with kelp, this is the most widely consumed of all the seaweeds. In English, this is called laver. Most often sold in sheets, its principal use is as a wrapper for sushi (see page 221). To lightly crisp Nori, releasing its delicate sweet flavour, pass the sheets over a flame, or place in a hot oven for a few minutes before crumbling over a salad or into a soup.

Wakame The seaweed that most resembles land vegetables, this has a mild flavour and lovely green colour; it is the ideal type for the first-time seaweed taster to try. The texture after reconstituting is very tender, making it popular in salads, sprinkled over rice dishes or added to pickles.

Hijiki This type requires little preparation as it is usually pre-cooked before drying. Looking very similar to tea leaves, this seaweed's bulk is increased immensely when soaked, so only very little is needed. Hijiki is very good sautéed, or dipped in batter and deep-fried for tempura.

Agar-agar Known also as *kanten* in Japan, this is most widely used as a gelling agent. Both varieties can be enjoyed on their own, though the white variety makes a delicious salad: soak the seaweed for a few minutes until it softens, then toss with cucumber strips, toasted almonds and a dressing of sesame oil and soy sauce.

Nidashi konbu

Konbu

Tororo konbu

Konbu rolls

FRESH SEAWEEDS

Many of the seaweeds found around the coasts of Europe can be used fresh, either cooked or raw. Laver is a bright green seaweed that has been a traditional food in the British Isles, where it is reduced to a spinach-like purée, then moulded into patties and mixed with oatmeal and called laver bread. It can be fried and served with grilled bacon or poached fish. Dulse and sea lettuce can be shredded for garnishes or salads. Not strictly a seaweed, samphire is a vegetable that grows near ocean shores. To best savour it, steam, toss with melted butter or vinaigrette, and serve as an accompaniment to seafood.

Laver bread

Samphire

Tissue thin, this Japanese seaweed is popular as an ingredient, flavouring and wrapping

Nori

Wakame

Hijiki

Red agar agar

White agar agar

An Asian staple
Seaweed is widely used in the cuisines of Japan, Korea and parts of China

LAVER BREAD AND POACHED SKATE

Serves 4

Juice of ½ lemon or to taste
60 g (2 oz) medium oatmeal
500 g (1 lb) laver, fresh or frozen
4 small skate wings
2 tbsp cider vinegar
4 tbsp oil
Lemon slices and parsley sprigs for garnish

In a bowl, mix together the lemon juice, oatmeal and laver. Mould into small patties, about 3 cm (1¼ in) in diameter, and spinkle lightly with a little more oatmeal. Place enough water to cover the skate wings in a shallow pan and bring to the boil. Add the vinegar and the skate, and poach for 8-10 minutes. Meanwhile, gently heat the oil in a frying pan and add the laver bread patties. Fry 2 minutes on either side. Serve with the skate and garnish with lemon and parsley.

PREPARING SUSHI

Nori sheets and rice in sweetened vinegar are mandatory for sushi, after that, the choice of fillings is up to the cook: mushrooms, spinach, pickled ginger and dried gourd shavings are just some examples.

1 Place a lightly toasted nori sheet on a bamboo mat. Spread with vinegared rice, leaving one edge of the nori exposed. Place the filling on top of the rice.

2 Use the mat to help roll the nori round the rice. Squeeze the mat gently to make it firmer. Leave the roll to rest for five minutes.

3 Unroll and remove the bamboo mat. Using a sharp knife, slice the sushi rolls into 2.5 cm (1 in) rounds. Serve with soy sauce and wasabi paste (see page 166).

OILS, VINEGARS & DAIRY PRODUCTS

OLIVE OIL

Olive oil is one of the oldest culinary oils. In ancient Athens, the olive was a symbol of the city's prosperity, and its oil was used both in cooking and as fuel for oil-burning lamps. The Romans also spread olive cultivation throughout their empire, from Africa to the Iberian peninsula. There was even an ancient Roman philosophy of longevity that linked two vital products of their daily life: wine and olive oil. Nowadays, olive oils are classified by category – from pure to extra-virgin – and these categories are determined by levels of acidity. This is important information because a high level of acidity detracts from the flavour of oil. It is this flavour that makes olive oil such a valuable ingredient, but with so many different categories and classifications, it can be difficult to ascertain the quality within from the label without. All olive oil labels should indicate the percentage of acidity, grade of oil, volume and country of origin. If the label also shows the name of the producer and the farm or village where it was made, this is a sign that it has been produced with care, on a small scale, and the quality should be high.

PRODUCTION

The traditional method for making olive oil is to crush the olives between two opposing stone wheels until the fruit is reduced to a pulp. This pulp is then spread on mats which are stacked one upon the other and pressed down with weights. There are other more modern production methods, but this is the method used for oils labelled "cold pressed." Because the pressure from the weights is relatively low, heat does not build up in the pulp, hence, the "cold" pressing. Heat allows more oil to be extracted but also results in an inferior flavour, so cold-pressed oils are superior in quality.

Olive oil is graded on a scale that rates its level of acidity. Other factors, such as colour, flavour and aroma, are also considered, but the quality is closely linked to the percentage of acidity. The higher the level, the less aromatic and refined the oil will be. Extra-virgin olive oil, with only 1 per cent maximum acidity, is the finest. It is followed by fine virgin olive oil, with a maximum acidity of 1.5 per cent, and virgin olive oil, which can have as much as 3 per cent. Pure olive oil also has a maximum acidity level of 3 per cent, but it is made from a blend of different grades of oil.

In the end, for olive oils, quality is synonymous with flavour, and the best way to wade through the many available oils is to let your own palate be the judge.

TYPES OF OLIVE OIL

Olive oil is produced in most of the countries near the Mediterranean; only the most prominent producers are listed here.
Italian Olive Oil The oils from Tuscany and Umbria are held to be the finest. Their renown is the fruit of an extensive marketing

The taste of the finest oils is light and fruity

Cloudy oil
Air, heat and light will cause olive oil to turn rancid, so it should be stored in a cool place in an airtight container. It should be refrigerated in hot weather and after opening. When chilled the oil may turn cloudy and even solidify. Such oil will turn clear again at room temperature so that cloudiness should not be taken as an indication of the oil being ruined.

The colour of olive oil ranges from pale golden yellow to a dark dense green

Oil pourer *with spout can be used with tins of olive oil to make pouring easier*

operation, which may partially account for their reputation. There is, however, a local consortium and rigorous quality controls to maintain good production methods.

Spanish Olive Oil After Italy, Spain is the world's largest olive oil producer, though there are years when climatic conditions are more favourable to Spain and production there will surpass that in Italy. The Spanish olive oil industry is governed by an internal body that has established a quality control called "label of origin." Borjas Blancas, in the north-eastern region of Lérida, is considered to produce some of the finest of the Spanish label of origin oils.

Greek Olive Oil In Greece, annual olive oil consumption is estimated to be around 23 litres (5 gallons) per person, which puts them at the head of worldwide per capita consumption. However, Greece is only the third largest producer. Also, quality tends to vary as controls are less strict than in other oil-producing countries.

French Olive Oil Unlike Greece, French olive oil production is low but quality is generally held to be high. Most of the oil producing groves are in the south, and oils from the areas surrounding Nyons and the Vallée des Baux are of superior quality.

Cooking with Olive Oil

Olive oil can be used in the same way that other cooking oils and fats are used, but some palates find its flavour too strong. For a less pronounced flavour, blend olive oil with a more neutral oil, such as sunflower or corn oil. (An overpoweringly unpleasant taste may simply indicate a low quality oil.)

In the countries that surround the Mediterranean, olive oil is vital to the cuisine. It is as much a seasoning as a cooking medium. It can be drizzled over a platter of sliced, ripe red tomatoes, or added to a hot vegetable soup just before serving, as is often done in Italy and France. Likewise, true Spanish *gazpacho* recipes call for the addition of a Spanish olive oil just before serving. All three countries have their own version

of grilled bread with olive oil. For Italian *bruscheta*, thick slices of country bread are grilled before being rubbed with garlic and topped with olive oil and sea salt. When crushed tomatoes are added, the Spanish call it *pan con tomate*. In France, croûtons fried in olive oil can be served with a purée of potatoes and salt cod (*brandade*) or bowls of saffron-scented bouillabaisse.

Olive oil is essential to all Italian pasta sauces; when combined with garlic and chillies, it is a sauce in itself, delicious with spaghetti. Mayonnaise made with olive oil and flavoured with crushed garlic is commonplace in southern Spain and France, and many uncooked, herb-based sauces, such as *pesto*, rely on olive oil.

While Europeans often use olive oil for cooking meats and sautéing vegetables, in the Middle East, it is generally reserved for seasoning cold starters and salads, such as aubergine purée or *hummus* (chick pea purée), or for frying fish.

Infused olive oils
Some Italian extra-virgin olive oils are already infused with truffles, porcini mushrooms or lemon; some French oils are available with herbs and spices. These lend themselves well to seasoning any dish that calls for ordinary olive oil.

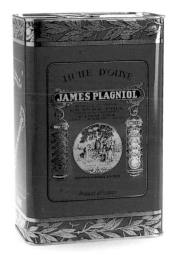

Storing oil
Light is the enemy of olive oil; it should be stored in a cool, dark place, preferably in a tin or a dark-coloured bottle. Oil purchased in bulk should always be poured into smaller containers.

NUT AND SEED OILS

For the cook, oils are a necessary ingredient. They add fat for browning and for consistency, and many oils add flavour. Oils derived from nuts and seeds, also contribute to a well-balanced diet. Much attention has been focused on mono-unsaturated, polyunsaturated and saturated fats – all of which can be present in nut and seed oils. These technical terms refer to the molecular structure of the oil, more specifically, to the number of hydrogen atoms present. Saturated fats, the least healthy, contain the maximum possible number of hydrogen atoms. The healthier polyunsaturated and mono-unsaturated fats have less than their maximum of hydrogen atoms, and so combine more easily with other substances within the body, such as oxygen. Olive oil is high in mono-unsaturated fats, while palm and coconut oils have the highest levels of saturated fats. Although there are general-purpose oils they can generally be divided into cooking oils – those which are fairly neutral in flavour and withstand heat well – and seasoning oils, which are best used to flavour uncooked dishes such as salads. Cooking oils include soy and corn oils; walnut and hazelnut oils can be heated, but are most successful as seasoning oils.

Almond Oil A pale oil made from sweet almonds, this is used in baking and confectionery. Use to coat cake tins or baking sheets when preparing delicate baked goods, or heat gently with flaked almonds and serve with fish or cooked green vegetables.

Avocado Oil Extracted from the stones of avocados, and sometimes from blemished fruit, this oil is colourless with a faint aniseed flavour. It is mainly used in North America.

Coconut Oil Extracted from the dried kernel of the coconut, this is often used in commercial food preparations and in certain Indian dishes. It is high in saturated fats.

Corn Oil One of the most economical and widely used all-purpose oils, this is deep yellow in colour and heavy in texture. Corn oil is high in polyunsaturated fats and has a high smoke point, so it is both healthy and ideal for most culinary preparations.

Cottonseed Oil Derived from the cotton plant, this is used in the production of margarine and blended cooking oils. It is also used in Egyptian cookery, where it lends a distinctive flavour.

Grapeseed Oil A pale, delicate oil extracted from grape pips, this can withstand a wide range of temperatures. When refrigerated it will not cloud, making it ideal for mayonnaise, and it has a very high smoke point so it is excellent for frying and general cookery. It is high in polyunsaturated fats.

Hazelnut Oil This is a delicious, richly flavoured oil extracted from the nut. Produced mainly in France, it is expensive and should be used with the finest vinegars for salad dressings, or as a marinade for fish or poultry. Its delicate flavour is lost when heated, but it can be whisked into a sauce at the last minute or used for baked goods in combination with hazelnuts.

OILS FOR FLAVOUR

Nut and seed oils are generally used as a flavouring for cold food, or added to hot dishes at the last minute. Pumpkin seed, walnut and hazelnut oils, Asian sesame oil, cold-pressed groundnut and pineseed oils all make superb salad dressings, vegetable seasonings and marinades. Because they are quite flavoursome – often to the point of being overpowering – they should always be used sparingly and in combination with a neutral oil, such as sunflower. They can also be used, much the same as a pat of butter, to flavour cooked foods; toss steamed or boiled green beans with walnut oil just before serving.

Groundnut Oil This is a very fine, almost tasteless oil for general use in salads, cooking and frying. The cold-pressed variety has a mild peanut flavour which is good with fruit-flavoured vinegars for salad dressings. Groundnut oil is moderately high in mono-unsaturates and low in saturates.

Palm Oil Also known as palm-nut oil or *dende oil*, this is extracted from the pulp of the fruit of oil palms. Orange-gold in colour, it has a pleasant nutty flavour. Although it is a general-purpose oil, being light in colour and taste and good for frying and making salad dressings, it does, however, turn rancid very rapidly.

Pineseed Oil With a distinctive pineseed flavour, this oil is produced on a small scale primarily in France. It is quite costly but the flavour will never disappoint. Use it for salads; it is especially delicious when added to a dipping sauce for artichokes.

Pumpkin Seed Oil This is a dark brown oil with a pleasant flavour of toasted pumpkin seeds. It is popular in Austria, where most of it is produced. Use as a last-minute seasoning for steamed vegetables or fish.

Rapeseed Oil A neutral-flavoured oil, this is suitable for frying, cooking or baking. It has a high smoke point and is very low in saturated fats.

Safflower Oil With a bright yellow colour, this oil is ideal for all culinary use, though the flavour is rather strong. Of all the cooking oils, this is the highest in polyunsaturated fats, lowest in saturated fats and a good source of vitamin E.

Sesame Oil There are several types of sesame oil. European or cold-pressed sesame oil is light in colour and nutty in flavour with a high smoke point, making it a good cooking oil. Asian sesame oil is made from

toasted sesame seeds, giving it a darker colour and more prominent taste. Middle Eastern sesame oils are lighter in flavour than Asian ones with a deep golden colour. They are aromatic and capable of being heated to a high temperature.

Soy Oil A major component of blended oils, this is a high quality, neutral-flavoured oil which is low in saturated fats.

Sunflower Oil This is one of the best all-purpose oils. It is high in polyunsaturates, tasteless, pale, light in texture and inexpensive. It can be used for frying, cooking, salad dressings and mixing with other more strongly flavoured oils.

Vegetable Oil This is an oil obtained from blending a number of oils in various proportions, and types and quantities are not necessarily given on the label. It may contain coconut or palm oils, which are high in saturated fats. Vegetable oil has little aroma or flavour, making it popular as a all-purpose culinary oil.

Walnut Oil A delicious topaz-coloured oil with a rich, nutty flavour. Walnuts from the Perigord and Dordogne in France are said to produce the best oil. In these regions, walnuts are strictly graded for quality; it is even possible for one tree to have two separate grades of walnut. Production is small, therefore this oil is expensive. Walnut oil does not keep long, either opened or unopened, so buy in small quantities and keep in a cool place, but not in the refrigerator. It makes a delicious salad dressing, and in baking it adds flavour to cakes, especially those which contain walnuts. It is also good with fish, poultry and vegetables, or use wherever a walnut taste will marry well with the ingredients.

Flavouring oils
Oils with a distinct taste should be chosen in order to enhance particular dishes; they are too overpowering to be used simply for general-purpose cooking. Such oils, particularly if they are not blended, tend also to be expensive so are best used where only a small amount is needed.

Grapeseed oil

Virgin sesame oil

Virgin pumpkin seed oil

Hazelnut oil

Walnut oil

BURNING POINT
If an oil is heated for too long to too high a temperature it may catch fire. Never use water to extinguish burning oil; instead smother it with a lid, a flameproof or fire blanket, or some aluminium foil.

FLAVOURED OILS

Oils infused with herbs and spices can add greatly to any recipe which calls for ordinary oil. There are a number of flavoured oils available in supermarkets and speciality shops, but these are also quite easy to prepare at home. Extra-virgin olive oil lends itself most naturally to flavouring. For something truly extraordinary, infuse a high-quality olive oil with a truffle; a small quantity of oil can even be flavoured with truffle shavings. Use the truffle oil to season pasta, risotto or salads. Herbs and spices can be added alone, or in combination. There are no rules, though the ingredients should always be complementary. While these oils are destined mainly for use as seasoning, not cooking, robust-flavoured herbs, such as thyme, rosemary and bay, make excellent additions to oil used for fondue.

SPICES

Spice-infused oils can be made year round using any spices at hand. To enhance the flavour, some spices such as caraway and fennel seeds, can be dry roasted before infusing. Spices can be left whole, or they can be crushed slightly to allow more flavour to escape. Appropriate choices include: cardamom, star anise, juniper, coriander seeds, nutmeg, cinnamon, cumin and cloves.

Cardamom

Juniper

Nutmeg

Saffron

HERBS

Making herb-flavoured oils is a good way of using summer herbs when they are inexpensive and plentiful. Use basil, bay, coriander leaves, oregano, marjoram, chervil, chives, dill, mint, parsley, rosemary, sage, tarragon and thyme. For the most reliable effect add herbs separately or combine with ingredients such as garlic and lemon peel for a more variable flavour.

Sage

Rosemary

Basil

Cinnamon oil　　　**Basil oil**

As an ingredient for frying and browning, oil is more versatile than butter and the range of possible flavours is more varied. To the already long list of different oils with their different perfumes, add the number of herbs, spices and other ingredients that can be infused, and discover an endless supply of seasoning alternatives. An excellent vehicle for flavour, oils need only be infused with a small amount of herbs or spices. Add a pinch of curry powder to oil and it will take on a delicious curry flavour, perfect for tossing with pasta or vegetables. Add a slice of ginger and it will become ginger oil, which can be brushed on beef marinated in soy sauce just before cooking. With a few star anise, oil becomes an excellent seasoning for chicken or shellfish dishes. Any store cupboard will benefit from a constant and plentiful supply of flavoured oils.

If using fresh herbs, wash and dry thoroughly, and bruise lightly to help release their flavour. Place the herbs in a clean bottle or jar with a clamp-top, and add oil to cover. Seal tightly and leave to stand in a cool, dark place for at least two weeks. Taste the oil; when it has a pronounced flavour it is ready to use. For a stronger flavour, add more herbs and leave to stand for a week longer. The oil can be left as it is, or the herbs can be strained. Bear in mind that the oil's flavour will strengthen on standing if it is not strained. However, the addition of a sprig of the appropriate herb is not only a most attractive finishing touch, it also makes the flavour of the oil readily identifiable. For spice-flavoured oils, both whole and ground spices can be used, though whole always have more flavour. Quantities are according to taste, the method is the same as for herb-flavoured oil.

COOKING WITH FLAVOURED OILS

Flavoured oil can be used as an alternative to ordinary oil though the results will not taste the same. A salad dressing made with olive oil is adequate, but can be delicious when made with a herb-infused olive oil. Chives, parsley and chervil – all excellent salad herbs – are ideal used alone, or in combination, to perfume a salad oil. A bottle of this oil is handy during seasons when these delicate herbs are hard to obtain. Herbs with a robust flavour (bay, rosemary, thyme and sage) impart an earthy flavour to oils. Use them to enhance marinades for meat and game, or as a marinade for small, firm goat cheeses. An excellent starter can be prepared from the marinated goat cheese: slice the cheese, place on rounds of French bread and grill until bubbly; serve on a bed of salad greens tossed with a dressing made from the marinade oil.

A groundnut oil spiced with cinnamon sticks makes a beautiful edible gift as well as a delicious oil for frying fruit fritters, cooking pancakes or waffles, or brushed on chicken for grilling. Groundnut oil can also be infused with fruit – strawberries, lemons, pears, apples, oranges and peaches – alone or in combination. Use the fruit-flavoured oil when making mayonnaise or dressings to accompany cold meats.

COOK'S CHOICE
PENNE WITH VEGETABLES AND CURRY OIL

Serves 2–4

8 tbsp extra-virgin olive oil
2 tsp curry powder
Salt
6 medium carrots, diced
500 g (1 lb) peas, fresh or frozen
1 large onion, diced
2 yellow peppers
500 g (1 lb) penne

One day before serving, infuse the oil with the curry. The day of serving, bring a saucepan of water to the boil. Add salt, place the carrots in a sieve and submerge in the water. Cook until just tender, about 2 minutes. Remove the carrots and return the water to the boil. Cook the peas in the water, about 3 minutes. Drain and set aside. In a frying pan, combine 2 tbsp of the curry oil, the onion and salt to taste. Cook over medium heat for 3 minutes. Add the peppers and cook until just soft, a further 1–2 minutes. Taste for seasoning. Cook the penne in boiling, salted water until just tender. Add the carrots and peas to the penne just to warm, then drain. Transfer to a bowl, add the onion mixture and remaining curry oil. Toss to coat and serve.

MAKING CHILLI OIL

While most oils can be flavoured cold, chilli oil is best heated. Keep the heat very low and supervise cooking; if the chillies are over-heated, they will give off throat-burning fumes. Any oil can be used, and milder, or hotter, chillies can be substituted. Oils, such as Asian sesame oil, are best added after the original mixture is cooked in order for their distinctive flavours to have the greatest effect. A Mediterranean-style version, made with extra-virgin olive oil, is delicious when drizzled over pasta, pizza, or brushed over grilled meats just before serving.

1 In a frying pan, mix 250 ml (8 fl oz) groundnut oil and 6 tbsp chopped dried red chillies. Cook 10 minutes over very low heat; leave to cool.

2 When cool, add 2–3 tsp ground cayenne pepper and 1–2 tbsp Asian sesame oil. Cover and let stand for at least 12 hours.

3 Strain through a lined funnel into a sterilized bottle. Add 2–3 whole chillies for a decorative effect. Keep in a cool, dark place.

VINEGAR

The term "vinegar" comes from the French *vin aigre,* or sour wine, and it is also used to describe other soured, alcohol-based liquids, such as those made from cider, malt or rice wine. Souring is a natural process which occurs when a liquid containing less than 18 per cent alcohol is exposed to the air. Bacteria present in the air react with the alcohol to produce a thick, mouldy-looking skin over the surface of the liquid, which is called the "mother." In simple scientific terms, the mother is a layer of yeast cells and bacteria that converts the alcohol into a natural acetic acid, and it is this acid that gives vinegar its characteristic sharpness. Although this reaction does occur naturally, it is not always consistent. To produce quality vinegars, the speed and temperature of this process must be controlled. This explains why it is not enough to leave an open bottle of wine or ale on the kitchen counter for a few days and expect it to turn into vinegar. If unmonitored, the souring process can result in loss of flavour, or in further bacterial action and the production of unpleasant bitter flavours. In the kitchen, wine vinegars are indispensable for salad dressings, marinades and deglazing (see page 249). Rice wine vinegar is vital for flavouring the rice in sushi, and malt vinegar is used in many pickles and, of course, on fish and chips.

TYPES OF VINEGAR

In general, wine vinegars are required to have at least 6 per cent acetic acid, and other vinegars range between 4–6 per cent acetic acid. Slight variations in acidity levels will be only slightly perceptible on the palate; they need only be of concern when preparing pickles or other preserves.

Wine, malt and cider vinegar are strong, but distilled and spirit vinegars are even stronger. While any vinegar can be distilled, malt vinegar is most often used for this process. The distillation concentrates the acetic acid, increasing the level above 6 per cent.

The vinegar made in any given country tends to reflect the produce. Wine-making countries, such as France, Italy and Spain, produce wine vinegars. Where apples are a main crop, as in parts of North America, cider vinegar represents the bulk of production. Beer-brewing countries, such as Britain, produce malt vinegar. In the Far East, where wine is made from rice, a mild variety of rice wine vinegar containing 2–4 per cent acetic acid is most widely used.

Wine Vinegar This is produced from both red and white wines, and the quality of the vinegar depends on the quality of the wine. The finest wine vinegars are made by the *Orléans* method, which allows wine to ferment slowly and naturally (at about 21°C; 70°F) in oak barrels until the mother forms on the surface. However, this method is lengthy and costly, and many manufacturers speed up the process by raising the temperature. This results in a less costly vinegar, but one that is also inferior in quality.

There are almost as many types of wine vinegar as there are wines. Champagne vinegar has a pale colour and delicate flavour, while Rioja vinegar has a deep red colour and a full rich taste. Sherry vinegar, with its deep caramel colour and well-rounded mellow flavour, is matured in wooden casks similar to those in which the sherry is made and can be expensive. As wine-making develops in America and Australia, new kinds of vinegars, such as those made from the California Zinfandel grape variety, are emerging.

A wine vinegar that is gaining recognition in cuisines around the world is *aceto balsamico,* or balsamic vinegar. Made in Modena in northern Italy, the name balsamic comes from the Italian for "balm" and refers to the smooth mellow character of this unique vinegar. Balsamic vinegar is made from unfermented grape juice that is

Distilled vinegar

Malt vinegar

Cider vinegar

Rice vinegar

Red wine vinegar   **White wine vinegar**

Balsamic vinegar   **Champagne vinegar**

Fine wine vinegars

Champagne vinegar is an elegant substitute in recipes which call for ordinary white wine vinegar. Balsamic vinegar can be very expensive, but a little goes a long way. Mixed with an extra-virgin olive oil, it makes a superb dressing for delicate salad leaves, or, sauce for fish such as poached sea bass.

aged in wooden casks. The quality of the finished product depends a great deal on the type of wood used and the skill of the vinegar-maker. The finest vinegars are aged for a minimum of ten years; the maximum ageing time can extend for many decades. Balsamic vinegar production demands an artistry equal to the production of a great wine. In Modena, fine, aged balsamic vinegar maybe served as an after-dinner drink. Traditionally-made balsamic vinegar can be costly, though an industrially-made version does exist and is an acceptable substitute for the traditional kind in most recipes.

Cider Vinegar Apple pulp or cider can be made into cider vinegar following the same method used to produce wine vinegar. There are recipes which call specifically for cider vinegar, but it has a strong, sharp flavour and should only be used where it complements the other ingredients. Commercial cider vinegars, which are filtered, are a pale brown colour. Home-produced versions can become cloudy, but this does not affect their taste or indicate an inferior quality. The flavour is not smooth and refined enough for most salad dressings, but it can be used successfully in fruit pickles.

Malt Vinegar Made from malted barley, this type is most often used as a pickling vinegar for onions and other vegetables. Malt vinegar has too strong a flavour for use in salad dressings, but is the perfect condiment for fish and chips. Powerful distilled malt vinegar, which is colourless, is for pickling vegetables, such as cucumber, which are likely to dilute the vinegar. It is also used in the manufacture of sauces and chutneys and is sometimes coloured with caramel to produce brown malt vinegar.

Spirit Vinegar The strongest of all vinegars and is used almost exclusively for pickling. It differs from distilled vinegar in that it contains a small quantity of alcohol.

Rice Vinegar Most common in the cuisines of Asia, this type is made from soured and fermented rice wines. Japanese rice vinegars are mellow and mild, while vinegar from China is sharp and sometimes slightly sour. Depending on the rice used, Chinese vinegars are red or white in colour. Like vinegars in the West, rice vinegar is often flavoured. Soy sauce and mirin, or sweet rice wine, can be added, along with spices and flavourings such as ginger, dried bonito flakes, chillies, sesame seeds, onions, horseradish and mustard. There is also a black Chinese vinegar, which is obtained from wheat, sorghum and millet instead of rice.

COOKING WITH VINEGAR

Vinegar is an essential ingredient in the kitchen and a highly versatile flavouring. Also used as a means of preserving foods, generally fruit, vinegar is also an excellent seasoning. High-quality vinegars can be costly so it is important that they are stored properly to ensure maximum shelf-life. Keep vinegars in a cool place away from light; they do not need to be refrigerated. Most vinegars can be kept almost indefinitely if stored correctly. Vinegar is commonly used in sauces and salad dressings – particularly where a sweet-and-sour flavour is desired – and it can be used as a preservative for fruits and vegetables. It is also one of the principal ingredients in fruit and vegetable pickles and chutneys.

The importance of vinegar to the flavour of the finished dish is often overlooked. The best vinegars are made from the finest raw ingredients, and this is especially true for wine vinegars. A high-quality sherry vinegar, for example, can transform a simple green salad; an ordinary vinegar, however, will result in an ordinary salad.

Certain kinds of vinegar are used to deglaze pan juices for piquant sauces or gravies. The addition of a little vinegar can enliven many sauces, especially tomato-based ones, but remember to use a light touch. Vinegar goes surprisingly well with soft fruits, such as raspberries and strawberries, and a dash of a mellow vinegar adds distinction to fresh fruit salad.

A classic dish from Modena pairs sliced strawberries and balsamic vinegar. Drizzle fresh strawberries with a good quality balsamic vinegar and leave to mellow for 30 minutes before serving. A few drops of balsamic vinegar, used to deglaze pan-fried liver or duck can transform an ordinary dish into something special.

When deciding which vinegar to use in a dish, always choose the most appropriate flavour. Malt vinegar is made from grain and is strongly flavoured, so it is best with straightforward food such as fish and chips, cold meats, or when preparing relishes and chutneys. Cider vinegar is the best choice for deglazing pork chops, accompanied by sautéed apples.

Wine vinegars are ideal for mayonnaise and all kinds of salad dressings. They are also used in many classic butter sauces, such as *béarnaise*, often made with white wine vinegar and served with fish. A dash of fine wine vinegar adds distinction to rich meat or game stews.

FLAVOURED VINEGARS

Flavoured vinegars have long been used in cookery and they are enjoying renewed popularity. Fine wine vinegars are the most appropriate choice for flavouring, and they can be enhanced by a wide variety of herbs, spices and flavourings. Flavoured vinegar can take the place of ordinary vinegar in most recipes provided that the marriage of flavours is judicious. White wine vinegar infused with herbs, such as tarragon, or with shallots, makes an ideal ingredient in dressings for robust salad greens, such as cos or curly endive. Or, blend it with oil, cream and seasonings and toss in a chicken or seafood salad. Flavoured red wine vinegars will give added depth to marinades, stews or meat dishes. They can also be used to perk up a salad made with ordinary lettuce, while garlic-infused red wine vinegar is a good choice for red cabbage salad. Wine vinegar can also be lightly perfumed with rose petals or imbued with the more distinctive flavour of flowers such as lavender, nasturtium and violet.

Stronger sherry vinegar, flavoured with sliced horseradish, rosemary, garlic cloves or chilli, makes an excellent, last-minute seasoning for meat and poultry.

Appropriate partnerships

Be sure to pair flavoured vinegars with appropriate partners. For example, a dash of tarragon vinegar at the end of cooking adds a pleasant touch to simple sautéed chicken breasts, and spiced vinegar is excellent with game.

MAKING HERB VINEGAR

Place 60 g (2 oz) fresh, clean herbs in a clean jar with a clamp-top lid. Bring 500 ml (16 fl oz) vinegar to the boil and pour over the herbs. Seal and leave to infuse for at least 2 weeks, shaking the jar occasionally. To store, strain the vinegar into a clean jar or bottle and seal with a cork (see page 233).

Rosemary vinegar　　**Nutmeg vinegar**

COOK'S CHOICE
SPICED VINEGAR

Makes 4.5 litres (8 pt)

4.5 litres (8 pt) wine vinegar
1 nutmeg
1 small piece fresh ginger, peeled
1/2 tsp whole cloves
10 g (1/2 oz) mustard seeds
60 g (2 oz) salt
1 tbsp black peppercorns
Peel of 1/2 orange
6 shallots, quartered

In a large earthenware crock or glass container with a lid, combine all the ingredients and stir to mix. Cover tightly and leave to steep in a warm place, or in the sun, for 3–4 weeks. Strain into a bowl, pressing to extract the flavour. Pour through a funnel into clean bottles and cork. Store in a cool, dark place. Use as a last-minute seasoning for grilled meats.

MAKING FRUIT VINEGAR

Any soft fruit, particularly summer fruit, can be used to enhance the flavour of vinegar. It is best to use white wine vinegar, which will take on the colour of the fruit. Herbs and spices, such as bay leaf and cinnamon, offer an unusual addition.

1 Combine 500 g (1 lb) fruit, such as raspberries, apricots or blueberries, and 1.25 litres (2 pt) vinegar in sterilized glass jars with non-reactive seals. Leave in a warm place to steep. Shake the jars occasionally.

2 Strain the vinegar into a saucepan, pressing the fruit against the sieve to extract as much flavour as possible. Add 1 tbsp caster sugar and stir to blend. Place over low heat and simmer for 10 minutes. Cool and transfer to sterilized jars. For an attractive presentation, add a few fresh berries.

MAKING FLAVOURED VINEGAR

There is no limit to the combinations possible when making flavoured vinegars at home. Use red or white wine vinegar with fresh ripe fruit, or very fresh, unblemished herbs, to produce distinctively flavoured vinegars. For maximum flavour, heat the vinegar gently before steeping. Use the seasonings alone or in combination with one another to add a personal touch. Some suitable combinations include lemon and thyme, rosemary and bay, or cranberries, cloves and honey. For fruit vinegar, frozen fruit can be used but do not use canned fruits in syrup as these contain an excess of sugar. For a more attractive presentation, add a few fresh berries or pieces of fruit to the bottle after straining. Fruit vinegars also benefit from the addition of honey.

Rose petal vinegar

Cherry vinegar

CORKING VINEGAR

When making vinegars at home, old bottles may be used over and over again provided that they are sterilized. Corks, however, cannot, and they should be replaced with each new batch of vinegar. New corks need to be trimmed to fit the bottles. They must then be sterilized in a pan of boiling water for a few minutes; this also helps to soften them slightly. To seal the bottles, push the corks into the bottles. With a wooden or rubber mallet, pound the corks into the neck of the bottle, leaving only 5 mm (¹/₄ in) exposed cork.

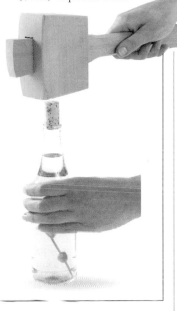

STORING FLAVOURED VINEGAR

A dark cupboard in a cool place, or a cellar, is the ideal place for keeping home-made flavoured vinegar. A low storage temperature is not only important for maintaining flavour – if the vinegar is kept in a warm environment, it may ferment and pop its cork. This fermentation is generally a sign that the vinegar is no longer fit for consumption and should be thrown away. As a rule, any home-bottled vinegar that develops a questionable appearance or odour should be disposed of in a safe manner.

BUTTERMILK, SOURED CREAM AND YOGURT

Milk or cream thickened by heat, or sharpened by bacterial cultures, or both, becomes buttermilk, soured cream or yogurt. These dairy products have a unique role in the kitchen. All three can be used as the basis for dips and dressings, in cake batters or bread doughs, and can greatly enhance many soups. Cuisines the world over use cultured dairy products in a number of ways. Soured cream is used extensively in the cuisines of Central and Eastern Europe. Yogurt is used in both sweet and savoury dishes throughout India and the Middle East, and in America, buttermilk flavours many baked goods, or serves as the foundation for refreshing fruit-flavoured drinks.

Cultured dairy products are difficult to use in cooking as they curdle when overheated, and for this reason, they must never be boiled. For best results, always add them at the end of cooking time, and stir in by spoonfuls. Alternatively, a teaspoon or so of cornflour can be stirred in before heating. This will help to stabilize these delicate ingredients and reduce the risk of curdling.

Yogurt Thought to be Turkish in origin, yogurt has been used for centuries throughout India, the Middle East, Turkey and the Balkan regions of Eastern Europe. There are many different types of this popular cultured dairy product. Much depends on the milk from which it is produced: either whole, semi-skimmed or skimmed cow's milk, or water buffalo, camel, goat or sheep's milk. Yogurt is produced by adding bacteria (that are beneficial to the digestive tract), to the milk, which is usually pasteurized and homogenized. These bacteria break down the milk sugar, or lactose, to produce lactic acid, which gives yogurt its characteristic sharpness. Yogurt can be enjoyed on its own, but it can also be used as a marinade to tenderize tough meats, or as a thickener for sauces. There are many different types of yogurt. *Plain yogurt* is the most basic; it is simply milk with the two yogurt cultures: *Lactobacillus bulgaricus* and *Streptococcus thermophilus.* Plain yogurt has been incubated in its carton will be soft-textured. A firmer set results when the yogurt is incubated in large tanks. Low-fat yogurt is made from skimmed milk and contains between 0.5–2 per cent fat. Very low-fat yogurt has less than 0.5 per cent fat. Commercially sweetened fruit yogurts are generally made using low-fat yogurt. Unflavoured, plain yogurt is ideal to use as a starter for home-made yogurt (see above).

Greek-style yogurt is made from either ewe's milk or cow's milk. It is characterized by a thick, creamy texture and an especially rich flavour. Ewe's milk yogurt is relatively low in fat (about 6 per cent) and is naturally thick. Cow's milk yogurt is much higher in fat (about 10 per cent) and it must be strained to remove the excess moisture, and to obtain the characteristic thickness. The acidity of cow's milk yogurt is balanced by the high fat content, giving it a sweeter, more mild flavour. *French-style yogurt* is generally set, and is made from low-fat homogenized milk. As a rule, set yogurts can be used for cooking, though they are best appreciated when eaten in their natural state, sweetened with vanilla sugar (see page 195) or enhanced with honey or fruit compotes. To avoid the crunchy texture of caster sugar, use icing sugar instead as this dissolves more easily and smoothly.

MAKING YOGURT

Bring 500 ml (16 fl oz) pasteurized milk to the boil, then lower the heat and simmer for 2 minutes. Transfer to a glass bowl, cover, and cool to 43°C (110°F). In another glass bowl, beat 2 tbsp plain yogurt until thin. Slowly whisk in the milk. Cover securely and leave to incubate for 8–10 hours in a warm place (about 24–29°C; 75–85°F). In warm weather, wrapping in a towel will often suffice. Alternatively, leave overnight in a gas oven with only the pilot light lit. Refrigerate and consume within 4 days.

Soured cream *is a versatile ingredient that can be used as a garnish for soups, a topping for potatoes or for dips*

Yogurt

Buttermilk *is particularly effective with certain baked goods where its acid helps the dough to rise*

Yogurt and mint

Cream cheese, buttermilk and dried apricots

Soured cream and watercress

Dairy products in dips
The slightly tangy flavour of soured milk products offers the perfect base for dips served with vegetable crudités, biscuits, breadsticks or toast.

Buttermilk A by-product of butter-making, this is the liquid which is drained from the churned milk after the fat has coagulated to form butter. Old-fashioned buttermilk was simply pasteurized before packaging, and it had a rich, full flavour. Nowadays, a culture is added and it is left to ferment for about 12–14 hours at a very low temperature, giving modern-day buttermilk a more acidic tang. Buttermilk marries well with the sweetness of fruits such as pears and cherries, and they can be processed together in a blender for a pleasant, non-alcoholic drink. In some recipes, where sharpness is welcome, buttermilk can be substituted for ordinary milk; try making fruit custards or flans with buttermilk. In baking, it is best to use recipes that are specially adapted for buttermilk as the quantities of yeast or baking powder are calculated to accommodate the acidity of buttermilk.

Soured Cream While soured cream is, in effect, sour, it is not ordinary cream which becomes sharp over time. Commercial soured cream is made from a homogenized cream, which has about the same fat content as single cream, and a bacterial culture. As with butter-milk, it is the culture that imparts the tang. Especially popular in the cuisines of Central and Eastern Europe, soured cream is essential in the classic Russian dish, beef stroganoff, and beetroot soup, or *borscht*, which is common to many cuisines of the area. Soured cream can be used like ordinary double cream to enrich meat or game casseroles, sauces and soups; soured cream with chopped fresh chives is the classic baked potato topping. Soured cream is also the ideal base for crudité dipping sauces and salad dressings. In North America, soured cream is a popular addition to chocolate cakes and to speciality yeast-dough cakes, known as coffee cakes.

COOK'S CHOICE
BUTTERMILK PANCAKES

Serves 2–4

250 g (8 oz) plain flour
1 tsp caster sugar
1 tsp salt
2 tsp bicarbonate of soda
1 ¹/₂ tsp baking powder
2 eggs
60 g (2 oz) unsalted butter, melted (or vegetable oil)
500 ml (16 fl oz) buttermilk
Melted butter or oil for frying
Maple syrup

In a large mixing bowl, sift together the flour, sugar, salt, bicarbonate of soda and baking powder. In another bowl, lightly beat the eggs and stir in the melted butter and buttermilk. Make a well in the centre of the flour mixture and slowly whisk in the egg mixture until thick. Allow to rest 20–30 minutes to thicken. If the batter is too thick, thin with a little more buttermilk. Heat a large, heavy-based frying pan and add enough butter or oil to coat. Ladle the batter into the pan to form pancakes. Cook over medium heat until golden brown on the edges and bubbles on upper-side burst open, 3–4 minutes. Turn and cook the other side until golden, 1–2 minutes. Transfer to plates and serve immediately with maple syrup.

CRÈME FRAÎCHE

An essential ingredient in all French kitchens, this is a much more distinctive version of soured cream. In some areas, crème fraîche is difficult to obtain, but it can easily be made at home. Place 500 ml (16 fl oz) double cream in a saucepan with 250 ml (8 fl oz) buttermilk. Cook over gentle heat until the mixture feels warm, but not hot, about 30°C (85°F). Transfer to a bowl, cover partially and leave at room temperature for 4–8 hours (hot weather will speed up the culturing process). Stir, cover securely and refrigerate.

BUTTER

Made simply by beating cream until it thickens and separates, butter has been used through the ages for a variety of culinary preparations. According to one theory, the technique of butter-churning was discovered unintentionally by early travellers in cold climates; milk carried on horseback for long journeys was churned into butter by the constant motion. Butter made from cow's milk is the norm in most countries, though goat and ewe's milk are used in Greece, water buffalo's milk is sometimes used in Italy, camel's milk in Africa, and yak's milk in Tibet. In the kitchen, heat alters the form and flavour of butter. It can be clarified (see page 237) for high-heat cooking methods, used alone as a spread or seasoned with a variety of flavourings (see page 238).

Salted butter

Unsalted butter

PRODUCTION

While there are many different types of butter, production methods are essentially the same. Pasteurized cream is placed in great vats and churned vigorously. This beating causes the fat globules to pull together and solidify, leaving a liquid which is known as buttermilk. The buttermilk is drawn off, leaving small lumps of solid butter that are washed and drained. If necessary, any additional flavouring, such as salt, or colouring is added at this stage. The butter is then churned until it forms a solid mass that is ready for packaging.

The flavour of butter varies according to the cow and its diet. Springtime butter is held to be the best because the cows have more opportunity to graze and feed on fresh grass. In the winter, when their diets are higher in grain, they tend to produce a less flavourful and less supple butter.

These factors also affect the colour. Some cows produce a deep yellow butter, others a paler one. For a consistent product year round, natural dyes such as annatto (see page 60) or carotene can be added.

TYPES OF BUTTER

By definition, pure dairy butter must be at least 80 per cent fat, but will also contain 10–18 per cent water and 2–4 per cent milk solids, or whey. There are two basic types of butter: sweet cream butter and lactic butter. Both of these may be salted or unsalted. Butter that is labelled "salted" contains at least 3 per cent salt; "slightly salted" butter contains only 1–2.5 per cent salt.

Sweet cream butter is made from pasteurized cream which is placed in a "cream-ageing" tank at a low temperature for about 12 hours before churning. This butter has a sweet creamy taste and a golden yellow colour, and is ideal for baked goods.

Pasteurized cream combined with a lactic acid culture produces lactic butter. During manufacture, the cream and lactic acid are blended and left at a higher temperature (18–20°C; 65-68°F), for a longer time than sweet cream butter. The resulting butter has a much lower moisture content, only about 10 per cent, while sweet cream butter can contain as much as 18 per cent moisture. For baked goods and pastries, especially puff pastry, low-moisture butter is preferable as humidity will interfere with the consistency of the finished dish.

COOKING WITH BUTTER

Butter adds substance, an unctuous texture and, above all, an inimitable flavour to many culinary preparations.

The choice of butter for cooking is generally a matter of taste, although unsalted lactic butter is the preferred type for most culinary preparations for several reasons. The absence of salt is an advantage, allowing the cook more control over the flavour of the finished dish. This type of butter also has a higher percentage of pure butterfat and a lower percentage of water and milk solids, allowing it to better withstand heat without

STORING BUTTER

Butter is best kept in the refrigerator, but as it easily absorbs other flavours, it should be well-wrapped and kept away from strong-smelling foods – especially melon and cauliflower. Before refrigeration, ceramic containers were often used to keep butter fresh. Butter in the lid was chilled by cold salt water in the base. Today, these offer an attractive presentation; iced water can be used in place of salt water.

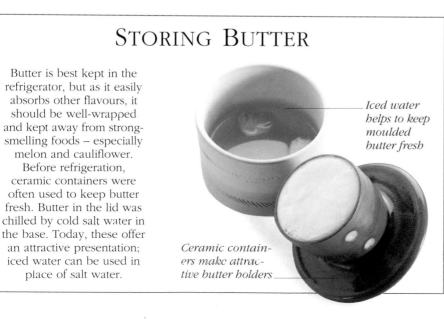

Iced water helps to keep moulded butter fresh

Ceramic containers make attractive butter holders

CLARIFYING BUTTER

Clarified butter is butter that has been melted to remove the water and milk solids, leaving pure butterfat, which has a much higher burning point: 180°C (350°F). Clarified butter can be made in large batches and stored, well wrapped, in the refrigerator where it will keep for several weeks.

1 Melt the butter over low heat without stirring. When completely melted, remove from the heat and skim the foam from the surface with a spoon.

2 Slowly pour the melted butter into a bowl leaving the milky solids behind. Alternatively, after skimming, pour through a sieve lined with muslin.

adding any unwanted moisture to delicate preparations, such as pastries and icings. Because butter contains water and milk solids, it burns at a lower temperature than other cooking fats. Adding oil to butter raises its smoke point and reduces the risk of burning. An indication of the water and milk-solid content of butter can be seen when it is heated. When the temperature reaches the boiling point of water, the butter sizzles. This is the sound of the water boiling and evaporating. If the temperature continues to rise, the milk solids will separate, appearing as a white sediment. Further heating causes the milk solids to brown, which can add a pleasant nutty flavour, followed by black, or burnt, butter which has a bitter flavour and is reputed to be unhealthy. With small quantities of butter,

such as the amount added to a frying pan for sautéing, black can follow quite rapidly from brown, so care should be taken when using high heat. For frying or other high-heat cooking methods, clarified butter (see above) is best, but bear in mind that butter with fewer milk solids has less flavour.

Butter is an essential ingredient in many classic sauce recipes. The simplest is *à la meunière*, which is melted butter enhanced by a squeeze of fresh lemon juice. Roux – a mixture of butter and flour – is the basis for béchamel, and it is also used to thicken gravies, soups and stews. Butter-mounted sauces are many, and they can be identified by their rich flavour and glossy appearance. *Beurre blanc* (see above) is a classic example, and any stock-based sauce can be mounted with butter by simply whisking in small cubes of cold butter just before serving.

A knob of butter has many uses: stirred into creamy scrambled eggs, it stops the cooking process and adds flavour; it prevents chocolate sauces and icings turning dull; and dotted over a fruit pie, it stops the filling from boiling over.

Butter stamps *are carved wooden implements that can be used to imprint butter with decorative patterns*

COOK'S CHOICE
BEURRE BLANC

Makes about 250 ml (8 fl oz)

1 large shallot, finely chopped
3 tbsp white wine vinegar
1 tbsp dry white wine
90 ml (3 fl oz) double cream or crème fraîche
8 oz (250 g) unsalted butter, chilled and cut into small cubes
Salt
Freshly ground white pepper

In a saucepan, combine the shallot, vinegar and wine over high heat. Cook until the liquid has almost evaporated, 1–2 minutes. Lower the heat, add the cream and cook until reduced and thickened, a further 1–2 minutes; whisk occasionally. Off the heat, whisk in the butter, a few cubes at a time, whisking constantly. Move the pan on and off the heat while adding the butter and never let the mixture boil. Season to taste and serve immediately. (Although difficult to keep hot for a long time, the sauce can be kept warm over a bowl of hot water for up to 30 minutes; stir often to prevent the sauce from separating.) Serve with poached fish.

COOK'S CHOICE
BEURRE NOIR

Makes about 80 ml (2³/₄ fl oz)

60 g (2 oz) unsalted butter
1 tsp white wine vinegar
2 tbsp lemon juice
1 tbsp capers, drained
Salt
Freshly ground white pepper
1 tbsp chopped fresh parsley

In a saucepan, melt the butter over medium heat until it browns; do not allow to burn. Pour immediately into a small bowl and leave to cool slightly. In the same pan used for the butter, combine the vinegar and lemon juice and cook over high heat until reduced by half. Stir in the capers and season to taste. Stir in the butter and parsley and serve with grilled or poached fish.

FLAVOURED BUTTER

On its own, butter is an excellent flavouring, but when combined with herbs, spices and other ingredients, its taste potential is even greater. Garlic butter is perhaps the most well-known, but the flavouring possibilities are endless. Anchovies, horseradish, tarragon, chives, basil, and chillies are just some of the choices for making savoury butters to spread on canapés or sandwiches, or serve alongside grilled meat or fish. Sweet butters can be made with many ingredients: honey, cinnamon, fresh or dried fruit, nuts, vanilla and chocolate, for example. Prepare with softened butter then chill until firm or use to make garnishes. Flavoured butter can also be frozen.

HERB BUTTER SHAPES

1 Spread softened butter between two sheets of greaseproof paper. Roll out evenly, about 5 mm (1/4 in) thick. Transfer to a baking sheet and refrigerate until firm.

2 With cutters, or a small glass, stamp out shapes or circles. Or, use a sharp knife and a ruler to cut out geometric shapes. Chill until ready to use.

BUTTER ROSES

1 Fill a piping bag fitted with a wide ribbon nozzle with softened, flavoured butter. The butter can be coloured with food colouring if desired. Chill until firm enough to pipe.

2 Attach a square of grease-proof paper to a small jar. Pipe a central strip, turning the jar, to form a tight spiral. To finish, twist the tip of the nozzle towards you in a single, steady movement.

3 Hold the nozzle at a 45° angle to the piped-out rose centre. Starting just before the seam, pipe out one petal; twist bottom towards you to finish. Continue piping petals, overlapping them slightly, and making them larger as you work away from the centre. Turn the jar while piping for even petals. Chill until serving.

COOK'S CHOICE
HERB BUTTER

Makes about 125 g (4 oz)

125 g (4 oz) unsalted butter, softened
1 tbsp chopped fresh chives
1 tbsp chopped flat-leaf parsley
1/2 tbsp chopped fresh tarragon
1 tsp whole-grain mustard
Salt
Freshly ground black pepper

Blend together the butter, chives, parsley, tarragon, mustard, and salt and pepper to taste. Let stand, covered, in a cool place for 1 hour to allow the flavours to develop. Chill to firm before serving with seafood, chicken or meat.

COOK'S CHOICE
RASPBERRY HONEY BUTTER

Makes about 125 g (4 oz)

350 g (12 oz) raspberries
2 tbsp honey
1 tsp lemon juice
125 g (4 oz) unsalted butter, softened

Purée raspberries in a food processor. Strain to remove the seeds, if desired. In a saucepan, combine the raspberries, honey and lemon juice and bring to the boil. Leave to cool. Blend together the butter and the raspberry mixture. Let stand, covered, in a cool place for 1 hour to allow the flavours to develop. Chill to firm before serving with warm croissants, scones or toast.

BUTTER BALLS

One of the simplest butter garnishes can be made with a melon ball tool. Use one size and group different flavoured butters, or make an assortment of balls using different-sized tools. Assemble into the grape cluster shown here, or serve individually. For example, serve chive balls with baked potatoes or honey butter balls with tea-time scones. Or, shape softened butter into balls and roll in herbs or spices to coat.

1 Dip a melon baller into cold water then press into a block of chilled butter. Plain butter balls can be rolled in spices or chopped herbs for flavour. Alternatively, prepare a flavoured butter, reshape into a block and chill until firm.

2 For textured butter balls, roll between two wooden butter shapers. Arrange an assortment of flavoured or plain butter balls atop fresh vine leaves in a cluster formation. The butter grape cluster makes a stunning buffet centrepiece.

Fresh leaves make an appropriately pretty and colourful background on which to display your butter "fruits"

Butter can be flavoured from within or without, and moulded into many different shapes

Nutmeg butter

Sesame butter

Chive butter

Paprika butter

Thyme butter

COOK'S CHOICE
CHOCOLATE HAZELNUT BUTTER

Makes about 175 g (6 oz)

20 g (³⁄₄ oz) plain chocolate, chopped

1 tsp caster sugar

1 tbsp hazelnut-flavoured liqueur

125 g (4 oz) unsalted butter, softened

1 tsp vanilla essence

30 g (1 oz) ground hazelnuts

In a bowl, combine the chocolate, sugar and liqueur and melt (see page 182). Leave to cool. Blend together the butter, chocolate mixture, vanilla and hazelnuts. Let stand, covered, in a cool place for 1 hour to allow the flavours to develop. Chill to firm before serving with warm croissants, scones or toast.

COOK'S CHOICE
MEDITERRANEAN BUTTER

Makes about 125 g (4 oz)

125 g (4 oz) unsalted butter, softened

2 tsp capers, chopped

2–3 anchovy fillets, chopped

1 garlic clove, chopped

1 tsp lemon juice

2 sun dried tomatoes, chopped

Salt

Freshly ground black pepper

Blend together the butter, capers, anchovies, garlic, lemon juice, tomatoes, and salt and pepper to taste. Let stand, covered, in a cool place for 1 hour to allow the flavours to develop. Chill to firm before serving with veal, chicken or seafood.

SAUCES, PRESERVES & CONDIMENTS

SOY SAUCE

Salted and fermented soy beans were among the very first Chinese condiments. A thin liquid known as *jiang*, was in use 2,000 years ago, and this is thought to be the ancestor of Chinese soy sauce. The sauce familiar today was developed in the 6th century. It is made from fermented soy beans and wheat, which are aged, sometimes for two years, before being strained and bottled.

Soy sauce was first used to preserve food for the winter months, though it is now a common seasoning and flavouring in kitchens from East to West. There are light and dark versions, each with their own uses – much like red and white wines – though traditional northern Chinese cooks use only dark soy sauce, while the Japanese, who developed their own style of soy sauce, use light sauce.

Soy beans

Light soy sauce

Dark soy sauce

The procedure for making soy sauce combines roasted soy beans and a lightly ground grain, usually wheat, with a special mould starter. After the culture has been growing for several days, yeast and brine are added, along with a bacteria starter, much like the ones used to make yogurt. The resulting mash is left to age, which can take as long as two years. The sauce is then strained and bottled.

Chinese Soy Sauce Soy sauce is used in China rather as salt is used in the West. It seasons all kinds of Chinese dishes, from soups and dipping sauces to stir-frys and stews. The Chinese produce both a light and dark soy sauce. The latter is aged much longer and it is also mixed with molasses. The resulting sauce therefore has a much stronger flavour and a deeper, caramel colour.

Each type of soy sauce has its own place in Chinese cooking. Dark soy is used to flavour and colour heartier dishes such as red-braised chicken, as well as many beef and pork dishes. Light soy sauce is used with seafood, vegetables and in soups and dipping sauces.

Mushroom soy is made from dark soy sauce that has been infused with Chinese straw mushrooms; this is rich and full-flavoured and can be used whenever dark soy is called for

Mushroom soy sauce

Japanese soy sauce

SOY BEAN SAUCES

Yellow bean sauce, popular in Northern and Western China, is used to flavour Peking noodles and was the traditional condiment for Peking Duck. In Sichuan and Hunan cooking, it is often seasoned with chillies. Hoisin sauce, which is much sweeter and spicier, is used in southern Chinese stir-fry dishes and is delicious as a marinade for meat and poultry, or as a basting sauce. Do not confuse hoisin sauce with Chinese barbecue sauce (see page 244), which is similar in appearance but not in flavour.

Yellow bean sauce

Hoisin sauce

A particularly dark version is made by infusing the soy sauce with straw mushrooms. Known as mushroom soy, this is rich and full-flavoured, and can be used whenever a recipe calls for dark soy sauce.

Japanese Soy Sauce The Chinese introduced soy sauce to Japan, and the Japanese then developed their own varieties to suit local cooking methods and styles of cuisine. The fermenting and ageing processes are similar, but Japanese soy sauce contains more wheat and is usually matured for no longer than six months. As a result, it is less salty and slightly sweeter.

The Japanese prefer much lighter versions of soy sauce; even their dark sauce would fall at the lighter end of the Chinese scale. In southern Japan, an especially light sauce is used, as the style of cuisine discourages the use of ingredients that obviously alter and "discolour" food.

The Japanese use soy sauce both as a table condiment and as a flavouring. Like the Chinese, the Japanese use the darker versions in red meat dishes and the lighter versions in clear soups and one-pot meals.

Other Soy Sauces True Japanese *tamari* sauce is a rich, dark sauce brewed without wheat. It is most commonly served in sushi restaurants and is rarely used in the home. In the West, the term tamari has been applied to a variety of Japanese-style soy sauces, mainly on offer in healthfood shops.

Southeast Asia also has many soy sauces that vary from region to region. *Ketjap manis* is a very thick and sweet type of soy sauce

Decorative soy servers *such as these attractive porcelain pouring containers are made for use at the table*

used in Indonesia. *Toyo mansi* is a light style soy sauce from the Philippines, flavoured with a native fruit similar to the lemon.

Soy-Based Condiments These rich, flavoursome pastes, made from fermented soy beans, are popular throughout China and Southeast Asia. The best are made with whole beans; ground bean sauces tend to be slightly more salty.

In Sichuan cooking, bean sauces, either plain or fired-up with a few chillies, are an integral part of most dishes. Hoisin is a soy bean sauce flavoured with five-spice mixture (see page 95) and dried chillies. When mixed with sugar and sesame oil, it becomes the dipping sauce served with Peking Duck.

COOK'S CHOICE
MASTER SAUCE CHICKEN

Serves 4–6

1 free-range chicken, weighing about 2 kg (4 lb)
Salt
300 ml (¹/2 pt) soy sauce
300 ml (¹/2 pt) dry sherry
150 g (5 oz) sugar
2–3 tbsp honey
1 star anise
1 small piece tangerine peel

Wash the chicken thoroughly and pat dry. Season the inside lightly with salt. In a large saucepan, combine the soy sauce, sherry, sugar, honey, star anise and tangerine peel. Bring to the boil, stirring to dissolve the sugar. Add the chicken. When boiling, reduce the heat and poach for 30 minutes, basting often. Turn the chicken and poach a further 20 minutes. Remove from the heat; leave the chicken in the pan and allow to stand for 20 minutes; baste occasionally. Serve warm or cold. The sauce can be re-used. Simply strain and refrigerate. Bring to the boil before using and adjust seasoning if necessary. The refrigerated sauce will keep for about 10 days.

USING TERIYAKI

Teriyaki glaze is a flavoursome topping for barbecued, pan-fried or baked food. Here, chicken breasts are dipped into teriyaki and grilled. Slice and top with the thickened glaze before serving.

1 For the teriyaki, bring 300 ml (¹/2 pt) each of mirin, Japanese soy sauce and chicken stock to the boil. Cool and pour into a shallow dish. Dip chicken breasts in the teriyaki, coating both sides.

2 In a saucepan, mix 3 tbsp of the teriyaki with 2¹/2 tsp of sugar and bring almost to the boil. Stir in 1¹/2 tsp cornflour dissolved in 2¹/2 tbsp water and the remaining teriyaki. Stir until thick.

3 Cook the chicken. A grill is best with teriyaki, but the chicken can be baked or pan-fried. To serve, slice the breasts across the grain and fan out on a plate. Spoon over the teriyaki glaze and serve.

FISH SAUCES

The fish sauces that are popular seasonings in Southeast Asian cuisine are distant relatives of the salted anchovy sauce of ancient Roman times, and the anchovy essence used by many cooks today. Often these sauces are a by-product of fish that are fermented, layered with salt and then placed in sealed crocks. The liquid that is drawn off from the fish by the salt is separated and strained for fish sauces; sometimes the remaining fish are pounded into a paste that is then used as a seasoning.

Western chefs using fish sauces to flavour stir-frys often add a pinch of sugar; the sweetness is a pleasant foil to the salty pungency of the fish sauce.

The main purpose of fermenting fish in Asian cuisines is to extract the juices for flavoursome seasoning sauces. In Vietnam and Thailand, however, the fermented fish are pounded into a pungent seasoning paste which can be used in place of fish sauce in some dishes. A particularly flavoursome version is made from ground anchovies mixed with fish sauce. Known as *mam nem xay*, the taste of this sauce has been likened to creamed anchovies.

Oyster Sauce This is a Cantonese speciality, originally made from oysters, salt and water, though nowadays cornflour and caramel are added as well. Used as an all-purpose seasoning for meat, fish, vegetables and noodles, it has a pleasant savoury flavour that is not overly fishy.

Fish Sauce Made from fish, usually anchovies or mackerel, fermented in salt, this sauce can be used as a kitchen seasoning or table condiment, much like soy sauce. Thai *nam pla*, Vietnamese *nuoc mam* and Filipino *patis* are some of the better known versions sold in the West.

Fine Shrimp Sauce Known as *kapee* in Thailand, this is also made by combining shrimps and salt, except it is left to ferment and dry in the sun, not in crocks. A similar sun-dried sauce is also made from squid.

Barbecue Sauce This is made of dried fish and shrimp, chillies, garlic, peanuts and spices. Use like a curry paste in stir-frys, or spread on meat for grilling.

Table condiments
A common ingredient in Asian sauces, stir-fries and dips, some of the milder fish sauces can be used much as soy sauce is with Chinese food, though the taste will be more pungent.

Fish by-products
include sauces that have a strongly concentrated and pungent flavour; these are widely used in Chinese and Southeast Asian cooking

Fine fish paste   **Oyster sauce**   **Fine shrimp sauce**   **Nam pla**   **Fish sauce**

CHILLI SAUCES

South American Indians were making chilli pepper sauces well before Columbus arrived, and chillies have remained a very important flavouring in the cuisines of Mexico and the Caribbean. Today, there are probably as many recipes as there are cooks, and chilli sauces are used to enhance a variety of dishes: from omelettes, grills and hamburgers, to salads, marinades and casseroles. Once discovered, chilli peppers were taken to Europe and the Far East, where pepper sauces became extremely popular. Chinese, Korean, Vietnamese and Thai cuisines all use hot sauces. Some are served on the side, others are used as an ingredient, resulting in a truly fiery dish.

Hot chilli sauces
In the Caribbean, each island has its own style of pepper sauce. Most are made by steeping chillies in vinegar. Some are red from tomatoes, others are yellow from turmeric, but the common denominator is lots of chilli-fired heat. Pepper sauces are used in preparations ranging from sautés to marinades, and as a table sauce. Tabasco Sauce is a North American condiment made from extremely hot Tabasco peppers and matured for several years in oak barrels. A few drops will be enough to give soups, casseroles and sauces a strongly piquant flavour.

Small, high-necked bottles are the standard containers for the fiery red chilli sauces

These sauces can be red, yellow or green in colour, and many contain minced pepper and onion

Saltier and thicker than their Caribbean counterparts, the chilli seeds are clearly visible

Chilli-flavoured sauces
Salsa is the Mexican word for sauce, but outside Mexico it has come to mean an uncooked tomato-based relish, flavoured in varying degrees by onions, fresh coriander and chillies; some salsas use the very hot and slightly smoky jalapeno peppers. Salsas can be used as a topping for Mexican-style dishes, such as tacos and tostadas, and are delicious with most bean, rice, egg and meat dishes. Tex-Mex inspired barbecue sauces show a Mexican influence in their often high chilli content. They are best brushed over charcoal-grilled steaks, ribs or chicken, before and after cooking.

Asian chilli sauces
The Chinese treat chilli peppers in much the same way as soy beans (see page 242). They are salted and fermented to produce pungent sauces, which are used in stews, stir-frys and soups. In China, chilli sauces are essential to the flavours of Sichuan and Hunan cuisine. They are also used in Korean cooking. In other parts of Southeast Asia, chillies are bottled fresh, retaining their red colour, and are used as a table sauce or mixed with other ingredients such as peanuts, dried fish and soy sauce to make sambals (see page 69) or satay sauce (see page 249).

COFFEE TEA & SPICED DRINKS

ROASTING AND BREWING

A good cup of coffee depends upon the correct choice of bean and grind for the occasion. Roasting is the first step to the final flavour as the application of heat develops the aromas of the bean. However, single types of beans, or blends, which are suitable for the breakfast table may not be appropriate after dinner. The type of grind will also affect the final flavour, as will the choice of equipment. For example, a very finely ground coffee is unsuitable in a percolator, but essential for espresso coffee.

Always make sure the equipment is clean and free from coffee residue. Use freshly drawn water and heat to just off the boil. Allow 1–2 teaspoons of coffee per 150 ml (1/4 pt) water. Timing is vital – brewed for too short a time, the flavour will be weak and sour; too long and the flavour will be destroyed, leaving only bitterness. For a stronger brew, add more coffee per cup. Freshness is essential; buy beans in small quantities and grind as needed. Also, be sure to match the grind with the preparation being used.

TYPES OF ROASTS

The degree of roast determines the delicacy or richness of a coffee; strength is determined by the amount of coffee used.

Light This roast is used for beans with subtle flavours that would be marred by stronger roasting and it gives them a light brown colour. Lightly-roasted coffee is the most suitable type for drinking with milk.

Medium With a more pronounced flavour and smell, this roast results in coffee that is good for breakfast drinking, with milk. It also makes good after-lunch or dinner coffee, which may be drunk without milk.

Dark This roast gives the beans a deep colour and a glossy finish. It provides a strong flavour and aroma, and is best for drinking black, after dinner.

Continental A very dark roast, full of strong smoky flavours, this is the preferred roast of those who like a powerful coffee.

Continental roast

Dark roast

Medium roast

Pale roast

GRINDERS

There is a wide selection of electrical, mechanical, modern and antique grinders. Choose one that has a means of controlling the degree of grind and ensure that it produces an even grind every time.

TYPES OF GRINDS

The coarseness or the fineness of the grind determines the surface area of the coffee that will come into contact with the water. Because some brewing methods have very long, or very short, contact period between grounds and water, they must always be matched with a suitable grind. For example, in expresso machines, the water spends very little time in contact with the grounds, so they must be very fine to ensure that the flavour is passed along to the water.

With a coffee grinder on hand, the beans can be ground to order. If not, buy ground in small quantities and store in an airtight container kept in the refrigerator. The flavour of coffee depends on its highly volatile oils, so it is best to buy freshly-roasted beans in small quantities.

Coarse Grind It is only possible to obtain this grind at home. It may be used for the jug method and for percolators and will produce a lighter brew than medium grind.

Medium Grind The most versatile grind, this is suitable for use in jugs, percolators, cafetières and Neapolitan flip pots. Use a fine sieve with jugs and percolators.

Fine Grind For coffee made by the filter or drip method, this is the grind to choose. It produces a large surface area of coffee that allows the water filtering through to take up the maximum flavour. The coffee will be strong as the fineness of the grind prevents the water from filtering through too fast, thereby lengthening the contact time between coffee and water.

Espresso Grind An especially fine grind, this is designed specifically for use in espresso machines and moka espresso pots.

Pulverized Sometimes known as powdered coffee, this is finest grind available. The heat generated during the grinding process contributes to the distinctive flavour.

Coarse grind

Medium grind

Medium fine grind

Percolators

As the brewing begins, boiling water is forced through ground coffee held in a basket. The disadvantage is that the same boiling liquid circulates continuously. With good temperature control, percolators can make good coffee, though coffee experts tend to frown on percolators as the coffee can become overheated and "stewed."

Cafetière

This is a refinement of the old-fashioned jug method. After the boiling water has been poured over the coffee, cover with the special lid and allow to infuse for a short while. Then slowly push down the plunger, forcing the coffee grounds to the bottom of the pot. Use only coarse or medium grinds or the coffee will be cloudy.

Neapolitan Flip Pots

Fill the bottom of the pot with cold water. Place the filter on top and fill with ground coffee to form a mound. Screw on the top and snap the upper pot into position. Place over a medium heat until steam starts to escape, then flip the pot over to allow the water to flow through the coffee grounds.

Espresso grind

Fine grind

Pulverized

Moka Espresso Pots

These are similar to the Neapolitan pots, but the hot water is forced through the filter by pressure into the upper chamber, so that the pot does not have to be turned over. A gurgling sound indicates that the coffee is ready; pour immediately or the coffee may burn. Use a fine grind for a good strong cup of coffee.

Filter

This method can be used for any style of coffee and any roast. Place the filter paper in the holder and place over a pot. Very slowly pour in the water, in time with the coffee dripping through. Keep the pot warm over a very low heat or an electric hot plate, and do not allow the coffee to boil.

Ibrik

Turkish coffee is traditionally made in a long-handled ibrik. To prepare, allow one heaped teaspoon each of coffee and sugar to each small cup. Bring to the boil, stir to dissolve the sugar and return to the boil. Remove from the heat, let stand, then return to the boil. Leave to settle; pour without straining.

265

COFFEES OF THE WORLD

Coffee is an international beverage, with universal popularity, but it is drunk by people with divergent tastes, cultures and traditions. As a result, each country has developed its own ways of coffee making, serving and drinking. Most European countries start the day with a version of "café au lait" and then move on to stronger cups of black coffee, usually after meals. Americans like to drink black coffee throughout the day as well as during and after meals. In the Middle East, coffee is drunk quite strong and strict rules of etiquette dictate the service.

The French morning ritual of coffee and croissants is copied throughout the world. Parisian cafés offer large mugs of frothy white coffee, called *grand crème*, while the more modest provincial establishments call it *café au lait*, and it may be served in deep bowls, as is done in most homes. It tastes quite different to the "milky" coffee made in Britain or America.

Later in the day, consumption continues with the smaller demi-tasse (literally half-cups), holding around 100 ml (3½ fl oz) of strong black coffee. The French prefer a bitter, high-roast coffee. In homes and offices, the filter or drip method is most prevalent, but it is also customary to step out, at any time of day, for an *express* at the local café.

The Italians, too, are a nation of dedicated coffee-drinkers and they have different tastes for different times of the day. Mornings usually start with *caffe latte*, a rich roast espresso that is made by blending the coffee with about three times as much hot milk. After lunch and dinner (and for some, throughout the day), the traditional strong, black espresso served in a demi-tasse is the preferred drink. This is made in special machines that force hot water through tightly packed, finely ground espresso coffee. It is often served with a twist of lemon.

Like the French, the Italians feel that coffee with milk is difficult to digest after a meal, and the well-loved cappuccino is most often drunk in-between meals. In principle, café au lait and cappuccino are similar, but the French and Italian versions never taste the same. Cappuccino is made with espresso coffee that is blended with steamed milk, often topped with a sprinkling of cinnamon or cocoa powder, and sometimes a dollop of cream as well. It is said to owe its name to its colour, which is similar to the mocha-coloured robes of the Cappuccine monks.

Strong black coffee is also popular in Spain and Portugal, where it is known as *café solo*. In Germany, there are tiny shops or booths where standing customers can consume small cups of strong, but not very bitter, black coffee.

In the coffee houses of Vienna, coffee is meant to be drunk with rich, cream-laden cakes, and the liking for this combination is echoed throughout Eastern Europe. The Austrians spend their *jause*, the equivalent of the British teatime, in a coffee shop or, failing that, at home in the company of

---

CAFÉ BRULOT
To prepare, place 1 tbsp demerara sugar, 5 whole cloves, a long strip each of lemon peel and orange peel, ½ cinnamon stick, ½ vanilla pod and 150 ml (¼ pt) brandy in a saucepan. Heat gently until the sugar dissolves and the brandy is warm. Ignite with a match and allow to burn for about 30 seconds. Pour into 4 cups that are three-quarters full of hot, strong coffee.

An international favourite
Appreciated morning, noon and night, coffee is a universal beverage that is served in a variety of ways.

Café au lait

Espresso

Viennese coffee

Turkish coffee

friends. As an additional flourish, the strong coffee, which is sometimes flavoured with dried figs, is often topped by a dollop of whipped cream that is sprinkled with ground cinnamon or nutmeg.

In Britain, coffee-drinking is fast catching on and, though tea is still the most popular breakfast beverage, coffee takes over at mid-morning and after meals. Both the British and the Americans prefer a softer, milder brew than the Continentals, but Americans do like their coffee black.

Iced coffee is popular on hot days in both Europe and America. It is made by brewing coffee strong, sweetening it and then chilling it. This is served with either iced water or milk. *Café frappé* is the French version, made frothy by vigorously shaking the coffee with ice cubes until chilled.

As could be expected, coffee is practically the national drink in Brazil, where the average consumption is estimated to be 20 tiny cups per person, per day. However, unlike Europeans, the Brazilians drink their coffee quite sweet. The morning black coffee is sugared heavily, while for the *cafézinho* drunk throughout the day, the cup seems to be almost filled with brown sugar before the coffee even goes in.

Coffee-drinking in Greece, Turkey and the Middle East is much more than a refreshing pause; it is often a ritual. Service can be elaborate, and there is a formal ceremony

Gaelic coffee *is an after-dinner drink made with Irish whisky and hot coffee topped with a layer of cream*

that dictates that the oldest and most re-spected guest is served first. The cups are never filled up to the brim as this shows disrespect and guests should take care not to drink the coffee to the last drop. Not only is this seen as bad manners, but the grounds settle into an unpalatably thick, sludge-like deposit at the bottom. Often, coffee will be flavoured with cinnamon sticks, vanilla pods, ginger or cardamom (see page 83). Sometimes orange flower water is added. In Sudan, cloves are a popular flavouring, and in Morocco, peppercorns are favoured.

AFTER-DINNER COFFEE

Combinations of strong coffee, cream and spirits or liqueurs offer a satisfying alternative to heavy desserts. For festive occasions, they can be made in tall glasses to show off the contrasting layers of coffee and cream. Heatproof glasses with handles are specially made for this purpose.

To prepare an after-dinner coffee, place a heaped teaspoon of brown sugar in a warmed glass with two tablespoons of liquor. Some of the more popular choices are: brandy, whisky, rum, vodka, crème de cacao, or almond or coffee flavoured liqueurs. Pour on a strong, medium-roast coffee. Stir well to dissolve the sugar. Rest the spoon against the rim of the glass and pour lightly whipped cream over the back and into the glass. If sufficient sugar is used, the cream will float in a thick layer on the top.

COFFEE SUBSTITUTES AND FLAVOURINGS

Roasted chicory root is a popular coffee extender in France and Belgium. In Britain, it is also added to cheap brands of instant coffee. The roots impart a characteristic bitter taste that is unpleasant to some. Dandelion root, which belongs to the same family as chicory, is toasted for a drink similar to coffee that is sold in healthfood shops as dandelion coffee. Toasted barley is used to produce a drink called "malted coffee." Spices and floral waters are often added in the Middle East, while in Austria, ground, dried figs are added for a thick, sweet flavour. Some coffees are sprayed with flavourings, such as oil of amaretto or vanilla.

MAKING GRANITA

This refreshing iced drink may be flavoured with brandy or rum and served with a spoonful of sweetened whipped cream.

1 Heat 250 ml (8 fl oz) water and 175 g (6 oz) sugar, stir and boil for 1 minute. Add 250 ml (8 fl oz) coffee and leave to cool.

2 Place in a shallow pan and freeze for 1 hour. Stir, and return to the freezer. Continue to stir and freeze for 2 hours.

TEA

One of the world's oldest beverages, tea was discovered by the Chinese – a more arduous task than it sounds, as they must have worked their way through a great number of indigenous plants before coming across the *camelia sinensis*, or tea plant. It then took many centuries to perfect the art of tea production, resulting in the variety of types available today. First adopted by the Japanese, and then by Europeans looking for cash crops to grow in their tropical colonies, tea is now cultivated most widely in India, Sri Lanka, Africa, Georgia and Japan, as well as in China. Tea was finally imported to Europe in the 17th century, and in its early days, it was a highly-prized luxury item. Nonetheless, it caught on quickly in many countries on the continent, though it is most often thought of as Britain's national drink. Today, Indian tea has taken over from China tea as the favourite.

GROWING TEA

The tea bush is an evergreen tropical plant with stiff, pointed, shiny green leaves. In order to flourish, it requires a wet, warm climate with at least 60 cm (2 ft) of rain a year. The bushes are planted in vast tea gardens at heights from 100 metres-2 km (300-7,000 ft) above sea level. At higher, cooler altitudes, tea bushes grow more slowly and produce smaller crops. For this reason, the flavour and characteristics of high-altitude teas are different from the faster-growing bushes on the lower slopes. In the cooler areas, such as northern India, the harvest is seasonal but elsewhere picking, or "plucking," carries on all year.

Young, soft shoots produce the finest tea and only the top two leaves and bud are plucked. This work is done mainly by women and demands great skill. A good plucker can gather between 30-35 kilos (60-77 lb) of leaf in a day, which will yield only about one-quarter to one-third that amount of tea after manufacture. An estimated 9,100 million bushes are required to meet the world's demand for tea.

Legend has it that tea was discovered by the Chinese Emperor Shen Nung around 2750 B.C. One day, while boiling drinking water, some leaves from an over-hanging tree fell into the pot. The resulting beverage was a pleasant infusion that tasted good and stimulated the senses, and a tradition was born. Tea drinking remained an essentially Chinese custom until about A.D. 800, when the beverage was introduced in Japan.

In the 17th century, when tea was finally introduced in Europe, the tea trade centred on Japan. But when Japan closed its borders to Europeans, China became the principal source of supply.

At first, tea was taken primarily as a tonic for the relief of a large number of maladies. One Dutch doctor advocated the drinking of at least 40 cups a day, but he was an employee of the East India Company. Tea-drinking really took off in Britain when Catherine of Braganza married Charles II in 1662 and brought a chest of tea as part of her dowry. Once it had the royal seal of approval, tea was able to move out of the smoky din of coffee-houses and into the drawing rooms of the wealthy. It soon became equally popular with the urban and rural working classes, who bought small quantities of the cheapest tea and brewed it weak. *Sligo*, an especially popular brand at the time, was advertised as being strong enough to endure as many as three or four changes of water.

The government of the day soon saw the value of instituting a tax on tea. This started off fairly low, but when it was increased to 100 per cent, housewives found it prudent to keep their supplies of tea under lock and key in special boxes called caddies. When this tax was extended to cover tea imports to the colonies, hundreds of Bostonians threw the first shipments of taxed tea into the harbour. This historical act is known as the Boston Tea Party, and it was one of the first rumblings that set the scene for the American War of Independence.

The tea clipper was introduced to Europe in the 1850's to keep supply in pace with the demands of the burgeoning tea trade. Prior to this development, the return trip from London to the Canton River could last almost as long as one year. These huge, three-masted ships, of American design, cut the sailing time by more than half, and captains would race each other to be the first to reach home port.

Meanwhile, the days of the East India Company's monopoly on trade with China were numbered, and the search began for alternative sources. Tea had been found growing wild in northern India, and culti-

Green tea

Black tea

Oolong tea

Tea caddies *were a protective as well as decorative means of storage when heavy taxes made tea a valuable commodity*

vation began first in Assam and Darjeeling, and later in Sri Lanka. Tastes have evolved along the lines of supply, and by the beginning of this century, Indian tea had taken over from Chinese tea as the preferred drink in Britain and North America.

PRODUCTION

The Chinese learned that by cultivating tea in different areas they could produce very different flavours of tea. They also developed and perfected a variety of production methods, which resulted in three quite different types of tea.

Green Tea As soon as these leaves are picked, they are left to wither until there is no moisture left. The whole leaves are then steamed and rolled, resulting in green grey balls. By processing whole, the leaves are able to retain the enzymes that prevent them from oxidizing, hence losing colour and flavour. The result is a pale, yellow-green

tea with a distinctly unusual flavour. The name Gunpowder Green was given to this tea by the first British colonists in China who named it for its likeness in form and colour to lead ball shot.

Oolong Tea This tea comes mainly from the southeast coast of China and Taiwan. After harvesting, the leaves are left to wither for a few hours to remove some of the moisture. They are then rolled by machine to release the juices, followed by a short fermentation period prior to oven-firing. After processing, the colour of the leaves changes to copper and the flavour is mild, falling mid-way between green tea and black tea.

Black Tea Produced in India as well as in China, these leaves are withered and rolled like Oolong. The fermentation period, however, is considerably longer, which breaks down the enzymes, producing a varnish that coats the leaf. The leaves are then dried and caramelized sugars are added to impart the colour, aroma and characteristic flavour of these teas.

GRADING TEA

Size and appearance are the criteria for tea grading. The two main grades – whole-leaf and broken-leaf – are used for black tea and are subdivided within each category.

Whole-leaf teas are classified as Flowery Orange Pekoe, Orange Pekoe or Pekoe. The broken-leaf grades are further classified by particle size. Broken-leaf is largest, followed by another series that includes fannings, orange fannings and dust, which is most commonly used for tea bags.

The flavour of all teas coming onto the market is judged by highly skilled tea tasters. They evaluate the flavour and aroma of the brewed tea, as well as the appearance and aroma of the fresh and dry leaves.

Black tea *is categorized according to leaf size, ranging from whole-leaf grades to dust, which is used in tea bags*

The largest of all the tea grades, this requires longer brewing to release the flavour

This is the best all-purpose tea as the size of the leaves reduces the necessary brewing time

The finest grade of tea, this is used primarily for tea bags

Whole-leaf tea　　**Broken-leaf tea**　　**Small-leaf tea**

TEA TYPES

Just like vines and wines, the taste of tea is dependent on where and how it is grown. The altitude, the soil and the climate all have a marked effect on the flavour. Teas grown at the highest altitudes, for example, mature more slowly and have a lower yield, resulting in a higher quality. The main tea producing countries are China, India and Japan, however there are a few other regions worthy of mention. Kenya is home to some very fine teas, particularly those cultivated east of the Great Rift Valley, where some of the tea gardens are at altitudes of 2 km (1¼ miles) above sea level. The teas are all black, with a brisk flavour. In Russia, tea is grown on the slopes of the Caucasus Mountains, and the leaves are fermented to produce black tea that gives a very mellow brew.

The way in which tea is harvested, dried and processed will affect the flavour of the brew: Indian tea tastes quite different to that from China or Ceylon, and teas from Assam in northern India differ in flavour to those from Nilgiri in the south. Some teas are blended according to special recipes.

Chinese Green Teas Most familiar as the tea served in Chinese restaurants, these teas are all mild, with a pleasant fruity flavour.

Gunpowder Green This is a classic tea that uses tightly rolled, unfermented leaves. It yields a very pale drink with a light flavour.

Chinese Oolong Teas In general, these teas are stronger than green teas, but milder than black teas.

Taiwan (Formosa) Oolong Considered by some experts to be one of the finest of teas, this has a natural fruity flavour that is not too strong.

Formosa Oolong Peach Blossom This tea does not contain peach blossom – it takes its name from its unique peachy flavour that is only found in the best-quality teas.

Chinese Black Teas These teas range in flavour from mild, to smoked, to strong.

Keemum A delicate and aromatic tea from northern China, this is low in tannins with a deep, rich flavour.

Lapsang Souchong A large-leaf tea that is rich and full bodied, this has a very distinctive, but delicate, smoky, tarry flavour.

Yunnan Western A tea containing a high proportion of the youngest leaves, this has a sweet taste and a light golden colour.

Indian Teas All of the teas produced in this country are black teas.

Assam One of the classic Indian teas, this is grown in the Brahmaputra valley in north-east India. The taste is strong and malty. The best quality Assam teas contain the "tips," or unopened buds, from the bushes and are known as Tippy Assam.

Darjeeling Another popular tea from northern India, this type is noted for its distinctive, delicate flavour. The small, broken-leaf grade

---

BLENDED TEAS

Most packets of commerical tea are made up of a blend of 15 or more leaves from different areas. There are also some rather special traditional teas which are also blended.

English Breakfast Tea is a blend of strong Indian teas which gives a full-bodied and fragrant liquor.

Earl Grey Tea is a blend of Keemun and Darjeeling teas flavoured with oil of bergamot. The recipe was given to the diplomat Earl Grey by a Chinese Mandarin, and the Earl brought the recipe back with him to England.

Russian Caravan Tea is a blend of fine teas from China, Formosa and India. It was originally transported to Russia from India via camel caravan, hence its name.

---

produces a light, golden drink with a subtle flavour. Bushes from the highest tea gardens in the foothills of the Himalayas, have large leaves that produce teas with a unique "muscatel" flavour of perfumed grapes. The most notable of all the various Darjeelings is Darjeeling Broken Orange Pekoe, which is sometimes called the champagne of tea.

Ceylon Teas The teas produced in Sri Lanka are all black teas.

Dimbula Grown at altitudes reaching 2 km (1¼ miles) and over, this tea has a fine quality and, like most Ceylon tea, a rich colour and flavour. Orange Pekoe and Broken Orange Pekoe are the usual leaf grades, resulting in a drink with an aromatic fragrance and a delicate, fresh taste.

Kandy This tea is noted for its full-bodied quality and strength, appealing particularly to those who like a robust brew.

Nuwara Eliya A light, "bright" tea with a fragrant flavour, this is excellent when served with lemon wedges.

Uva This is a fine-flavoured tea from the eastern slopes of the central mountains.

Japanese Green Teas These are quite different from Chinese green teas as the flavour of some can be decidedly strong.

Sencha These long, green leaves make a light, bright easy-to-drink tea that is good for everyday drinking.

Sencha Brancha This is a combination of tea leaves and rice that results in a drink with a nutty flavour.

FLAVOURED TEA

In addition to the many types of teas that vary in flavour, there is also a wide range of flavoured teas. They are flavoured with flowers or fruits, or with essences, such as chocolate, mint or brandy. Many teas are flavoured naturally with dried fruit, flowers and spices; some are flavoured artificially. The Chinese have long been flavouring their teas with flowers and each region has

Passion fruit tea

Rose-violet tea

Orange blossom tea

Chrysanthemum tea

Apricot tea

Coconut tea

Rose tea

Jasmine tea

its own traditional blend. The flowers are dried with the tea so that the delicate flavour permeates throughout.

Jasmine Tea Traditionally served with dim sum dishes, this is a classic Chinese tea. It is a green tea, exotically scented with the addition of real jasmine flowers.

Rose Pouchong Tea From the province of Guangdong, this is made by interspersing flower petals with the tea leaves during drying. It makes a pale, soothing tea. *Rose Congou* is another rose-scented tea.

Chrysanthemum Tea This is medium-strength black China tea blended with chrysanthemum flowers.

Orchid Tea This is obtained by blending a semi-fermented Oolong tea with crushed orchid flowers. It makes a light, delicate and fragrant brew, considered to be the tea of connoisseurs.

Lychee Tea This is a traditional Chinese blend that is perfumed with the husks of the lychee fruit.

Fruit Tea Modern blends are produced using varied fruits: apricots, blackcurrants, apples, wild cherries, passion fruit, oranges, lemons and mangos. The producers of fruit teas carefully blend their own mixtures of China, Indian and Ceylon teas to go with the chosen fruit.

Fruit and flower teas *are best appreciated on their own, without milk, lemon and sometimes even sugar*

TEAS AROUND THE WORLD

Tea is drunk in many countries of the world and each one has its own particular ways for preparation and service. The Chinese always drink tea black, the Tibetans lace it with yak butter and the Moroccans flavour theirs with mint or sage. In Europe, there is a choice of milk and lemon, while in Russia, they might add jam. The containers used to brew the tea, along with the bowls, cups and mugs in which to serve it are equally variable. Tea can be served hot or cold, or it can be the base for other drinks such as punches and fruit cups. It is even used to impart flavour and colour to foods. Though tea is an everyday drink, it is often associated with hospitality and every country has its own special customs and ceremonies, which range from the simple to the elaborate.

The Chinese were the first to document the etiquette of tea. The third volume of a book, published in 780 A.D. by the writer Lu Yu, set out the various ways in which each type of tea should be prepared and served. It also included detailed instructions on the implements to be used and even how these should be made.

The teapot and the tea bowl are both Chinese inventions. The latter had no handles and the first European tea cups were very similar. Handles were soon found to be an advantage, though the two styles were in production simultaneously for some years. Saucers followed, and even the handleless cup was given a deep saucer from which the tea could also be drunk. The first European teapots were made of ceramic or fine porcelain china, but silver eventually took over. By the mid-19th century, ornate silver tea services, with huge tea urns on swivel stands, were much in demand. Other equipment included laqueur trays to carry the tea services, sieves and caddy spoons, sugar-bowls, small milk jugs and slop bowls, and tea cosies made of quilted silk or velvet.

At first, tea was served at any time of the day. But in Britain, the seventh Duchess of Bedford founded the very English habit of serving afternoon tea. According to the footnotes of history, the Duchess was prone to light bouts of hunger in the afternoon. One day she ordered a pot of tea and some snacks to be brought to her room. She so enjoyed the experience that she began to invite guests to accompany her in the new

MAKING TEA
Proper brewing is essential for good flavour. Use freshly drawn water from the cold tap and bring to a rolling boil. Warm the teapot with hot water, empty out the water and add the tea. Pour on the water, stir, and leave to stand for 3-5 minutes. Stir again before serving.
Iced tea is very popular in North America and on the Continent. It is made by doubling the quantity of tea brewed to allow for the addition of ice which dilutes it. Tall glasses with plenty of crushed ice are commonly used for serving; garnish with a slice of lemon and a sprig of fresh mint. Cold tea also serves as a base to both alcoholic and non-alcoholic punches and fruit cups.

Customs and Ceremonies
In many countries, tea is more than just a drink, it is the focus of ceremonies that can be steeped in tradition or simply a pretext for gathering with friends.

Moroccan mint tea

Japanese tea

Chinese tea

European tea

Iced tea
Brew tea extra strong as the addition of ice cubes will dilute the taste.

repast. Soon all London was sipping tea and nibbling little sandwiches in the middle of the afternoon.

Serving tea is also associated with hospitality in many Arab countries, and guests are offered steaming cups of special flavoured tea to sip with sweetmeats and other delicacies.

In Japan, there is a very formal ceremony attached to tea service. There are two stages of the ceremony, named for the types of tea served. *Koicha* is a thick and bitter tea, *Ususha* is a much thinner tea. *Koicha* takes place in a special tea room. The host makes the tea and acts as servant to his guests. The principal guest is the first to drink from the bowl and he then passes it on to the other guests. There are also strict rules that govern the topic of conversation, and at this stage it is most polite to discuss the tea-making equipment. *Ususha* is held in another room where guests may chat in a more relaxed atmosphere.

FLAVOURINGS

The Chinese and the Japanese have always believed that tea should be allowed to show off its aroma and flavour without any additions. But even in these countries, all kinds of flavourings may be added.

In Western countries, tea is usually served with milk, a habit that dates from the 18th century in Britain. In those days, it was thought that pouring boiling tea into a delicate china tea bowl would break it, so the milk was added first. Modern experts agree that the milk should go first, but for different reasons. Research has shown that milk poured in after the tea is likely to form a fatty layer on the top. Sugar is frowned upon by the experts as it denatures the flavour. The Russians, however, take sugar in their lemon tea and the Anatolians drink tea through a cube of sugar held in the mouth.

In Arab countries, herbs such as mint, sage and basil are popular. Black tea is drunk strong, often with the addition of a stick of cinnamon, some cardamom pods or a mixture of aniseed and chopped walnuts. Moroccan mint tea is made by infusing sweetened green tea with fresh or dried mint leaves. Lemon verbena or scarlet geranium can also be added.

One of the most exotically flavoured teas is *Kashmiri tea*, which is a blend of green and Darjeeling tea flavoured with a mix of crushed green cardamoms, cinnamon, cloves, chopped almonds and pine nuts.

COOK'S CHOICE
TEA PUNCH

Serves 10–12

600 ml (1 pt) freshly made double-strength Ceylon tea
250 ml (8 fl oz) Amontillado sherry
250 ml (8 fl oz) rum
Juice of 1 lemon
2 tbsp lime juice cordial
Sugar
600 ml (1 pt) crushed ice (or more ice cubes)
Orange and lemon slices for garnish

Mix the hot tea with the sherry, rum, lemon juice and lime cordial. Add sugar to taste and stir until it dissolves. Leave the mixture to cool. Transfer to a punch bowl. Add the ice and leave to stand again until about half the ice has melted. Stir, float slices of orange and lemon on the top and serve.

COOK'S CHOICE
HOT TODDY

Serves 4

300 ml (½ pt) freshly made Darjeeling tea
50 ml (2 fl oz) whisky
50 ml (2 fl oz) ginger wine
4 cloves
1 cinnamon stick

In a saucepan, combine the tea, whisky, wine, cloves and cinnamon. Warm over a gentle heat; do not boil. Leave to infuse for 3–5 minutes. Strain into mugs and serve immediately.

TEA-SMOKING

In parts of China, tea-smoking is used to colour and flavour foods, such as duck and chicken. Peking duck was originally smoked with camphor wood, but this is not widely available and tea is now used instead. Unlike the Western technique of hot-smoking, this process does not cook the food.
To proceed, mix a few tablespoons of loose black tea with brown sugar and herbs or spices, such as aniseed. Rice or flour could also be added for more smoke. Line a heavy wok and its lid with aluminium foil, place the smoking mixture in the base of the wok and place a rack or several crossed chopsticks over the top. Place the food to be smoked on the rack, (or chopsticks) and replace the lid. Place the wok over a very high heat and leave to smoke for about 15 minutes. Care should be taken to open the kitchen windows as the room is likely to fill with smoke. Turn off the heat and leave to stand for a further 10 minutes. The food is now ready to cook as required.

Tea-smoking adds colour and a smoky flavour, but it does not cook foods

TISANES

Herbal infusions have been used through the ages for their medicinal properties. Indeed, the word "tisane" comes from the Greek for medicinal brew. Tisanes contain none of the tannin and caffeine found in conventional teas and many herbal mixtures make refreshing beverages that can be drunk either hot or cold. In Europe, tisanes have never gone out of fashion, and they are gaining renewed popularity in many other countries.

Tisanes are made by infusing the leaves, fruit and flowers of almost any edible plant. Infusions can be chosen for their stimulating or relaxing properties, and advocates of homeopathic remedies, recommend tisanes for their healing properties.

Tisanes are made in very much the same way as ordinary tea but usually in smaller quantities; allow 15 g ($^1/_2$ oz) dried herbs or 30 g (1 oz) fresh herbs for every 600 ml (1 pt) boiling water. Lemon juice and honey have an affinity for many hot tisanes, or they can be served ice cold with a sprig of the fresh herb for garnish.

Leaves Most of the well known culinary herbs also have medicinal properties. Rosemary makes a strongly flavoured tea that stimulates the circulation and can help ease migraines. Sage is said to be good for sore throats, and thyme sweetened with honey makes a soothing cough mixture. Mint – with its 200 varieties – is valued as an aid to digestion and combines well with other herbs; it is especially refreshing with lime blossom. Spearmint and peppermint tea make good revitalizing drinks, especially when served iced. The menthol in hot peppermint tea can be useful for clearing head colds. Less well-known leaves include comfrey, verbena, lemon verbena and raspberry leaves. Lemon balm, sometimes known as melissa, makes a very fragrant tea with a calming effect on the nerves; it is also good for the digestion.

Fruits and Flowers Chamomile flowers have a pungent, grassy flavour when infused and the tea is good for the digestive system, calming the nerves and aiding sleep. In Italy, it is frequently used to calm nursing mothers and their babies.

An infusion of lavender will soothe and relax, while elderflowers and elderberries have long been used in tisanes to calm the nerves, and reduce insomnia and migraines. They remain a popular remedy for soothing inflamed throats, coughing and other symptoms of headcolds. Rose petals and violets, sweetened with honey, also produce a tisane to soothe a cough.

Rich in vitamin C, hibiscus lends a sharp, fruity taste and crimson colour to herbal mixtures. Only the red petals are used in tisanes. Rosehips, also rich in vitamin C, come from the dog rose. Its stimulating properties are quite potent, so always use in moderate doses. The sharp, fruity flavour combines particularly well with hibiscus.

Very fine or crushed leaves should be infused with a fine-mesh strainer

Infusing mugs have strainer baskets to hold the tea and lids to keep the liquid hot

Infusing mug

Infusers
Infusing spoons and balls can be used to make individual cups of herbal teas.

Spoon-sized strainers allow for the proper dosage of leaves for a single cup

REVIVING MORNING TISANE

Tisanes made with selected ingredients result in an invigorating brew for the morning – or any time of day – that can be drunk instead of coffee or tea.

Herbs with invigorating and bracing properties include fresh or dried nettles, blackcurrant and blackberry leaves, peppermint, rosemary, angelica, sweet cicely, borage, lemon verbena, hibiscus blossoms, rosehips and roses.

Combine 2 teaspoons each lemon verbena, peppermint, dried roses, hibiscus, nettle and rosehip (for extra colour and flavour, add more rosehip). Pour some boiling water in the teapot, swirl it round to warm, then discard. Place the mixture in the teapot and pour over 500 ml (16 fl oz) boiling water. Leave to infuse for 5 minutes. Strain before serving and sweeten to taste.

Rosehip

Lemon verbena

Dried roses

Nettle

Hibiscus

Peppermint

Orange peel

Hops

Scullcap

Chamomile

Lemon balm

Lime flower

RELAXING EVENING TISANE

After a heavy meal or an exhausting day a soothing tisane is most welcome. Herbs with calming and sedative properties include basil, begamot lavender, anise leaves, marjoram, violet flowers and leaves, mallow flowers, fennel, dill and all the ingredients listed below.

Mix together ½ teaspoon each of chamomile, lime flower, lemon balm, vervain, scullcap, hops and dried orange peel. Crush half a liquorice stick and add to the herbs. Pour some boiling water in the teapot, swirl it round to warm, then discard. Place the mixture in the teapot and pour over 500 ml (16 fl oz) boiling water. Leave to infuse for 5 minutes. Strain before serving and sweeten with honey to taste.

NON-ALCOHOLIC DRINKS

Fruit and vegetable juices are delicious on their own, but they can also be combined and flavoured with herbs and spices for refreshing and unusual drinks. Dairy products such as milk, yogurt and buttermilk can also be used for flavoursome drinks. Another pleasant preparation involves the addition of yeast to herbal infusions or juices, resulting in a light, naturally sparkling drink. All of these beverages are easily prepared at home, offering a wide variety of satisfying alternatives to traditional alcoholic cocktails. The possibilities for mixed drinks are almost endless, limited only by individual taste. It is easy to build up a repertoire of interesting and unusual non-alcoholic cups, coolers and cocktails. Start by mixing two familiar drinks and then go on to experiment with more unusual flavour combinations, sweetening with sugar or honey and herbs and spices to taste.

HERBS FOR DRINKS

Fresh herbs can be used both to flavour and decorate non-alcoholic drinks. Mint is the most widely used herb with fruit drinks, but borage, parsley, lemon balm, thyme, basil and dill all work well. Stronger herbs such as chives, coriander and tarragon are better with vegetable juices.

Lemon verbena

Ginger mint

Salad burnet

Pineapple sage

A refreshing pause
Use a variety of fresh herbs and spices to flavour fruit and vegetable juices or milk-based drinks.

Fruit and vegetable juices and dairy drinks

COOK'S CHOICE
ST. CLEMENT'S CUP

Serves 4

125 g (4 oz) sugar
Grated zest and juice of 2 oranges
Soda water
Juice of 1 lemon
Fresh lemon balm and lemon slices for garnish

In a saucepan, combine the sugar with 600 ml (1 pt) water over medium heat, stirring until the sugar dissolves. Add the orange zest and juice, lemon juice and a sprig of lemon balm and leave to cool. Add the soda water. Chill for at least 3 hours before serving. Garnish each glass with a small sprig of lemon balm and a slice of lemon.

COOK'S CHOICE
LASSI

Serves 4

250 ml (8 fl oz) natural yogurt
1/2 tsp salt
1-2 sprigs mint, leaves only
1/2 tsp dry roasted cumin seeds
Freshly ground black pepper
Fresh mint sprigs for garnish

In a blender, combine the yogurt, salt, mint and 600 ml (1 pt) water, and process until smooth. Chill for at least 3 hours. Pour into tall glasses, sprinkle with the cumin and pepper to taste. Garnish with sprigs of mint.

The juice of citrus fruits lends itself very well to drinks. Orange and grapefruit juice are the quintessential breakfast juices, and freshly squeezed lemon juice mixed with sugar and water is lemonade to some, *citron pressé* to others. However, there is no need to stick to single-juice mixtures.

The tartness of lemon juice can be deliciously subdued with orange juice and a spoonful of honey. Grapefruit juice can be blended with orange juice and a sprig of fresh herbs can be added for flavour and eye appeal: lemon balm, sweet cicely and peppermint are all suitable.

Herb flowers, such as borage or lemon thyme, make beautiful garnishes for fruit drinks. For festive occasions, remove the thorns and leaves from untreated long-stem roses and place the flowers in tall glasses filled with grapefruit juice, cranberry juice and a squeeze of fresh lime.

More elaborate fruit cups and coolers are made by mixing a variety of bottled and home-pressed fruit juices together. Try apple with strawberry juice, peach with tangerine juice, or pineapple with mango juice. Some of these mixtures need the acidity of lemon, lime or grapefruit juice to balance the sweetness. Top up with soda water or ginger beer, add ice cubes and decorate with sliced fruit and sprigs of fresh herbs before serving.

Fresh fruit juices also have an affinity for fruit syrups (see page 204). Tart fruit juices, such as lime and grapefruit, work best as the syrups are sugar-based. Floral syrups (see page 213) can be blended to great effect with delicate fruits, such as strawberry.

Almost all vegetables can be processed for their juice but carrot, tomato and cucumber are the most appropriate. A juice extractor is the best tool for the job. For extra flavour, add basil, lovage or parsley to tomato juice, dill or chives to cucumber juice, and tarragon or mint to carrot juice.

A refreshing drink can be made from a borscht-like combination of beets, cucumber and apple. Likewise, carrot and coriander are natural partners in the soup pot, and the addition of orange juice helps in the transition from bowl to glass.

Tangy buttermilk is ideal for drinks. It can be used alone, or subdued with milk or yogurt. Strawberries, bananas and honey mixed in a blender with some chilled buttermilk make a delicious and wholesome summertime drink, with an appealing froth on the top. Serve in tall glasses, garnished with fresh mint sprigs.

Flavoured milk is a familiar drink base, generally made with cocoa powder or fruit syrups, such as strawberry. Drinking yogurt is becoming increasingly popular, though in the East, yogurt has long been the base of refreshing drinks. Lassi, the traditional Indian yogurt drink, can be either sweet – flavoured with mint or rose water – or savoury, flavoured with cumin and cardamom. Lassis are meant to tame the fire of spicy curries, but they are refreshing drinks in their own right

Releasing citrus juices
Before squeezing citrus fruits, roll on the worktop, pressing down, to help release a maximum of juice.

COOK'S CHOICE
CARROT-GAZPACHO COCKTAIL

Serves 4

450 ml (½ pt) carrot juice
450 ml (½ pt) tomato juice
7.5 cm (3 in) cucumber, grated
2 tbsp chopped fresh coriander, basil or dill
Salt
Freshly ground black pepper
Ice cubes

Mix the juices in a large jug and chill for 1 hour. Stir in the remaining ingredients. Pour into glasses and serve garnished with sprigs of the chosen herb.

MAKING GINGER BEER

Ginger beer is a traditional British drink, somewhat old-fashioned, but delicious and refreshing nonetheless. Serve chilled in tall glasses.

1 With the flat edge of a knife, crush 30 g (1 oz) peeled ginger. Add to a bowl with 500 g (1 lb) sugar, 5 litres (8 ¾ pt) boiling water and the juice of 2 lemons.

2 In a small bowl, dissolve 1 sachet dried beer yeast in tepid water. Leave to stand for 3-4 minutes so the yeast develops, then stir with a spoon.

3 Add the yeast to the ginger mixture, stir to blend and leave for 24 hours. Strain then pour into clean bottles and seal or cork (see page 233), leaving about 2.5 cm (1 in) at the top.

ALCOHOLIC DRINKS

As long as alcoholic drinks have been distilled, they have served as the basis for warming and soothing spiced drinks; sometimes they were thickened with egg yolks, sometimes they were sweetened with raisins, honey or sugar. Mulled wine and beer used to be heated with a red hot poker, though today, specialities like glühwein and punch are more likely to be steeped on the hob. Punch originated in India, where it was made with a locally produced spirit. It became the custom to use five ingredients in the mix, and since the Indian word for five was *pantsch*, this soon became anglicized to punch.

Wine cups and punches are festive and flavoursome uses for ordinary bottles of still or sparkling wine. They can be enhanced with spirits or liqueurs, teas or tisanes, and fruit or floral syrups (see Index). Flavourings that have an affinity for alcoholic drinks include citrus fruits and spices, such as cinnamon and cloves. Beer and lager feature less frequently in mixed drinks; the exception is Black Velvet, which is a mixture of Champagne and Guinness. There are many ways to enjoy flavoured alcoholic drinks: from a simple blend of rum, hot water, honey and lemon, to a more elaborate punch blending several spirits with fruits and spices.

COOK'S CHOICE
TOASTED ALE PUNCH

Serves 6

60 g (2 oz) light brown sugar
1 lemon, sliced
¹/₄ tsp ground cloves
¹/₄ tsp ground cinnamon
150 ml (¹/₄ pt) brandy
600 ml (1 pt) light ale
1 slice white bread, toasted and cut into small shapes
Freshly grated nutmeg

In a large bowl, combine the sugar and 300 ml (¹/₂ pt) water and stir to dissolve. Add the lemon, cloves, cinnamon, brandy and ale. Stir to blend and add the bread. Sprinkle with grated nutmeg and serve.

Flavouring drinks
The addition of herbs and spices adds greatly to alcoholic drinks, both warmed and chilled.

COOK'S CHOICE
WHITE WINE CUP

Serves 8-10

2 bottles dry white wine
¹/₂ bottle dry sherry
Juice of 2 lemons
2.5 cm (1 in) fresh ginger, peeled
Soda water
Sugar
Cucumber slices for garnish

Mix together the wine, sherry, lemon juice and ginger and chill for 2 hours. To serve, remove the ginger, transfer to glasses, add soda water to taste and sweeten if desired. Add cucumber slices and serve.

COOK'S CHOICE
MADEIRA MILK PUNCH

Serves 6

1 egg
1.25 litres (2 pt) milk
125 g (4 oz) sugar
300 ml (¹/₂ pt) Madeira
150ml (¹/₄ pt) brandy
Freshly grated nutmeg

Whisk together the egg and 150 ml (¹/₄ pt) of the milk. In a saucepan, bring the remaining milk and sugar to the boil. Whisk a little of the hot milk into the egg mixture, then return all to the saucepan. Whisk in the Madeira and brandy; do not boil. When frothy, pour into mugs, sprinkle with grated nutmeg and serve.

Mulling spices

Mulled drinks and punches

MAKING MULLED WINE

Mulled wine is a traditional festive drink in many parts of the world, but this delicious and warming wine is suitable for any cold winter evening. Mulled beer can be made in the same way, but without the sugar and lemon.

1 In a pan, combine 1 sliced lemon, 4 bottles red wine, 600 ml (1 pint) water and 175 ml (6 fl oz) brandy. Add a cinnamon stick, several allspice berries and 2–3 cloves. Bring just to the boil; taste and add sugar if desired.

2 Cover and leave to infuse for at least 30 minutes. Just before serving, return to the heat to warm but do not allow to boil. Strain into a heated bowl, or individual mugs, and serve with slices of lemon

FLAVOURING LIQUEUR

Flavoured liqueurs can easily be made at home by steeping fresh fruits in a mixture of alcohol and sugar syrup. Fruits to choose include whole oranges or just the zest, pears, peaches, sloes, damsons or plums. Large fruit should be sliced; small fruit should be pricked all over to help release the flavoursome juices. Simply place the fruit in a clean jar and cover with a mixture of three parts alcohol – gin, rum, brandy or vodka – to one part sugar syrup (see page 196). Spices, herbs, citrus peel and even coffee beans can be added for flavour.

1 To make an unusual orange and coffee bean liqueur, cut three slits down the side of an orange and insert some coffee beans in each of the incisions.

2 Place the orange in a jar and add a handful of coffee beans. Pour on a mixture of one-third sugar syrup to two-thirds tequila and seal. Chill for 3 months before using.

Warm, spiced drinks such as Toddies, Nogs and Grogs were all the rage in the 18th century, though they are somewhat less popular today.

Hot toddies are easy-to-make drinks for cold winter nights. Pour a measure of whisky, rum or brandy into a tall, heatproof glass. Add a teaspoon of sugar, a pinch of spice, and top up with boiling water. Good flavour combinations include brandy with allspice or nutmeg, and rum with cloves or cinnamon. For a Tam O'Shanter, mix two parts Scotch whisky and one part brandy, sweeten with brown sugar and sprinkle with allspice. To transform this drink into a nog, whisk together brown sugar to taste and one egg and pour on some boiling milk. Whisk the mixture over low heat until thick and frothy but do not boil or the eggs will curdle. Divide the same amount of whisky and brandy between coffee mugs and pour on the hot milk mixture to fill.

Grog refers to a mix of rum, lemon juice, brown sugar, cinnamon and sultanas. The name comes from the slang for the water-diluted rum, instigated by a naval Admiral, nicknamed Old Grog, that was allotted to British sailors.

The original five ingredients in Punch were spirits, tea, sugar, fruit juice and water. Nowadays, punches have fallen from favour, being replaced by mulled wines that combine red wine, rum or brandy, sugar, lemon and a variety of spices.

Wine cups and coolers are lighter, more refreshing drinks, in which spirits are replaced with wine, sherry or vermouth. Flavourings include fresh fruit or juice, and perhaps a sprig of mint.

Sangria is a familiar wine-based drink traditionally made by adding sugar and ice to red Spanish wine. The recipe can be more elaborate, adding brandy or even orange liqueur. The Spanish also make a hot red wine cup with nutmeg and lemon called *bollam*. The German, Swiss and Austrian *glühwein* is similar, but has a more elaborate mix of spices.

Frosted glasses
To frost a glass, dip the rim into a saucer of diluted gum arabic and then into a saucer of caster sugar and leave to dry.

INDEX

BIBLIOGRAPHY

Anderson, J: Green Thumb Preserving Guide, New York, 1984

Arasaki, S & T: Vegetables from the Sea, Tokyo, 1983

Arctander, S: Perfume and Flavouring Materials of Natural Origin, New Jersey, 1960

Bailey, A: Cook's Ingredients, London, 1990

Bayless, R with Bayless D G: Authentic Mexican Cooking, London, 1987

Bissell, F: Sainsbury's Book of Food, London, 1989

Bonar, A: Herbs, London, 1989

Boxer, A & Back, P: The Herb Book, London, 1989

Bremness, L: The Complete Book of Herbs, London, 1988

Brennan, G & Glen, C: Peppers Hot and Chile, Berkeley, 1988

Brissenden, R: South East Asian Food, London, 1969

Brown, C, R and B: The Wine Cook Book, Boston, 1941

Brumichitr, V: The Taste of Thailand, London, 1988

Cavage, B: The Elegant Onion, Vermont, 1988

Chapman, P: The Curry Club Indian Restaurant Cookbook, London, 1984

Chapman, P: The Curry Club Middle Eastern Cookbook, London, 1989

Clair, C: Of Herbs and Spices, London, 1961

Clifton, C: Edible Flowers, London, 1983

Cordero-Fernando, G: The Culinary Culture of the Philippines, Manila, 1976

Cost, B: Foods from the Far East, London, 1990

David, E: A Book of Mediterranean Food, London, 1950

David, E: French Provincial Cooking, London, 1970

David, E: Spices, Salt and Aromatics In The English Kitchen, London, 1975

Delaveau, P: Les Epices, Paris, 1987

Dimbleby, J: The Cook's Companion, London, 1991

Dowell, P; Ortiz, E L; Radecka, H: The Book of Ingredients, London, 1980

Garland, S: The Herb & Spice Book, London, 1985

Glasse, H: The Art of Cookery Made Plain and Easy, London, 1747

Goldstein, D: A Taste of Russia, London, 1985

Good Housekeeping: Complete Book of Preserving, London,1991

Grant, R: Caribbean and African Cookery, London, 1988

Greenberg, S and Ortiz, E L: The Spice of Life, London, 1983

Grieve, M: A Modern Herbal, London, 1931

Grigson, J: Jane Grigson's Vegetable Book, London, 1980

Grigson, J: Jane Grigson's Fruit Book, London, 1983

Grigson, S: Sophie Grigson's Ingredients Book, London, 1991

Gubser, M: America's Bread Book, New York, 1968

Halici, N: Nevin Halici's Turkish Cookbook, London, 1989

Hallgarten, P: Spirits & Liqueurs, London 1983

Harrison, Masefield, Wallis: The Oxford Book of Food Plants, Oxford, 1969

Hazan, M: The Classic Italian Cookbook, London, 1981

Hemphill, J and R: Herbs, Their Cultivation and Usage, London, 1984

Hemphill, R: The Penguin Book ofHerbs and Spices, London, 1968

Hériteau, J: Potpourris and Other Fragrant Delights, London, 1975

Hillier, M: Roses, London, 1991

Hobhouse, C: Great European Chefs, London, 1990

Hodgson, M: The Hot & Spicy Cookbook, New York, 1989

Jaffrey, M: An Invitation to Indian Cooking, London, 1976

Kennedy, D: The Art of Mexican Cooking, New York, 1989

Kwaham, R: La Cuisine Arabe, Paris, 1970

Kitchiner, W: The Cook's Oracle, London, 1817

Leeming, M & May Huang Man-Hui, Far-Eastern Vegetarian Cooking, London, 1985

Leyel, C F: Herbal Delights, London, 1987

Lowenfeld, C and Back, P: The Complete Book of Herbs and Spices, Newton Abbot, 1974

Mackley, L: A Gourmet's Book of Tea & Coffee, London, 1989

Man, R & Weir, R: The Compleat Mustard, London, 1988

Marcus, G and N: Forbidden Fruits and Forgotten Vegetables, London, 1983

McCormick: Spices of the World Cookbook, New York, 1964

Millon, M and K: Flavours of Korea, London, 1991

Miloradovich, M: Cooking with Herbs and Spices, New York, 1950

Molyneux, J with Grigson, S: The Carved Angel Cookery Book, London, 1990

Mulherin, J: Spices & Natural Flavourings, London, 1988

Nathan, A: Salad, San Francisco, 1985

Norman, J: The Complete Book of Spices, London, 1990

Odarty, B: A Safari of African Cooking, Detriot, 1976

Ortiz, E L: Carribean Cookery, London, 1975

Ortiz, E L: The Book of Latin American Cooking, London, 1985

Owen, S: Indonesian Food and Cookery, London, 1986

Passmore, J: The Letts Companion to Asian Food & Cooking, London, 1991

Phillips, R. Mushrooms, London, 1981

Prudhomme, P: Chef Paul Prudhomme's Louisiana Kitchen, New York, 1984

Roden, C: A New Book of Middle Eastern Food, London, 1986

Rohde, E S: Gardens of Delight, London, 1934

Rosengarten, F: The Book of Spices, Pennsylvania, 1969

Rosso, J & Lukins, S: The New Basics Cookbook, New York, 1989

Rubinstein, H: The Chocolate Book, London, 1982

Sahni, J: Classic Indian Cooking, London, 1986

Sheen, J: Lavender, London, 1991

Simon, A L: A Concise Encyclopedia of Gastronomy, New York, 1981

Smith, B S: Gourmet Gifts, Victoria, 1985

Smires, L B: La Cuisine Marocaine, Paris 1971

Sonntag, L: The Little Tofu Book, London 1987

Spring Books: The World Atlas of Food, London, 1988

Steele, L: The Book of Hot & Spicy - Nibbles - Dips - Dishes, London 1987

Stern, J and M: Square Meals, New York, 1985

Stobart, T: Herbs, Spices and Flavourings, London, 1977

Tannahill, R: Food in History, London, 1973

Taw Kritikara, M L and Pimsai Amranand, M R: Modern Thai Cooking, Bangkok, 1977

Time-Life Books: Foods of the World Series, Alexandria, 1968

Time-Life Books: The Good Cook Series, Amsterdam, 1979

Trewby, M: A Gourmet's Book of Herbs and Spices, London, 1989

Tropp, B: The Modern Art of Chinese Cooking, New York, 1982

Tsuji, S: Japanese Cooking, Tokyo, 1980

Willan, A: Reader's Digest Complete Guide to Cookery, London, 1989

Wolfert, P: The Cooking of South West France, London, 1987

Yan-kit, S: Yan-kit's Classic Chinese Cookbook, London, 1984

ACKNOWLEDGEMENTS

The editors would particularly like to thank **Vanessa Kramer,** whose advice, research and hard work made a large contribution to the scholarship of this book.

The following authors contributed text:
Angelika Duval
Fergus Fleming
Christopher Middleton
Judy Ridgway
Elizabeth Wolf-Cohen

Editorial Assistants:
Judy Bastyra, Elizabeth Godfray, Rosie Kindersley, Beverly LeBlanc, Sally Poole, Madeline Weston, Ian Wood

Photographer's Assistant:
Jules Selmes

Home Economists:
Sandra Baddeley
Elizabeth Burkwood
Annie Nichols

Additional Typesetting:
Rowena Feeny

For information and fact-finding, the editors wish to thank the following individuals and organizations:

Bui Xuan Khoa, Second Secretary of the Vietnamese Embassy; Coffee News Information Centre; Deborah Gillat and Zeba Mirza at the Ministry of Agriculture, Fisheries and Food; Terril Jones; Korea National Tourism Corporation; Melody Meade; Jill Norman; Royal Thai Embassy; Alan Wylie at Peacock Salt Ltd; Sarah Wynter

For their help, advice and supply of herbs, spices and flavourings for photography, many thanks to the following:

Rosemary Titterington
Iden Croft Herbs Ltd.
Frittenden Road
Staplehurst
Kent TN12 0DH

Nathalie Lopez
A Touch of Spice Ltd.
21 The Highlands
Bexhill-on-Sea
East Sussex TN39 5HL

Charles Carey
The Oil Merchant
47 Ashchurch Grove
London W12 9BU

Angelika Duval
Thyme Cottage
87 World's End Lane
Green Street Green
Kent BR6 6AE

Thanks also to the following, who kindly supplied props for photography:

Neal Street East
5-7 Neal Street
London WC2H 9PU

Covent Garden General Store
111 Long Acre
London WC2N 4BA

The Tea Council Ltd
Sir John Lyon House
5 High Timber Street
London EC4 3NJ

Villeroy & Boch Tableware Ltd
203 Regent Street
London W1R 2DE

Whittard of Chelsea Ltd
73 Northcote Road
Battersea
London SW11 6PJ

Algerian Coffee Stores Ltd
52 Old Compton Street
London W1V 6PV

40-414-3